ANNUAL EDITIONS

Psychology 09/10
Fortieth Edition

EDITOR

William Buskist
Auburn University

William Buskist is the Distinguished Professor in the Teaching of Psychology at Auburn University and a Faculty Fellow at Auburn's Biggio Center for the Enhancement of Teaching and Learning. He is a past president of the Society for the Teaching of Psychology (Division 2 of the American Psychological Association) and a member of the National Institute on the Teaching of Psychology (NITOP) planning committee. He is published widely in the teaching of psychology and has received several teaching awards, including the Robert S. Daniel award from the Society and The Gerald and Emily Leischuck Presidential Award for Excellence in Teaching from Auburn University. He is a Fellow of APA Divisions 1 (General Psychology) and 2 and is a past president of Division 2.

Higher Education

Boston   Burr Ridge, IL   Dubuque, IA   New York   San Francisco   St. Louis
Bangkok   Bogotá   Caracas   Kuala Lumpur   Lisbon   London   Madrid   Mexico City
Milan   Montreal   New Delhi   Santiago   Seoul   Singapore   Sydney   Taipei   Toronto

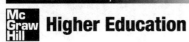

The McGraw·Hill Companies

McGraw Hill Higher Education

ANNUAL EDITIONS: PSYCHOLOGY, FORTIETH EDITION

Published by McGraw-Hill, a business unit of The McGraw-Hill Companies, Inc., 1221 Avenue of the Americas, New York, NY 10020.
Copyright © 2010 by The McGraw-Hill Companies, Inc. All rights reserved. Previous edition(s) 2007, 2008, 2009. No part of this publication
may be reproduced or distributed in any form or by any means, or stored in a database or retrieval system, without the prior written consent
of The McGraw-Hill Companies, Inc., including, but not limited to, in any network or other electronic storage or transmission, or broadcast
for distance learning.

Some ancillaries, including electronic and print components, may not be available to customers outside the United States.

Annual Editions® is a registered trademark of The McGraw-Hill Companies, Inc.
Annual Editions is published by the **Contemporary Learning Series** group within The McGraw-Hill Higher Education division.

1 2 3 4 5 6 7 8 9 0 QPD/QPD 0 9

ISBN 978–0–07–351639–4
MHID 0–07–351639–2
ISSN 0272–3794

Managing Editor: *Larry Loeppke*
Senior Managing Editor: *Faye Schilling*
Developmental Editor: *Debra Henricks*
Editorial Coordinator: *Mary Foust*
Editorial Assistant: *Nancy Meissner*
Production Service Assistant: *Rita Hingtgen*
Permissions Coordinator: *Lenny J. Behnke*
Senior Marketing Manager: *Julie Keck*
Marketing Communications Specialist: *Mary Klein*
Marketing Coordinator: *Alice Link*
Project Manager: *Sandy Wille*
Design Specialist: *Tara McDermott*
Senior Production Supervisor: *Laura Fuller*
Cover Graphics: *Kristine Jubeck*

Compositor: Laserwords Private Limited
Cover Images: Debra Henricks (inset); © Royalty-Free/Corbis (background)

Library in Congress Cataloging-in-Publication Data
Main entry under title: Annual Editions: Psychology 2009/2010.
  1. Psychology—Periodicals. I. Buskist, William, *comp*. II. Title: Psychology
658'.05

www.mhhe.com

Editors/Advisory Board

Members of the Advisory Board are instrumental in the final selection of articles for each edition of ANNUAL EDITIONS. Their review of articles for content, level, currentness, and appropriateness provides critical direction to the editor and staff. We think that you will find their careful consideration well reflected in this volume.

Preface

In publishing ANNUAL EDITIONS we recognize the enormous role played by the magazines, newspapers, and journals of the public press in providing current, first-rate educational information in a broad spectrum of interest areas. Many of these articles are appropriate for students, researchers, and professionals seeking accurate, current material to help bridge the gap between principles and theories and the real world. These articles, however, become more useful for study when those of lasting value are carefully collected, organized, indexed, and reproduced in a low-cost format, which provides easy and permanent access when the material is needed. That is the role played by ANNUAL EDITIONS.

Scientific psychology is barely 130 years old. In 1879, Wilhelm Wundt, a German scientist, founded the first research laboratory in psychology and became the first person to claim the title of a psychologist. With the crudest of methodology, at least by modern standards, Wundt searched for the basic elements of human consciousness. From these humble beginnings, Wundt probably could not have possibly imagined the mushrooming of psychology into what it has become today—A vital and healthy science that serves as the basis for psychological practice in just about every corner of the world. Each year, psychological science and practice is studied by hundreds of thousands of students across the globe. And each year, thousands of young men and women graduate with PhDs in psychology and begin careers in which they either conduct research in psychology, practice psychology to improve the human condition, or do a combination of both.

To be sure, there is no aspect of human behavior, thought, or emotion that psychological scientists and practitioners leave unexamined—the entire spectrum of human nature is fair game. After all, human nature is the most complex and fascinating subject matter in all science, and to understand it, even its most basic and mundane elements must be examined.

Unlike in Wundt's time, when no psychological journals existed, today there are literally hundreds of thousands of science reports in numerous journals each year. Also, unlike in Wundt's time, the scientific methodology and instruments are as complex as they are technical; and it often takes advance study in psychology to even begin to understand many of these articles. For this reason, McGraw-Hill publishes its *Annual Editions*—an anthology of recent articles about psychology. The editorial staff at McGraw-Hill has designed *Annual Editions: Psychology 09/10* to meet the needs of lay people and students who are curious about psychological science and its practice. *Annual Editions: Psychology 09/10* provides a large selection of readable, informative articles primarily from popular magazines and newspapers. Most of these articles are written by journalists, but a few of them are by psychologists.

We selected those articles for this volume that are representative of current research and thinking in psychology. They provide clear examples of the types of research and issues discussed in most introductory classes. As in any science, some of the topics discussed in this collection are revolutionary; others confirm things that we already know.

Some articles invite speculation about social and personal issues; others encourage careful thought about potential misuse of research findings. Your teacher will expect that you read assigned articles carefully and critically, so that you will come to understand how psychologists view their subject matter, and what issues loom large on the horizon in need of further investigation.

We assume that you will find this collection of articles readable and useful. I suggest that you look at the organization of this book and compare it to the organization of your textbook and course syllabus. By examining the topic guide provided after the table of contents, you can identify those articles that best match any particular unit of study in your course. Your instructor may provide some help in this effort or assign articles to supplement the text. As you read the articles, try to connect their contents with the principles you are learning from your text and classroom lectures. Some of the articles will help you better understand a specific area of psychology; others will help you connect and integrate information from diverse research areas. Both of these strategies are key to learning about psychology or any other science. It is only through careful study and thoughtful integration of research findings from many studies that we are able to discover and apply new knowledge.

Please take time to provide us with feedback about *Annual Editions: Psychology 09/10* by completing and returning the article rating form in the back of the book. Your comments and suggestions will help guide the annual revision of this anthology. With your help, this collection will be even better next year.

The McGraw-Hill editorial staff wishes you the very best of success with your studies this year.

Bill Buskist

William Buskist
Editor

Note: Karen Duffy served as the editor for the previous editions of *Annual Editions: Psychology*. I am indebted to her for her outstanding judgment in selecting wonderful articles and essays, many of which appear in this volume.

Contents

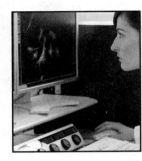

UNIT 1
The Science of Psychology

UNIT 2
Biological Bases of Behavior

The concepts in bold italics are developed in the article. For further expansion, please refer to the Topic Guide.

UNIT 3
Perceptual Processes

The concepts in bold italics are developed in the article. For further expansion, please refer to the Topic Guide.

UNIT 4
Learning and Remembering

UNIT 5
Cognitive Processes

The concepts in bold italics are developed in the article. For further expansion, please refer to the Topic Guide.

UNIT 6
Emotion and Motivation

UNIT 7
Development

The concepts in bold italics are developed in the article. For further expansion, please refer to the Topic Guide.

UNIT 8
Personality Processes

The concepts in bold italics are developed in the article. For further expansion, please refer to the Topic Guide.

UNIT 9
Social Processes

UNIT 10
Psychological Disorders

The concepts in bold italics are developed in the article. For further expansion, please refer to the Topic Guide.

UNIT 11
Psychological Treatments

The concepts in bold italics are developed in the article. For further expansion, please refer to the Topic Guide.

Correlation Guide

The *Annual Editions* series provides students with convenient, inexpensive access to current, carefully selected articles from the public press. **Annual Editions: Psychology 09/10** is an easy-to-use reader that presents articles on important topics such as *development, motivation, psychological disorders,* and many more. For more information on *Annual Editions* and other *McGraw-Hill Contemporary Learning Series* titles, visit www.mhcls.com.

This convenient guide matches the units in **Annual Editions: Psychology 09/10** with the corresponding chapters in three of our best-selling McGraw-Hill Psychology textbooks by Lahey and Feldman.

Annual Editions: Psychology 09/10	Psychology: An Introduction, 10/e by Lahey	Understanding Psychology, 9/e by Feldman	Essentials of Understanding Psychology, 8/e by Feldman
Unit 1: The Science of Psychology	**Chapter 1:** Introduction to Psychology **Chapter 2:** Research Methods in Psychology	**Chapter 1:** Introduction to Psychology **Chapter 2:** Psychological Research	**Chapter 1:** Introduction to Psychology
Unit 2: Biological Bases of Behavior	**Chapter 3:** Biological Foundations in Behavior **Chapter 4:** The Interplay of Nature and Nurture	**Chapter 3:** Neuroscience and Behavior **Chapter 11:** Sexuality and Gender	**Chapter 2:** Neuroscience and Behavior
Unit 3: Perceptual Processes	**Chapter 5:** Sensation and Perception **Chapter 6:** States of Consciousness	**Chapter 4:** Sensation and Perception **Chapter 5:** States of Consciousness	**Chapter 3:** Sensation and Perception **Chapter 4:** States of Consciousness
Unit 4: Learning and Remembering	**Chapter 7:** Basic Principles of Learning **Chapter 8:** Memory	**Chapter 6:** Learning **Chapter 7:** Memory	**Chapter 5:** Learning **Chapter 6:** Memory
Unit 5: Cognitive Processes	**Chapter 9:** Cognition, Language, and Intelligence	**Chapter 8:** Cognition and Language **Chapter 9:** Intelligence	**Chapter 7:** Thinking, Language, and Intelligence
Unit 6: Emotion and Motivation	**Chapter 11:** Motivation and Emotion **Chapter 13:** Stress and Health	**Chapter 10:** Motivation and Emotion	**Chapter 8:** Motivation and Emotion **Chapter 11:** Health Psychology
Unit 7: Development	**Chapter 10:** Developmental Psychology	**Chapter 12:** Development **Chapter 14:** Health Psychology	**Chapter 9:** Development
Unit 8: Personality Processes	**Chapter 12:** Personality Theories and Assessment	**Chapter 13:** Personality	**Chapter 10:** Personality
Unit 9: Social Processes	**Chapter 16:** Social Psychology	**Chapter 17:** Social Psychology	**Chapter 14:** Social Psychology
Unit 10: Psychological Disorders	**Chapter 14:** Abnormal Behavior	**Chapter 15:** Psychological Disorders	**Chapter 12:** Psychological Disorders
Unit 11: Psychological Treatments	**Chapter 15:** Therapies **Chapter 17:** Psychology Applied to Business and Other Professions	**Chapter 16:** Treatment of Psychological Disorders	**Chapter 13:** Treatment of Psychological Disorders

Topic Guide

This topic guide suggests how the selections in this book relate to the subjects covered in your course. You may want to use the topics listed on these pages to search the Web more easily.

On the following pages a number of Web sites have been gathered specifically for this book. They are arranged to reflect the units of this Annual Editions reader. You can link to these sites by going to *http://www.mhcls.com*.

All the articles that relate to each topic are listed below the bold-faced term.

Internet References

The following Internet sites have been selected to support the articles found in this reader. These sites were available at the time of publication. However, because Web sites often change their structure and content, the information listed may no longer be available. We invite you to visit http://www.mhcls.com for easy access to these sites.

Annual Editions: Psychology 09/10

General Sources

McGraw-Hill Contemporary Learning Seris
http://www.mhcls.com/online/contentsmain.mhtml

This site is the home page for support materials for McGraw-Hill's texts, including the Annual Edition anthology your instructor has assigned for your class. This site will allow you to test your knowledge of reading materials and provide you additional resources to support your study of psychology.

APA Resources for the Public
http://www.apa.org/topics/homepage.html

Use the site map or search engine to access APA Monitor, the American Psychological Association newspaper, APA books on a wide range of topics, PsychINFO, an electronic database of abstracts on scholarly journals, and the HelpCenter.

Health Information Resources
http://www.health.gov/nhic/Pubs/tollfree.htm

Here is a long list of toll-free numbers that provide health-related information. None offer diagnosis and treatment, but some do offer recorded information; others provide personalized counseling, referrals, and/or written materials.

Mental Help Net
http://mentalhelp.net

This comprehensive guide to mental health online features thousands of individual resources. Information on mental disorders and professional resources in psychology, psychiatry, and social work is presented.

Psychology: Online Resource Central
http://www.psych-central.com

Thousands of psychology resources are currently indexed at this site. Psychology disciplines, conditions and disorders, and self-development are among the most useful.

School Psychology Resources Online
http://www.schoolpsychology.net

Numerous sites on special conditions, disorders, and disabilities, as well as other data ranging from assessment/evaluation to research, are available on this resource page for psychologists, parents, and educators.

Social Psychology Network
http://www.socialpsychology.org

The Social Psychology Network is the most comprehensive source of social psychology information on the Internet, including resources, programs, and research.

UNIT 1: The Science of Psychology

Association for Psychological Science
http://www.psychologicalscience.org/

This site is the home page for APS, which is large national organization of scientifically-oriented psychologists. t features up-to-date news items on the science of psychology as well as descriptions of APS activities and events.

American Psychological Association
http://www.apa.org/

This site is the home page for APA, the largest organization of professional psychologists in the United States. This site will give you access to all of APA's resources on the net, including news updates, publications, and topical information.

Psychological Research on the Net
http://psych.hanover.edu/Research/exponnet.html

This site provides information on research experiments in psychology. Biological psychology/neuropsychology, clinical psychology, cognition, developmental psychology, emotions, health psychology, personality, sensation/perception, and social psychology are some of the areas covered.

UNIT 2: Biological Bases of Behavior

Behavioral Genetics
http://www.ornl.gov/hgmis/elsi/behavior.html

This government-backed Web site includes helpful information on behavioral genetics.

Institute for Behavioral Genetics
http://ibgwww.colorado.edu/index.html

Dedicated to conducting and facilitating research on the genetic and environmental bases of individual differences in behavior, this University of Colorado site provides links to genetic sites, statistical sites, and the Biology Meta Index, as well as to search engines.

Serendip
http://serendip.brynmawr.edu/serendip/

Serendip, which is organized into 10 subject areas (e.g., brain and behavior, complex systems, genes and behavior, science and culture, and science education), contains interactive exhibits, articles, links to other resources, and a forum area.

Society for Neuroscience
http://www.sfn.org/

This site is the home page for the Society of Neuroscience and contains information and links to the most recent research and theory regarding biological bases of behavior.

UNIT 3: Perceptual Processes

Five Senses Home Page
http://www.sedl.org/scimath/pasopartners/senses/welcome.html

This site provides information about human sensory systems for school teachers, but much of the information is interesting and be useful to you in your study of perception at the college level.

Psychology Tutorials and Demonstrations
http://psych.hanover.edu/Krantz/tutor.html

Interactive tutorials and simulations, in the area of sensation and perception, as well as several other areas, are available here.

Internet References

Visual and Optical Illusions
http://dragon.uml.edu/psych/illusion.html

This site hosts a wide range of compelling visual illusions.

UNIT 4: Learning and Remembering

Classical Conditioning
http://chiron.valdosta.edu/whuitt/col/behsys/classcnd.html

This site provides a thorough overview of the basic principles of classical conditioning.

Operant Conditioning
http://psychology.about.com/od/behavioralpsychology/a/introopcond.htm

This site provides basic information about the principles of operant conditioning.

Social Learning Theory
http://teachnet.edb.utexas.edu/~lynda_abbott/Social.html

This site provides an overview of the fundamentals of modern social learning theory.

UNIT 5: Cognitive Processes

American Association for Artificial Intelligence (AAAI)
http://www.aaai.org/AITopics/index.html

This AAAI site provides a good starting point to learn about artificial intelligence (AI)—what artificial intelligence is and what AI scientists do.

Cognition and Thinking
http://library.thinkquest.org/26618/en-5.1.1 = mental%20imagery.htm

This helpful site provides an introduction to the basic principles of cognition.

UNIT 6: Emotion and Motivation

Motivation
http://chiron.valdosta.edu/whuitt/col/motivation/motivate.html

This site provides an abundance of information on psychological research on motivation.

Emotion
http://www.psychology.org/links/Environment_Behavior_Relationships/Emotion/

This site contains brief descriptions and links to Web articles on all facets of emotion.

Mind Tools
http://www.psychwww.com/mtsite/

Useful information on stress management can be found at this Web site.

UNIT 7: Development

American Association for Child and Adolescent Psychiatry
http://www.aacap.org

This site is designed to aid in the understanding and treatment of the developmental, behavioral, and mental disorders that could affect children and adolescents. There is a specific link just for families about common childhood problems that may or may not require professional intervention.

Developmental Psychology
http://psychology.about.com/od/developmentalpsychology/Developmental_Psychology.htm

This site presents a very good overview of development, especially in childhood. It also contains many helpful links to Web sites on related issues.

The Opportunity of Adolescence
http://www.winternet.com/~webpage/adolescencepaper.html

According to this site, adolescence is the turning point, after which the future is redirected and confirmed. The opportunities and problems of this period are presented with quotations from Erik Erikson, Jean Piaget, and others.

UNIT 8: Personality Processes

Great Ideas in Personality
http://www.personalityresearch.org/

This site provides links to discussions of the major ideas and issues in the psychological study of personality.

The Personality Project
http://personality-project.org/personality.html

This Personality Project (by William Revelle) is meant to guide those interested in personality theory and research to the current personality research literature.

UNIT 9: Social Processes

Nonverbal Behavior and Nonverbal Communication
http://www3.usal.es/~nonverbal/

This Web site has a detailed listing of nonverbal behavior and nonverbal communication sites, including the work of historical and current researchers.

The Social Psychology Network
http://www.socialpsychology.org/

This site is the "one-stop shopping center" for information on social psychology. It contains over 1500 links to social psychology on the Web.

UNIT 10: Psychological Disorders

American Association of Suicidology
http://www.suicidology.org

The American Association of Suicidology is a nonprofit organization dedicated to the understanding and prevention of suicide. This site is designed as a resource to anyone concerned about suicide.

Ask NOAH About: Mental Health
http://www.noah-health.org/en/mental/

Information about child and adolescent family problems, mental conditions and disorders, suicide prevention, and much more is available here.

Mental Health Net Disorders and Treatments
http://www.mentalhelp.net/

Presented on this site are links to psychological disorders, which include anxiety, panic, phobic disorders, schizophrenia, and violent/self-destructive behaviors.

Internet References

National Clearinghouse for Alcohol and Drug Information
http://ncadi.samhsa.gov

Information on drug and alcohol facts that might relate to adolescence and the issues of peer pressure and youth culture is presented here. Resources, referrals, research and statistics, databases, and related Net links are available.

National Women's Health Resource Center (NWHRC)
http://www.healthywomen.org

NWHRC's site contains links to resources related to women's substance abuse and mental illnesses.

UNIT 11: Psychological Treatments

Abraham A. Brill Library
http://plaza.interport.net/nypsan/service.html

Containing data on over 40,000 books, periodicals, and reprints in psychoanalysis and related fields, the Abraham A. Brill Library has holdings that span the literature of psychoanalysis from its beginning to the present day.

The C.G. Jung Page
http://www.cgjungpage.org

Dedicated to the work of Carl Jung, this is a comprehensive resource, with links to Jungian psychology, news and opinions, reference materials, graduate programs, dreams, multilingual sites, and related Jungian themes.

Knowledge Exchange Network (KEN)
http://www.mentalhealth.org

Information about mental health (prevention, treatment, and rehabilitation services) is available via toll-free telephone services, an electronic bulletin board, and publications.

NetPsychology
http://netpsych.com/index.htm

This site explores the uses of the Internet to deliver mental health services. This is a basic cybertherapy resource site.

Sigmund Freud and the Freud Archives
http://plaza.interport.net/nypsan/freudarc.html

Internet resources related to Sigmund Freud, which include a collection of libraries, museums, and biographical materials, as well as the Brill Library archives, can be found here.

UNIT 1

The Science of Psychology

Unit Selections

Key Points to Consider

- What is psychology? Why study psychology?

- What exactly do psychologists do? Are there different types of psychology?

- How does psychology make a difference in day-to-day life?

- How can we distinguish good science from pseudoscience?

- Can psychological research be biased? How so?

- What can we do to diminish the effects of any bias in psychological research?

- In what ways can research results be misused or abused?

Student Web Site
www.mhcls.com

Internet References

Association for Psychological Science
http://www.psychologicalscience.org/
American Psychological Association
http://www.apa.org/
Psychological Research on the Net
http://psych.hanover.edu/Research/exponnet.html

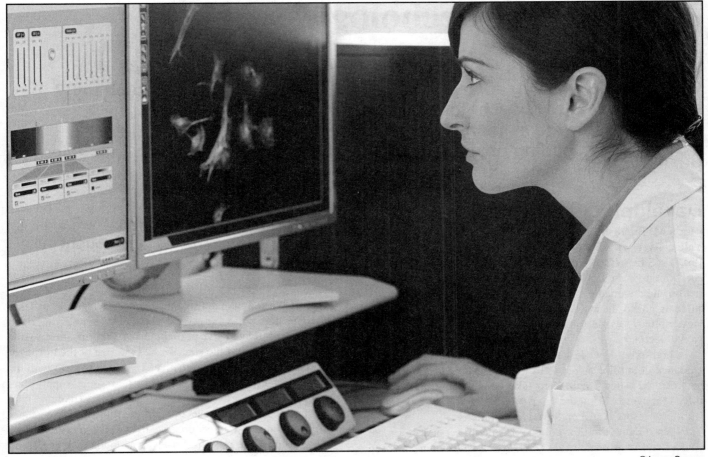

Contemporary psychology is defined *as the science of mental activity and behavior.* This definition reflects the two parent disciplines from which psychology emerged: philosophy and biology. Compared to its parents, psychology is very much a new discipline. Some aspects of modern psychology are particularly biological, such as neuroscience, perception, psychophysics, and behavioral genetics. In fact, many of our recent advances in understanding thinking and behavior emanate from neuroscience.

Today's psychologists work in a variety of settings. Many psychologists are academics, teaching and conducting psychological research on university campuses. Others work in applied settings such as hospitals, mental health clinics, industry, and schools. Most psychologists specialize in a particular field of psychology in graduate training.

Industrial psychologists specialize in human performance in organizational settings, while clinical psychologists are concerned about the assessment, diagnosis, and treatment of individuals with mental disorders. Each specialty typically requires a graduate education and sometimes requires a license to practice. Despite its varied nature, psychology remains a viable and exciting field.

Why Study Psychology?

**Why did psychology's leading researchers take that first course?
Was it the compelling advice of a master? Perhaps a sudden [epiphany]?
Why did you study psychology?
There probably are as many reasons as there are people in the field.
In this series, leading psychology researchers talk about getting into science.**

Developing a Supertaste

Linda M. Bartoshuk
Yale University School of Medicine
PhD 1965 from Brown University

As a kid growing up in Aberdeen, South Dakota, I read science fiction and dreamed of astronomy. Junior high had a career day; students got to interview members of the profession to which they aspired. I asked for a scientist, but was assigned to interview a secretary.

In high school, when I signed up for math and science, my guidance counselor suggested these were unrealistic choices, but relented when I agreed to take bookkeeping and typing. Fifty-four words a minute later (not bad in the world before word processors) I still preferred trigonometry.

When it came time for college, I came in second in a math contest and won a slide rule (for anyone who has never used one, they are amazing little devices). I headed to Rapid City to tour the South Dakota School of Mines and Technology. Women were welcomed but few went, and I was not attracted to the prospect. Carleton College had a telescope and an astronomy major. The cost was daunting but a National Merit Scholarship came to my aid and I was off. Again, few women turned up in math and science, but we were treated well by our instructors.

Not so in the real world. I learned that some observatories banned women from using the telescopes; those big, complex machines were too much for us. I had had it. I remember the night my roommate and I sat with the Carleton course book and discovered that a psychology major would give me credit for all the math and science I had taken. Wow! As a junior I signed up for introductory psychology taught by John Bare, the new department chair. The class scintillated. When we got to psychophysics, I knew I was home. Astronomy had taught me that measurement of the perceived brightness of stars played a role in measuring the size of the universe. The farther away the star, the dimmer it appears from earth. If we only knew how bright it was at the source, we could calculate the distance.

Discovering that some supertasters live in neon taste worlds has brought me full circle.

One of the few women in astronomy provided the missing link; some stars pulse and we can see their brightness wax and wane. Theory related the periodicity of the pulsation to the absolute brightness of the star. We had the size of the universe! John Bare sent me to Brown University to study taste with his mentor, Carl Pfaffmann. Discovering that some supertasters live in neon taste worlds compared to non tasters (like me) who live in pastel taste worlds has brought me full circle. We cannot share experiences, so how could we discover that taste is more vivid to some? The missing link was a standard. If we could find some sensation that was not correlated with taste, everyone could express taste intensities relative to that standard. Assuming any variability in perception of the standard to be roughly equal across groups, we could compare tastes across groups. To my delight, one of the best standards we have tested is the brightness of the sun.

An APS Fellow and Charter Member, Bartoshuk has served on the APS Board of Directors. She will give the Bring the Family Address at the 16th Annual Convention.

The Children Come First

Patrice Marie Miller
Salem State College
EdD 1988 from Harvard University

It is hard to choose a major or a career when you have never really been exposed to it. Thinking back, though, it seems as if the issues that I am involved in as a developmental psychologist started as early as ninth grade. At that time, I was living in Rio de Janeiro, Brazil. Rio, then as now, was a city full of natural beauty and poverty. In the ninth grade I worked on a project started by my history professor, in which we visited one of the *favelas* (the hillside slums) on Saturdays and engaged in games and crafts activities with the children. The idea was to try and have a positive impact on their development by giving them something constructive to do and some contact with other models for doing things.

Based on that experience, I decided that I wanted to do something that would have a positive impact on the lives of children, especially poor children. In high school and the early years of college, I tried different ways of having an impact on the lives of children, such as tutoring in East Harlem and working as a teacher's assistant. I enjoyed these experiences in many ways, but I felt as if we did not know enough about how children developed to know how best to help them.

I decided that I wanted to do something that would have a positive impact on the lives of children, especially poor children.

My senior year at New York University, I was still wondering what to do. I thought I might teach for a few years—perhaps back in Rio—while I figured out my future. The August before senior year, while at a psychological meeting with my mother, a school psychologist, I met a professor teaching behavior analysis at NYU. Second semester of that year, I worked with him on a research project involving autistic children. This experience pushed me into thinking of a different kind of career, one as an academic psychologist. I enjoy the problem solving involved in planning, carrying out, analyzing and writing up research. Thinking out issues and having things work out the way you had hoped is a special kind of thrill that I only experienced when I began to do research.

When I finished my BA, I still was not ready to forge ahead. First, I had to go back and learn some of the mathematics I had managed to duck. During this time, I worked on several research projects, along with my psychologist husband (surely, also, a reinforcing influence in all this). When we moved to Cambridge, Massachusetts, I obtained my doctorate in human development from Harvard's Graduate School of Education. My dissertation on very young infants' reactions to being taken care of by a stranger versus their mother was an attempt to look at whether and in what ways young infants differentiated between their mothers and other caregivers. It was the first of several projects I have been engaged in since on early social and emotional development of children. Teaching, which I also do, allows me to communicate some of my passions to newer students.

The way I think about it now is that my work ideally combines intellectual activities that I greatly enjoy, with an opportunity to work on issues in a field that, as a whole, I believe makes a difference in the lives of children.

Miller is a developmental psychologist specializing in social and emotional development.

Clinical Cognition

Teresa A. Treat
Yale University
PhD 2000 from Indiana University

Throughout my undergraduate and graduate years at Indiana University, I was inspired by Dick McFall's vision of an integrative psychological science. Dick spoke eloquently about a new generation of clinical scientists who were fully trained in both clinical and cognitive science, or in clinical and neural science, such that they were viewed as legitimate in both fields. And he wondered whether such hybrid scholars would view psychopathology from a novel vantage that might help to move forward our understanding, assessment, and treatment of psychological problems. I tested the waters by taking a mathematical psychology course with Jim Townsend during my first year in the clinical-science program. The course damn near killed me—granted, this is not an uncommon experience in a Townsend course—but Jim was unfailing in his support and encouragement, and I emerged with numerous ill-formed notions about the potential utility of formal mathematical modeling of clinically relevant cognitive processing.

In the meantime, McFall, Rick Viken, and I had begun developing photo stimulus sets that would allow us to use cognitive science models and methods to investigate men's perceptions of women's sexual interest (with implications for our understanding of acquaintance-initiated sexual aggression), as well as women's perceptions of other women's shape- and weight-related information (with implications for our understanding of eating disorders). The resulting photo stimulus sets were a far cry from the simpler, well-controlled stimuli that cognitive scientists typically used to investigate normative cognitive processes. Thus, it was unclear whether the principles and paradigms developed in this more highly controlled context would generalize to the messiness of investigations of clinically relevant individual differences in complex social perception.

As the work progressed, I became accustomed to hearing cognitive scientists insist that "those are the most uncontrolled stimuli I've ever seen!" In contrast, of course, many clinical scientists claimed that they were "the most over-controlled stimuli" they'd ever seen. Fortunately Rob Nosofsky, John Kruschke, and David MacKay—as well as two extremely gifted graduate students at the time, Tom Palmeri and Mike Erickson—worked with us every step of the way on these two lines of research and spent countless hours training me in the rudiments of multidimensional scaling, formal models of categorization and learning, and computational modeling.

Eventually, I had completed all the coursework necessary for a joint degree in clinical and cognitive science, but I had yet to declare my additional major. It felt presumptuous to call myself a clinical-cognitive scientist, because that implied that I was a "real" cognitive scientist as well as a "real" clinical scientist. The latter had been a central piece of my academic identity for years, but I had yet to recognize the former. Three years of working side by side with cognitive students in Kruschke's lab finally changed this. And then one day, when I was musing out loud in the lab about whether to declare the joint degree, one of my lab mates challenged me by saying, "What's wrong with you? You're as much a cognitive scientist as the rest of us." Soon thereafter, I remember nervously marching upstairs to the cognitive-science office to officially declare the joint major and choose a career as a clinical-cognitive scientist—long after I already was living and loving a career in McFall's "integrative psychological science."

Treat is a clinical and counseling psychologist who specializes in cognitive science.

Redefining a Career

Milton D. Hakel
Bowling Green State University
PhD 1966 from the University of Minnesota

It wasn't pretty. It wasn't easy. But especially in the perspective offered by the passage of over 40 years, choosing a major, then choosing to pursue graduate study, and then deciding study for the PhD was a chaotic, sometimes frantic, and always exciting process.

As a teen, I knew I wanted to go to college, but I had no clear direction in mind. When I was a high school junior, I wanted to go anyplace but the University of Minnesota. After investigating the costs, and considering my grades (which made me a weak competitor for scholarships), dissonance reduction worked its magic and I applied only to the University of Minnesota. It was a fortunate application (and acceptance), and I have always appreciated the excellent and challenging education I received there.

As an undergraduate beginning in 1959, I ran through a succession of 12 declared and undeclared majors, hoping to find something that could suit me for the long run. Some majors lasted as little as three weeks, until I got the results of a mid-term or final that I interpreted as a signal to apply my efforts elsewhere. Other majors lasted much longer, and I graduated with a double major in philosophy and psychology. But by my senior year I knew I wanted to pursue graduate study in psychology. Many small but significant events led to that career direction.

As a third-quarter freshman, I talked my way into a limited-enrollment honors section of an introductory laboratory course (my grades put me just below the formal cut score). The course offered hands-on experience in research. In trios we collected data to replicate a one trial learning experiment originally published by William K. Estes, and individually we analyzed and reported the findings. I concluded that I could learn how to design and conduct research. All three of us in my group eventually earned PhDs, and it was a special pleasure many years later to actually meet Estes, when he became the editor of *Psychological Science* (I was part of the original APS Publication Committee that invited him to be the founding editor).

As a junior I quit commuting and moved on campus, meeting that first day a delightful and spirited woman who became my wife within a year. I took two courses in individual differences; in retrospect, they are the most important courses I ever

had—thank you Jim Jenkins and Marv Dunnette. The issues I first studied there continue to animate scientific discourse and public policy: testing and learning, heritability, group differences. I also took a course in vocational guidance, and heard about "varch" as an attribute of a career, variety, and change. I knew this was what I wanted, and guessed that a career in research would offer it.

In defining my career I redefined a few key words: chaos, frantic, excitement.

I hung out in the psychology building, getting to know graduate students and some faculty. When an opening occurred for an undergraduate teaching assistant (they needed someone to sharpen mark-sense pencils and do other tasks too menial for graduate students), I applied and got the job, and my exposure to psychology and psychologists expanded.

As a senior in 1962–63 I did a voluntary research project under Dunnette's guidance. The work I did in that "job sample" was sufficient as a demonstration of capability to get me into graduate school. I applied to only one, but my grades and scores were borderline, so I was admitted on probation (the US Air Force was my other "employment" option, and one could already see that the Vietnam War was getting ugly). The senior project eventually became my first publication.

In graduate school to pursue a master's, I found it considerably surprising when I was invited at the end of my first year to bypass the MA and work directly toward the doctorate. I became interested in how people form impressions of others and use those impressions to make consequential decisions, such as who to hire. The topic was partly a consequence of having been interviewed by about 50 different potential employers (and being rejected by 40 of them) while looking for summer jobs. I completed the degree, and research that Dunnette and I proposed was supported by the National Science Foundation in 1966. I stayed at Minnesota for two years as a postdoc, and then moved to Ohio State, Houston, and Bowling Green.

My experiences sensitized me to the fallibility of predictors and the need to devise effective and equitable systems for 1) selecting employees/admitting students, and 2) enabling people to develop their capabilities fully. These continue to be engaging issues.

So in defining my career I redefined a few key words. Chaos—going from no direction through 12 majors to one. Frantic—marrying while still an undergraduate, having two children while in graduate school, and worrying about employment and the draft raised occasional anxieties. Excitement—enough for a lifetime, and that was just the beginning.

Hankel is an APS Fellow and Charter Member and has served on the APS Board of Directors. He is an industrial/organizational psychologist.

Does Psychology Make a Significant Difference in Our Lives?

The intellectual tension between the virtues of basic versus applied research that characterized an earlier era of psychology is being replaced by an appreciation of creative applications of all research essential to improving the quality of human life. Psychologists are positioned to "give psychology away" to all those who can benefit from our wisdom. Psychologists were not there 35 years ago when American Psychological Association (APA) President George Miller first encouraged us to share our knowledge with the public. The author argues that psychology is indeed making a significant difference in people's lives; this article provides a sampling of evidence demonstrating how and why psychology matters, both in pervasive ways and specific applications. Readers are referred to a newly developed APA Web site that documents current operational uses of psychological research, theory, and methodology (its creation has been the author's primary presidential initiative): www.psychologymatters.org.

PHILIP G. ZIMBARDO

Does psychology matter? Does what we do, and have done for a hundred years or more, really make a significant difference in the lives of individuals or in the functioning of communities and nations? Can we demonstrate that our theories, our research, our professional practice, our methodologies, our way of thinking about mind, brain, and behavior make life better in any measurable way? Has what we have to show for our discipline been applied in the real world beyond academia and practitioners' offices to improve health, education, welfare, safety, organizational effectiveness, and more?

Such questions, and finding their answers, have always been my major personal and professional concern. First, as an introductory psychology teacher for nearly six decades, I have always worked to prove relevance as well as essence of psychology to my students. Next, as an author of the now classic basic text, *Psychology and Life* (Ruch & Zimbardo, 1971), which claimed to wed psychology to life applications, I constantly sought to put more psychology in our lives and more life in our psychology (Gerrig & Zimbardo, 2004; Zimbardo, 1992). To reach an even broader student audience, I have coauthored *Core Concepts in Psychology* (Zimbardo, Weber, & Johnson, 2002) that strives to bring the excitement of scientific and applied psychology to students in state and community colleges.

In order to further expand the audience for what is best in psychology, I accepted an invitation to help create, be scientific advisor for, and narrator of the 26-program PBS TV series, *Discovering Psychology* (1990/2001). For this general public audience, we have provided answers—as viewable instances—to their "so what?" questions. This award-winning series is shown both nationally and internationally (in at least 10 nations) and has been the foundation for the most popular telecourse among all the Annenberg CPB Foundation's many academic programs (see www.learner.org). Finally, as the 2002 president of the American Psychological Association, my major initiative became developing a compendium of exemplars of how psychology has made a significant difference in our lives. This Web-based summary of "psychology in applied action" has been designed as a continually modifiable and updateable repository of demonstrable evidence of psychological knowledge in meaningful applications. In a later section of this article, the compendium will be described more fully and some of its examples highlighted.

I was fortunate in my graduate training at Yale University (1954–1960) to be inspired by three exceptional mentors, each of whom modeled a different aspect of the relevance and applicability of basic psychology to vital issues facing individuals and our society. Carl Hovland developed the Yale Communication and Attitude Change Program after coming out of his military assignment in World War II of analyzing the effectiveness of propaganda and training programs (Hovland, Lumsdaine, & Sheffield, 1949). He went on to transform what was at that time a complex, global, and vague study of communication and persuasion into identifiable processes, discrete variables, and integrative hypotheses that made possible both experimental research and applications (Hovland, Janis, & Kelley, 1953). Neal Miller always straddled the fence between basic and applied research, despite being known for his classic experimental and theoretical formulations of motivation and reward in learning and conditioning. His World War II experience of training pilots to overcome fears so that they could return to combat was an applied precursor of his later role in developing biofeedback through his laboratory investigations of conditioning autonomic nervous system responses (N. E. Miller, 1978, 1985, 1992). The last of my Yale mentors, Seymour Sarason, moved out from his research program on test anxiety in children into the community as one of the founders of Community Psychology (Sarason, 1974). It was a daring move at that time in a field that honored only the scientific study of *individual* behavior.

Psychology of the 50s was also a field that honored basic research well above applied research, which was typically accorded second-class status, if not denigrated by the "experimentalists," a popular brand name in that era. Psychology at many major universities aspired to be "soft physics," as in the heady days of our Germanic forebears, Wundt, Fechner, Ebbinghaus, Titchner, and others (see Green, Shore, & Teo, 2001). Anything applied was seen at best as crude social engineering by tinkerers, not real thinkers. Moreover, behaviorism was still rampant, with animal models that stripped away from learning what nonsense syllable memory researchers had deleted from memory—merely the context, the content, the human meaning, and the culture of behavior. The most prominent psychologist from the 50s through the 80s, B.F. Skinner, was an anomaly in this regard. Half of him remained a Watsonian radical behaviorist who refused to admit the existence of either motivation or cognition into his psychology (Skinner, 1938, 1966, 1974). Meanwhile, the other Skinner side applied operant conditioning principles to train pigeons for military duties and outlined a behaviorist Utopia in *Walden Two* (Skinner, 1948).

Giving Psychology Away: The Call for Societal Accountability

And then along came George Miller whose American Psychological Association (APA) presidential address in 1969 stunned the psychological establishment because one of its own firstborn sons committed the heresy of exhorting them to go public, get real, get down, give it up, and be relevant. Well, that is the way I think I heard it back then when George Miller (1969) told his audience that it was time to begin "to give psychology away to the public." It was time to stop talking only to other psychologists. It was time to stop writing only for professional journals hidden away in library stacks. It was time to go beyond the endless quest for experimental rigor in the perfectly designed study to test a theoretically derived hypothesis. Maybe it was time to begin finding answers to the kinds of questions your mother asked about why people acted the way they did. Perhaps it was acceptable to start considering how best to translate what we knew into a language that most ordinary citizens could understand and even come to appreciate.

I for one applauded George Miller's stirring call to action for all these reasons. It was heady for me because I believed

that coming from such a distinguished serious theorist and researcher—not some do-gooder, liberal communitarian whom the establishment could readily dismiss—his message would have a big impact in our field Sadly, the banner raised by Miller's inspirational speech, did not fly very high over most psychology departments for many years to come. Why not? I think for four reasons: Excessive modesty about *what* psychology really had of value to offer the public, ignorance about *who* was "the public," cluelessness about *how* to go about the mission of giving psychology away, and lack of sufficient concern about *why* psychology needed to be accountable to the public.

How shall we counterargue against such reasoning? First, scanning the breadth and depth of our field makes apparent that there is no need for such professional modesty. Rather, the time has come to be overtly proud of our past and current accomplishments, as I will try to demonstrate here. We have much to be proud of in our heritage and in our current accomplishments. Second, the public starts with our students, our clients, and our patients and extends to our funding agencies, national and local politicians, all nonpsychologists, and the media. And it also means your mother whose "bubba psychology" sometimes needs reality checks based on solid evidence we have gathered. Third, it is essential to recognize that the media are the gatekeepers between the best, relevant psychology we want to give away and that elusive public we hope will value what we have to offer. We need to learn how best to utilize the different kinds of media that are most appropriate for delivering specific messages to particular target audiences that we want to reach. Psychologists need to learn how to write effective brief press releases, timely op-ed newspaper essays, interesting articles for popular magazines, valuable trade books based on empirical evidence, and how best to give radio, TV, and print interviews. Simple awareness of media needs makes evident, for example, that TV requires visual images, therefore, we should be able to provide video records of research, our interventions, or other aspects of the research or therapeutic process that will form a story's core.

"Media smarts" also means realizing that to reach adolescents with a helpful message (that is empirically validated), a brief public service announcement on MTV or an article in a teen magazine will have a broader impact than detailed journal articles or even popular books on the subject.[1] Thus, it becomes essential to our mission of making the public wiser consumers of psychological knowledge to learn how to communicate effectively to the media and to work with the media.

Finally, we can challenge the fourth consideration regarding societal accountability with the awareness that taxpayers fund much of our research as well as some of the education of our graduate students. It is imperative that we convey the sense to the citizens of our states and nation that we are responsive to society's needs and, further, that we feel responsible for finding solutions to some of its problems (Zimbardo, 1975). It has become standard operating procedure for most granting agencies now to require a statement about the potential societal value of any proposed research. That does not mean that all research must be applied to dealing with current social or individual problems because there is considerable evidence that research that originally seemed esoterically "basic" has in time found valuable applications (see Swazey, 1974). It does mean that although some of our colleagues begin with a focus on a problem in an applied domain, the others who start with an eye on theory testing or understanding some basic phenomena should feel obligated to stretch their imaginations by considering potential applications of their knowledge. I believe we have much worthy applicable psychology, basic research, theory, and methodology that is awaiting creative transformations to become valuable applied psychology.

The Profound and Pervasive Impact of Past Psychological Knowledge

Before I outline some recent, specific instances of how psychological research, theory, and methodology have been applied in various settings, I will first highlight some of the fundamental contributions psychology has already made in our lives. Many of them have become so pervasive and their impact so unobtrusively profound that they are taken for granted. They have come to be incorporated into the way we think about certain domains, have influenced our attitudes and values, and so changed the way individuals and agencies behave that they now seem like the natural, obvious way the world should be run. Psychology often gets little or no credit for these contributions—when we should be deservedly proud of them.

Psychological Testing and Assessment

One of psychology's major achievements has been the development and the extensive reliance on objective, quantifiable means of assessing human talents, abilities, strengths, and weaknesses. In the 100 years since Alfred Binet first measured intellectual performance, systematic assessment has replaced the subjective, often biased judgments of teachers, employers, clinicians, and others in positions of authority by objective, valid, reliable, quantifiable, and normed tests (Binet, 1911; Binet & Simon, 1915). It is hard to imagine a test-free world. Modern testing stretches from assessments of intelligence, achievement, personality, and pathology to domains of vocational and values assessment, personnel selection, and more. Vocational interest measures are the backbone of guidance counseling and career advising. The largest single application of classified testing in the world is the Armed Services Vocational Aptitude Battery that is given to as many as 2 million enlisted personnel annually. Personnel selection testing has over 90 years of validity research and proven utility.

We are more familiar with the SAT and GRE standardized testing, currently being revised in response to various critiques, but they are still the yardstick for admission to many colleges and universities (Sternberg, 2000). Workplace job skills assessment and training involves huge numbers of workers and managers in many countries around the world (DuBois, 1970). Little wonder, then, that such pervasive use of assessments has spawned a multibillion dollar industry. (Because I am serving here in this article in the capacity as cheerleader for our discipline, I will not

raise questions about the political misuse or overuse of testing nor indeed be critical of some of the other contributions that follow; see Cronbach, 1975.)

Positive Reinforcement

The earlier emphasis in schools and in child rearing on punishment for errors and inappropriate behavior has been gradually displaced by a fundamentally divergent focus on the utility of positive reinforcement for correct, appropriate responding (Straus & Kantor, 1994). Punishing the "undesirable person" has been replaced by punishing only "undesirable behavioral acts." Time-outs for negative behavior have proven remarkably effective as a behavior-modification strategy (Wolfe, Risley, & Mees, 1965). It has become so effective that it has become a favorite technique for managing child behavior by parents in the United States. "Half the parents and teachers in the United States use this nonviolent practice and call it 'time-out,' which makes it a social intervention unmatched in modern psychology," according to the American Academy of Pediatrics' (1998) publication.

Animal training has benefited enormously from procedures of shaping complex behavioral repertoires and the use of conditioned reinforcers (such as clickers' soundings paired with food rewards). An unexpected value of such training, as reported by animal caregivers, is that they enhance the mental health of many animal species through the stimulation provided by learning new behaviors (*San Francisco Chronicle,* 2003). Skinner and his behaviorist colleagues deserve the credit for this transformation in how we think about and go about changing behavior by means of response-contingent reinforcement. Their contributions have moved out of animal laboratories into schools, sports, clinics, and hospitals (see Axelrod & Apsche, 1983; Druckman & Bjork, 1991; Kazdin, 1994; Skinner, 1974).

Psychological Therapies

The mission of our psychological practitioners of relieving the suffering of those with various forms of mental illness by means of appropriately delivered types of psychological therapy has proven successful. Since Freud's (1896/1923, 1900/1965) early cases documenting the efficacy of "talk therapy" for neurotic disorders, psychotherapy has taken many forms. Cognitive behavior modification, systematic desensitization, and exposure therapies have proven especially effective in treating phobias, anxiety disorders, and panic attacks, thanks to the application of Pavlovian principles of classical conditioning (Pavlov, 1897/1902, 1897/1927), first developed by Joseph Wolpe (1958). Even clinical depression is best treated with a combination of psychotherapy and medication, and psychotherapy has been shown to be as effective as the drugs alone (Hollon, Thase, & Markowitz, 2002). At a more general level, psychology has helped to demystify "madness," to bring humanity into the treatment of those with emotional and behavioral disorders, and to give people hope that such disorders can be changed (Beck, 1976). Our practitioners and clinical theorists have also developed a range of treatments designed especially for couples, families, groups, for those in rehabilitation from drugs or physical disabilities, as well as for many specific types of problems such as, addictions, divorce, or shyness.

Self-Directed Change

The shelves of most bookstores in the United States are now as likely to be filled with "self-help" books as they are with cooking and dieting books. Although many of them can be dismissed as bad forms of "pop psych" that offer guidance and salvation without any solid empirical footing to back their claims, others provide a valuable service to the general public. At best, they empower people to engage in self-directed change processes for optimal personal adjustment (see Maas, 1998; Myers, 1993; Zimbardo, 1977). In part, their success comes from providing wise advice and counsel based on a combination of extensive expert experience and relevant research packaged in narratives that ordinary people find personally meaningful.

Dynamic Development Across the Life Span

Earlier conceptions of children as small adults, as property, and later as valuable property were changed in part by the theories and research of developmental psychologists (see McCoy, 1988; Pappas, 1983). In recent times, the emerging status of "the child as person" has afforded children legal rights, due process, and self-determination, along with the recognition that they should be regarded as competent persons worthy of considerable freedom (Horowitz, 1984). Psychology has been a human service profession whose knowledge base has been translated into support for a positive ideology of children (Hart, 1991). The human organism is continually changing, ever modifying itself to engage its environments more effectively, from birth through old age. This fundamental conception has made evident that babies need stimulation of many kinds for optimal development, just as do their grandparents. There is now widespread psychological recognition that infants do experience pain; learning often depends on critical age-related developmental periods; nature and nurture typically interact in synergistic ways to influence our intelligence and many attributes; mental growth follows orderly progressions, as does language acquisition and production; and that the elderly do not lose their mental agility and competence if they continue to exercise their cognitive skills throughout life (see Baltes & Staudinger 2000; Bee, 1994; Erikson, 1963; Piaget, 1954; Pinker, 1994; Plomin & McClearn, 1993; Scarr, 1998). These are but a few of the fundamental contributions of psychology to the way our society now thinks about human development over the course of a lifetime because of decades of research by our developmentalist colleagues.

Parenting

Advice by psychologists on best parental practices has varied in quality and value over time. However, there now seems to be agreement that children need to develop secure attachments to parents or caregivers and that the most beneficial parenting style for generating an effective child-parent bond is authoritative. Authoritative parents make age-appropriate demands on children while being responsive to their needs, autonomy, and freedom (see Baumrind, 1973; Collins, Maccoby, Steinberg, Hetherington, & Bornstein, 2000; Darling & Steinberg, 1993; Maccoby, 1980, 1992, 2000).

Psychological Stress

Is there any day in our modern lives that stress does not seem to be omnipresent? We are stressed by time pressures on us, by our jobs (Maslach, 1982), by our marriages, by our friends or by our lack of them. Back when I was a graduate student, stress was such a novel concept that it was surprising when our professor Irving Janis (1958) wrote one of the first books on the subject of psychological stress. The concept of psychological stress was virtually unrecognized in medical care in the 50s and 60s. Psychosomatic disorders baffled physicians who never recognized stress as a causal factor in illness and disease. Since then, psychological research and theorizing has helped to move the notion of stress to the center of the biopsychosocial health model that is revolutionizing medical treatments (Ader & Cohen, 1993; Cohen & Herbert, 1996). Psychologists have shown that our appraisals of stress and our lifestyle habits have a major impact on many of the major causes of illness and death (see Lazarus, 1993; Lazarus & Folkman, 1984). We have made commonplace the ideas of coping with stress, reducing lifestyle risk factors, and building social support networks to enable people to live healthier and longer lives (see Coe, 1999; Cohen & Syme, 1985; Taylor & Clark, 1986).

Unconscious Motivation

Psychology brought into the public mind, as did dramatists such as William Albee, Arthur Miller, and Tennessee Williams, that what we think and do is not always based on conscious decisions. Rather, human behavior may be triggered by unconscious motivations of which we have no awareness. Another nod of thanks goes out to the wisdom of Sigmund Freud and of Carl Jung (1936/1959) for helping to illuminate this previously hidden side of human nature. In a similar vein, slips of the tongue and pen are now generally interpreted as potentially meaningful symptoms of suppressed intentions. It is relatively common in many levels of U.S. society for people to believe that accidents may not be accidental but motivated, that dreams might convey important messages, and also that we use various defense mechanisms, such as projection, to protect fragile egos from awareness of negative information.

Prejudice and Discrimination

Racial prejudice motivates a range of emotions and behaviors among both those targeted and those who are its agents of hatred. Discrimination is the overt behavioral sequeala of prejudiced beliefs. It enforces inequalities and injustices based on categorical assignments to presumed racial groups. Stereotypes embody a biased conception of the attributes people presumably possess or lack. The 1954 decision by the Supreme Court of the United States (*Brown v. Board of Education of Topeka, KS*) that formally desegregated public schools was based on some critical social psychological research. The body of empirical research by Kenneth and Mamie Clark (1939a, 1939b, 1940, 1950) effectively demonstrated for the Court that the segregated educational conditions of that era had a negative impact on the sense of self-worth of Negro (the then-preferred term) school children. The Court, and the thoughtful public since then, accepted the psychological premise that segregated education, which separates the races, can never be really equal for those being stigmatized by that system of discrimination. Imposed segregation not only is the consequence of prejudice, it contributes further to maintaining and intensifying prejudice, negative stereotypes, and discrimination. In the classic analysis of the psychology of prejudice by Gordon Allport (1954), the importance of equal status contact between the races was advanced as a dynamic hypothesis that has since been widely validated in a host of different contexts (Pettigrew, 1997).

Humanizing Factory Work

Dehumanizing factory assembly lines in which workers were forced to do the same repetitive, mindless task, as if they were robots, initially gave Detroit automakers a production advantage. However, Japanese automakers replaced such routinized assembly lines with harmonious, small work teams operating under conditions of participatory management and in-group democratic principles. The remarkable success of the Japanese automakers in overtaking their American counterparts in a relatively short time is due in part to their adaptation of the principles of group dynamics developed by Kurt Lewin, his colleagues and students at the Massachusetts Institute of Technology, and the University of Michigan (Lewin, 1947a, 1947b, 1948). Paradoxically, U.S. auto manufacturers are now incorporating this Japanese work model into their factories, decades after they should have done so. This is one way in which psychological theory can be credited with a humanizing impact on industrial work. But psychologists working in the industrial/organizational framework have done even more to help businesses appreciate and promote the importance of goal setting, worker-job fit, job satisfaction, and personnel selection and training.

Political Polling

It is hard to imagine elections without systematic polling of various segments of the electorate using sampling techniques as predictors of election outcomes. Polling for many other purposes by Gallup, Roper, and other opinion polling agencies has become big business. Readers might be surprised to learn that psychologist Hadley Cantril (1991) pioneered in conducting research into the methodology of polling in the 1940s. Throughout World War II, Cantril provided President Roosevelt with valuable information on American public opinion. He also established the Office of Public Opinion Research, which became a central archive for polling data.

How and Why Psychology Matters in Our Lives

I am proud to be a psychologist. As the 2002 APA president, one of my goals was to spread that pride far and wide among my colleagues as well as among all students of psychology. For starters, we can all be proud of the many contributions we have made collectively to enrich the way people think about the human condition, a bit of which was outlined above. I am also proud of the fact that our scientific approach to understanding the behavior of individuals has guided some policy and improved some operating procedures in our society. We have always been one of the most vigilant and outspoken proponents of the use of the scientific method for bringing reliable evidence to bear on a range of issues (Campbell, 1969). Given any intervention or new policy, psychologists insist on raising the question, "but does it really work?" and utilizing evaluative methodologies and meta-analyses to help make that decision. Psychologists have modeled the approach to reducing errors in advancing behavior-based conclusions through random assignment, double-blind tests, and sensitivity to the many biases present in uncontrolled observations and research procedures. Many of us have also been leaders in advancing a variety of innovations in education through our awareness of principles of attention, learning, memory, individual differences, and classroom dynamics. In addition, I am proud of our discipline's dedication to relieving all forms of human suffering through effective therapeutic interventions along with promoting prevention strategies and appropriate environmental change. As psychologists, we should also be pleased by discovering that our theories, research, and methodologies are serving to influence individual and societal actions, as will be shown next.

Psychologymatters.org

The scaffolding for such pride in psychology might best be manifest in a newly developed compendium, which shows society what we have done and are doing to improve the quality of life. I wanted to have available in one easily accessible and indexed source a listing of the research and theories that have been translated into practice. Such a resource would indicate how each item is being applied in various settings, such as schools, clinics, hospitals, businesses, community services, and legal and governmental agencies. It would establish the fact that psychology makes a significant difference in our lives by means of these concrete exemplars of its relevant applications. Ideally, this compendium would indicate how psychological contributions have saved lives, reduced or prevented suffering, saved money, made money, enhanced educational goals, improved security and safety, promoted justice and fairness, made organizations operate more effectively, and more. By designing this compendium as a Web-based open file, it can be continually updated, modified, and expanded as promising research meets the criterion of acceptability as having made a practically significant difference.

This effort to devise a compendium began with the help of APA's Science Directorate, by issuing a call for submissions to many e-mail lists serving APA members and through requests in APA's Monitor on Psychology and on the www.apa.org Web site. The initial set of items was vetted independently by Len Mitnick (formerly of the National Institute of Mental Health) and me. A "blue-ribbon" task force of journal editors, textbook authors, and senior scientists was formed to further vet these final items, help revise them, and then to work at expanding our base.[2]

Because this compendium offers the opportunity to portray an attractive, intelligent face of psychology to the public, final drafts have been edited or rewritten by science writers in APA's Public Communication's office, ably directed by Rhea

Farberman. Ideally, the submissions appear in a jargon-free, readable style appealing to the nonpsychologist public, as well as to our professional colleagues. In addition to having the individual items categorized into many general topical domains, readily searchable by key words or phrases, we have expanded the value of this site by adding an extensive glossary of psychological terms, a historical timeline of major psychological events and contributors, and basic information on "how to be a wiser consumer of research." We will include other extensions as appropriate based on feedback from colleagues and the public we are serving.

The criteria for inclusion are that each submission be presented (a) in sufficient detail to allow an independent assessment; (b) with evidence of significant statistical effects obtained within the study; (c) with reported application or extension of the submitted research, methodology, or theory in some specific domain of relevance; and (d) with evidence of where and how it has made a significant difference, such as citation of a new law, policy, standardized procedure, or operating system that was based on the submitted item. Items with *promise* of such applicability in the future (because they were too new to have been subject to any evaluation of outcome effectiveness) are being held in a "wait-and-check-back-later" file. I should mention in passing that many submitted items described research that was interesting, including some classic studies, but they have never met the test of societal applicability.

I welcome the feedback of *American Psychologist* readers on this first phase of our efforts, while also issuing a cordial invitation to add your voice to this compendium with additional worthy submissions. The reach of these initial efforts will hopefully be extended by having this compendium serve as a model to the psychological associations of countries around the world, adding to psychology's global relevance.

Please visit us at www.psychologymatters.org. But please wait a moment before booting up your computer, until you finish reading the next section of this article, which highlights a sampling of what you will find there.

Highlights of Psychology's Real World Relevance

I want to conclude with a dozen or so examples taken from our compendium that illustrate a range of its different topics and domains of applicability. This presentation will end with one extended instance of what I consider a model collaboration of theory, research, media applicability, and global dissemination of psychological knowledge conveyed in a unique format—soap operas! It is the ingenious application of the theory of social modeling by Albert Bandura (1965, 1977) in the design of scenarios used in soap operas to encourage literacy, birth control, the education of woman, environmental sustainability, and more.

Human Factors

Traffic safety has been improved by researchers in the area of human factors and ergonomics through a better understanding of visual perception. We now know that changing the standard color of red emergency trucks to a lime-green color reduces accidents because that greenish hue is better perceived in dim light. Similarly, changing traffic sign fonts to increase their recognition at night is another safety improvement resulting from psychological research by Allen (1970), Solomon and King (1985), and Garvey, Pietrucha, and Meeker (1997).

Scott Geller's (2001, 2003) research program applies Skinnerian behavior analysis to increase safe behaviors, reduce at-risk behaviors, and prevent unintentional injuries at work and on the road. Such unintentional injury is the leading cause of death to people ages 44 years and under. The behavior-based safety (BBS) approach for increasing safety identifies critical behaviors that are targeted for change, establishes baselines, applies change interventions, and evaluates workers' change away from specific risky behaviors to more beneficial directions. This approach has been applied in thousands of organizations with great success, such as in having people wear seat belts and in occupational safety programs. The rate of reported injuries after five years of implementation of this behavioral approach decreased by as much as an average 72% across a number of organizations (for a summary of the evidence for the extent of injury reduction, see the report by Beth Sulzer-Azaroff & John Austin, 2000). One indicator of the social significance of applying behavior analysis is apparent in the *Clinical Practice Guidelines* of New York States' (1999) Department of Health, Early Intervention Program: "It is recommended that principles of applied behavior analysis (ABA) and behavior intervention strategies be included as important elements in any intervention program for young children with autism" (p. 13).

Navigational aids for the blind and visually impaired people have been developed by psychologists Roberta Klatsky and Jack Loomis, working with geographer Reginald Golledge (Loomis, Klatsky, & Golledge, 2001) over several decades. They utilize principles of spatial cognition along with those of space and auditory perception to guide locomotion. Their new technology is now in development funded by the National Institute for Disability and Rehabilitation Research.

Criminal Justice

Cognitive and social psychologists have shown that eyewitness testimony is surprisingly unreliable. Their research reveals the ease with which recall of criminal events is biased by external influences in interrogations and police line-ups. The seminal work of Beth Loftus (1975, 1979, 1992) and Gary Wells (Wells & Olson, 2003), among others, has been recognized by the U.S. Attorney General's office in drawing up national guidelines for the collection of accurate and unbiased eyewitness identification (see Malpass & Devine, 1981; Stebley, 1997).

The Stanford Prison Experiment has become a classic demonstration of the power of social situational forces to negatively impact the behavior of normal, healthy participants who began to act in pathological or evil ways in a matter of a few days (Zimbardo, Haney, Banks, & Jaffe, 1973). It added a new awareness of institutional power to the authority power of Stanley Milgram's (1974) blind obedience studies (see Blass, 1999; Zimbardo, Maslach, & Haney, 1999). The lessons of this research have gone well beyond the classroom. In part as a consequence of my testimony before a Senate judiciary committee on crime and prisons (Zimbardo, 1974), its committee chair, Senator Birch Bayh, prepared a new law for federal prisons requiring juveniles in pretrial detention to be housed separately from adult inmates (to prevent their being abused). Our participants were juveniles in the pretrial detention facility of the Stanford jail. A video documentary of the study, "Quiet Rage: The Stanford Prison Experiment," has been used extensively by many agencies within the civilian and military criminal justice system as well as in shelters for abused women. I recently discovered that it is even used to educate role-playing military interrogators in the Navy SEAR (survival, evasion, and resistance) program about the dangers of abusing their power against others role-playing pretend spies and terrorists (Annapolis Naval College psychology staff, personal communication, September 18, 2003). The Web site for the Stanford Prison Experiment gets more than 500 visitors daily and has had more than 13 million unique page views in the past four years (www.prisonexp.org). Those surprising figures should be telling us that we must focus more effort on utilizing the power of the Web as a major new medium for disseminating psychology's messages directly to a worldwide audience.

Education

Among the many examples of psychology at work in the field of education, two of my favorites naturally have a social psychological twist. Elliot Aronson and his research team in Austin, Texas, dealt with the negative consequences of desegregated schools by creating "jigsaw classrooms." Prejudice against minority children was rampant, those children were not performing well, and elementary school classes were marked by high degrees of tension. But when all students were taught to share a set of materials in small learning teams where each child has one set of information indispensable to the rest of the team, and on which tests and grades depend, remarkable things happened. All kids started to listen to the other kids, especially minority kids who they used to ignore or disparage, because such attention and cooperation is essential to getting a good grade. Not only did the self-esteem of the minority children escalate, but so did their academic performance, as prejudice and discrimination went down. The techniques of the jigsaw classroom are inexpensive for teachers to learn and to operationalize, so it is no wonder that Aronson's simple concept is now being incorporated into the curricula of hundreds of schools in many states, with similarly impressive results (Aronson, 1990; Aronson, Blaney, Stephan, Sikes, & Snapp, 1978; Aronson & Gonzalez, 1988; Aronson & Patnoe, 1997).

Teaching young children interpersonal cognitive problem solving skills, known as ICPS, reduces physical and verbal aggression, increases coping with frustrations, and promotes positive peer relationships. This research program developed by Myrna Shure and George Spivak (1982) over the past several decades is a major violence prevention approach being applied in schools and family agencies in programs called "Raising a Thinking Child" and by the U.S. Department of Education's "I Can Problem Solve" program.

Health

Environmental health is threatened by a host of toxic substances, such as lead, mercury, solvents, and pesticides. Experimental psychologists, behavioral analysts, and psychometricians have helped create the field of behavioral toxicology that recognizes the nervous system as the target for many toxins, with defects in behavior and mental processes as the symptomatic consequences. Pioneering work by psychologist Bernard Weiss (1992, 1999) and others has had a significant impact on writing behavioral tests into federal legislation, thereby better regulating the use of a wide range of neurotoxins in our environment. That research documents the vulnerability of children's developing brains to chemicals in the environment.

Among the many negative consequences of America's involvement in the Vietnam War was the explosion of the phenomenon of posttraumatic stress disorder (PTSD). Many veterans were experiencing this debilitating disorder that was uncovered during their psychotherapy treatments. The more we discovered about this delayed, persistent, intense stress reaction to violence and trauma, the more we realized that veterans of earlier wars had also experienced PTSD, but it was unlabeled. That was also the case with many civilian victims of trauma, among them rape victims and those who had experienced child abuse. PTSD has become a well-recognized and publicly acknowledged phenomenon today because it was one of the mental health consequences of the monumental trauma from the terrorist attacks on September 11, 2001, in New York City and Washington, DC. Credit for the early recognition, identification, measurement, and treatment of PTSD goes to the programs of research funded by the Veteran's Administration, which was pioneered by the research team of clinical psychologist Terry Keane (Keane, Malloy, & Fairbank, 1984; Weathers, Keane, & Davidson, 2001).

The Magic of Touch

One of the consequences of a host of amazing medical advances is saving the lives of many premature infants who would have died even just a decade ago. With modern intensive care, preemies weighing only a few pounds now survive, but the essential hospital costs are staggering, up to $10,000 a day for weeks or months! One simple solution for sending them home sooner depends on accelerating their growth by means of touch therapy. Psychologist Field extended earlier research she had done with biologist Saul Schanberg (Field, 1998; Field & Schanberg, 1990; Field et al., 1986) on massaging infant rat pups that were motherless. Just as the infant rats rapidly grew in response to that vigorous touch, so did the human preemies. Massaging them several times a day for only 15 minutes was sufficient to stimulate growth hormones. On average, such massaged infants are able to go home six days sooner than comparison preemies treated in the conventional way. Given 470,000 premature infants are born each year in the United States alone, it is evident that billions of dollars in health care costs could be saved if this simple, inexpensive treatment was made standard procedure in more hospital intensive care units (see also Meltz, 2000).

To establish the societal value of any intervention designed to save lives or enhance health and well-being, one must systematically evaluate its cost-effectiveness. That means establishing a ratio of the benefits compared with various cost estimates of putting the intervention into operation and sustaining it over time. Such a ratio was developed for dollar costs per year of life saved and applied to more than 500 life-saving interventions (Tengs et al., 1995). Across all of these interventions, the median cost was $42,000 per year of life saved. Although some programs save more resources than they cost, others cost millions of dollars for each year of life they save and thus become of questionable social value. Using this standard measure, we discover that new neonatal intensive care for low-birth-weight infants (preemies) costs a whooping $270,000 for each year of their lives saved. By that yardstick, the inexpensive touch therapy intervention would dramatically reduce that cost-effectiveness ratio.

The puzzling issue then is why such a simple procedure is not now standard operating procedure in every such intensive care unit in the nation or the world? One goal of our compendium development team is also to investigate why some potentially useful interventions have not been applied in the venues where they could make a significant difference. For instance, social psychologists have shown convincingly that elderly patients in a home for the aged who were given a sense of control and responsibility over even minor events became healthier and lived significantly longer than comparison patients (Langer & Rodin, 1976; Rodin & Langer, 1977). Amazingly, this simple, powerful intervention has not ever been utilized—even in the institution where the research was conducted.

Undoing Dyslexia via Video Games

Treatment for dyslexia by speech therapists and counselors is a slow, long, expensive, and frustrating experience for professionals, parents, and children. Cognitive neuroscientist, Paula Tallal, is using new functional magnetic resonance imaging techniques to identify the source of reading dyslexia in brain regions that do not adequately process fast appearing sound-sight phonemic combinations. She then worked with a computer-programming agency to develop special video games that systematically shape these children's ever-faster responses to various sights and sounds in the games. With this new technology, children treat themselves in an atmosphere of entertainment and adventure, rely only on intrinsic motivation of game playing, get personalized feedback, and need minimal supervision by highly skilled professionals.

The special computerized video game is called "Fast For-Word." It provides intensive, highly individualized adaptive training across a large number of cognitive, linguistic, and reading skills that are vital for academic success. By adapting trial by trial to each child's performance, progress in aural and written language skills of children with dyslexia is reduced to but a few weeks from what had been typically years of intervention efforts. Approximately 375,000 individuals have completed such training across 2,200 public schools nationwide, and over 2,000 private practice professionals use Fast ForWord programs in their clinics (for more information, visit www.scientificlearning.com and www.brainconnection.com).

This sensitive application of psychological knowledge and new methods blended with high technology has resulted in enhanced quality of life for these children as well as their families and teachers, not to mention much money and resources saved (see Holly Fitch & Tallal, 2003; Tallal & Benasich, 2002; Tallal, Galaburda, Llinas, & Von Euler, 1993).

An Idealized Example of Psychology Applied Globally

The use of intrinsically interesting media, such as video games and Tele-Health dynamic systems, enables adults as well as children to play central roles in individualized health-management programs. The power of the media also has been extended to television as a far-reaching medium to convey vital persuasive messages about behavior changes that are essential to cope with many of the social, economic, political, and health problems facing individuals around the globe. Can psychology contribute to effectively dealing with the population explosion in many countries, increase the status and education of women, and minimize or prevent AIDS? A tall order, for sure. However, it is now happening through a remarkable collaboration of a wise TV producer, a brilliant psychologist, and an international agency that distributes their unusual messages worldwide (Bandura, 2002; Smith, 2002).

Promoting Family Planning

The explosion in population around the world is one of our most urgent global problems. Ecologically sustainable development and growth is being challenged by a variety of entwined phenomena, such as high fertility rates in many countries coupled with suboptimal birth rates in others, dramatically increased longevity in some nations along with the spread of deadly communicable diseases in others. One means of population control in overpopulated countries involves women and men actively engaged in their own family planning. However, the question is how to do so effectively and efficiently because most previous efforts have met with minimal success?

A TV producer in Mexico, Miguel Sabido, created soap operas that were serialized daily dramas, with prosocial messages about practicing family planning and also others that promote literacy and education of women. Woven into the narrative of his commercial dramas were elements taken from Albert Bandura's sociocognitive theory of the importance of social models in shaping desired behaviors (Bandura, 1965, 1977, 1986). In many Spanish-speaking countries, most family members watch soap operas fervently each day as their plots unfold over many weeks or months. Viewers identify with attractive, desirable models and dis-identify with those whose actions seem repulsive or create unwanted problems for the "good" guys. In some scenarios, there are also actors who represent "transitional models," starting off engaging in high-risk or undesirable behaviors but then changing in socially appropriate directions. After some programs, there is informational or community support for the cause being projected, by celebrities, government officials, or members of the clergy. This secondary influence path for behavior change adds the key element of making connections to the viewers' personal social networks and community settings in addition to the direct path from the media message to desired changes in target behaviors.

Does it really work? After watching the Mexican programs promoting family planning, many women enrolled in family planning clinics. The 32% increase of woman starting to use this service was similar to the increase in contraceptive users. This was true even though there was never an explicit message about contraception for family planning (in deference to the negative position on this birth control issue by the Catholic Church). Another key result was that the greater the level of media exposure to these family-oriented TV soap operas, the greater was the percentage of women using contraceptives and also discussing family planning with spouses "many times" (Bandura, 2002).

Preventing the Spread of AIDS

These dramas were shown in one region of Tanzania, Africa, and their effects compared with a control region where TV viewers were not exposed to the dramas (later on they got to see the same soap operas). One of the many prosocial effects was an increase in new family planning adopters following the viewing of these dramatic serials compared with no change in the control region. Seventeen segments were included in dramas in Tanzania to prevent the spread of the AIDS virus, a special problem among truck drivers who have unprotected sex with hundreds of prostitutes working at truck stop hubs. Actors portrayed positive models who adopt safe sex practices or negative ones who do not—and then they die of AIDS! Condom distribution soared following viewing this series, whereas it remained low in the control, no soap opera region. Along with this critical change in behavior were also reports of reduced number of sexual partners, more talk about HIV infection, and changed beliefs in personal risk of HIV infection from unprotected sex. Such attitudinal and behavioral changes are vital to slowing the spread of AIDS, which is estimated to make orphans of up to 25 million children worldwide in the next half dozen years (Naik, 2002; The Straits Times, 2002).

Female Literacy

Education of women is one of the most powerful prophylaxes for limiting population growth, so these soap opera programs in many countries show stories that endorse women continuing with their education as one way of liberating young women from male and matriarchal dominance. In one village in India, there was an immediate 30% increase in women going to school after the airing of these soap operas.

A Potent Blending of Talents, Wisdom, and Resources for Social Good

So here we have the unique case of a wise person in the media borrowing ideas from a psychologist and then extending the scope of influence by pairing up with a nonprofit agency, Population

Communications International (PCI) to disseminate these dramas worldwide. PCI's "mission is to work creatively with the media and other organizations to motivate individuals and communities to make choices that influence population trends encouraging development and environmental protection" (PCI, 2002). PCI's efforts at social diffusion span more than 17 countries worldwide with radio and TV serial dramas, comic books, and videos for classroom use. Finally, there is a fourth essential component: systematic evaluation of outcomes by an independent organization of all of these entertainment-educational change programs (see www.population.org).

It is evident that these serial dramatizations use the power of narrative story telling over an extended time, which the public views voluntarily, to motivate specific behavior change in directions guided by the information conveyed in the drama, which in turn has its origins in sound psychological theory and research. What also becomes evident is that when psychologists want to give psychology away to the public, we need to collaborate with those who understand best *how* to reach the public, namely those intimately involved with the mass media. They are our gatekeepers to the audiences we want to reach and influence. We have to find ways of inviting and intriguing media with the utility of psychological knowledge for crafting entertaining stories that can make a significant difference in the quality of lives of individuals and society.

Accentuating Psychology's Positive Messages

The collaboration between psychologist Albert Bandura, media master Miguel Sabido, and the resourcefulness of the PCI agency is an ideal model for us to emulate and extend in spreading more of our positive messages. Among those new messages are the two exciting directions that psychology can be expected to take in the next decade. The emergence of Martin Seligman's (2002) revolutionary "Positive Psychology" enterprise is creating a new vital force for recognizing and enriching the talents, strengths, and virtues of even ordinary people (see Diener, 2000; Myers, 2002; Snyder & Lopez, 2002). It is shifting attention away from deficits, disabilities, and disorders toward a focus on what is special about human nature like our resilience in the face of trauma, our joys, our sense of wonder and curiosity, and our capacity for goodness and love.

The fertile field of "behavioral economics" integrates psychology with economics and neuroscience to understand the economically irrational human element in judgments under uncertainty (see Kahneman & Tversky, 1979; Simon, 1955; Tversky & Kahneman, 1974, 1986). We can anticipate that Daniel Kahneman's winning the 2003 Nobel Prize in economics has made him a role model for the next generation of professional psychologists to emulate and to enter this exciting domain of relevant inquiry.

In conclusion, I repeat the questions that got me to this point and the simple answer that I now feel is justified—and I hope readers of this article agree with its positive bias.

Does psychology matter? Can psychological research, theory, methods, and practice make a significant difference in the lives of individuals, communities, and nations? Do we psychologists have a legacy of which we can be proud? Can we do more and better research that has significant applicable effects in the real world? Are we ready now "to give psychology away to the public" in useful, accessible ways? And finally, can we learn how better to collaborate with the media, with technology experts, with community leaders, and with other medical and behavioral scientists for psychology to make an even more significant difference in the coming decade?

My final answer is simply YES, YES indeed! May the positive forces of psychology be with you, and with our society.

Notes

1. Recognizing the importance of bringing psychology's understanding that violence is a learned behavior to the public, APA has joined with the National Association for the Education of Young Children and the Advertising Council to create a national multimedia public service advertising campaign designed to remind adults of the role they play in teaching children to use or avoid violence and then empower these adults to model and teach the right lessons. The campaign, first launched in 2000, has reached over 50 million households. At the community level, the campaign includes collaborations with local groups in a train-the-trainer model to bring early childhood violence prevention awareness and know-how to parents, teachers, and other caregivers.

2. The task force selected to identify and evaluate the research, theory, and methodology in psychology that qualified for inclusion in the Psychology Matters compendium has been ably cochaired by David Myers and Robert Bjork. Other members have included Alan Boneau. Gordon Bower, Nancy Eisenberg, Sam Glucksberg, Philip Kendall, Kevin Murphy, Scott Pious, Peter Salovey, Alana Conner-Snibbe, Beth Sulzer-Azaroff, Chris Wickens, and Alice Young. They have been assisted by the addition of Brett Pelham and David Partenheimer. Rhea Farberman and her staff in APA's Office of Public Communications have played a vital role in the development and continuing evolution of this project. The staff of the Science Directorate aided in the early development of the survey that was circulated to initiate electronic input of candidate items from APA constituent groups.

References

Ader, R., & Cohen, N. (1993). Psychoneuroimmunology: Conditioning and stress. *Annual Review of Psychology, 44,* 53–85.

Alien, M. J. (1970). *Vision and highway safety.* Philadelphia: Chilton.

Allport, G. (1954). *The nature of prejudice.* Reading, MA: Addison-Wesley.

American Academy of Pediatrics, Committee on Psychosocial Aspect of Child and Family Health. (1998). Guidance for effective discipline. *Pediatrics, 101,* 723–728.

Aronson, E. (1990). Applying social psychology to desegregation and energy conservation. *Personality and Social Psychology Bulletin, 16,* 118–132.

Aronson, E., Blaney, N., Stephan, C., Sikes, J., & Snapp, M. (1978). *The jigsaw classroom.* Beverly Hills, CA: Sage.

Aronson, E., & Gonzalez, A. (1988). Desegregation jigsaw, and the Mexican-American experience. In P. A. Katz & D. Taylor (Eds.),

Eliminating racism: Profiles in controversy (pp. 301–314). New York: Plenum Press.

Aronson, E., & Patnoe, S. (1997). *The jigsaw classroom: Building cooperation in the classroom* (2nd ed.). New York: Addison Wesley Longman.

Axelrod, S., & Apsche, H. (1983). *Effects of punishment on human behavior.* New York: Academic Press.

Baltes, P. B., & Staudinger, U. M. (2000). Wisdom: A metaheuristic (pragmatic) to orchestrate mind and virtue toward excellence. *American Psychologist, 55,* 122–136.

Bandura, A. (1965). Influence of models' reinforcement contingencies on the acquisition of imitated responses. *Journal of Personality and Social Psychology. 1,* 589–595.

Bandura, A. (1977). *Social learning theory.* Englewood Cliffs, NJ: Prentice Hall.

Bandura, A. (1986). *Social foundations of thought and action: A social cognitive theory.* Englewood Cliffs, NJ: Prentice Hall.

Bandura, A. (2002). Environmental sustainability by sociocognitive deceleration of population growth. In P. Schmuck & W. Schultz (Eds.), *The psychology of sustainable development* (pp. 209–238). Dordrecht, the Netherlands: Kluwer.

Baumrind, D. (1973). The development of instrumental competence through socialization. In A. Pick (Ed.), *Minnesota Symposium on Child Development* (Vol. 6, pp. 3–46). Minneapolis: University of Minnesota Press.

Beck, A. T. (1976). *Cognitive therapy and emotional disorders.* New York: International Universities Press.

Bee, H. (1994). *Lifespan development.* New York: HarperCollins.

Binet, A. (1911). *Les idé es modernes sur les enfants* [Modern ideas about children]. Paris: Flammarion.

Binet, A., & Simon. T. (1915). *A method of measuring the development of intelligence of young children.* Chicago: Chicago Medical Books.

Blass, T. (Ed.). (1999). *Obedience to authority: Current perspectives on the Milgram Paradigm* (pp. 193–237). Mahwah, NJ: Erlbaum.

Campbell. D. T. (1969). Reforms as experiments. *American Psychologist, 24,* 409–429.

Cantril, A. H. (1991). *The opinion connection: Polling, politics, and the press.* Washington, DC: CQ Press.

Clark, K. B., & Clark, M. K. (1939a). The development of consciousness of self and the emergence of racial identification in negro preschool children. *Journal of Social Psychology, 10,* 591–599.

Clark, K. B., & Clark, M. K. (1939b). Segregation as a factor in the racial identification of negro preschool children: A preliminary report. *Journal of Experimental Education, 8,* 161–163.

Clark, K. B., & Clark, M. K. (1940). Skin color as a factor in racial identification of negro preschool children. *The Journal of Social Psychology, II,* 159–169.

Clark, K. B., & Clark, M. K. (1950). Emotional factors in racial identification and preference in negro children. *Journal of Negro Education, 19,* 341–350.

Coe, C. L. (1999). Psychosocial factors and psychoneuroimmunology within a lifespan perspective. In D. P. Keating & C. Hertzman (Eds.), *Developmental health and the wealth of nations: Social, biological, and educational dynamics* (pp. 201–219). New York: Guilford Press.

Cohen, S., & Herbert, T. B. (1996). Health psychology: Psychological factors and physical disease from the perspective of human psychoneuroimmunology. *Annual Review of Psychology, 47,* 113–142.

Cohen, S., & Syme, S. L. (Eds.). (1985). *Social support and health.* Orlando, FL: Academic Press.

Collins, W. A., Maccoby, E. E., Steinberg, L., Hetherington, E. M., & Bornstein, M. H. (2000). Contemporary research on parenting: The case for nature and nurture. *American Psychologist, 55,* 218–232.

Cronbach, L. J. (1975). Five decades of public controversy over mental testing. *American Psychologist, 30,* 1–14.

Darling, N., & Steinberg, L. (1993). Parenting style as context: An integrative model. *Psychological Bulletin, 113,* 487–496.

Diener, E. (2000). Subjective well-being: The science of happiness and a proposal for a national index. *American Psychologist, 55,* 34–43.

Discovering psychology [Television series]. (1990; updated 2001). Boston: WGBH, with the American Psychological Association. (Funded and distributed by the Annenberg CPB Foundation, Washington, DC)

Druckman. D., & Bjork, R. A. (1991). *In the mind's eye: Enhancing human performance.* Washington, DC: National Academy Press.

DuBois, P. H. (1970). *A history of psychological testing.* Boston: Allyn & Bacon.

Erikson, E. H. (1963). *Childhood and society* (2nd ed.). New York: Norton.

Field, T. (1998). Massage therapy effects. *American Psychologist, 53,* 1270–1281.

Field, T., & Schanberg, S. M. (1990). Massage alters growth and catecholamine production in preterm newborns. In N. Gunzenhauser (Ed.), *Advances in touch* (pp. 96–104). Skillman, NJ: Johnson & Johnson.

Field, T., Schanberg, S. M., Scafidi, F., Bauer, C. R., Vega-Lahr, N., Garcia, R., et al. (1986). Tactile/kinesthetic stimulation effects on preform neonates. *Pediatrics, 77,* 654–658.

Freud, S. (1923). *Introductory lectures on psycho-analysis* (J. Riviera, Trans.). London: Allen & Unwin. (Original work published 1896)

Freud, S. (1965). *The interpretation of dreams.* New York: Avon. (Original work published 1900)

Garvey, P. M., Pietrucha, M. T., & Meeker, D. (1997). Effects of font and capitalization on legibility of guide signs. *Transportation Research Record No. 1605,* 73–79.

Geller, E. S. (2001). *The psychology of safety handbook.* Boca Raton, FL: CRC Press.

Geller, E. S. (2003). Behavior-based safety in industry: Realizing the large-scale potential of behavior analysis to promote human welfare. *Applied & Preventive Psychology, 10,* 87–105.

Gerrig, R., & Zimbardo, P. G. (2004). *Psychology and life* (17th ed.). Boston: Allyn & Bacon.

Green, C. D., Shore, M., & Teo, T. (2001). *The transformation of psychology: Influences of 19th century philosophy, technology, and natural science.* Washington, DC: American Psychological Association.

Hart, S. N. (1991). From property to person status: Historical perspective on children's rights. *American Psychologist, 46,* 53–59.

Hollon, S. D., Thase, M. E., & Markowitz, J. C. (2002). Treatment and prevention of depression. *Psychological Science in the Public Interest, 3,* 39–77.

Holly Fitch, R., & Tallal, P. (2003). Neural mechanisms of language-based learning impairments: Insights from human populations and animal models. *Behavior and Cognitive Neuroscience Reviews, 2,* 155–178.

Horowitz, R. M. (1984). Children's rights: A look backward and a glance ahead. In R. M. Horowitz & J. B. Lazar (Eds.), *Legal rights of children* (pp. 1–9). New York: McGraw-Hill.

Hovland, C. I., Janis, I. L., & Kelley, H. H. (1953). *Communication and persuasion.* New Haven, CT: Yale University Press.

Hovland, C. I., Lumsdaine, A. A., & Sheffield, F. D. (1949). *Experiments on mass communication.* Princeton, NJ: Princeton University Press.

Janis, I. L. (1958). *Psychological stress: Psychoanalytical and behavioral studies of surgical patients.* New York: Wiley.

Jung, C. G. (1959). The concept of the collective unconscious. In *The archetypes and the collective unconscious, collected works* (Vol. 9, Part 1, pp. 54–74). Princeton, NJ: Princeton University Press. (Original work published 1936)

Kahneman, D., & Tversky, A. (1979). Prospect theory: An analysis of decision under risk. *Econometrica, 47,* 263–291.

Kazdin, A. E. (1994). *Behavior modification in applied settings* (5th ed.). Pacific Grove, CA: Brooks/Cole.

Keane, T. M., Malloy, P. F., & Fairbank, J. A. (1984). Empirical development of an MMPI subscale for the assessment of PTSD. *Journal of Consulting and Clinical Psychology, 52,* 138–140.

Langer, E. F., & Rodin, J. (1976). The effects of choice and enhanced personal responsibility for the aged: A field experiment in an institutionalized setting. *Journal of Personality and Social Psychology, 34,* 191–198.

Lazarus, R. S. (1993). From psychological stress to the emotions: A history of changing outlooks. *Annual Review of Psychology, 44,* 1–21.

Lazarus, R. S., & Folkman, S. (1984). *Stress, appraisal, and coping.* New York: Springer.

Lewin, K. (1947a). Frontiers in group dynamics: Concept, method and reality in social science; social equilibria and social change. *Human Relations, 1,* 5–41.

Lewin, K. (1947b). Frontiers in group dynamics: II. Channels of group life; social planning and action research. *Human Relations, 1,* 143–153.

Lewin, K. (1948). *Resolving social conflicts.* New York: Harper.

Loftus, E. F. (1975). Leading questions and the eyewitness report. *Cognitive Psychology, 7,* 560–572.

Loftus, E. F. (1979). Eyewitness testimony. Cambridge, MA: Harvard University Press. Loftus, E. F. (1992). When a lie becomes memory's truth: Memory distortion after exposure to misinformation. *Current Directions in Psychological Science, 1,* 121–123.

Loomis, J. M., Klatsky, R. L., & Golledge, R. G. (2001). Navigating without vision: Basic and applied research. *Optometry and Vision Science, 78,* 282–289.

Maas, J. (1998). *Power sleep: The revolutionary program that prepares your mind for peak performance.* New York: Villard.

Maccoby, E. E. (1980). *Social development: Psychological growth and the parent-child relationship.* San Diego, CA: Harcourt Brace Jovanovich.

Maccoby, E. E. (1992). The role of parents in the socialization of children: An historical overview. *Developmental Psychology, 28,* 1006–1017.

Maccoby, E. E. (2000). Parenting and its effects on children: On reading and misreading behavior genetics. *Annual Review of Psychology, 51,* 1–27.

Malpass, R. S., & Devine, P. G. (1981). Eyewitness identification: Lineup instructions and the absence of the offender. *Journal of Applied Psychology, 66*, 482–489.

Maslach, C. (1982). *Burnout: The cost of caring.* Englewood Cliffs, NJ: Prentice Hall.

McCoy, E. (1988). Childhood through the ages. In K. Finsterbush (Ed.), *Sociology 88/89* (pp. 44–47). Guilford, CT: Dushkin.

Meltz, B. F. (2000, November 2). Do you touch your baby enough? *Boston Globe*, p. H1.

Milgram, S. (1974). *Obedience to authority.* New York: Harper & Row.

Miller, G. (1969). Psychology as a means of promoting human welfare. *American Psychologist, 24*, 1063–1075.

Miller, N. E. (1978). Biofeedback and visceral learning. *Annual Review of Psychology, 29*, 373–404.

Miller, N. E. (1985). The value of behavioral research on animals. *American Psychologist, 40*, 423–440.

Miller, N. E. (1992). Introducing and teaching much-needed understanding of the scientific process. *American Psychologist, 47*, 848–850.

Myers, D. G. (1993). *The pursuit of happiness.* New York: Avon.

Myers, D. G. (2002). *Intuition: Its powers and perils.* New Haven, CT: Yale University Press.

Naik, G. (2002, July 5). Uganda AIDS study suggests education stems spread of HIV. *Wall Street Journal*, p. A14.

New York State. (1999). *Clinical practice guidelines.* New York: Department of Health, Early Intervention Program, Autism.

Pappas. A. M. (1983). Introduction. In A. M. Pappas (Ed.), *Law and the status of the child* (pp. xxvii–lv). New York: United Nations Institute for Training and Research.

Pavlov, I. P. (1902). *The work of the digestive glands* (W. H. Thompson, Trans.) London: Griffin. (Original work published in 1897)

Pavlov, I. P. (1927). *Conditioned reflexes* (G. V. Anrep, Trans.). London: Oxford University Press. (Original work published 1897)

Pettigrew, T. F. (1997). Generalized intergroup contact effects on prejudice. *Personality and Social Psychology Bulletin, 23*, 173–185.

Piaget, J. (1954). *The construction of reality in the child.* New York: Basic Books.

Pinker, S. (1994). *The language instinct: How the mind creates language.* New York: Morrow.

Plomin, R., & McClearn, G. E. (1993). *Nature, nurture, and psychology.* Washington, DC: American Psychological Association.

Population Communications International. (2002). *15th anniversary: Keeping pace with change.* New York: Author.

Rodin, J., & Langer, E. F. (1977). Long-term effects of a control-relevant intervention with the institutionalized aged. *Journal of Personality and Social Psychology. 35*, 897–902.

Ruch, F. L., & Zimbardo, P. G. (1971). *Psychology and life* (8th ed.). Glenview, IL: Scott, Foresman.

Sarason, S. B. (1974). *The psychological sense of community: Prospects for a community psychology.* Oxford, England: Jossey-Bass.

Scarr, S. (1998). American child care today. *American Psychologist, 53*, 95–108.

Seligman, M. (2002). *Authentic happiness: Using the new positive psychology to realize your potential for lasting fulfillment.* New York: Free Press.

Shure, M. B., & Spivak, G. (1982). Interpersonal problem solving in children: A cognitive approach to prevention. *American Journal of Community Psychology, 10*, 341–356.

Simon, H. (1955). A behavioral model of rational choice. *Quarterly Journal of Economics, 69*, 99–118.

Skinner, B. F. (1938). *The behavior of organisms: An experimental analysis.* New York: Appleton-Century.

Skinner, B. F. (1948). *Walden two.* New York: Macmillan.

Skinner, B. F. (1966). What is the experimental analysis of behavior? *Journal of the Experimental Analysis of Behavior, 9*, 213–218.

Skinner, B, F. (1974). *About behaviorism.* New York: Knopf.

Smith, D. (2002). The theory heard "round the world." *Monitor on Psychology, 33*, 30–32.

Snyder, C. R., & Lopez, S. J. (2002). *Handbook of positive psychology.* New York: Oxford University Press.

Solomon, S. S., & King, J. G. (1985). Influence of color on fire vehicle accidents. *Journal of Safety Research, 26*, 47.

Stebley, N. M. (1997). Social influence in eyewitness recall: A meta-analytic review of line-up instruction effects. *Law and Human Behavior, 21*, 283–298.

Sternberg, R. J. (Ed.). (2000). *Handbook of intelligence.* Cambridge, England: Cambridge University Press.

The Straits Times. (2002, July 12). *The HIV orphan mega-crises.* Hong Kong: 14th International AIDS Conference.

Straus, M. A., & Kantor, G. K. (1994). Corporal punishment of adolescents by parents: A risk factor in the epidemiology of depression, suicide, alcohol abuse, child abuse, and wife beating. *Adolescence, 29*, 543–561.

Sulzer-Azaroff, B., & Austin, J. (2000, July). Does BBS work? Behavior-based safety and injury reduction: A survey of the evidence. *Professional Safety*, 19–24.

Swazey, J. P. (1974). *Chlorpromazine in psychiatry: A study of therapeutic innovation.* Cambridge, MA: MIT Press.

Tallal, P., & Benasich, A. A. (2002). Developmental language learning impairments. *Development and Psychopathology, 14*, 559–579.

Tallal, P., Galaburda, A. M., Llinas, R. R., & Von Euler, C. (Eds.). (1993). *Temporal information processing in the nervous system: Special reference to dyslexia and dysphasia* (Vol. 682). New York: New York Academy of Sciences.

Taylor, S. E., & Clark, L. F. (1986). Does information improve adjustments to noxious events? In M. J. Saks & L. Saxe (Eds.), *Advances in applied social psychology* (Vol. 3, pp. 1–28). Hillsdale, NJ: Erlbaum.

Tengs, T, O., Adams, M. E., Pliskin, J. S., Safan, D. G., Siegel, J. E., Weinstein, M. C., & Graham, J. D. (1995). Five-hundred life-saving interventions and their cost effectiveness. *Risk Analysis, 15*, 369–390.

Tversky, A., & Kahneman, D. (1974). Judgment under uncertainty: Heuristics and biases. *Science, 185*, 1124–1131.

Tversky, A., & Kahneman, D. (1986). The framing of decisions and the psychology of choice. *Science, 211*, 453–458.

Weathers, F. W., Keane, T. M., & Davidson, J. R. T. (2001). Clinicians' administered PTSD scale: A review of the first ten years of research. *Depression & Anxiety, 13*, 132–156.

Weiss, B. (1992). Behavioral toxicology: A new agenda for assessing the risks of environmental pollution. In J. Grabowski & G. VandenBos (Eds.), *Psychopharmacology: Basic mechanisms and applied interventions. Master lectures in psychology* (pp. 167–207). Washington, DC: American Psychological Association.

Weiss, B. (1999, May). *The vulnerability of the developing brain to chemicals in the environment.* Paper presented at the New York Academy of Medicine conference on Environmental Toxins and Neurological Disorders, New York.

Wells, G. L., & Olson, E. A. (2003). Eyewitness testimony. *Annual Review of Psychology, 54,* 277–295.

Wolfe, M. M., Risely, T. R., & Mees, H. L. (1965). Application of operant conditioning procedures to behavior problems of an autistic child. *Research and Therapy, 1,* 302–312.

Wolpe, J. (1958). *Psychotherapy by reciprocal inhibition.* Stanford, CA: Stanford University Press.

Zimbardo, P. G. (1974). *The detention and jailing of juveniles* (pp. 141–161) [Hearings before U. S. Senate Committee on the Judiciary Subcommittee to Investigate Juvenile Delinquency, September 10, 11, 17, 1973], Washington, DC: U.S. Government Printing Office.

Zimbardo, P. G. (1975). On transforming experimental research into advocacy for social change. In M. Deulsch & H. Hornstein (Eds.), *Applying social psychology: Implications for research, practice and training* (pp. 33–66). Hillsdale, NJ: Erlbaum.

Zimbardo, P. G. (1977). *Shyness: What it is, what to do about it.* Reading, MA: Addison-Wesley.

Zimbardo, P. G. (1992). *Psychology and life* (13th ed.). New York: HarperCollins.

Zimbardo, P. G., Haney, C., Banks, W. C., & Jaffe, D. (1973, April 8). The mind is a formidable jailer: A Pirandellian prison. *The New York Times Magazine,* Section 6, pp. 38–46.

Zimbardo, P. G., Maslach, C., & Haney, C. (1999). Reflections on the Stanford prison experiment: Genesis, transformations, consequences. In T. Blass (Ed.), *Obedience to authority: Current perspectives on the Milgram Paradigm* (pp. 193–237). Mahwah, NJ: Erlbaum.

Zimbardo, P. G., Weber, A. L., & Johnson, R. L. (2002). *Psychology: Core concepts* (4th ed.). Boston, MA: Allyn & Bacon.

Editor's note—Philip G. Zimbardo was president of APA in 2002. This article is based on his presidential address, delivered in Toronto, Canada, at APA's 111th Annual Convention on August 9, 2003. Award addresses and other archival materials, including presidential addresses, are peer reviewed but have a higher chance of publication than do unsolicited submissions. Presidential addresses are expected to be expressions of the authors' reflections on the field and on their terms as president. Both this address and that of Robert J. Sternberg, the 2003 APA president, were presented at this convention to catch up on the year lag that had developed in the last decade of giving presidential addresses.

Author's note—Correspondence concerning this article should be addressed to Philip G. Zimbardo, Department of Psychology, Stanford University Building 430, Mail Code 380, Stanford, CA 94305. E-mail: zim@stanford.edu

The 10 Commandments of Helping Students Distinguish Science from Pseudoscience in Psychology

Scott O. Lilienfeld

"Professor Schlockenmeister, I know that we have to learn about visual perception in your course, but aren't we going to learn anything about extra-sensory perception? My high school psychology teacher told us that there was really good scientific evidence for it."

"Dr. Glopelstein, you've taught us a lot about intelligence in your course. But when are you going to discuss the research showing that playing Mozart to infants increases their I.Q. scores?"

"Mr. Fleikenzugle, you keep talking about schools of psychotherapy, like psychoanalysis, behavior therapy, and client-centered therapy. But how come you've never said a word about sensory-motor integration therapy? My mother, who's an occupational therapist, tells me that it's a miracle cure for attention-deficit disorder."

The Pseudoscience of Popular Psychology

If you're like most introductory psychology instructors, these sorts of questions probably sound awfully familiar. There's a good reason: much of the popular psychology "knowledge" that our students bring to their classes consists of scant more than pseudoscience. Moreover, our students are often fascinated by dubious claims on the fringes of scientific knowledge: extrasensory perception, psychokinesis, channeling, out-of-body experiences, subliminal persuasion, astrology, biorhythms, "truth serum," the lunar lunacy effect, hypnotic age regression, multiple personality disorder, alien abduction reports, handwriting analysis, rebirthing therapy, and untested herbal remedies for depression, to name but a few. Of course, because some of these claims may eventually be shown to contain a core of truth, we should not dismiss them out of hand. Nevertheless,

what is troubling about these claims is the glaring discrepancy between many individuals' beliefs in them and the meager scientific evidence on their behalf.

Yet many introductory psychology instructors accord minimal attention to potentially pseudoscientific topics in their courses, perhaps because they believe that these topics are of, at best, marginal relevance to psychological science. Moreover, many introductory psychology textbooks barely mention these topics. After all, there is already more than enough to cover in psychology courses, so why tack on material of doubtful scientific status? Furthermore, some instructors may fear that by devoting attention to questionable claims they will end up sending students the unintended message that these claims are scientifically credible.

Benefits of Teaching Students to Distinguish Science from Pseudoscience

So why should we teach psychology students to distinguish science from pseudoscience? As personality theorist George Kelly (1955) noted, an effective understanding of a construct requires an appreciation of both of its poles. For example, we cannot grasp fully the concept of "cold" unless we have experienced heat. Similarly, students may not grasp fully the concept of scientific thinking without an understanding of pseudoscientific beliefs, namely those that at first blush appear scientific but are not.

Moreover, by addressing these topics, instructors can capitalize on a valuable opportunity to impart critical thinking skills, such as distinguishing correlation from causation and recognizing the need for control groups, by challenging students' misconceptions regarding popular psychology. Although many students find these skills to be "dry" or even deadly dull when presented in the abstract, they often enjoy acquiring these skills in the context of lively and controversial topics (e.g., extrasensory perception) that stimulate their interest. Students often learn about such topics from various popular psychology sources that they seek out in everyday life, such as magazine articles, Internet sites, and television programs.

Indeed, for many beginning students, "psychology" is virtually synonymous with popular psychology. Yet because so much of popular psychology consists of myths and urban legends, such as most people use only 10 percent of their brains, expressing anger is usually better than holding it in, opposites attract in interpersonal relationships, high self-esteem is necessary for psychological health, people with schizophrenia have more than one personality, among a plethora of others, many students probably emerge from psychology courses with the same misconceptions with which they entered. As a consequence, they often depart college incapable of distinguishing the wheat from the chaff in popular psychology.

Teaching students to distinguish science from pseudoscience can prove immensely rewarding. Foremost among these rewards is producing discerning consumers of the popular psychology literature. Indeed, research evidence supports the efficacy of teaching psychology courses on pseudoscience and the paranormal. For example, Morier and Keeports (1994) reported that undergraduates enrolled in a "Science and Pseudoscience" seminar demonstrated a statistically significant reduction in paranormal beliefs relative to a quasi-control group of students enrolled in a psychology and law class over the same time period (see also Dougherty, 2004). They replicated this effect over a 2-year period with two sections of the course. Wesp and Montgomery (1998) found that a course on the objective examination of paranormal claims resulted in a statistically significant improvement in the evaluation of reasoning flaws in scientific articles. Specifically, students in this course were better able to identify logical errors in articles and provide rival explanations for research findings.

The 10 Commandments

Nevertheless, teaching students to distinguish science from pseudoscience brings more than its share of challenges and potential pitfalls. In my introductory psychology course (in which I emphasize strongly the distinction between science and pseudoscience in psychology) and in my advanced undergraduate seminar, "Science and Pseudoscience in Psychology," I have learned a number of valuable lessons (by first making just about every mistake about which I'll warn you).

In the following section, I summarize these teaching tips, which I refer to as the "10 Commandments" of teaching psychology students to distinguish science from pseudoscience. To avoid being accused of failing to separate Church from State, I have worded all of these injunctions in the positive rather than the negative to distinguish them from the (only slightly better known) biblical 10 Commandments. I urge readers of this column to inscribe these commandments on impressive stone tablets to be mounted outside of all psychology departments.

First Commandment

Thou shalt delineate the features that distinguish science from pseudoscience. It's important to communicate to students that the differences between science and pseudoscience, although not absolute or clear-cut, are neither arbitrary nor subjective. Instead, philosophers of science (e.g., Bunge, 1984) have identified a constellation of features or "warning signs" that characterize most pseudoscientific disciplines. Among these warning signs are:

- A tendency to invoke ad hoc hypotheses, which can be thought of as "escape hatches" or loopholes, as a means of immunizing claims from falsification.
- An absence of self-correction and an accompanying intellectual stagnation.
- An emphasis on confirmation rather than refutation.
- A tendency to place the burden of proof on skeptics, not proponents, of claims.
- Excessive reliance on anecdotal and testimonial evidence to substantiate claims.
- Evasion of the scrutiny afforded by peer review.
- Absence of "connectivity" (Stanovich, 1997), that is, a failure to build on existing scientific knowledge.
- Use of impressive-sounding jargon whose primary purpose is to lend claims a facade of scientific respectability.
- An absence of boundary conditions (Hines, 2003), that is, a failure to specify the settings under which claims do not hold.

Teachers should explain to students that none of these warning signs is by itself sufficient to indicate that a discipline is pseudoscientific. Nevertheless, the more of these warning signs a discipline exhibits, the more suspect it should become.

Second Commandment

Thou shalt distinguish skepticism from cynicism. One danger of teaching students to distinguish science from pseudoscience is that we can inadvertently produce students reflexively dismissive of any claim that appears implausible. Skepticism, which is the proper mental set of the scientist, implies two seemingly contradictory attitudes (Sagan, 1995): an openness to claims combined with a willingness to subject these claims to incisive scrutiny. As space engineer James Oberg (see Sagan, 1995) reminded us, we must keep our minds open but not so open that our brains fall out. In contrast, cynicism implies close-mindedness. I recall being chastised by a prominent skeptic for encouraging researchers to keep an open mind regarding the efficacy of a novel psychotherapy whose rationale struck him as farfetched. However, if we foreclose the possibility that our preexisting beliefs are erroneous, we are behaving unscientifically. Skepticism entails a willingness to entertain novel claims; cynicism does not.

Third Commandment

Thou shalt distinguish methodological skepticism from philosophical skepticism. When encouraging students to think critically, we must distinguish between two forms of skepticism: (1) an approach that subjects all knowledge claims to scrutiny with the goal of sorting out true from false claims, namely methodological (scientific) skepticism, and (2) an approach that denies the possibility of knowledge, namely philosophical skepticism. When explaining to students that scientific knowledge is inherently tentative and open to revision, some students may mistakenly conclude that genuine knowledge is impossible. This view, which is popular in certain postmodernist circles, neglects to distinguish knowledge claims that are more certain from those that are less certain. Although absolute certainty is probably unattainable in science, some scientific claims, such as Darwin's theory of natural selection, have been extremely well corroborated, whereas others, such as the theory underpinning astrological horoscopes, have been convincingly refuted. Still others, such as cognitive dissonance theory, are scientifically controversial. Hence, there is a continuum of confidence in scientific claims; some have acquired virtual factual status whereas others have been resoundingly falsified. The fact that methodological skepticism does not yield completely certain answers to scientific questions and that such answers could in principle be overturned by new evidence does not imply that knowledge is impossible, only that this knowledge is provisional. Nor does it imply that the answers generated by controlled scientific investigation are no better than other answers, such as those generated by intuition (see Myers, 2002).

Fourth Commandment

Thou shalt distinguish pseudoscientific claims from claims that are merely false. All scientists, even the best ones, make mistakes. Sir Isaac Newton, for example, flirted with bizarre alchemical hypotheses throughout much of his otherwise distinguished scientific career (Gleick, 2003). Students need to understand that the key difference between science and pseudoscience lies not in their content (i.e., whether claims are factually correct or incorrect) but in their approach to evidence. Science, at least when it operates properly, seeks out contradictory information and—assuming that this evidence is replicable and of high quality—eventually incorporates such information into its corpus of knowledge. In contrast, pseudoscience tends to avoid contradictory information (or manages to find a way to reinterpret this information as consistent with its claims) and thereby fails to foster the self-correction that is essential to scientific progress. For example, astrology has changed remarkably little over the past 2,500 years despite overwhelmingly negative evidence (Hines, 2003).

Fifth Commandment

Thou shalt distinguish science from scientists. Although the scientific method is a prescription for avoiding confirmatory bias (Lilienfeld, 2002), this point does not imply that scientists are free of biases. Nor does it imply that all or even most scientists are open to evidence that challenges their cherished beliefs. Scientists can be just as pigheaded and dogmatic in their beliefs as anyone else. Instead, this point implies that good scientists strive to become aware of their biases and to counteract them as much as possible by implementing safeguards against error (e.g., double-blind control groups) imposed by the scientific method. Students need to understand that the scientific method is a toolbox of skills that scientists have developed to prevent themselves from confirming their own biases.

Sixth Commandment

Thou shalt explain the cognitive underpinnings of pseudoscientific beliefs. Instructors should emphasize that we are all prone to cognitive illusions (Piatelli-Palmarini, 1994), and that such illusions can be subjectively compelling and difficult to resist. For example, class demonstrations illustrating that many or most of us can fall prey to false memories (e.g., Roediger & McDermott, 1995) can help students to see that the psychological processes that lead to erroneous beliefs are pervasive. Moreover, it is important to point out to students that the heuristics (mental shortcuts) that can produce false beliefs, such as representativeness, availability, and anchoring (Tversky & Kahneman, 1974), are basically adaptive and help us to make sense of a complex and confusing world. Hence, most pseudoscientific beliefs are cut from the same cloth as accurate beliefs. By underscoring these points, instructors can minimize the odds that students who embrace pseudoscientific beliefs will feel foolish when confronted with evidence that contradicts their beliefs.

Seventh Commandment

Thou shalt remember that pseudoscientific beliefs serve important motivational functions. Many paranormal claims, such as those concerning extrasensory perception, out-of-body experiences, and astrology, appeal to believers' deep-seated needs for hope and wonder, as well as their needs for a sense of control over the often uncontrollable realities of life and death. Most believers in the paranormal are searching for answers to profound existential questions, such as "Is there a soul?" and "Is there life after death?" As psychologist Barry Beyerstein (1999) noted (in a play on P.T. Barnum's famous quip), "there's a seeker born every minute" (p. 60). Therefore, in presenting students with scientific evidence that challenges their paranormal beliefs, we should not be surprised when many of them become defensive. In turn, defensiveness can engender an unwillingness to consider contrary evidence.

One of the two best means of lessening this defensiveness (the second is the Eighth Commandment) is to gently challenge students' beliefs with sympathy and compassion, and with the understanding that students who are emotionally committed to paranormal beliefs will find these beliefs difficult to question, let alone relinquish. Ridiculing these beliefs can produce reactance (Brehm, 1966) and reinforce students' stereotypes of science teachers as close-minded and dismissive. In some cases, teachers who have an exceptionally good rapport with their class can make headway by challenging students' beliefs with good-natured humor (e.g., "I'd like to ask all of you who believe in psychokinesis to please raise my hand"). However, teachers must ensure that such humor is not perceived as demeaning or condescending.

Eighth Commandment

Thou shalt expose students to examples of good science as well as to examples of pseudoscience. In our classes, it is critical not merely to debunk inaccurate claims but to expose students to accurate claims. We must be careful not merely to take away student's questionable knowledge, but to give them legitimate knowledge in return. In doing so, we can make it easier for students to swallow the bitter pill of surrendering their cherished beliefs in the paranormal. Students need to understand that many genuine scientific findings are at least as fascinating as are many scientifically dubious paranormal claims. In my own teaching, I have found it useful to intersperse pseudoscientific information with information that is equally remarkable but true, such as lucid dreaming, eidetic imagery, subliminal perception (as opposed to subliminal persuasion, which is far more scientifically dubious), extraordinary feats of human memory (Neisser & Hyman, 2000), and appropriate clinical uses of hypnosis (as opposed to the scientifically unsupported use of hypnosis for memory recovery; see Lynn, Lock, Myers, & Payne, 1997). In addition, we should bear in mind the late paleontologist Stephen Jay Gould's (1996) point that exposing a falsehood necessarily affirms a truth. As a consequence, it is essential not only to point out false information to students, but also to direct them to true information. For example, when explaining why claims regarding biorhythms are baseless (see Hines, 2003), it is helpful to introduce students to claims regarding circadian rhythms, which, although often confused with biorhythms, are supported by rigorous scientific research.

Ninth Commandment

Thou shalt be consistent in one's intellectual standards. One error that I have sometimes observed among skeptics, including psychology instructors who teach critical thinking courses, is to adopt two sets of intellectual standards: one for claims that they find plausible and a second for claims that they do not. The late psychologist Paul Meehl (1973) pointed out that this inconsistency amounts to "shifting the standards of evidential rigor depending on whose ox is being gored" (p. 264). For example, I know one educator who is a vocal proponent of the movement to develop lists of empirically supported therapies, that is, psychological treatments that have been shown to be efficacious in controlled studies. In this domain, he is careful to draw on the research literature to buttress his assertions regarding which psychotherapies are efficacious and which are not. Yet he is dismissive of the research evidence for the efficacy of electroconvulsive therapy (ECT) for depression, even though this evidence derives from controlled studies that are every bit

as rigorous as those conducted for the psychotherapies that he espouses. When I pointed out this inconsistency to him, he denied emphatically that he was adhering to a double standard. It eventually became apparent to me that he was casting aside the evidence for ECT's efficacy merely because this treatment struck him as grossly implausible. Why on earth, he probably wondered, should inducing an epileptoid seizure by administering electricity to the brain alleviate depression? But because surface plausibility is a highly fallible barometer of the validity of truth claims, we must remain open to evidence that challenges our intuitive preconceptions and encourage our students to do so as well.

Tenth Commandment

Thou shalt distinguish pseudoscientific claims from purely metaphysical religious claims. My final commandment is likely to be the most controversial, especially for skeptics who maintain that both pseudoscientific and religious beliefs are irrational. To appreciate the difference between these two sets of beliefs, we must distinguish pseudoscience from metaphysics. Unlike pseudoscientific claims, metaphysical claims (Popper, 1959) cannot be tested empirically and therefore lie outside the boundaries of science. In the domain of religion, these include claims regarding the existence of God, the soul, and the afterlife, none of which can be refuted by any conceivable body of scientific evidence. Nevertheless, certain religious or quasi-religious beliefs, such as those involving "intelligent design" theory, which is the newest incarnation of creationism (see Miller, 2000), the Shroud of Turin, and weeping statues of Mother Mary, are indeed testable and hence suitable for critical analysis alongside of other questionable naturalistic beliefs. By conflating pseudoscientific beliefs with religious beliefs that are strictly metaphysical, instructors risk (a) needlessly alienating a sizeable proportion of their students, many of whom may be profoundly religious; and (b) (paradoxically) undermining students' critical thinking skills, which require a clear understanding of the difference between testable and untestable claims.

Conclusion

Adherence to the Ten Commandments can allow psychology educators to assist students with the crucial goal of distinguishing science from pseudoscience. If approached with care, sensitivity, and a clear understanding of the differences between skepticism and cynicism, methodological and philosophical skepticism, the scientific method and the scientists who use it, and pseudoscience and metaphysics, incorporating pseudoscience and fringe science into psychology courses can be richly rewarding for teachers and students alike. In a world in which the media, self-help industry, and Internet are disseminating psychological pseudoscience at an ever-increasing pace, the critical thinking skills needed to distinguish science from pseudoscience should be considered mandatory for all psychology students.

References

Beyerstein, B. L. (1999). Pseudoscience and the brain: Tuners and tonics for aspiring superhumans. In S. D. Sala (Ed.), *Mind myths: Exploring popular assumptions about the mind and brain* (pp. 59–82). Chichester, England: John Wiley.

Brehm, J. (1966). *A theory of psychological reactance.* New York: Academic Press.

Bunge, M. (1984, Fall). What is pseudoscience? *Skeptical Inquirer, 9,* 36–46.

Dougherty, M. J. (2004). Educating believers: Research demonstrates that courses in skepticism can effectively decrease belief in the paranormal. *Skeptic, 10*(4), 31–35.

Gilovich, T. (1991). How we know what isn't so: *The fallibility of human reason in everyday life.* New York: Free Press.

Gleick, J. (2003). *Isaac Newton.* New York: Pantheon Books.

Gould, S. J. (1996, May). Keynote address, *"Science in the age of (mis)information."* Talk presented at the Convention of the Committee for the Scientific Investigation of Claims of the Paranormal, Buffalo, New York.

Hines, T. (2003). Pseudoscience and the paranormal: A critical examination of the evidence. Buffalo, NY: Prometheus.

Kelly, G. A. (1955). *The psychology of personal constructs, Vols. 1 and 2.* New York: Norton.

Lilienfeld, S. O. (2002). When worlds collide: Social science, politics, and the Rind et al. child sexual abuse meta-analysis. *American Psychologist, 57,* 176–88.

Lilienfeld, S. O., Lohr, M., & Morier, D. (2001). The teaching of courses in the science and pseudoscience of psychology. *Teaching of Psychology, 28,* 182–191.

Lilienfeld, S. O., Lynn, S. J., & Lohr, J. M. (2003). *Science and pseudoscience in clinical psychology.* New York: Guilford.

Lynn, S. J., Lock, T. G., Myers, B., & Payne, D. G. (1997). Recalling the unrecallable: Should hypnosis be used to recover memories in psychotherapy? *Current Directions in Psychological Science, 6,* 79–83.

Meehl, P. E. (1973). Psychodiagnosis: Selected papers. Minneapolis, MN: University of Minnesota Press.

Miller, K. (2000). *Finding Darwin's God: A scientist's search for common ground between God and evolution.* New York: Cliff Street Books.

Morier, D., & Keeports, D. (1994). Normal science and the paranormal: The effect of a scientific method course on students' beliefs in the paranormal. *Research in Higher Education, 35,* 443–453.

Myers, D. G. (2002). *Intuition: Its powers and perils.* New Haven: Yale University Press.

Neisser, U., & Hyman, I. E. (2000). *Memory observed: Remembering in natural contexts.* New York: Worth Publishers.

Piatelli-Palmarini, M. (1994). *Inevitable illusions: How mistakes of reason rule our minds.* New York: John Wiley & Sons.

Popper, K. R. (1959). *The logic of scientific discovery.* New York: Basic Books.

Roediger, H. L., & McDermott, K. B. (1995). Creating false memories: Remembering words not presented in lists. *Journal of Experimental Psychology: Learning, Memory, and Cognition, 21,* 803–814.

Ruscio, J. (2002). *Clear thinking with psychology: Separating sense from nonsense.* Pacific Grove, CA: Wadsworth.

Sagan, C. (1995). *The demon-haunted world: Science as a candle in the dark.* New York: Random House.

Shermer, M. (2002). *Why people believe weird things: Pseudo-science, superstition, and other confusions of our time.* New York: Owl Books.

Stanovich, K. (1997). *How to think straight about psychology* (4th ed.). New York: HarperCollins.

Tversky, A., & Kahneman, D. (1974). Judgment under uncertainty: Heuristics and biases. *Science, 185,* 1124–1131.

Wesp, R., & Montgomery, K. (1998). Developing critical thinking through the study of paranormal phenomena. *Teaching of Psychology, 25,* 275–278.

Science vs. Ideology

Psychologists fight back against the misuse of research.

REBECCA A. CLAY

When psychologist Rebecca A. Turner, PhD, heard that a Bush administration appointee was citing her research as evidence for why the unmarried shouldn't have sex, she was dumbfounded.

In a 1999 study published in *Psychiatry* (Vol. 62, No. 2), Turner and her co-authors reported preliminary findings about the link between emotion and the hormone oxytocin. A physician who went on to become the administration's top family-planning official pointed to the paper as proof that sex with multiple partners damages women's ability to bond.

"We couldn't have imagined in our wildest dreams that someone could misinterpret our research that way," says Turner, now a professor of organizational psychology at Alliant International University in San Francisco.

Of course, Turner is not the only psychologist whose research has been co-opted, misinterpreted or attacked. While researchers working in such contentious areas as homosexuality, divorce or abortion are the most frequent targets, even those studying such seemingly innocuous areas as depression have been misconstrued.

What the strategies have in common, says Turner, is an emphasis on ideology rather than science.

But psychological researchers are fighting back, providing accurate, unbiased information to policy-makers, courts and the media. They're also noting methodological problems in research that contradict established science. And, perhaps most important, they're promoting the need for review by peers rather than politicians.

Setting the Record Straight

For Robert-Jay Green, PhD, it was the "accumulation of distortions of research" by anti-gay groups that spurred him into action.

"I just reached a point where I felt that those who know the most about lesbian/gay/bisexual/transgender (LGBT) issues—legitimate social scientists and mental health professionals who have spent their entire careers studying the issues—had lost their voice in the national debate," he explains.

To counter the distortions, Green founded the nonpartisan Rockway Institute at Alliant International University, where he is a clinical psychology professor.

Educating the media is especially important. In many instances, Green says, journalists become unwitting allies of well-funded anti-gay groups. Whether they're trying to achieve balance or feed their thirst for controversy, he says, journalists sometimes rely on spokespeople from groups that "frequently and categorically dismiss all reputable existing research on LGBT issues" or rely on dubious findings from discredited researchers.

Green points to a 2006 *Time* article by Focus on the Family chairman James Dobson, PhD, as an example, noting that Dobson ignored an extensive body of quantitative and qualitative literature when he claimed that children do best when raised by heterosexual couples. "In one fell swoop, Dobson dismisses all that research," notes Green. And because corrections or rebuttals often receive less attention than the original assertion, he adds, the damage is done.

To counter such misinformation, the Rockway Institute draws on the expertise of behavioral scientists, mental health professionals and physicians who can provide accurate information. The institute also conducts its own research to fill knowledge gaps, with Green, fellow faculty members and doctoral students exploring such topics as same-sex marriage and coming out. Green and a colleague are currently seeking funding for a study that will supplement the many qualitative studies of gay male parenting with a longitudinal study of outcomes of children raised by gay men. In another study in the planning stages, Green and colleagues will examine the impact of an LGBT-affirmative curriculum being used in health science classes taken by ninth-graders in Los Angeles. The goal, says Green, is to "answer some of the most pressing public policy questions related to LGBT issues."

Funding for the institute's dual roles comes from private donations, faculty research grants and paid research assistantships.

Emphasizing Methodology

In other issue areas, special-interest groups have assumed the trappings of science to bolster ideology-driven claims. One example is so-called "post-abortion syndrome," a scientific-sounding name for something most researchers say doesn't exist.

Nancy E. Adler, PhD, a professor of medical psychology at the University of California, San Francisco, is one of them. She has found that the rate of distress among women who've had abortions is the same as that of women who've given birth. Adler and other experts reviewed the literature in the late 1980s as part of an APA panel and found no evidence of a post-abortion syndrome. Even the anti-abortion Surgeon General C. Everett Koop, MD, refused to issue a report on abortion's supposed psychological impact when President Ronald Reagan asked him to, citing the lack of evidence of harm.

Since then, says Adler, anti-abortion advocates have become more world-wise.

"They're using scientific terminology," she points out. They're also gaining credibility by getting published in mainstream journals.

But such research often has methodological problems, Adler claims.

"Women are not randomly assigned to have abortions," she points out. "Women who are having abortions are having them in the context of an unwanted pregnancy, which usually has some other very stressful aspects. Their partners may have left them. They may have been raped."

In addition, says Adler, proponents of the syndrome don't mention the base rate of depression and other psychological problems in society as a whole. And they always attribute such problems to abortion rather than any other possible causes.

A new APA Task Force on Mental Health and Abortion will examine such issues in a report later this year.

Trying to explain methodological deficiencies can be tough, adds Adler, who is not a member of the new task force. "I don't know that the 10 o'clock news is going to cover the problem of reverse causation," she says.

Defending Peer Review

Researchers working on controversial topics aren't the only ones who have had trouble.

If You're a Target

What should you do if you're targeted by Congress or people more interested in ideology than science? Karen Studwell, JD, senior legislative and federal affairs officer in APA's Science Directorate, offers these tips:

- **Prevent attacks from happening.** Think about the public health relevance of your research even before you publish your results. Drawing on your grant application, develop a one-page statement about why your research is important, why the federal government should be funding it and what conclusions can be drawn from your findings.
- **Engage the media.** If your research is being misrepresented, contact journalists or write a letter to the editor. Write op-eds about your research findings. Take advantage of media training, often available through your university's public affairs office or at APA advocacy training events. But keep in mind that sometimes it's best not to engage with everyone who misrepresents your research—particularly those outside the mainstream media whose primary role is to generate controversy. "They want attention and debate, so no response could be the best response," advises Studwell.
- **Remember you're not alone.** Contact your university's public affairs office, APA, the Rockway Institute or other issue specific organizations. APA is also a founding member of the Coalition to Protect Research, a group of 60 scientific societies dedicated to monitoring congressional attempts to rescind funding for individual grants and protecting the peer review process.
- **Stay calm.** Even after a congressional attack on your research, it's unlikely you will lose your federal funding. APA responds to these attacks by working with Congress to ensure that as a bill makes its way through the lengthy legislative process, language targeting individual grants is removed.

—R. Clay

Sam Gosling, PhD, an associate professor of psychology at the University of Texas in Austin, was startled to learn that Congress thought his research on mood was frivolous. In 2004, a member of Congress added an amendment to an appropriations bill attacking Gosling's grant as a waste of National Institute of Mental Health funding.

"I don't want federal funding to be frivolous either," says Gosling, noting that his study analyzed the effect of personal living environments on college students' moods. "My research can easily be made to sound frivolous, but depression is a serious issue among students."

Because the research was nearly complete, Gosling was never in danger of losing his funding. But the experience of being part of what he calls "a political gesture" left him shaken.

"It's incredibly chilling and scary—the idea of having government interference in these things," he says. "It has made me much more reluctant to submit a grant."

While Congress does have a legitimate role in setting the research agenda, he emphasizes, politicians should leave the review of individual grants to scientists.

REBECCA A. CLAY is a writer in Washington, D.C.

UNIT 2

Biological Bases of Behavior

Unit Selections

Key Points to Consider

- What contributes more to an individual's psychological being—nature or nurture?

- How does the environment contribute to an individual's psychological being?

- How do genes influence human psychological characteristics and behaviors?

- How has genetic research advanced our understanding of various psychological disorders?

- How is neuroscience enhancing our understanding of the brain and its relation to behavior?

- What important roles do hormones play in our everyday lives?

Student Web Site
www.mhcls.com

Internet References

Behavioral Genetics
http://www.ornl.gov/hgmis/elsi/behavior.html
Institute for Behavioral Genetics
http://ibgwww.colorado.edu/index.html
Serendip
http://serendip.brynmawr.edu/serendip/
Society for Neuroscience
http://www.sfn.org/

As a child, Angelina vowed she did not want to turn out like either of her parents. Angelina's mother was passive and acquiescent about her father's drinking. When Dad was drunk, Mom always called his boss to report that Dad was "sick" and then acted as if there was nothing wrong at home. Angelina's childhood was a nightmare. Her father's behavior was erratic and unpredictable. If he drank just a little bit, most often he was happy. If he drank a lot, which was usually the case, he frequently but not always became belligerent.

Despite vowing not to become like her father, as an adult Angelina found herself in the alcohol rehabilitation unit of a large hospital. Angelina's employer could no longer tolerate her on-the-job mistakes or her unexplained absences from work. Angelina's supervisor therefore referred her to the clinic for help. As Angelina pondered her fate, she wondered whether her genes pre-ordained her to follow in her father's inebriated footsteps, or whether the stress of her childhood had brought her to this point in her life. After all, being the child of an alcoholic is not easy.

Like Angelina, psychologists are concerned with discovering the causes of human behavior. Once the cause is known, treatments for problematic behaviors can be developed. In fact, certain behaviors might even be prevented when the cause has been pre-identified. But for Angelina, prevention was too late.

One of the paths to understanding humans is the task of understanding the biological underpinnings of their behavior. Genes and chromosomes, the body's chemistry (as found in hormones, neurotransmitters, and enzymes), and the nervous system comprised of the brain, spinal cord, nerve cells, and other parts are all implicated in human behavior. All represent the biological aspects of behavior and ought, therefore, to be worthy of study by psychologists.

Physiological psychologists and neuroscientists examine the role of biology in behavior. These psychologists often utilize one of a handful of techniques to understand the biology-behavior connection. Animal studies involving manipulation, stimulation, or destruction of certain parts of the brain offer one method of study, but these studies remain controversial with animal rights activists. There is also an alternative technique available that involves the examination of unfortunate individuals born with malfunctioning brains or those whose brains are damaged later by accidents or disease. We can also use animal models to understand genetics. Also, by studying an individual's behavior in comparison to

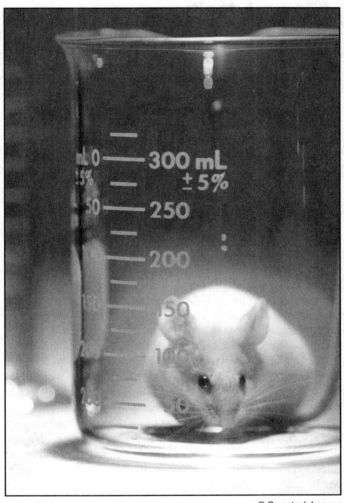

© Comstock Images

both natural and adoptive parents, or by studying identical twins reared together or apart, we can begin to understand the role of genetics and the environment in human behavior.

The articles in this unit are designed to familiarize you with the knowledge psychologists have gleaned by using these and other such techniques to study the biological processes involved in human behavior. Each article should interest you and make you more curious about the role of biology in the psychological functioning of human beings.

The Amazing Brain

Is Neuroscience the Key to What Makes Us Human?

RICHARD RESTAK

While in medical school, V. S. Ramachandran, director of the Center for Brain and Cognition at the University of California at San Diego, encountered a patient given to episodes of alternately weeping and laughing uncontrollably. This display of emotional mercuriality struck Ramachandran as a replay of the human condition. "Were these just mirthless joy and crocodile tears, I wondered? Or was he actually feeling alternately happy and sad, the same way a manic-depressive might, but on a compressed scale?"

During his professional career as a neurologist and researcher, Ramachandran has retained his curiosity and formulated about his patients the "kinds of very simple questions that a schoolboy might ask but are embarrassingly hard for experts to answer."

For example, "Why does this patient display these curious symptoms? What do the symptoms tell us about the working of the normal brain?" In the process, Ramachandran has learned that many patients with damage in a localized part of the brain often suffer a highly selective loss of one specific function with other functions remaining unaffected—an indication that the damaged area is normally involved somehow in mediating the impaired function. Further, some of these selective impairments can be both fascinating and informative.

Consider David, a patient of Ramachandran's who emerged from a coma mentally intact, with the exception of the bizarre delusion that his mother had been replaced by an impostor.

Further evaluation revealed an important distinction: Although David couldn't recognize his mother when encountering her face to face, he had no trouble identifying her when talking to her on the telephone. What could account for such an anomaly?

It turns out that separate pathways lead from the auditory and visual regions of the brain to the amygdala, an important component of the brain's emotional circuitry. In David's case, the fibers connecting the visual center to the amygdala were no longer functioning normally. As a result, whenever he looked at his mother he no longer got that warm feeling of recognition that normally accompanies seeing one's parent. He therefore accused her of being an impostor.

The auditory fibers in David's brain, in contrast, retained their normal connections with the amygdala. Consequently, the emotional linkage of voice and person remained intact and David recognized his mother's voice.

"This is a lovely example . . . of neuroscience in action; of how you can take a bizarre, seemingly incomprehensible neurological syndrome . . . and then come up with a simple explanation in terms of the known neural pathways in the brain," writes Ramachandran.

Other bizarre but informative disorders taken up in this wide-ranging book include phantom limb (the sensation that an amputated arm or leg is still present); synesthesia (a condition in which the senses are mingled so that the affected person tastes a shape, or sees a color in a sound or a number); and achromotopsia (seeing the world in shades of gray, like a black-and-white film).

"By studying neurological syndromes which have been largely ignored as curiosities or mere anomalies, we can sometimes acquire novel insights into the functions of the normal brain," the author writes. Moreover, he suggests, "the study of patients with neurological disorders has implications for the humanities, for philosophy, maybe even for aesthetics and art."

While all this sounds reasonable, Ramachandran sometimes comes across like the proverbial carpenter who approaches all issues as resolvable via the use of hammer and nail. Specifically, he claims that neuroscience can answer (or soon will) "some lofty questions that have preoccupied philosophers since the dawn of history: What is free will? What is body image? What is art? What is the self? Who am I?"

At times, his reductionism pushes the envelope a bit: "We recognize that life is a word loosely applied to a collection of processes—DNA replication and transcription, Krebs cycle, Lactic acid cycle, etc., etc." At another point, after naming several brain structures he asserts, "Know how they perform their individual operations, how they interact, and you will know what it means to be a conscious human being."

Despite such extravagant and hubristic statements, no one so far has been able to perform the alchemical conversion whereby "To be or not to be" can be understood in terms of neurotransmitters and brain structures. Nor is such a conversion ever likely since, as philosopher Gilbert Ryle pointed out, it would invoke the category mistake: intermingling separate and distinct orders of discourse.

For example (Ryle's own example, incidentally), the university that I attended cannot be equated except associatively with the buildings comprising it. True, the buildings when considered together may loosely be referred to as "the university"; but the entity defined by that word is far more nuanced than just real estate.

Likewise, can the mind be explained totally in terms of the brain? Ramachandran thinks so and while, on the whole, I tend to agree with him, I also have to admit to a trace of agnosticism on the question.

Not surprisingly, when discussing mental illness, Ramachandran is strictly in the neuropsychiatric camp: Neurology and psychiatry are so interpenetrated that future treatments and cures can only come about via increased knowledge about the brain. As a neurologist and neuropsychiatrist myself, I certainly don't disagree with that claim. Many psychiatrists, however, may find Ramachandran's phrasing of the matter a bit off-putting ("it is only a matter of time before psychiatry becomes just another branch of neurology").

But his heart is in the right place. Freudianism and other guru-driven "isms" are dead, replaced by an emphasis on the brain. Indeed, so much has been learned about mental illness in the past two decades as a result of brain research that it's difficult to imagine any alternative approach.

My principal criticism of this book concerns its odd arrangement: 112 pages of text accompanied by 44 pages of endnotes. As he mentions in his introduction, Ramachandran holds a rather quirky notion about endnotes ("the real book is in the endnotes"). Perhaps that's true, but the delegation of large parts of the narrative to the endnotes presents several difficulties.

For one, this text-endnote dichotomy makes it too easy for both author and editor to forsake their most important duty: organizing the material into a free-flowing narrative. Second, on occasion—such as his description of the more exotic forms of synesthesia—the endnotes prove even more interesting than the main text.

Finally, material in the text is sometimes repeated in the endnotes, such as Ramachandran's explanation of the origin of the ear. And given this emphasis on the endnotes, why are the notes corresponding to the last two citations in the final chapter missing?

Admittedly, these are minor quibbles that detract not at all from a perfectly marvelous book. Overall, reading Ramachandran in *A Brief Tour of Human Consciousness* is like listening to a John Coltrane solo: The man is here, there, and everywhere; he's inventive, inspired, wildly speculative, and yet disciplined by the demands of his craft. Give him a fact about the brain and he'll link it with a quote from Shakespeare; a nanosecond later he'll suggest an experiment that you can carry out in your living room to learn more about the fact.

To Ramachandran, the brain is more than an enchanted loom, and wider than the sky; it's an endless source for manic excitement, intriguing questions, profound reflections and a zany humor ("our brains . . . if raised in a culture-free environment like Texas would barely be human"). And like Coltrane, Ramachandran leaves you marveling at how he does it; wondering how he's learned all that he knows; and spinning like a top from the effort of trying to absorb all the wonderful things that he's telling you.

A Brief Tour of Human Consciousness is well worth the effort. You'll be entertained, provoked, amused and—most important of all—eager to learn more.

RICHARD RESTAK a neurologist and neuropsychiatrist, is the author of *Poe's Heart and the Mountain Climber: Exploring the Effects of Anxiety on Our Brains and Our Culture,* 2004.

The Threatened Brain

The human brain's distinct reactions to distant dangers and nearby threats may be deregulated in anxiety disorders.

STEPHEN MAREN

The world is a dangerous place. Every day we face a variety of threats, from careening automobiles to stock market downturns. Arguably, one of the most important functions of the brain and nervous system is to evaluate threats in the environment and then coordinate appropriate behavioral responses to avoid or mitigate harm.

Imminent threats and remote threats produce different behavioral responses, and many animal studies suggest that the brain systems that organize defensive behaviors differ accordingly[1]. On page 1079 of this issue, Mobbs and colleagues make an important advance by showing that different neural circuits in the human brain are engaged by distal and proximal threats, and that activation of these brain areas correlates with the subjective experience of fear elicited by the threat[2]. By pinpointing these specific brain circuits, we may gain a better understanding of the neural mechanisms underlying pathological fear, such as chronic anxiety and panic disorders.

To assess responses to threat in humans, Mobbs and colleagues developed a computerized virtual maze in which subjects are chased and potentially captured by an "intelligent" predator. During the task, which was conducted during high-resolution functional magnetic resonance imaging (fMRI) of cerebral blood flow (which reflects neuronal activity), subjects manipulated a keyboard in an attempt to evade the predator. Although the virtual predator appeared quite innocuous (it was a small red circle), it could cause pain (low- or high-intensity electric shock to the hand) if escape was unsuccessful. Brain activation in response to the predatory threat was assessed relative to yoked trials in which subjects mimicked the trajectories of former chases, but without a predator or the threat of an electric shock. Before each trial, subjects were warned of the contingency (low, high, or no shock). Hence, neural responses evoked by the anticipation of pain could be assessed at various levels of threat imminence not only before the chase, but also during the chase when the predator was either distant from or close to the subject.

How does brain activity vary as a function of the proximity of a virtual predator and the severity of pain it inflicts? When subjects were warned that the chase was set to commence, blood oxygenation level-dependent (BOLD) responses (as determined by fMRI) increased in frontal cortical regions, including the anterior cingulate cortex, orbitofrontal cortex, and ventromedial prefrontal cortex. This may reflect threat detection and subsequent action planning to navigate the forthcoming chase. Once the chase commenced (independent of high- or low-shock trials), BOLD signals increased in the cerebellum and periaqueductal gray. Activation of the latter region is notable, as it is implicated in organizing defensive responses in animals to natural and artificial predators[3, 4]. Surprisingly, this phase of the session was associated with decreased activity in the amygdala and ventromedial prefrontal cortex. The decrease in amygdala activity is not expected, insofar as cues that predict threat and unpredictable threats activate the amygdala[5, 6].

However, activity in these brain regions varied considerably according to the proximity of the virtual predator and the shock magnitude associated with the predator on a given trial. When the predator was remote, blood flow increased in the ventromedial prefrontal cortex and lateral amygdala. This effect was more robust when the predator predicted a mild shock. In contrast, close proximity of a predator shifted the BOLD signal from these areas to the central amygdala and periaqueductal gray, and this was most pronounced when the predator predicted an intense shock. Hence, the prefrontal cortex and lateral amygdala were strongly activated when the level of threat was low, and this activation shifted to the central amygdala and periaqueductal gray when the threat level was high.

The shift in neural activity from the forebrain to the midbrain may reflect increases in fear as the predator approaches. In support of this view, Mobbs *et al.* also showed that BOLD signals in the periaqueductal gray and the nearby dorsal raphe nucleus were highly correlated with the degree to which subjects feared the predator and how confident they were that they could escape. In animals, similar variations in fear define the topography of behavior along a "predatory imminence continuum"[7]. According to this view, the prefrontal cortex and lateral amygdala may coordinate behavior (such as avoidance) in the face of a distal threat, whereas the central amygdala and periaqueductal gray may coordinate defensive responses (such as freezing) when threat is imminent[8]. Forebrain systems engaged by a remote predator may even inhibit midbrain defense systems to promote escape behavior. Indeed, when escape fails and capture becomes inevitable (when control is lost), prefrontal inhibition of amygdala activity[9] and midbrain defense circuits may be released to shift behavior into a defensive mode[10]. Although Mobbs *et al.* show that subjects were motivated to escape the virtual predator, it would be of interest to know whether the brain activation patterns they observed predicted fear responses (such as sweating or tachycardia) during the task.

The majority of fMRI studies investigating the neural substrates of aversive emotions—including fear—have used tasks in which the imminence of the threat does not vary, or varies in a way that would elude detection in a neuroimaging study[11]. For example, many studies have used Pavlovian fear conditioning procedures, in which a conditioned stimulus is paired with an aversive event (shock, loud noise, or a fear-evoking image). In this situation, the imminence of the aversive outcome does not vary, at least in a spatial domain, when the conditioned stimulus is presented. Although imminence might vary during the conditioned stimulus as the unconditioned stimulus approaches in time, modern fMRI techniques cannot resolve brain activity during the short conditioned stimuli (2 to 4 s) typically used in these experiments. Nonetheless, these approaches have identified brain responses to stimuli that predict aversive outcomes, and activation of the amygdala also figures prominently in this response[12-15].

What do the findings tell us about human anxiety and panic? As the imminence of a threat increases, the successive activation of neural circuits in the forebrain and midbrain may yield qualitative changes in the subjective experience of fear: Activation of the prefrontal cortex by distal, unpredictable threats might foster anxiety, whereas activation of the periaqueductal gray by proximal threats that predict pain may fuel panic. Dysfunction in these circuits is therefore likely to yield a variety of chronic anxiety disorders[16-18]. Indeed, decoupling of the midbrain periaqueductal gray from cortical-amygdaloid regulation may contribute to panic disorder, which is characterized by intense somatic and autonomic fear responses to stimuli or situations that pose no immediate threat. Mobbs and colleagues have now set the stage for future efforts to explore this intriguing possibility in patients with anxiety disorders.

References

1. M. S. Fanselow, *Psychon. Bull. Rev.* **1,** 429 (1994).
2. D. Mobbs *et al.*, *Science* **317,** 1079 (2007).
3. B. M. De Oca, J. P. DeCola, S. Maren, M. S. Fanselow, *J. Neurosci.* **18,** 3426 (1998).
4. R. Bandler, M. T. Shipley, *Trends Neurosci.* **17,** 379 (1994).
5. G. Hasler *et al.*, *J. Neurosci.* **27,** 6313 (2007).
6. S. Maren, G. J. Quirk, *Nat. Rev. Neurosci.* **5,** 844 (2004).
7. M. S. Fanselow, L. S. Lester, in *Evolution and Learning,* R. C. Bolles, M. D. Beecher, Eds. (Erlbaum, Hillsdale, NJ, 1988), pp. 185–211.
8. P. Amorapanth, J. E. LeDoux, K. Nader, *Nat. Neurosci.* **3,** 74 (2000).
9. G. J. Quirk, E. Likhtik, J. G. Pelletier, D. Paré, *J. Neurosci.* **23,** 8800 (2003).
10. J. Amat *et al.*, *Nat. Neurosci.* **8,** 365 (2005).
11. C. Buchel, R. J. Dolan, *Curr. Opin. Neurobiol.* **10,** 219 (2000).
12. K. S. LaBar, J. C. Gatenby, J. C. Gore, J. E. LeDoux, E. A. Phelps, *Neuron* **20,** 937 (1998).
13. D. C. Knight, D. T. Cheng, C. N. Smith, E. A. Stein, F. J. Helmstetter, *J. Neurosci.* **24,** 218 (2004).
14. J. S. Morris, A. Ohman, R. J. Dolan, *Nature* **393,** 467 (1998).
15. E. A. Phelps *et al.*, *Nat. Neurosci.* **4,** 437 (2001).
16. C. Grillon, S. M. Southwick, D. S. Charney, *Mol. Psychiatry* **1,** 278 (1996).
17. I. Liberzon, B. Martis, *Ann. N.Y. Acad. Sci.* **1071,** 87 (2006).
18. M. R. Milad, S. L. Rauch, R. K. Pitman, G. J. Quirk, *Biol. Psychology* **73,** 61 (2006).

The author is in the Department of Psychology and Neuroscience Program, University of Michigan, Ann Arbor.

Phantom Pain and the Brain

An actual touch, or an imaginary one? It's all the same to (some parts of) your brain.

SADIE F. DINGFELDER

Scientists have long conceptualized the part of the brain known as the primary somatosensory cortex (S1) as where it first registers touch sensations. Prick your finger and S1 springs into action, sending raw information about the injury's location to higher brain areas for further interpretation, according to most neuroscience textbooks.

Those textbooks may need new editions. S1 doesn't simply catalogue physical sensations: It also registers sensory illusions that are generated elsewhere in the brain, according to a recent study in *PLOS Biology* (Vol. 4, No. 3, pages 459–466). In fact, as far as S1 is concerned, there's no difference between a real or imaginary touch, says lead author Felix Blankenburg, PhD, a neuroscience researcher at University College London (UCL). Other researchers, including David Ress, PhD, a neuroscience professor at Brown University, are finding similar results in S1's cousin, the primary visual cortex.

Together, the research paints a picture of a deeply integrated brain, one that begins making sense of information at the earliest stages of perception, says Ress.

"You use a lot of your brain to make a visual decision," he says. "The whole system is probably used as an integrated whole in order to create visual consciousness."

Tactile Illusions

Tap people's arms rapidly at the wrist and then at the elbow, and they will feel a phantom tap right in the middle, as if a rabbit were hopping the arm's length. Blankenburg and his colleagues, including Jon Driver, PhD, director of the Cognitive Neuroscience Institute at UCL, harnessed this phenomenon, known as the cutaneous rabbit illusion, to see how tactile illusions play out in the brain.

The researchers strapped electrodes to the arm of 10 adult participants, placing the electrodes at three points between each participant's elbow and wrist. While the participants lay in a functional magnetic resonance imaging (fMRI) machine, the researchers delivered pulses to the electrodes. In one condition, participants experienced real sensations hopping up their

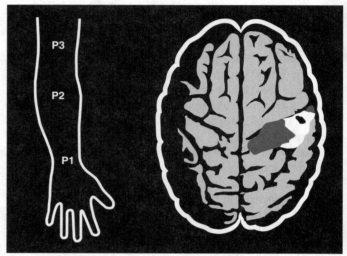

The cutaneous rabbit illusion activates the same area of the brain that would respond if that body site (P2) had actually been touched.

arms, as experimenters activated the three electrodes in succession. In another condition, participants only thought they felt the sensation hopping up their arms, as researchers delivered pulses first to the electrode near their wrist and then to one by their elbow.

Participants reported feeling the illusory touch and the real one equally strongly, and their brains agreed—the S1 area registered both sensations at the same location in the brain and with a similar amount of neural activity.

"This is quite remarkable because traditionally we thought S1 formed a map of the body that faithfully represents the actual touch on the skin, but our results suggest this is not always the case," says study author Christian Ruff, PhD, a psychology and neuroscience researcher at UCL. Instead, S1 seems to be representing what we feel—not what is actually there, he adds.

Where is S1 getting its false information? One possibility is that higher areas of the somatosensory cortex, the ones that would integrate information about the time and location of a tap on the skin, also register raw sensory information and then force their interpretation on S1, says Ress, who also studies perception.

In fact, while S1 showed no differences in activation during real and imagined touch, the right premotor cortex showed increased activation during the illusory touch, and that area may be at least part of the illusion's source, Ruff observes.

"It could be that signals from higher-level brain structures can influence the primary sensory cortex via neural feedback connections," Ruff notes.

Visual Mistakes

Researchers who study an entirely different sense—vision—are coming to similar conclusions. Scientists traditionally claim that the primary visual cortex, or V1, registers sensory information and then kicks it to higher-level areas for processing. A study published in a 2003 issue of *Nature Neuroscience* (Vol. 6, No. 4, pages 414–420) suggests otherwise.

The study's four adult participants lay in an fMRI machine while watching a screen that showed a faint vertical grating on a similarly patterned background, or just the background alone. Participants had one second to view the screen and then one second to press a button indicating whether they had seen the vertical grating—a process repeated several hundred times for each participant.

Analysis of their brain activity showed high levels of activity in V1 both when the participants saw the grating and when they just thought they saw it. What's more, the V1 area was similarly quiet when participants did not see the grating as when they just missed it.

This line of research could eventually help amputees who suffer from phantom limb pain. If phantom pain comes from the lowest level of the sensory system, effective drugs or therapy could target that area.

These results, like those of the Blankenburg study, help explain why false perceptions sometimes feel quite real, says Ress.

"If you think you perceive a sensation, then the lower-level primary sensory area that is associated with that false perception actually becomes involved," he notes.

However, he cautions that fMRI data doesn't always match up with the electrical activity of the brain.

"It's a very indirect measure of neural activity, and we are still not exactly sure what it means," he notes.

That said, this line of research could eventually help amputees who suffer from phantom limb pain, Blankenburg says. If phantom pain comes from the lowest level of the sensory system, effective drugs or therapy could target that area.

In the distant future, research on the translation of sensation to perception may lead to machines that transmit visual signals directly into the brains of blind people, allowing them to see. But if higher level areas of the brain feed information to the lower areas, as is suggested by this line of research, such applications wouldn't just be able to transmit raw data straight into people's primary cortices, Ress posits.

"The design of something that emulates cortical processing becomes more complicated when the brain is a recursive network," he says.

The Home Team Advantage . . . and Other Sex Hormone Secrets

Testosterone and estrogen drive touchdowns and boost brainpower, but they work their magic with a selectivity that science is only beginning to understand. A primer on how these counterintuitive chemicals truly shape us.

SHERRY BAKER

Playing in front of a wildly cheering hometown crowd, the Canadian ice hockey team whizzed around the ice with more speed and sizzle than usual, scoring goal after goal and winning the game. And it wasn't just that night, either. The high-energy performance of the all-star team, hailing from northern Ontario, *always* peaked during home games, suggesting a home-field advantage.

Hoping to learn their secret, psychologists Cameron Muir and Justin Carre of Brock University in Ontario studied the team over a season, measuring testosterone levels in saliva before and after each game. As they expected, the increase in status following a win always resulted in a rise. But the surprise came in measurements *prior* to the games: Whenever the competition was on home turf, testosterone increased ahead of time, suggesting the hormone provided impetus for defending one's territory. "Just as a dog defends its yard, these players are encouraged to defend home ice," Carre said.

The Brock scientists found that testosterone ebb and flow tracked emotional states: Self-confidence increased for home games, and, according to player reports, slid back down when players were away. The bottom line: Testosterone changes are directly related to personality, mood, and aggression—and not just in sports.

For men and women alike, sex hormones (including testosterone, produced by the testes, and estrogen, from the ovaries) are power players in myriad human abilities and behaviors. Language, cognition, libido, and health all fluctuate as hormone levels change. Yet the impact is nuanced and often counterintuitive. Testosterone revs aggression in status-hungry men, but has little effect in more laid-back souls. Estrogen has long been thought to keep memory sharp before menopause—but for women who start taking estrogen supplements years after going through menopause, the result may be memory problems instead. Finally, just as sex hormones influence behavior, changing situations

often modulate the hormones. "The causal arrow between hormones and behavior points in both directions," says University of Nevada anthropologist Peter Gray. The subject is complex and often confusing. But given the common manipulation of sex hormones through prescription drugs and supplements, unraveling their hidden forces has never been more critical.

Testosterone Warriors
Why One Man's Triumph Is Another Man's Torment

A Humble Priest Renowned for his Wisdom, Peter Morrone wanted nothing more than to live out his days in the hermetic monastery near his home in Italy. But his dream came crashing down when he was tapped to succeed Pope Nicholas IV in 1294. As the new Pope Celestine V, Morrone lacked the assertiveness of his predecessor and soon became a pawn of King Charles II. Unsuited for the job, he abdicated the papacy after four short months. But the next pope, Boniface VIII, so feared Celestine's popularity that he hunted him down and threw him in jail where, 10 months later, he died.

According to Robert Josephs, a social endocrinologist at the University of Texas, Celestine's reaction to the lofty status of pope can be seen through the lens of testosterone: Naturally low levels of testosterone could explain his shrinking-violet personality and his failure to rise to the challenge when his status demanded it most. High levels of testosterone, meanwhile, might explain why Boniface went to such extremes to put Celestine in his place.

When Josephs arrived on the endocrine scene in the late 1990s, the research connecting sex hormones and human behavior was contradictory. A strong connection had been shown in many animal species. But human experiments found no consistent connection and experts theorized that our developed prefrontal cortex simply overrode messages the sex hormones sent to the midbrain.

Josephs soon demonstrated that humans are hardly exempt from the passions of other animals—those passions are just more complex. As with Celestine and Boniface, testosterone plays out differently depending upon whether an individual is driven by status or prefers a more modest leadership role. Men motivated by the quest for power have higher baseline levels of testosterone—and the more they feel threatened, the higher their testosterone (and their aggression).

One study, for instance, tracks testosterone after loss of a game. Baseline testosterone drops, it turns out, *only* in those who don't much care about dominance or whether they win or lose. These less-competitive players start out with modest testosterone levels and after a loss, their levels fall. But in those with high-baseline testosterone—typically of competitive mindset—the levels soar. "High-T men react to a loss as if in the throes of testosterone addiction—the more testosterone climbs, the more testosterone they crave, and they can get more only by challenging the winner and playing again," Josephs explains.

He found the rule applied not just to competition in sports or games, but also to competition for mates. In one study, Josephs paired male college students and sent them into a room with an attractive female confederate. Each was to try to woo her, doing whatever it took. Students with high testosterone routinely slammed the other man, making fun, putting him down, refusing to laugh at his jokes.

Josephs also found that high-testosterone men communicate stress to their dogs. In a study of pet owners who had entered their dogs in a contest of agility, high-T men experienced surging testosterone after a loss. They yelled at or shoved their dogs. Josephs compares the phenomenon to injecting steroids. "If you put testosterone in muscle fibers they will fire more frequently," he says. "The more they fire the more you'll be able to punch, and the more you punch the more testosterone you need." Women and low-T men (who had still had lower testosterone following a loss) were sympathetic to pets that lost, petting and hugging them. All pet owners, men and women alike, responded with no change in testosterone when their dogs won—and usually treated the victorious dogs in the same, positive way. But no matter how much testosterone a woman had at baseline or how badly her dog lost, all females reacted like low-T men, soothing the losing pets.

Baseline testosterone even impacts cognition, Josephs found. In experiments, when status-striving, high-testosterone men are stripped of their status, they become angry, excited, and cognitively impaired. But more surprising, men with low resting-testosterone, without much impetus for status, become angry and impaired when placed in high-status positions they simply do not want.

Men with low testosterone become angry and impaired when placed in high status positions they simply do not want.

The studies point to innate human hierarchies every bit as immutable as those seen in primates or dogs. At first blush, says Joseph, "striving for status seems sensible because with it come resources and goodies that ensure survival." Yet from an adaptive perspective, the differences appear to make evolutionary sense. "If you look across the landscape of our species you'll see a high variation in resting testosterone, with each person seeking his particular place in the hierarchy and few people wanting to be out of their zone. If everyone were an alpha we'd have fights all the time. The group is more stable and life is more harmonious when hormone level and social niche correspond."

Brain-Building Hormones
Prenatal Testosterone Steers Spatial Reasoning, but Only to a Point

The ability to read a map or engineer a bridge isn't due to gender *per se*, but rather to the way sex hormones influence the structure and function of the brain. Before we're even born, testosterone in the womb influences development of brain regions handling spatial tasks. And as adults, optimum levels of testosterone and estrogen hone these skills yet again. In animals, there is a direct relationship between testosterone and spatial ability—for humans, that's not the case.

In fact, it was hard for scientists to study testosterone's impact in humans at all until researchers discovered that a high "2D4D" digit ratio—a ring finger longer than the index finger—is linked to high exposure to prenatal testosterone. In women, who as a rule don't receive as much exposure, ring and index fingers are often equal in length, while in males the ring finger tends to be longer.

Scientists at the University of Giessen in Germany used the association to correlate mathematical and spatial skill with pre-birth testosterone levels. It was already known that men outscore women on spatial and numerical tests overall. But last year in the journal *Intelligence,* the German scientists reported that women with a "male-like" finger ratio (and therefore higher levels of prenatal testosterone) scored better than those whose wedding finger was shorter—and they also outperformed the men on the numerical tests.

While prenatal testosterone enhances performance of spatial tasks, the relationship is complex and varies from skill to skill. Using finger ratios to estimate, University of Cambridge psychologists graphed prenatal testosterone against three spatial tasks: mental rotation (recognizing two-dimensional representations of three-dimensional shapes), targeting (literally hitting a target on a computer screen), and figure-disembedding (finding a smaller simple form that is part of a larger, complex picture).

Their findings, published last year in the *Journal of Biological Psychology,* show that the exclusive predictor for mental rotation ability is gender, with men beating women. Because testosterone level played no role whatsoever, the researchers theorize that the advantage comes from more exposure to the task, and thus, more practice.

Hormone Fixes

Adjusting your hormones may rev everything from your mental faculties to your libido. But get the full facts before any do-it-yourself hormone shift.

Hormone Replacement Therapy

Prescription hormone replacement therapy, consisting of estrogen and progesterone or estrogen-only replacement, for women without a uterus, may help mood.

Testosterone for Men

Supplements may give low-testosterone men a mood boost and increase their libido. Side effects range from thickened blood to enlarged prostate, but may be averted with monitoring.

Testosterone for Women

May help a tanking libido recover after menopause. Testosterone and estrogen therapy given together may be especially effective.

"Bioidentical" Hormones

An alternative to traditional HRT, these nonpharmaceutical plant-derived estrogens supposedly mimic the optimum female hormonal environment. But "bioidenticals" may be created without much regard to the way natural hormones are metabolized.

DHEA

This steroid precursor to testosterone and estrogen declines rapidly after age 25. DHEA supplements are a popular, nonprescription way to supposedly rejuvenate hormones. But recent research concludes it has no anti-aging, nor mind- and strength-sparking benefits.

Phytoestrogens

Studies have found black cohosh relieves depression and anxiety better in menopausal women than Valium or Premarin. The plant contains phytoestrogens that bind to the estrogen receptors and work much like natural estrogen.

Finger ratio alone, on the other (ahem) hand, predicted targeting and figure-disembedding performance. For figure disembedding, the more prenatal testosterone, the better the performance. But for targeting, the level of prenatal testosterone helped only to a degree. In fact, the relationship was what researchers called "curvilinear"—the best performance required a highly favorable level of prenatal testosterone. Too much or too little, and the skill fell off. This could explain why men excel overall in targeting but also why some women may make better sharpshooters or pilots than many men.

The picture is also complex for free-flowing testosterone in adulthood. Instead of equating high-T with spatial skills, the relationship is reversed. It turns out that lower testosterone signals

greater skill, University of Cincinnati psychologist Julie Yonker reported in the journal *Cortex* in 2006.

The results show just how complex the interactions are. In both men and women, excess testosterone is converted to estradiol, a form of estrogen. Studies of women in their childbearing years have found that visual-spatial performance declines during ovulation, when estrogen levels are highest, and is enhanced during menstruation, when estrogen is low. "We infer that estradiol binds to the brain receptors directing visuospatial tasks, hindering performance," Yonker states.

Bottom line: We've got to get away from the idea of "female" brains and "male" brains and start thinking in terms of high- and low-testosterone and estrogen brains to understand how spatial skills develop.

Supercharging Memory with Estrogen
Why Timing Is Key in Hormone Therapy

For years the debate over estrogen loss and hormone replacement therapy has raged: As women enter and then pass through menopause, does the loss of estrogen cause not only hot flashes and mood swings but also memory impairment? And can hormone replacement therapy (HRT) protect cognitive sharpness that might otherwise be lost? Many experts have long insisted that memory problems emerge at midlife not because estrogen tanks but because of psychological factors—stressed-out and sleep-deprived women are naturally going to feel less mentally sharp. Therefore, when it comes to protecting memory, HRT would do little good and might even hurt.

Yet the naysayers based their conclusions on studies of older women—in one pivotal study, the average age was 72. Should we really extend the reaction of elderly women to younger women, whose hormones were just *starting* to decline? To find out, McGill sex-hormone researcher Barbara Sherwin studied working memory in a group of young women whose menopause had been temporarily induced during treatment for tumors. Sherwin's research, published in the journal *Psychoneuroendocrinology* in 2006, showed that memory scores in the young women given the estrogen-lowering drug Lupron plummeted but, when estrogen was added back, working memory deficits were restored. The clear conclusion was that estrogen supplements, timed correctly, kept working memory sharp.

Sherwin cautions that more research is needed because not all estrogen is identical and different forms of the hormone might affect cognition in different ways. She also notes that the route of administration, via patch instead of a pill, might affect what estrogen does to memory, the brain, and the rest of the body. In fact, a 2006 study from the San Francisco VA Medical Center found that extremely low doses of estradiol delivered through a patch had no ill effects on the cognitive abilities or general health of older women. If estrogen can be taken safely and if it does, in fact, preserve memory in women entering menopause, when is the best time to take it? "Probably in the late perimenopause, just around the time of menopause, around age 49," Sherwin says.

The Daddy Profile
The "Low-T," Long-Term Commitment Guy

High testosterone males might be less emotionally connected, sure, but that doesn't mean they're violent, sexually craven cave men. That, at least, is the conclusion of a recent study on testosterone and language. To do the research, James Pennebaker of the University of Texas followed two people receiving testosterone therapy—a man for improvement of upper body strength, and an individual who was female-to-male transgendered. For both, he found that the higher the levels went, the less likely they were to use emotional, socially connecting words in written notes. The level of anger and sexual content, however, remained unchanged. Testosterone steers written language—and presumably, the writer—away from social connections but not necessarily toward anger or preoccupation with sex.

The findings are in line with a host of other studies showing Low-T guys and gals provide us with social glue. Testosterone tends to be low in family men raising children and high in single men playing the field. "Lower levels of testosterone may increase the likelihood men will stay home and care for their wives and kids and decrease the likelihood they will go out drinking with the guys and chasing other women," says Harvard anthropologist Peter T. Ellison, who has studied the phenomenon for years.

The allure of the Low-T man was illuminated in the journal *Psychoneuroendocrinology* in 2006. Heterosexual men and lesbian and bisexual women with partners all had lower testosterone than their footloose counterparts. But gay and bisexual men with partners had similar levels of testosterone whether or not they had partners.

Forget the concept of "male" versus "female" brain. High-T and Low-T personalities are the real buzzwords.

"The findings suggest that lower testosterone individuals might be more attractive for long-term relationships," says Sari M. van Anders of Simon Fraser University, the neuroendocrinologist who led the work. Van Anders notes that heterosexual men and lesbian women are both interested in women. "So one fascinating possibility is that females prefer long-term partners—whether male or female—with lower T." Another obvious way to interpret van Ander's data is that lower-T people, male or female, are just more interested in long-term relationships.

Because the "chicken or egg" conundrum of hormones and behavior is still unresolved, the effect of artificial hormones on marriage, parenting, or friendship is also a gray area. "Taking testosterone may improve relationships for some people; as testosterone is raised, improved mood, libido, and self-worth could be the result," speculates Nevada's Peter Gray. "For others, the supplements could do harm." The fact is that studies showing the precise connections between our hormones and our minds and personality have yet to be done. Even when we understand specific mechanisms, the low-T and high-T among us may be loathe to change. Would a satisfied family man or woman really relinquish social comfort and connectivity to battle on the corporate front? Perhaps even more absurd: the idea that a Lothario would agree to suppress his testosterone just to appease a spouse.

The emotional and cognitive pull of sex hormones is undeniable, but with so many twists and turns that the idea of gender-specific traits has given way to the reality of hormone-associated tendencies. Forget the concept of the "male brain" and "female brain." High-T and Low-T personalities and estrogen-driven smarts are the real buzzwords.

SHERRY BAKER is a health and medical writer living outside Atlanta.

UNIT 3
Perceptual Processes

Unit Selections

Key Points to Consider

- How does sensation differ from perception?

- What are altered states of consciousness?

- Why are sleeping and dreaming so important to psychologists?

- How do humans learn to recognize faces?

Student Web Site
www.mhcls.com

Internet References

Five Senses Home Page
   http://www.sedl.org/scimath/pasopartners/senses/welcome.html
Psychology Tutorials and Demonstrations
   http://psych.hanover.edu/Krantz/tutor.html
Visual and Optical Illusions
   http://dragon.uml.edu/psych/illusion.html

Marina and her roommate have been friends since their first year of college. Because they share so much in common, they decided to become roommates in their sophomore year. They both want to travel abroad one day. Both date men from the same college, both are education majors, and both want to work with young children after graduation. Today they are at the local art museum. As they walk around the galleries, Marina is astonished at her roommate's taste in art. Whatever her roommate likes, Marina hates. The paintings and sculptures that Marina admires are the very ones to which her roommate turns up her nose. "How can our tastes in art be so different when we share so much in common?" Marina wonders. What Marina and her roommate experience is a difference in perception—the interpretation of the sensory stimulation provided by the artwork. Perception and its sister area of psychology, sensation, are the focus of this unit.

For many years, it was popular for psychologists to consider sensation and perception as two distinct processes. Sensation was defined in passive terms as the simple event of some stimulus energy (e.g. a sound wave) impinging on a specific sensory organ that then reflexively transmitted appropriate information to the central nervous system. Perception, on the other hand, was defined as integrative and interpretive processes that the higher centers of the brain supposedly accomplish, based on sensory information and available memories of similar events.

The strict dichotomy of sensation and perception is no longer widely accepted by today's psychologists. The revolution came in the mid-1960s, when a psychologist published a then radical treatise in which he reasoned that perceptual processes included *all* sensory events that he believed were directed by an actively searching central nervous system. This viewpoint provided that certain perceptual patterns, such as recognition of a piece of artwork, may be species-specific. That is, all humans, independent of learning history, should share some of the same perceptual repertoires. This unit on perceptual processes is designed to further your understanding of these complex and interesting processes.

© Goodshoot/PictureQuest

Extreme States

Out-of-body experiences? Near-death experiences? Researchers are beginning to understand how they occur and how they may alter the brain.

STEVEN KOTLER

I was 17 years old and terrified. The whole "let's go jump out of an airplane" concept had been dreamed up at a Friday night party, but now I was Saturday-morning sober and somehow still going skydiving. To make matters worse, this was in 1984, and while tandem skydiving was invented in 1977, the concept had yet to make its way to the airfield in mid-Ohio where I had wound up. So my first jump wasn't done with an instructor tethered to my back handling any difficulties we might encounter. Instead, I jumped alone 2,000 feet, my only safety net an unwieldy old Army parachute, dubbed a "round."

Thankfully, nobody expected me to pull my own rip cord. A static line, nothing fancier than a short rope, had been fixed between my rip cord and the floor of the airplane. If everything went according to plan, 15 feet from the plane, when I reached the end of my rope, it would tug open the chute. *Getting* to this point was more complicated.

As the plane flew along at 100 miles per hour, I had to clamber out a side door, ignore the vertiginous view, step onto a small metal rung, hold onto the plane's wing with both hands, and lift one leg behind me, so that my body formed a giant T. From this position, when my instructor gave the order, I was to jump. If all this wasn't bad enough, when I finally leaped out of the plane, I also leaped out of my body.

It happened the second I let go of the wing. My body started falling through space, but my consciousness was hovering about 20 feet away, watching me descend. During training, the instructor had explained that rounds opened, closed, and opened again in the first milliseconds of deployment. He had also mentioned that it happened too fast for the human eye to see and that we shouldn't worry about it. Yet in the instant I began falling, I was worried. I was also watching the chute's open-close-open routine, despite knowing that what I was watching was technically impossible to see.

My body began to tip over, tilting into an awkward position that would produce quite a jerk when the chute caught. In what might best be described as a moment of extracorporeal clarity, I told myself to relax rather than risk whiplash. In the next instant, my chute caught with a jerk. The jerk snapped my consciousness back into my body, and everything returned to normal.

Out-of-body experiences belong to a subset of not-so-garden-variety phenomena broadly called the paranormal, although the dictionary defines that word as "beyond the range of normal experience or scientific explanation," and out-of-body experiences are neither. This type of experience has been reported in almost every country in the world for centuries. Mystics of nearly every faith, including all five of the world's major religions, have long told tales of astral projection. But this phenomenon is not reserved for only the religious. The annals of action sports are packed with accounts of motorcyclists who recall floating above their bikes, watching themselves ride, and pilots who occasionally find themselves floating outside their airplane, struggling to get back inside. However, most out-of-body tales do not take place within the confines of an extreme environment. They transpire as part of normal lives.

The out-of-body experience is much like the near-death experience, and any exploration of one must include the other. While out-of-body experiences are defined by a perceptual shift in consciousness, no more and no less, near-death experiences start with this shift and then proceed along a characteristic trajectory. People report entering a dark tunnel, heading into light, and feeling an all-encompassing sense of peace, warmth, love, and welcome. They recall being reassured along the way by dead friends, relatives, and a gamut of religious figures. Occasionally, there's a life review, followed by a decision of the "should I stay or should I go?" variety. A 1990 Gallup poll of American adults found that almost 12 percent of Americans, roughly 30 million individuals, said they have had some sort of near-death experience.

Both phenomena have had a serious credibility problem. Much of it stems from the scientists who did the earliest investigations. Charles Tart, a psychologist at the University of California at Davis, who did the first major study of out-of-body experiences in 1969, and Raymond Moody, a psychiatrist recently retired from the University of Nevada at Las Vegas who did the same for near-death experiences in the early 1970s, designed experiments of questionable rigor and made matters worse by ignoring the peer-review process and publishing their results in best-selling books. Both Tart and Moody later wrote follow-up books partially debunking and partially recanting their previous ones.

Unfortunately, many researchers studying these extreme states of consciousness are unaware of these follow-up books and still point to the original work as evidence that none of this should be taken seriously. Simultaneously, many skeptics are unaware of much of the research done since then. But forget for the moment this troubled history and concentrate on more recent work. And there is plenty.

In 1982, while a children's brain cancer researcher and finishing his residency in pediatrics at Children's Hospital in Seattle, Melvin Morse was also moonlighting for a helicopter-assisted EMT service. One afternoon he was flown to Pocatello, Idaho, to perform CPR on 8-year-old Crystal Merzlock, who had apparently drowned in the deep end of a community swimming pool. When Morse arrived on the scene, the child had been without a heartbeat for 19 minutes; her pupils were already fixed and dilated. Morse got her heart restarted, climbed into the chopper, and went home. Three days later Crystal regained consciousness.

A few weeks passed. Morse was back at the hospital where Crystal was being treated, and they bumped into each other in the hallway. Crystal pointed at Morse, turned to her mother, and said, "That's the guy who put the tube in my nose at the swimming pool." Morse was stunned. "I didn't know what to do. I had never heard of OBEs [out-of-body experiences] or NDEs [near-death experiences]. I stood there thinking: How was this possible? When I put that tube in her nose, she was brain dead. How could she even have this memory?"

Morse decided to make a case study of Crystal's experience, which he published in the *American Journal of Diseases of Children*. He labeled the event a fascinoma, which is both medical slang for an abnormal pathology and a decent summary of the state of our knowledge at the time. He was the first to publish a description of a child's near-death experience.

He started by reviewing the literature, discovering that the classic explanation—delusion—had been recently upgraded to a hallucination provoked by a number of different factors, including fear, drugs, and a shortage of oxygen to the brain. But it was drugs that caught Morse's eye. He knew that ketamine, used as an anesthetic during the Vietnam War, frequently produced out-of-body experiences and that other drugs were suspected of being triggers as well. Morse decided to study halothane, another commonly used anesthetic, believing his study might help explain the many reports of near-death experiences trickling out of emergency rooms. "It's funny to think of it now," he says, "but really, at the time, I set out to do a long-term, large-scale debunking study."

Morse's 1994 report, commonly referred to as the Seattle study and published in *Current Problems in Pediatrics*, spanned a decade. During that period, he interviewed 160 children in the intensive care unit at Children's Hospital in Seattle who had been revived from apparent death. Every one of these children had been without a pulse or sign of breathing longer than 30 seconds. Some had been in that state for as long as 45 minutes; the average apparent death lasted between 10 and 15 minutes. For a control group, he used hundreds of other children also in intensive care, also on the brink of death, but whose pulse

and breathing hadn't been interrupted for more than 30 seconds. That was the only difference. In other dimensions—age, sex, drugs administered, diseases suffered, and setting—the groups were the same. In setting, Morse not only included the intensive care unit itself but also scary procedures such as insertion of a breathing tube and mechanical ventilation. These are important additions because fear has long been considered a trigger for a near-death experience (and might have been the trigger responsible for what happened when I skydived).

Morse graded his subjects' experiences according to the Greyson scale, a 16-point questionnaire designed by University of Virginia psychiatrist Bruce Greyson that remains the benchmark for determining whether or not an anomalous experience should be considered a near-death experience. Using this test, Morse found that 23 out of 26 children who experienced apparent death—the cessation of heartbeat and breathing—reported a classic near-death experience, while none of the other 131 children in his control group reported anything of the kind.

Morse later videotaped the children recalling their experiences, which included such standard fare as long tunnels, giant rainbows, dead relatives, and deities of all sorts. But many descriptions—augmented by crayon drawings—included memories of the medical procedures performed and details about doctors and nurses whose only contact with the child occurred while the child was apparently dead.

Other scientists have duplicated Morse's findings. Most recently, cardiologist Pim van Lommel, a researcher at Rijnstate Hospital in Arnhem, the Netherlands, conducted an eight-year study involving 344 cardiac-arrest patients who seemed to have died and were later revived. Out of that total, 282 had no memories, while 62 reported a classic near-death experience. Just as in Morse's study, van Lommel examined the patients' records for any factors traditionally used to explain near-death experiences—such as setting, drugs, or illness—and found no evidence of their influence. Apparent death was the only factor linked to near-death experiences. He also found that one person in his study had difficult-to-explain memories of events that happened in the hospital while he was presumed dead.

Possible clues to the biological basis of these unusual states turned up in studies conducted in the late 1970s, when the Navy and the Air Force introduced a new generation of high-performance fighter planes that underwent extreme acceleration. Those speeds generated tremendous g-forces, which pulled too much blood out of the pilots' brains, causing them to black out. The problem, known as G-LOC, for g-force-induced loss of consciousness, was serious, and James Whinnery, a specialist in aerospace medicine, was in charge of solving it.

Over a 16-year period, working with a massive centrifuge at the Naval Air Warfare Center in Warminster, Pennsylvania, Whinnery spun fighter pilots into G-LOC. He wanted to determine at what force tunnel vision occurred. More than 500 pilots accidentally blacked out during the study, and from them Whinnery learned how long it took pilots to lose consciousness under acceleration and how long they remained unconscious after the acceleration ceased. By studying this subset he also learned how long they could be unconscious before brain damage started.

He found that G-LOC could be induced in 5.67 seconds, that the average blackout lasted 12 to 24 seconds, and that at least 40 of the pilots reported some sort of out-of-body experience while they were unconscious. Not knowing anything about out-of-body experiences, Whinnery called these episodes dreamlets, kept detailed records of their contents, and began examining the literature on anomalous unconscious experiences. "I was reading about sudden-death episodes in cardiology," Whinnery says, "and it led me right into near-death experiences. I realized that a smaller percentage of my pilots' dreamlets, about 10 to 15 percent, were much closer in content to a classic NDE."

When Whinnery reviewed his data, he noted a correlation: The longer his pilots were knocked out, the closer they got to brain death. And the closer they got to brain death, the more likely it was that an out-of-body experience would turn into a near-death experience. This was the first hard evidence for what had been long suspected—that the two states are not two divergent phenomena, but two points on a continuum.

Whinnery found that G-LOC, when gradually induced, produced tunnel vision. "The progression went first to grayout (loss of peripheral vision) and then to blackout," he explains, and the blindness occurred just before a person went unconscious. "This makes a lot of sense. We know that the occipital lobe (the portion of the brain that controls vision) is a well-protected structure. Perhaps it continued to function when signals from the eyes were failing due to compromised blood flow. The transition from grayout to unconsciousness resembles floating peacefully within a dark tunnel, which is much like some of the defining characteristics of a near-death experience. The pilots also recalled a feeling of peace and serenity as they regained consciousness.

The simplest conclusion to draw from these studies is that, give or take some inexplicable memories, these phenomena are simply normal physical processes that occur during unusual circumstances. After all, once scientists set aside the traditional diagnosis of delusion as a source of these unusual mental states and began looking for biological correlates, there were plenty of possibilities. Compression of the optic nerve could produce tunnel vision; neurochemicals such as serotonin, endorphins, and enkephalins could help explain the euphoria; and psychotropics like LSD and mescaline often produce vibrant hallucinations of past events. But no one has directly tested these hypotheses.

What researchers have studied is the effect of a near-death experience. Van Lommel conducted lengthy interviews and administered a battery of standard psychological tests to his study group of cardiac-arrest patients. The subset that had had a near-death experience reported more self-awareness, more social awareness, and more religious feelings than the others.

Van Lommel then repeated this process after a two-year interval and found the group with near-death experience still had complete memories of the event, while others' recollections were strikingly less vivid. He found that the near-death experience group also had an increased belief in an afterlife and a decreased fear of death compared with the others. After eight years he again repeated the whole process and found those two-year effects significantly more pronounced. The near-death experience group was much more empathetic, emotionally

vulnerable, and often showed evidence of increased intuitive awareness. They still showed no fear of death and held a strong belief in an afterlife.

Morse, too, did follow-up studies long after his original research. He also did a separate study involving elderly people who had a near-death experience in early childhood. "The results were the same for both groups," says Morse. "Nearly all of the people who had had a near-death experience—no matter if it was 10 years ago or 50—were still absolutely convinced their lives had meaning and that there was a universal, unifying thread of love which provided that meaning. Matched against a control group, they scored much higher on life-attitude tests, significantly lower on fear-of-death tests, gave more money to charity, and took fewer medications. There's no other way to look at the data. These people were just transformed by the experience."

Morse has gone on to write three popular books about near-death experiences and the questions they raise about the nature of consciousness. His research caught the attention of Willoughby Britton, a doctoral candidate in clinical psychology at the University of Arizona who was interested in post-traumatic stress disorder. Britton knew that most people who have a close brush with death tend to have some form of post-traumatic stress disorder, while people who get that close and have a near-death experience have none. In other words, people who have a near-death experience have an atypical response to life-threatening trauma. No one knows why.

Britton also knew about work done by legendary neurosurgeon and epilepsy expert Wilder Penfield in the 1950s. Penfield, one of the giants of modern neuroscience, discovered that stimulating the brain's right temporal lobe—located just above the ear—with a mild electric current produced out-of-body experiences, heavenly music, vivid hallucinations, and the kind of panoramic memories associated with the life review part of the near-death experience. This helped explain why right temporal lobe epilepsy was a condition long defined by its most prominent symptom: excessive religiosity characterized by an intense feeling of spirituality, mystical visions, and auditory hallucinations of the voice-of-God variety. And given what Whinnery has found, it is possible that his pilots' near-death-like dreamlets were related to brief episodes of compromised blood flow in the temporal lobe.

Britton hypothesized that people who have undergone a near-death experience might show the same altered brain firing patterns as people with temporal lobe epilepsy. The easiest way to determine if someone has temporal lobe epilepsy is to monitor the brain waves during sleep, when there is an increased likelihood of activity indicative of epilepsy. Britton recruited 23 people who had a near-death experience and 23 who had undergone neither a near-death experience nor a life-threatening traumatic event. Then, working at a sleep lab, she hooked up her subjects to electrodes that measured EEG activity all over the brain—including the temporal lobes—and recorded everything that happened while they slept.

She then asked a University of Arizona epilepsy specialist who knew nothing about the experiment to analyze the EEGs.

Two features distinguished the group with near-death experience from the controls: They needed far less sleep, and they went into REM (rapid eye movement) sleep far later in the sleep cycle than normal people. "The point at which someone goes into REM sleep is a fantastic indicator of depressive tendencies," says Britton. "We've gotten very good at this kind of research. If you took 100 people and did a sleep study, we can look at the data and know, by looking at the time they entered REM, who's going to become depressed in the next year and who isn't."

Normal people enter REM at 90 minutes. Depressed people enter at 60 minutes or sooner. Britton found that the vast majority of her group with near-death experience entered REM sleep at 110 minutes. With that finding, she identified the first objective neurophysiological difference in people who have had a near-death experience.

Britton thinks near-death experience somehow rewires the brain, and she has found some support for her hypothesis regarding altered activity in the temporal lobe: Twenty-two percent of the group with near-death experience showed synchrony in the temporal lobe, the same kind of firing pattern associated with temporal lobe epilepsy. "Twenty-two percent may not sound like a lot of anything," says Britton, "but it's actually incredibly abnormal, so much so that it's beyond the realm of chance."

She also found something that didn't fit with her hypothesis. The temporal lobe synchrony wasn't happening on the right side of the brain, the site that had been linked in Penfield's studies to religious feeling in temporal lobe epilepsy. Instead she found it on the left side of the brain. That finding made some people uncomfortable because it echoed studies that pinpointed, in far more detail than Penfield achieved, the exact locations in the brain that were most active and most inactive during periods of profound religious experience.

Over the past 10 years a number of different scientists, including neurologist James Austin from the University of Colorado, neuroscientist Andrew Newberg, and the late anthropologist and psychiatrist Eugene D'Aquili from the University of Pennsylvania, have done SPECT (single photon emission computed tomography) scans of the brains of Buddhists during meditation and of Franciscan nuns during prayer. They found a marked decrease in activity in the parietal lobes, an area in the upper rear of the brain. This region helps us orient ourselves in space; it allows us to judge angles and curves and distances and to know where the self ends and the rest of the world begins. People who suffer injuries in this area have great difficulties navigating life's simplest landscapes. Sitting down on a couch, for example, becomes a task of Herculean impossibility because they are unsure where their own legs end and the sofa begins. The SPECT scans indicated that meditation temporarily blocks the processing of sensory information within both parietal lobes.

When that happens, as Newberg and D'Aquili point out in their book *Why God Won't Go Away*, "the brain would have no choice but to perceive that the self is endless and intimately interwoven with everyone and everything the mind senses. And this perception would feel utterly and unquestionably real." They use the brain-scan findings to explain the interconnected cosmic unity that the Buddhists experienced, but the results could also explain what Morse calls the "universal, unifying thread of love" that people with near-death experience consistently reported.

These brain scans show that when the parietal lobes go quiet, portions of the right temporal lobe—some of the same portions that Penfield showed produced feelings of excessive religiosity, out-of-body experiences, and vivid hallucinations—become more active. Newberg and D'Aquili also argue that activities often found in religious rituals—like repetitive chanting—activate (and deactivate) similar areas in the brain, a finding that helps explain some of the more puzzling out-of-body experience reports, like those of the airplane pilots suddenly floating outside their planes. Those pilots were as intensely focused on their instrumentation as meditators focused on mantras. Meanwhile, the sound of the engine's spinning produces a repetitive, rhythmic drone much like tribal drumming. If conditions were right, says Newberg, these two things should be enough to produce the same temporal lobe activity to trigger an out-of-body experience.

Neuropsychologist Michael Persinger of Laurentian University in Sudbury, Ontario, has conducted other studies that explore the generation of altered mental states. Persinger built a helmet that produces weak, directed electromagnetic fields. He then asked over 900 volunteers, mostly college students, to wear the helmets while he monitored their brain activity and generated variations in the electromagnetic field. When he directed these fields toward the temporal lobes, Persinger's helmet induced the sort of mystical, free-of-the-body experiences common to right temporal lobe epileptics, meditators, and people who have had near-death experiences.

None of this work is without controversy, but an increasing number of scientists now think that our brains are wired for mystical experiences. The studies confirm that these experiences are as real as any others, because our involvement with the rest of the universe is mediated by our brains. Whether these experiences are simply right temporal lobe activity, as many suspect, or, as Britton's work hints and Morse believes, a whole brain effect, remains an open question. But Persinger thinks there is a simple explanation for why people with near-death experience have memories of things that occurred while they were apparently dead. The memory-forming structures lie deep within the brain, he says, and they probably remain active for a few minutes after brain activity in the outer cortex has stopped. Still, Crystal Merzlock remembered events that occurred more than *19 minutes* after her heart stopped. Nobody has a full explanation for this phenomenon, and we are left in that very familiar mystical state: the one where we still don't have all the answers.

A Matter of Taste

Are you a supertaster? Just stick out your tongue and say "yuck."

MARY BECKMAN

There's good taste, and according to scientists, there's supertaste. Blue food coloring is going to tell me where I lie on the continuum. Armed with a bottle of blue dye No. 1 and a Q-tip, I paint my tongue cobalt, swish some water in my mouth and spit into the bathroom sink. In the mirror I see a smattering of pink bumps—each hiding as many as 15 taste buds apiece—against the lurid blue background. Now I'm supposed to count how many of those bumps, called fungiform papillae, appear inside a circle a quarter-inch in diameter, but I don't need to do that. Obviously, I have fewer than the 30 that would qualify me as having an extraordinary palate. I am not a supertaster. Thank goodness.

Normally, people prize highly acute senses. We brag about twenty-twenty vision or the ability to eavesdrop on whispers from across the room. But taste is not so simple: supertaste may be too much of a good thing, causing those who have it to avoid bitter compounds and find some spicy foods too hot to handle. This unusual corner of perception science has been explored by Linda Bartoshuk of Yale University, who first stumbled upon supertasting about 15 years ago while studying saccharin. While most people found the sugar substitute sweet and palatable, others sensed a bitter aftertaste. She went on to test hundreds of volunteers with a host of chemicals found in food. About one in four, she discovered, qualified as supertasters, a name she coined.

To find what made them special, Bartoshuk zeroed in on the tongue's anatomy. She found that people have different numbers of fungiform papillae, with tongue topography ranging from, say, sparse cactus-pocked deserts to lush lawns. To qualify for supertasterdom, which is a genetically inherited trait, a person has to have wall-to-wall papillae on his or her tongue and also have an ability to readily taste PROP, a bitter synthetic compound also known as 6-*n*-propylthiouracil, which is used as a thyroid medication.

As it happens, Bartoshuk is a non-taster—she's among another one in four who can't detect PROP at all—and likes it that way. "I prefer the dumb, happy life I lead," she says. "'Super' connotes superiority, but supertaste often means sensory unpleasantness." In the course of her research she has relied on volunteers and colleagues to perceive what she cannot, such as the difference in creaminess between skim and 2 percent milk. "PROP tastes like quinine," says Laurie Lucchina, a supertaster who made this discovery about ten years ago when she worked with Bartoshuk. Another person in the lab, Valerie Duffy, now at the University of Connecticut, is a medium taster. Bartoshuk routinely tested "the junk food of the month," sent to the lab through a food subscription service, on the two women. "Once she brought in a cookie that she thought was very bland. But to me, it tasted just right," recalls Lucchina.

"Mother's milk reflects the culture into which babies are born."

Perhaps not surprisingly, supersensitive taste influences what people eat. Bartoshuk and other researchers found that supertasters tend to shun or restrict strong-flavored foods and drinks—coffee, frosted cake, greasy barbequed ribs, hoppy hand-crafted ales. Also, supertasters tend to crave neither fats nor sugars, which probably helps explain why researchers have found that supertasters also tend to be slimmer than people without the sensitivity. When it comes to rich desserts, Lucchina says, "I usually eat just a bite or two and then I'm done."

Taste sensitivity may also affect health. According to recent studies, supertasters have better cholesterol profiles than the norm, helping reduce their risk of heart disease. Yet supertasting may also have a downside. Some scientists have speculated that supertasters don't eat enough bitter vegetables, which are believed to protect against various types of cancer. And in a still-preliminary study of 250 men by Bartoshuk and co-workers, nontasters had fewer colon polyps, a risk factor for colon cancer, than did medium tasters or supertasters. To be sure, not everyone is convinced that supertasters put themselves in harm's way by skimping on vegetables. Adam Drewnowski, a nutrition scientist at the University of Washington, says a dollop of butter or maybe a splash of cheese sauce may be all a supertaster needs to find spinach or broccoli palatable. Still, the new data intrigue medical researchers, who don't usually consider taste an inherited factor in disease risk.

Of course, there's more to satisfaction than meets the tongue. Flavors are a combination of taste and odors, which float up through the back of our mouths to activate a suite of smell receptors in the nose. (Hold your nose while tasting a jellybean. You can tell it's sweet but not what flavor it is. Then unplug your nose. See?) Each smell tingles a different constellation of neurons in the brain, and with experience we learn what these different patterns mean—it's bacon sizzling in the kitchen, not liver. Nature may dictate whether or not we're supertasters, but it's nurture that shapes most of our food preferences.

And taste training starts earlier than one might think—during breast-feeding or even in the womb, according to biopsychologist Julie Mennella of the Monell Chemical Senses Center in Philadelphia. She asked pregnant women and breast-feeding mothers to drink carrot juice for three weeks. In both cases, when it came time to switch to solid food, babies of these mothers liked carrots better than babies whose mothers never drank the stuff. "These are the first ways they learn what foods are safe," Mennella says. "Mother's milk reflects the culture into which babies are born."

Learning can even trump innate good sense, according to a study Mennella reported this past April. She found that 7-month-old babies normally disliked bitter and sour flavors, and when given a bottle with a slightly bitter, sour formula, they pushed it away and wrinkled their angelic faces in disgust. But 7-month-olds who had been introduced to the bitter formula months earlier happily drank it again. In another study of babies who'd never been fed carrots, she found that those who'd been exposed to a variety of other vegetables clearly enjoyed carrots more than did babies who'd dined on a more monotonous diet. She suggests that early exposure to a diversity of flavors enables babies to trust new foods later in life. "Clearly experience is a factor in developing food habits," says Mennella. "But we don't know how that interacts with genetics."

Beyond genes and even learning lies a more ineffable aspect of taste: its emotional content. Certain foods can bring back unpleasant experiences; it may take only one rotten hot dog to put you off franks for life. Other tastes unlock happy memories. To an extent that researchers are still trying to understand, learning which foods are safe to eat while in the security of mother's arms may be the source of some of our most enduring desires. This learning process could be, Mennella says, "one of the foundations of how we define what is a comfort food."

MARY BECKMAN, a freelance writer in Idaho, specializes in the life sciences.

What Dreams Are Made Of

Technologies that reveal the inner workings of the brain are beginning to tell the sleeping mind's secrets.

MARIANNE SZEGEDY-MASZAK

Strange images appear from long-forgotten memories. Or out of nowhere: You're roller-skating on water; your mother flashes by on a trapeze; your father is in labor; a friend dead for years sits down at the dinner table. Here are moments of unspeakable terror; there, moments of euphoria or serenity. Shakespeare wrote, "We are such stuff as dreams are made on," and 300 years later, Sigmund Freud gave the poetry a neat psychoanalytic spin when he called dreams "the royal road to the unconscious." The movies that unfold in our heads some nights are so powerfully resonant they haunt us for days—or inspire us. Mary Shelley dreamed of Frankenstein before she created him on paper; the melody to "Yesterday" came to Paul McCartney as he slept.

Everybody dreams—yet no one, throughout history, has fully grasped what the dreaming mind is doing. Are the nightly narratives a message from the unconscious to the conscious mind, as Freud believed? Or are they simply the product of random electrical flashes in the brain? Today, researchers aided by powerful technologies that reveal the brain in action are concluding that both schools of thought hold truth. "This is the greatest adventure of all time," says Harvard psychiatrist and dream researcher J. Allan Hobson. "The development of brain imaging is the equivalent of Galileo's invention of the telescope, only we are now exploring inner space instead of outer space."

Freud saw dreams as buried wishes disguised by symbols.

Mind-brain dance. The dream researchers' new tools, functional magnetic resonance imaging and positron emission tomography (PET) scanning, have been used for some time to capture the waking brain at work—making

decisions, feeling frightened or joyous, coping with uncertainty. And those efforts have shown clearly that psychology and physiology are intimately related: In someone suffering from an anxiety disorder, for example, the fear center of the brain—the amygdala—"lights up" as neurons fire in response to images that trigger anxiety; it flickers in a minuet with the center of memory, the hippocampus. Scanning people who are sleeping, too, suggests that the same sort of mind-brain dance continues 24 hours a day.

"Psychology has built its model of the mind strictly out of waking behavior," says Rosalind Cartwright, chair of the department of behavioral science at Rush University Medical Center in Chicago, who has studied dreams for most of her 83 years. "We know that the mind does not turn off during sleep; it goes into a different stage." Brain cells fire, and the mind spins. Problems find solutions; emotional angst seems to be soothed; out-of-the-box ideas germinate and take root.

> The door between the kitchen and the garage was split, so you could open the top half without opening the bottom half. It was the only safe way of doing it, because we had a rhinoceros in the garage. The garage was a lot bigger, though; it was also sort of a basement, and led underneath the rest of the house. My mother was cooking dinner, and I went into the bathroom where my brother Stuart was. The rhinoceros punched a hole in the floor with his horn.
>
> **Madeline,** third grade

What to make of young Madeline's dream? To Freud, had he met her, Madeline's rhinoceros horn would almost certainly have symbolized a penis, and the animal's violence would have been an expression of normal but threatening sexual feelings toward her brother—or perhaps of a fear of men in general. Freud saw dreams as deeply

Frankenstein and Mary Shelley

A Dream Come True

Can man create life? A talk on evolution that considered the possibility so disturbed Mary Godwin that she went to bed and dreamed up Frankenstein. She and three other writers, including her soon-to-be-husband, Percy Shelley, were staying at Lake Geneva in Switzerland during that summer of 1816, entertaining one another by telling and competing to write the best ghost stories. Shelley's vivid dream, in which she saw a "hideous phantasm of a man stretched out" and a scientist using a machine to try to bring him to life, inspired hers. She began to write the next day.

—Betsy Querna

Joseph and a Word from God

A Dream Come True

When Joseph discovered that Mary was pregnant during their engagement, he was "just crushed," says Father Gerald Kleba, a Roman Catholic priest in St. Louis who wrote the historical novel *Joseph Remembered*. Assuming that she had committed adultery, Joseph figured he would have to leave her. But an angel visited him in a dream, according to the Bible, and told him not to be afraid. Mary had conceived through the Holy Spirit and would bear a special child. That "huge aha moment" shaped the rest of Joseph's life, says Kleba, and still speaks to many Christians of the power of faith.

—B.Q.

buried wishes disguised by symbols, a way to gratify desires unacceptable to the conscious mind. His ideas endured for years, until scientists started systematically studying dream content and decided that actually, something less exotic is going on.

"Dreams do enact—they dramatize. They are like plays of how we view the world and oneself in it," says William Domhoff, who teaches psychology and sociology at the University of California-Santa Cruz. "But they do not provide grandiose meanings." Domhoff bases his view on a study of themes and images that recur in a databank of some 16,000 dreams—including Madeline's—that have been collected as oral narratives and are held at Santa Cruz. (The narratives can be read at www.dreambank.net.)

Post-Freudians might argue that the monsters lurking in children's dreams signal a growing awareness of the world around them and its dangers. Young children describe very simple and concrete images, while the dreams of 9- and 10-year-olds get decidedly more complex. A monster that goes so far as to chase or attack might represent a person who is frightening to the child during waking hours. "Dreaming serves a vital function in the maturation of the brain and in processing the experiences of the day," says Alan Siegel, professor of psychology at UC-Berkeley and author of *Dream Wisdom*.

The experience of dreaming is as universal as a heartbeat.

Nonsense. Physiology purists, who would say that Madeline's brain is simply flashing random images, got their start in 1953 with the discovery of rapid eye movement sleep. Using primitive electroencephalograms,

researchers watched as every 90 minutes, sleepers' eyes darted back and forth and brain waves surged. Then, in 1977, Harvard psychiatrists Hobson and Robert McCarley reported that during sleep, electrical activity picked up dramatically in the most primitive area of the brain—the pons—which, by simply stimulating other parts of the brain, produced weird and disconnected narratives. Much like people looking for meaning in an inkblot, they concluded, dreams are the brain's vain attempt to impose coherence where there is none.

Or maybe that's not the whole story, either, said a young neuropsychologist at the Royal London School of Medicine 20 years later, when his findings hinted that dreaming is both a mental and a physical process. Mark Solms showed that dreams can't be explained as simple physical reactions to flashes from the primitive pons, since some of the most active dreamers in his study had suffered brain damage in that area. On the other hand, in those with damage to regions of the brain associated with higher-order motivation, passionate emotions, and abstract thinking, the nightly movies had stopped. That seemed a sign that dreams might indeed express the mind's ideas and motivations. "It is a mistake to think that we can study the brain using the same concepts we use for the liver," says Solms.

"From my perspective, dreaming is just thinking in a very different biochemical state," says Deirdre Barrett, who teaches psychology at Harvard and is editor of the journal *Dreaming*. The threads can be "just as complex as waking thought and just as dull. They are overwhelmingly visual, and language is less important, and logic is less important."

I am a traveler carrying one light bag and looking for a place to spend the night. I . . . discover a hostel of a sort in a large indoor space big enough to house a gymnasium. I find a spot near a corner and

Paul McCartney and "Yesterday"

A Dream Come True

"I woke up with a lovely tune in my head," Paul McCartney recalled to his biographer, Barry Miles. "I thought, 'That's great. I wonder what that is?'" He got up that morning in May 1965, went to the piano, and began playing the melody what would become "Yesterday." At first, lacking lyrics, he improvised with "Scrambled eggs, oh my baby, how I love your legs." While he really liked the tune, he had some reservations: "Because I'd, dreamed it, I couldn't believe I'd written it." Today, with more than 1,600 covers, that song holds the Guinness world record for most recorded versions.

—B.Q.

prepare for bed. I think to myself, "Luckily, I have my high-tech pillow." I take out of my bag a light, flat panel about 8 by 10 inches and the thickness of a thick piece of cardboard. "It works by applying a voltage," I say. "There's a new kind of material which fluffs up when you apply a voltage." On the face of the panel is a liquid-crystal display with two buttons, one labeled "on" and one labeled "off." I touch the "on" button with my index finger, and the flat panel magically inflates to the dimensions of a fluffy pillow. I lay it down on the ground and comfortably go to sleep.

Chuck, scientist (from Dreambank.net)

If Chuck's experience is an example of logic gone to sleep, no wonder dreamers so often wake up shouting, "Eureka!" Indeed, history is filled with examples of inspiration that blossomed during sleep and eventually led to inventions or works of art or military moves. Exactly what happens to inspire creativity is unclear, but the new technology is providing clues.

Crazy smart. Brain scans performed on people in REM sleep, for example, have shown that even as certain brain centers turn on—the emotional seat of the brain and the part that processes all visual inputs are wide awake— one vital area goes absolutely dormant: the systematic and clear-thinking prefrontal cortex, where caution and organization reside. "This can explain the bizarreness you see in dreams, the crazy kind of sense that your brain is ignoring the usual ways that you put things together," says Robert Stickgold, associate professor of psychiatry at Harvard and director of the Center for Sleep and Cognition at Beth Israel Deaconess Medical Center. "This is what you want in a state in which creativity is enhanced. Creativity is nothing more and nothing less than putting

memories together in a way that they never have been before."

No wonder dreamers so often wake up shouting, "Eureka!"

Putting memories together is also an essential part of learning; people integrate the memory of new information, be it how to tie shoelaces or conjugate French verbs, with existing knowledge. Does dreaming help people learn? No one knows—but some sort of boost seems to happen during sleep. Many studies by sleep researchers have shown that people taught a new task performed it better after a night of sleep.

A study of how quickly dreamers solve problems supports Stickgold's theory that the sleeping mind can be quite nimble and inventive. Participants were asked to solve scrambled word puzzles after being awakened during both the REM phase of sleep and the less active non-REM phase. Their performance improved by 32 percent when they worked on the puzzles coming out of REM sleep, which told researchers that that phase is more conducive to fluid reasoning. During non-REM sleep, it appears, our more cautious selves kick into gear.

Indeed, PET scans of people in a non-REM state show a decline in brain energy compared with REM sleep and increased activity in those dormant schoolmarmish lobes. Does this affect the content of dreams? Yes, say researchers from Harvard and the Boston University School of Medicine.

Since people should theoretically be more uninhibited when the controlling prefrontal cortex is quiet, the team tracked participants for two weeks to see if their REM dreams were more socially aggressive than the ones they reported during non-REM sleep. The REM dreams, in fact, were much more likely to involve social interactions and tended to be more aggressive.

I had a horrible dream. Howard was in a coffin. I yelled and screamed at his mom that it was all her fault. I kicked myself that I hadn't waited to become a widow rather than a divorcée in order to get the insurance. I woke up feeling miserable, the dream was so icky.

Barb (from Dreambank.net)

To many experts, Barb's bad dream would be a good sign, an indication that she would recover from the sorrow of her divorce. A vivid dream life, in which troubled or anxious people experience tough emotions while asleep, is thought to act, in the words of Cartwright, as "a kind of internal therapist."

Saddam and His Winning Strategy

A Dream Come True

Saddam Hussein used his dreams to guide policy, sometimes to the befuddlement of his closest advisers. The dictator's personal secretary told U.S. military investigators in an interview in 2003 that Hussein would sleep on difficult problems and report the solutions the next morning. One time that his dream got it right: During the Iran-Iraq War of the 1980s, Hussein dreamed that the Iranians would launch an offensive through a large marshland, so he ordered more troops there. His generals thought the move illogical but acquiesced. The Iranians attacked there, and the Iraqis prevailed.

—B.Q.

Jack Nicklaus and His Grip

A Dream Come True

In the summer of 1964, Jack Nicklaus was in a slump: "It got to the point where a 76 looked like a great score to me," the golfer told the Cleveland *Plain Dealer.* One night, during the Cleveland Open, he dreamed he was hitting the ball with a different grip—and it worked better. So he tried it the next day, shot a 68, then a 65, and ended the tournament tied for third place. For the year, he shot about a 70 average, the lowest in professional golf. "I'm almost embarrassed to admit how I changed my grip this week," he told the reporter at the time. "But that's how it happened. It's kinda crazy, isn't it?"

—B.Q.

The enduring and vexing question is: How much of value do dreams say? Despite all the efforts to quantify, to measure, no one has an answer yet. But dreams have played a role in psychotherapy for over a century, since Freud theorized that they signal deep and hidden motivations. "A dream is the one domain in which many of a patient's defenses are sufficiently relaxed that themes emerge that ordinarily would not appear in waking life," says Glen Gabbard, professor of psychiatry and psychoanalysis at Baylor College of Medicine.

A vivid dream life is thought to act as an "internal therapist."

Sometimes, dreams can be a helpful diagnostic tool, a way of taking the emotional temperature of a patient. The dreams of clinically depressed people are notable for their utter lack of activity, for example.

Might there be a physiological reason? Eric Nofzinger, director of the Sleep Neuroimaging Research Program at the University of Pittsburgh medical school, has studied PET scans of depressed patients and has found that the difference between their waking and sleeping states is far less dramatic than normal. On the one hand, he says, "we were shocked, surprised, and amazed at how much activity" there was in the emotional brain of healthy people during sleep. In depressed patients, by contrast, the vigilant prefrontal cortex, which normally is not active during sleep, worked overtime. Never surrendering to the soothing power of dreams, the brain is physically constrained, and its dream life shows it.

Healing power. Is it possible that dreaming can actually heal? "We know that 60 to 70 percent of people who go through a depression will recover without treatment," says Cartwright, who recently tested her theory that maybe they are working through their troubles while asleep. In a study whose results were published this spring in the journal *Psychiatry Research,* she recruited 30 people going through a divorce and asked them to record their dreams over five months. Depressed patients whose dreams were rich with emotion—one woman reported seething while her ex-husband danced with his new girlfriend—eventually recovered without the need for drugs or extensive psychotherapy. But those whose dreams were bland and empty of feeling were not able to recover on their own.

I've sat straight up in bed many times, reliving it, reseeing it, rehearing it. And it's in the most absurd ways that only a dream could depict . . . the one that comes to mind most, dreaming of a green pool in front of me. That was part of the radarscope. It was a pool of gel, and I reached into the radarscope to stop that flight. But in the dream, I didn't harm the plane. I just held it in my hand, and somehow that stopped everything.

Danielle O'Brien, air traffic controller for American Airlines Flight 77, which crashed into the Pentagon on Sept. 11, 2001 (in an interview with ABC News)

Many clinicians working with traumatized patients have found that their nightmares follow a common trajectory. First, the dreams re-create the horrors; later, as the person begins to recover, the stories involve better outcomes. One way to help victims of trauma move on is to encourage them to wake themselves up in the midst of a horrifying dream and consciously take control of the narrative, to take action, much as O'Brien appears to have done in her dream. This can break the cycle of nightmares by offering a sense of mastery. "If you can change the dream content," says Harvard's Barrett, author of *Trauma and Dreams,* "you see a reduction in all the other post-traumatic symptoms."

Cartwright recalls helping a rape victim who came in suffering from nightmares in which she felt an utter lack of control; together, they worked to edit the young woman's dreams of being in situations where she was powerless—of lying on the floor of an elevator without walls as it rose higher and higher over Lake Michigan, for example. "I told her, 'Remember, this is your construction. You made it up, and you can stop it,'" says Cartwright, who coached the woman to recognize the point at which the dream was becoming frightening and try to seize control. At the next session, the woman reported that, as the elevator rose, she decided to stand in her dream and figure out what was happening. The walls rose around her until she felt safe.

A window? A royal road? A way for the brain to integrate today with yesterday? While definitive answers remain elusive, the experience of dreaming is clearly as universal as a heartbeat and as individual as a fingerprint—and rich with possibilities for both scientist and poet.

About Face

Facial processing research has come a long way, but debates within the field and potential applications haven't quite reached a head.

Eric Jaffe

The motorcycle accident happened in August of 1980 and life would never be the same for the 39-year-old driver. His right arm endured significant damage, and he was right-handed. His judgment of construction design disappeared, and he was a city planner. Scenic landscapes and potential mates, once alluring sights, now aroused in him nothing, blending instead into indistinguishable images he could describe only as "dull."

If after the collision the patient inspected himself in a mirror, he might not have recognized the face looking back, but not because unfamiliar bandages or bruises distorted the view. Rather, this lack of recognition would have been caused by the patient's most prominent, and likely most painful, consequence of the accident: prosopagnosia, a disorder that renders a person unable to identify a face, be it the mailman's, a spouse's, or even one's own.

"It's an amazingly devastating disorder, to wake up and not be able to distinguish your family member," says Russell Bauer of the University of Florida, who studied the victim for many years and is co-editing an upcoming special issue on face processing for the *Journal of Neuropsychology.*

Deficits in facial perception caused by brain damage have been described by psychologists since the late 19th century, but the roots of the modern understanding of prosopagnosia are traced to Joachim Bodamer, who coined the term some 60 years ago. The condition is simultaneously comical, horrifying, and fascinating. It serves as the subject of one of Oliver Sacks' most beloved clinical stories, *The Man Who Mistook His Wife for a Hat.* Normally, people see another person "through his *persona,* his face," writes Sacks. But for the patient with prosopagnosia, "there was no *persona* in this sense—no outward *persona,* and no person within."

The disorder's complexity and curiosity sparked a scientific interest in face processing that continues today. Research in the field, once primarily focused on clinical cases, has evolved to include functional imaging and genetic research.

For all its advancements, however, face perception remains a contentious area. Scientists agree that one region of the brain, dubbed the fusiform face area, plays a major role in facial recognition. They disagree, though, on whether that area plays other roles as well and on whether face processing occurs innately or through gradual expertise.

"Face processing has been something that has interested people for many, many years," says Bauer of the decision to prepare a special issue of the journal. "We felt it was time to take stock of where we were."

Face First

From the moment they're born, infants begin gathering information on faces. Studies have shown that, within just a few exposures, newborns become so familiar with their mother's face that they prefer it to a stranger's. Almost as quickly, infants seem to gaze longer at faces that adults deem attractive than to those considered unattractive.

"We've come to know more in the last five to ten years about how infants respond to the social attributes of faces," says APS Fellow Paul Quinn of the University of Delaware.

Some of these findings seem counter-intuitive. After all, shouldn't a newborn seek out novelty—the stranger as well as the parent, the ugly as well as the beautiful—so as to grow familiar with a range of colors and characters? In 1964, Robert Fantz reported in *Science* that babies do indeed show more attention to new stimuli.

But that general rule goes out the window when human faces enter the picture, says Quinn. Many years ago, Quinn reported that infants just a few months old prefer silhouettes of human heads to those of animals. In a 2002 issue of *Science,* researchers reported that 6-month-old infants can individualize the faces of monkeys, but that this ability disappears by 9 months and remains generally absent in adults. More recently, Quinn found that by the time infants are 3 months old, those reared primarily by women prefer female faces—and vice versa for those cared for mostly by men.

"This suggests to me that infant-looking is directed by two systems of motivation," Quinn says. "A social system which directs attachment relationships with familiar objects, and then a non-social system that directs infants to explore properties of novel objects in their environment."

Recently, Quinn and a group of researchers led by David J. Kelly of the University of Sheffield in England wondered whether a preference for facial familiarity leads to a recognition bias toward certain races, as it does for genders and species. Do *they,* as the objectionable cliche goes, truly all look the same to *you?*

To find out, the researchers gathered an equal split of nearly 200 Caucasian infants who were 3-, 6-, and 9-months old. Sitting on their mother's laps, the infants looked at images of faces from four ethnic groups, African, Asian, Middle Eastern, and Caucasian, projected onto a screen. Meanwhile, experimenters recorded the eye movement and gaze length of the tiny faces, to determine if recognition had occurred.

By 9 months, infants only recognized faces within their own racial group, the researchers reported in the December 2007 *Psychological Science.* Six-month-olds tended toward this direction. The youngest group, meanwhile, recognized faces of all different races.

Perhaps frequent exposure to a certain race leads infants to "process same-race faces as individuals, but other-race faces at the . . . category level," Quinn says. "You come into the world with a representation of a face that is unspecified with respect to these social attributes. Then, depending on the type of experience you have, your face representation becomes tuned to particular values."

Expertise vs. Specialty

The findings in infants represent both sides of the larger debate of how people process faces. On one hand, the fact that infants nail down a mother's face after just a few looks implies some specialized, innate understanding. On the other hand, the impact of the caregiver's gender and race on facial perception suggests some gradual acquisition of facial expertise.

"Although we know that faces are a special class, we still don't know if they require a special module in the brain. We haven't really nailed down the effects of learning," Bauer says. "The balance is something we don't quite understand."

Brain imaging evidence suggests that several areas of the brain play a role in face processing—perhaps none more than the fusiform gyrus, which is located behind the right ear. In many studies, this region has responded so much more strongly to facial images than to non-facial objects that it has acquired a more telling name: the fusiform face area.

Researchers who believe that this area innately specializes in face perception can point to a bundle of evidence. Patients with prosopagnosia cannot recognize faces after their right temporal lobe is damaged, but patients with other types of brain damage retain the ability to recognize faces but can't distinguish objects. Research in monkeys has long shown areas of the brain that respond highly to facial images; in a 2006 issue of *Science,* a group of researchers reported an area of macaque brains in which 97 percent of neurons responded resoundingly more to faces than to other stimuli.

More recently, a team of researchers including Bradley C. Duchaine of University College London delivered transcranial magnetic stimulation, or TMS, to subjects' right occipital face area, another region thought to play a large role in facial perception. TMS disrupted the ability to process faces but had no impact on the perception of houses, the authors reported in a September 2007 issue of *Current Biology.*

Earlier in 2007, Duchaine and two other researchers argued that the growing evidence for facial specialty has reached a point where one can claim a "clear resolution" of the debate. "Cognitive and neural mechanisms engaged in face perception are distinct from those engaged in object perception," they conclude in the January issue of *TRENDS in Cognitive Science.*

Not everyone is convinced. "I think if you split object recognition and face recognition apart, you lose something," says Isabel Gauthier of Vanderbilt University. Some areas of the brain indeed respond highly to faces, she says. But those same areas are also active, for example, when a car expert processes cars or when a bird expert watches birds.

"I happen to not think faces are special for any innate reason," Gauthier says. "I think [face processing] is something we learn. There's a good chance it happens through experience."

In 1997, as part of her dissertation, Gauthier created objects called "greebles." She wanted to know if the brain would respond the same way to these abstractions as it did to faces. These novel objects are pointy, faceless figures that appear plucked from the mind of Picasso. After seven hours of studying them, however, subjects became expert enough to learn their names and notice distinguishing characteristics. In other words, subjects treated the greebles as they treat the different hairlines, eye levels, and nose lengths that make human faces unique.

Gauthier used functional imaging to track activity in the fusiform face area before and after subjects became familiar with greebles. Sure enough, as greeble training increased, so did brain response in this region. "A lot of people have come up with hallmarks of face processing," she says. "For me, these effects are doors into understanding expertise."

Some behavioral scientists have expressed skepticism over Gauthier's greeble work. (One of them, Nancy Kanwisher of the Massachusetts Institute of Technology, a leading voice for the specialized theory, was unable to comment for this story.) Gauthier points to some of her more recent work for further evidence that object and face perception might not be mutually exclusive. When car experts were asked to process faces and automobiles simultaneously, Gauthier found competition in the fusiform face area, she reported in a 2005 issue of *Current Directions in Psychological Science.* As car expertise increased, so did this neural interference.

"This tells you that whatever is special with faces," Gauthier says, "it's not unique."

For Autistic Children, a Face Lift

Recall, for a moment, the motorcycle victim mentioned earlier. After the accident, Russell Bauer showed the man faces of relatives or celebrities, and the victim could not identify the person, Bauer reported in *Neuropsychologia* in 1984. When given multiple-choice options, Bauer found, the victim performed at chance.

Oddly, though, skin conductance tests indicated a greater, subliminal recognition going on when the victim saw faces that he would have known before the accident. *Something* in the brain knew that a familiar face, even by no name at all, should smell as sweet.

Subsequent studies have confirmed this paradox: people with prosopagnosia can't recognize a face, but their fusiform face area is active when they look at one. The situation gets stranger, though, when considering people with autism. They're by no means prosopagnosic. Still, many of them have difficulty processing faces. What's more, when people with autism do look at faces, they don't show activity in the fusiform gyrus.

Exactly why this occurs is unclear, says Jim Tanaka of the University of Victoria in Canada. One plausible explanation fits in well with the expertise theory of face perception. The trouble that autistic patients have with face processing might stem from their social attention deficits, Tanaka says. "They won't respond to faces that typically developing children do, so if they're not looking at faces, they're unlikely to develop the expertise most of us have."

To address the problem, Tanaka and a group led by neuropsychologist Robert Schultz recently created a computer activity called Let's Face It. Children with autism tend to process faces by their individual parts, Tanaka says. They might see the eyes, nose, and mouth, for example, as separate and perhaps isolated features. Let's Face It aims to improve holistic facial perception.

Using a computer, children search for several faces hidden within a landscape scene. The faces are hairless and often appear blurred or even upside down. As the levels progress, the faces become harder to distinguish, often merging almost seamlessly into a waterfall, hillside, or even the ear of a tiger. In addition to the computer program, Let's Face It includes several other activities, such as building a face from individual parts.

In a five-year study, which concluded in August, the researchers administered Let's Face It activities to children with autism for two months. Other children received no other therapy. Tanaka did not want to go into details because the paper is currently being written, but he did say the children who engaged in the activities seemed to improve their face perception, "mostly in holistic processing."

All Shook Up

This article began with the story of a 39-year-old who lost the ability to recognize faces, even those of celebrities, after a motorcycle accident. It picks up now with another 39-year-old.

When shown a face of Elvis Presley, this woman identified The King as none other than Brooke Shields. Is she just a huge "Suddenly Susan" fan who cares not for "Heartbreak Hotel"? That's unknown (and, of course, unlikely). What is known is that this woman's prosopagnosia did not start after a brain injury. Her condition occurred naturally.

Once considered rare, congenital prosopagnosia is now thought to impact as much as 2 percent of the population. Recently, a group of researchers studied the aforementioned woman and nine of her relatives—many of whom had reported difficulty recognizing faces. The family members performed poorly on tasks involving face memory and judgment of facial similarity, the authors wrote in the June 2007 issue of *Cognitive Neuropsychology*. (Given the field's debate, it should be noted that the family members also had difficulty on some object recognition tasks.)

The genetic aspects of prosopagnosia and face perception, though still poorly understood, are gaining attention among researchers. In a paper in press for the upcoming *Journal of Neuropsychology* special issue, a group of Australian cognitive scientists, led by Laura Schmalzl, studied 13 members of a family, ranging in age from 4 to 87, and found a "wide spectrum of face processing impairments." They contend that genetic prosopagnosia "is not a single trait but a cluster of related subtypes," and that this disease profile is identifiable at an early age.

"We're becoming familiar with the idea that these disorders can occur congenitally rather than in an acquired fashion," Bauer says. Prosopagnosia is "becoming increasingly recognized as something that doesn't just happen once every billion years."

Still, he says, many important questions remain, including why prosopagnosics can't fully rehabilitate their facial perception. Bauer says he is not aware of a single case of complete recovery by a prosopagnosic. "That tells me we don't have a handle on the mechanism," he says.

In this sense, at least, the motorcycle victim is not unique. As of seven or eight years ago, when Bauer stopped following the case, the man had failed to regain any faculties of face processing. Like Oliver Sacks' patient, the motorcycle victim found some solace in music, but the pain of his impairment also led to drinking problems. "Last I heard," Bauer says, "he was continuing to cope, but had not had any recovery at all."

ERIC JAFFE is a writer in New York City.

UNIT 4
Learning and Remembering

Unit Selections

Key Points to Consider

- How is computer modeling and robotics changing our understanding of how people learn?

- In what ways can praise motivate students to learn? In what ways can it impair learning?

- In terms of learning, what is the difference between a "fixed mind-set" and a "growth mind-set"?

- In what types of jobs do people need effective learning abilities and fine-tuned memories? What can we learn from these individuals?

- Are "knowing" and "remembering" the same thing? Either way, why?

Student Web Site
www.mhcls.com

Internet References

Classical Conditioning
   http://chiron.valdosta.edu/whuitt/col/behsys/classcnd.html
Operant Conditioning
   http://psychology.about.com/od/behavioralpsychology/a/introopcond.htm
Social Learning Theory
   http://teachnet.edb.utexas.edu/~lynda_abbott/Social.html

Do you remember your first week of classes at college? There were so many new buildings and so many people's names to remember. You had to recall accurately where all your classes were as well as your professors' names. Just remembering your class schedule was problematic enough. For those of you who lived in residence halls, the difficulties multiplied. You had to remember where your residence was, recall the names of individuals living on your floor, and learn how to navigate from your room to other places on campus, such as the dining halls and library. Then came examination time. Did you ever think you would survive college exams? The material, in terms of difficulty level and amount, was perhaps more than you thought you could manage. What a stressful time you experienced when you first came to campus! Much of what created the stress was the strain on your learning and memory systems, two complicated processes unto themselves. Indeed, most of you survived just fine—and with your memories, learning strategies, and mental health intact.

Today, with their sophisticated experimental techniques, psychologists have distinguished several types of memory processes and have discovered what makes learning more complete, so that subsequent memory is more accurate. We also have discovered that humans aren't the only organisms capable of these processes. All types of animals can learn, even if the organism is as simple as an earthworm or amoeba.

Psychologists too know, that rote learning and practice are not the only forms of learning. For instance, at this point in time, in your introductory psychology class, you might be studying operant and classical conditioning, two important forms of learning of which humans and even simple organisms are capable. Both types of conditioning can occur without our awareness or active participation in them. The articles in this unit examine such processes of learning and memory.

Conversing with Copycats

Psychologists are using computer models to re-evaluate how humans learn their first tongue.

AMY CYNKAR

Is language hard-wired? As everyone knows from intro psych, Noam Chomsky thought so. He theorized that babies base language acquisition on an innate linguistic knowledge known as universal grammar—a system of principles and rules common to all languages.

Now that view's being challenged as psychologists re-evaluate it using advances in statistical learning and computational modeling. And their findings may provide new insight into how children acquire and process language, something cognitive scientists still grapple with. And as new research continues to unfold, it may lead to new treatments for children who have language disorders.

"It's been a major tenet of the field of linguistics that language could not be learnable, so it had to be innate," says Jay McClelland, PhD, a professor of psychology at Stanford University and a pioneer in using neural network modeling to better understand language acquisition. "What we're finding today is that this has to be rethought."

Reproducing Language Acquisition

In his book "The Language Instinct" (William Morrow, 1994), Stephen Pinker, PhD, argues that children begin learning words at a rate of one every two hours by their second birthday. While notably incompetent at many other activities at this age, children develop a firm grasp on language, without much error, relatively quickly. Morten Christiansen, PhD, a psychology professor at Cornell University, and a team of international psychologists are using neural network simulations and computer-based analyses of child-directed speech to unearth just how they do it.

Their findings suggest that children absorb the rules of language from adult conversations, particularly those directed specifically to them, much more than scientists originally thought. Specifically, children heed multiple cues related to how a word sounds, its length, pitch and where it occurs in a phrase or sentence.

Christiansen tested this multiple-cue integration theory using a series of computer simulations. The results, presented at the 2001 Cognitive Science Society conference, indicate that heeding multiple cues bolsters language learning. They also suggest that computer modeling accurately simulates a toddler's ability to recognize words and comprehend simple sentences.

Follow-up experiments show that children appear to use these multiple cues when learning new words. While initial research looked only at language acquisition in English, Christiansen and his colleagues recently tested their multiple-cue integration analyses in French, Dutch and Japanese, with similar results.

"We don't know yet whether we can completely discard the notion of innate knowledge in the classical Chomskyan sense, but we do know that it's likely to be much less important to explaining language acquisition," Christiansen says.

Some experts caution, however, that computational modeling cannot yet fully reproduce the complexities of social processes at the foundation of language learning. "A lot of what we do in understanding language is make inferences about what our listener knows, and what kind of knowledge we share in common," says James Morgan, PhD, professor of cognitive and linguistic sciences at Brown University. "It's tremendously difficult to program that kind of information into computers."

Developmental psycholinguists, such as Nancy Budwig, PhD, professor of developmental psychology at Clark University in Worchester, Mass., underscore this point, adding that social participation is an essential ingredient in the language-learning process for the human infant.

Modeling Language Impairment

If neural networking proves to be a good model for human language-learning, however, Christiansen's research may give new hope to people with language disorders.

His research may change how we think about language impairment, particularly among the 6 to 7 percent of U.S. children affected by Specific Language Impairment (SLI), a communication disorder in which a child has difficulty understanding or using words in sentences. SLI is also often referred to as developmental language disorder, language delay or developmental dysphasia.

"The classical view suggests that SLI is caused by a breakdown in one or more language modules, due to some sort of genetic impairment," he says. "However, an emerging perspective suggests that SLI is not a language disorder but rather a broader deficit in underlying learning mechanisms."

This new characterization could perhaps spur new SLI treatments that target the cognitive skills that underlie language, rather than focusing exclusively on a child's language impairment.

In fact, in collaboration with experts in speech and hearing, Christiansen is planning to use neural network modeling to evaluate the potential of such treatments. The modeling allows them to vet experimental approaches before trying them out on actual children, where the wrong approach might negatively affect a child's ability to process language.

"We don't know yet whether we can completely discard the notion of innate knowledge in the classical Chomskyan sense, but we do know that it's likely to be much less important to explaining language acquisition."

—Morten Christiansen
Cornell University

"Is this work going to lead to computers that can actually learn and use language in the same manner that humans do—probably not in our lifetime," says Morgan. "But this research is really central to illuminating what the nature of human nature is."

Move Over, Mice

Robots that learn may be the hot new research subjects for developmental psychologists, lending new insights on human development and learning.

Sadie F. Dingfelder

Babysit a robot. That was the strange summer assignment for research assistants in the machine learning lab at the University of California, San Diego (UCSD) in 2003. The robot wasn't much to look at—just a doll with a camera stuck to its head and an umbilical cord linking to a laptop—but the students gamely took on the task of bouncing the robot and cooing at it as if it were a real baby.

Lab leader Javier Movellan, PhD, had assigned the task to the students as part of an experiment, to see if the robot could learn, through a regular baby's experience, to recognize human faces. This is a feat that human babies can perform just minutes after birth, spurring the theory that we are born with knowledge about what faces look like. The baby robot had no such knowledge programmed in, so the baby robot's creators, including graduate students Ian Fasel and Nick Butko, expected the robot wouldn't catch on quickly. They planned to run the experiment for several months. But the robot astounded everyone: It learned to recognize human faces after just six minutes of life, accurately drawing squares around its babysitters' faces.

"We thought this would be a very difficult problem, and we are experts in machine learning," says Movellan. "We were very surprised that by six minutes it was already doing so well."

Movellan's finding suggests that human infants, like the baby robot, might not start out with any information about human faces. Rather, they could be extremely quick to learn that their mothers' faces tend to go along with interesting environmental cues—a lullaby, for instance, or movement. If a baby robot with the equivalent of only one million neurons in its programming can recognize human faces so quickly, imagine what a human baby, with its 10 billion neurons, can do, Mollevan says.

The baby robot is just one example of how machines that learn are contributing to theories of human development, says Terri Lewis, PhD, a psychology professor at McMaster University in Ontario. In fact, psychologists are increasingly teaming up with computer scientists to write programs that allow machines to interact with their environments and change from their experiences. The result: Robots can perform tasks that stump typical computers, even though standard computers are born into the world with gads of information preprogrammed into them. But aside from the practical applications, learning machines are starting to serve psychologists as a new model animal—one whose brain you can simply crack open and watch work.

"It is certainly a fascinating area of research and it's changing the way we think about the role of experience in development," Lewis says.

Robot University

Most computers are developmentally stunted. The ATM machine is not going to get faster at counting out cash; your e-mail software won't get better at recognizing spam. That's because programmers imbued them with a set of fixed rules: If an e-mail is not from a known address, then send it to the trash. The computer simply puts such rules in action.

However, computer programmers are increasingly writing programs that can change their own code, says Tony Jebara, PhD, a computer science professor at Columbia University. These programs are often based on "machine learning algorithms"—a handful of relatively simple rules that allow machines to get better at whatever it is they are supposed to do.

The inner workings of these programs are modeled on what we know about the structure of the human brain. Just as we have neurons, the baby robot's program has little units of information analysis that take in data and then produce a signal that affects the next "neuron" down the line. Such artificial neural networks result in systems that are much less likely to break than traditional programs—if one neuron malfunctions the system is relatively unaffected.

> **"What are the guiding principles that find meaningful patterns in the world—that is the Holy Grail for the future of machine learning and even human intelligence."**
>
> —Tony Jebara
> Columbia University

In addition to being more resilient than traditional systems, neural networks are producing human-like learning in machines. For instance, Movellan's baby robot was born knowing only that it should take note of sights and sounds that happen relatively rarely. So the hum of a nearby laptop was not very interesting to the robot—it heard that sound all the time. However, the voice of a graduate student talking to the robot was a special event, so it took note. The robot also knew to link interesting events, associating unusual sights with sounds, and unusual sounds with sights.

As the research assistants hefted the baby robot around, it took snapshots of the world with a built-in camera. Sometimes human faces would be in the picture, and the robot discovered that people often appeared at the same time it recorded unusual sounds. After just a few minutes, the robot learned that human faces were a particularly interesting aspect of its environment.

This amazed the researchers because previous computer programs were not very good at locating faces in busy backgrounds, says Mollevan. Impressively, the baby robot could find a human face in a sea of similarly shaped objects. It could recognize a face in profile and it could locate a face that was partially covered by hair, according to results presented at the 2006 International Conference on Development and Learning, in Bloomington, Ind.

And after a few more hours of training, the baby robot sometimes recognized that a line drawing of a face was the same kind of thing it had seen before, on the heads of graduate students.

The results are similar to that of an experiment with human infants, published in *Psychological Science* (Vol. 10, No. 5, pages 419–422) in 1999. In this study, Lewis and her colleagues tested infants' preference for faces just minutes after birth. They found that if you show an infant two cards, one with a face that has right-side-up features and one with those features turned upside down, the infant tends to look toward the right-side-up face.

At the time, the most likely explanation was that babies are born preferring face-like images—a tendency with clear evolutionary advantages, says Lewis.

"You want to be quick to orient to faces because there is definitely a survival benefit," Lewis notes. "Those faces are going to provide food for the baby."

But given the recent performance of the baby robot, the possibility that infants rapidly learn about faces seems just as plausible, she says.

"The people who do neural network modeling . . . are in the business of showing that the blank mind can learn a lot very quickly," she says.

Human-Like Mistakes

Learning machines are helping psychologists understand not only what people can learn, but also how we do it. Once researchers have built a computer that processes information like a human would, they can run experiments on it that would never work with living humans, says Gedeon Deak, PhD, a cognitive science professor at UCSD.

"We can simulate different kinds of processing models . . . and find out which ones most closely simulate the kinds of detailed decisions and errors that humans make," Deak notes.

One study, by Marian Bartlett, PhD, and her colleagues in the UCSD Machine Learning Lab, did just that: The researchers pitted two different face-processing programs against each other to see which worked best.

Linking faces to names has proven very difficult for computer programs. Past programs told computers to analyze the distance between features such as eyes. That approach resulted in computers that were not very good at seeing that two different pictures could be of the same person. A shadow could throw the program off entirely.

Bartlett and her colleagues took a different approach. Instead of giving the computer rules for analysis, they fed the computer hundreds of images. The computer figured out how to identify the images on its own, using one of two tools provided by the researchers.

Both tools required the computer to represent the image as a two-dimensional grid of pixels—much like how the retina registers light. The computer then took note of the brightness of each pixel, and flagged those that were near others of a markedly different brightness. The program used this technique to determine boundaries between different features.

However, one of the tools, known as Eigenfaces, only allowed the computer to make simple associations between pixels, while the other tool—Independent Component Analysis (ICA)—gave the computer the ability to make higher-order associations.

Both learning tools resulted in a program that was better at recognizing faces than past attempts, but the ICA version worked best. And when ICA did made mistakes, they were similar to the ones humans would make, according to results in-press at *Neurocomputing*. For example, when the program was trained with a set of faces that were mostly white, it had more difficulty distinguishing between Asian faces, just as people often have trouble distinguishing between individuals of other races.

"There are a number of effects in human-face perception research that are consistent with our model," Bartlett says.

The results suggest that human brains may follow a rule similar to ICA, whereby it takes in patterns of light and dark and performs high-level statistical analysis to determine which dark patches form noses and which are just shadows—something we probably learn to do as infants, Deak says.

"All normal developing humans are expert face processors, and this [study] suggests that we do incredibly powerful computations to identify faces," he notes.

Computers that can identify individuals may have anti-terrorism applications—allowing security cameras to flag people entering a building who are on a known-criminal list, for instance, or even identifying someone who had never been in the building before. But Deak is more excited by the contributions that machine learning can make to psychological research.

For instance, once you have a model of human-face recognition, you can change a little bit of the program and see whether the resulting mistakes look like human malfunctions—a process that could provide insight into disorders like autism. Similarly, researchers can investigate how a baby robot develops when it's neglected or abused—something they would obviously never try with real infants.

However, computers have a lot of catching up to do before they can approach the capabilities of the human brain, says Deak. And even with state-of-the-art computers, programmers will need findings from neuroscience and behavioral science to know if their models are true-to-life, says Jebara. But the biggest hurdle—and the point of the entire endeavor—will be figuring out the underlying program that allows humans to learn so much, despite having relatively little knowledge to begin with, he notes.

"What are the guiding principles that find meaningful patterns in the world—that is the Holy Grail for the future of machine learning and even human intelligence," says Jebara.

The Perils and Promises of Praise

**The wrong kind of praise creates self-defeating behavior.
The right kind motivates students to learn.**

CAROL S. DWECK

We often hear these days that we've produced a generation of young people who can't get through the day without an award. They expect success because they're special, not because they've worked hard.

Is this true? Have we inadvertently done something to hold back our students?

I think educators commonly hold two beliefs that do just that. Many believe that (1) praising students' intelligence builds their confidence and motivation to learn, and (2) students' inherent intelligence is the major cause of their achievement in school. Our research has shown that the first belief is false and that the second can be harmful—even for the most competent students.

As a psychologist, I have studied student motivation for more than 35 years. My graduate students and I have looked at thousands of children, asking why some enjoy learning, even when it's hard, and why they are resilient in the face of obstacles. We have learned a great deal. Research shows us how to praise students in ways that yield motivation and resilience. In addition, specific interventions can reverse a student's slide into failure during the vulnerable period of adolescence.

Fixed or Malleable?

Praise is intricately connected to how students view their intelligence. Some students believe that their intellectual ability is a fixed trait. They have a certain amount of intelligence, and that's that. Students with this fixed mind-set become excessively concerned with how smart they are, seeking tasks that will prove their intelligence and avoiding ones that might not (Dweck, 1999, 2006). The desire to learn takes a backseat.

Other students believe that their intellectual ability is something they can develop through effort and education. They don't necessarily believe that anyone can become an Einstein or a Mozart, but they do understand that even Einstein and Mozart had to put in years of effort to become who they were. When students believe that they can develop their intelligence, they focus on doing just that. Not worrying about how smart they will appear, they take on challenges and stick to them (Dweck, 1999, 2006).

More and more research in psychology and neuroscience supports the growth mind-set. We are discovering that the brain has more plasticity over time than we ever imagined (Doidge, 2007); that fundamental aspects of intelligence can be enhanced through learning (Sternberg, 2005); and that dedication and persistence in the face of obstacles are key ingredients in outstanding achievement (Ericsson, Charness, Feltovich, & Hoffman, 2006).

Alfred Binet (1909/1973), the inventor of the IQ test, had a strong growth mind-set. He believed that education could transform the basic capacity to learn. Far from intending to measure fixed intelligence, he meant his test to be a tool for identifying students who were not profiting from the public school curriculum so that other courses of study could be devised to foster their intellectual growth.

The Two Faces of Effort

The fixed and growth mind-sets create two different psychological worlds. In the fixed mind-set, students care first and foremost about how they'll be judged: smart or not smart. Repeatedly, students with this mind-set reject opportunities to learn if they might make mistakes (Hong, Chiu, Dweck, Lin, & Wan, 1999; Mueller & Dweck, 1998). When they do make mistakes or reveal deficiencies, rather than correct them, they try to hide them (Nussbaum & Dweck, 2007).

They are also afraid of effort because effort makes them feel dumb. They believe that if you have the ability, you shouldn't need effort (Blackwell, Trzesniewski, & Dweck, 2007), that ability should bring success all by itself. This is one of the worst beliefs that students can hold. It can cause many bright students to stop working in school when the curriculum becomes challenging.

Finally, students in the fixed mind-set don't recover well from setbacks. When they hit a setback in school, they *decrease* their efforts and consider cheating (Blackwell et al., 2007). The idea of fixed intelligence does not offer them viable ways to improve.

Let's get inside the head of a student with a fixed mind-set as he sits in his classroom, confronted with algebra for the first time. Up until then, he has breezed through math. Even when he barely paid attention in class and skimped on his homework, he always got *A*s. But this is different. It's hard. The student feels anxious and thinks, "What if I'm not as good at math as I thought? What if other kids understand it and I don't?" At some level, he realizes that he has two choices: try hard, or turn off. His interest in math begins to wane, and his attention wanders. He tells himself, "Who cares about this stuff? It's for nerds. I could do it if I wanted to, but it's so boring. You don't see CEOs and sports stars solving for *x* and *y*."

By contrast, in the growth mind-set, students care about learning. When they make a mistake or exhibit a deficiency, they correct it (Blackwell et al., 2007; Nussbaum & Dweck, 2007). For them, effort is a *positive* thing: It ignites their intelligence and causes it to grow. In the face of failure, these students escalate their efforts and look for new learning strategies.

Let's look at another student—one who has a growth mind-set—having her first encounter with algebra. She finds it new, hard, and confusing, unlike anything else she has ever learned. But she's determined to understand it. She listens to everything the teacher says, asks the teacher questions after class, and takes her textbook home and reads the chapter over twice. As she begins to get it, she feels exhilarated. A new world of math opens up for her.

It is not surprising, then, that when we have followed students over challenging school transitions or courses, we find that those with growth mind-sets outperform their classmates with fixed mind-sets—even when they entered with equal skills and knowledge. A growth mind-set fosters the growth of ability over time (Blackwell et al., 2007; Mangels, Butterfield, Lamb, Good, & Dweck, 2006; see also Grant & Dweck, 2003).

The Effects of Praise

Many educators have hoped to maximize students' confidence in their abilities, their enjoyment of learning, and their ability to thrive in school by praising their intelligence. We've studied the effects of this kind of praise in children as young as 4 years old and as old as adolescence, in students in inner-city and rural settings, and in students of different ethnicities—and we've consistently found the same thing (Cimpian, Arce, Markman, & Dweck, 2007; Kamins & Dweck, 1999; Mueller & Dweck, 1998): Praising students' intelligence gives them a short burst of pride, followed by a long string of negative consequences.

In many of our studies (see Mueller & Dweck, 1998), 5th grade students worked on a task, and after the first set of problems, the teacher praised some of them for their intelligence ("You must be smart at these problems") and others for their effort ("You must have worked hard at these problems"). We then assessed the students' mind-sets. In one study, we asked students to agree or disagree with mind-set statements, such as, "Your intelligence is something basic about you that you can't really change." Students praised for intelligence agreed with statements like these more than students praised for effort did. In another study, we asked students to define intelligence. Students praised for intelligence made significantly more references to innate, fixed capacity, whereas the students

praised for effort made more references to skills, knowledge, and areas they could change through effort and learning. Thus, we found that praise for intelligence tended to put students in a fixed mind-set (intelligence is fixed, and you have it), whereas praise for effort tended to put them in a growth mind-set (you're developing these skills because you're working hard).

We then offered students a chance to work on either a challenging task that they could learn from or an easy one that ensured error-free performance. Most of those praised for intelligence wanted the easy task, whereas most of those praised for effort wanted the challenging task and the opportunity to learn.

Next, the students worked on some challenging problems. As a group, students who had been praised for their intelligence *lost* their confidence in their ability and their enjoyment of the task as soon as they began to struggle with the problem. If success meant they were smart, then struggling meant they were not. The whole point of intelligence praise is to boost confidence and motivation, but both were gone in a flash. Only the effort-praised kids remained, on the whole, confident and eager.

When the problems were made somewhat easier again, students praised for intelligence did poorly, having lost their confidence and motivation. As a group, they did worse than they had done initially on these same types of problems. The students praised for effort showed excellent performance and continued to improve.

Finally, when asked to report their scores (anonymously), almost 40 percent of the intelligence-praised students lied. Apparently, their egos were so wrapped up in their performance that they couldn't admit mistakes. Only about 10 percent of the effort-praised students saw fit to falsify their results.

Praising students for their intelligence, then, hands them not motivation and resilience but a fixed mind-set with all its vulnerability. In contrast, effort or "process" praise (praise for engagement, perseverance, strategies, improvement, and the like) fosters hardy motivation. It tells students what they've done to be successful and what they need to do to be successful again in the future. Process praise sounds like this:

- You really studied for your English test, and your improvement shows it. You read the material over several times, outlined it, and tested yourself on it. That really worked!
- I like the way you tried all kinds of strategies on that math problem until you finally got it.
- It was a long, hard assignment, but you stuck to it and got it done. You stayed at your desk, kept up your concentration, and kept working. That's great!
- I like that you took on that challenging project for your science class. It will take a lot of work—doing the research, designing the machine, buying the parts, and building it. You're going to learn a lot of great things.

What about a student who gets an *A* without trying? I would say, "All right, that was too easy for you. Let's do something more challenging that you can learn from." We don't want to make something done quickly and easily the basis for our admiration.

What about a student who works hard and *doesn't* do well? I would say, "I liked the effort you put in. Let's work together some more and figure out what you don't understand." Process praise keeps students focused, not on something called ability that they may or may not have and that magically creates success or failure, but on processes they can all engage in to learn.

Motivated to Learn

Finding that a growth mind-set creates motivation and resilience—and leads to higher achievement—we sought to develop an intervention that would teach this mind-set to students. We decided to aim our intervention at students who were making the transition to 7th grade because this is a time of great vulnerability. School often gets more difficult in 7th grade, grading becomes more stringent, and the environment becomes more impersonal. Many students take stock of themselves and their intellectual abilities at this time and decide whether they want to be involved with school. Not surprisingly, it is often a time of disengagement and plunging achievement.

We performed our intervention in a New York City junior high school in which many students were struggling with the transition and were showing plummeting grades. If students learned a growth mind-set, we reasoned, they might be able to meet this challenge with increased, rather than decreased, effort. We therefore developed an eight-session workshop in which both the control group and the growth-mind-set group learned study skills, time management techniques, and memory strategies (Blackwell et al., 2007). However, in the growth-mind-set intervention, students also learned about their brains and what they could do to make their intelligence grow.

They learned that the brain is like a muscle—the more they exercise it, the stronger it becomes. They learned that every time they try hard and learn something new, their brain forms new connections that, over time, make them smarter. They learned that intellectual development is not the natural unfolding of intelligence, but rather the formation of new connections brought about through effort and learning.

Students were riveted by this information. The idea that their intellectual growth was largely in their hands fascinated them. In fact, even the most disruptive students suddenly sat still and took notice, with the most unruly boy of the lot looking up at us and saying, "You mean I don't have to be dumb?"

Indeed, the growth-mind-set message appeared to unleash students' motivation. Although both groups had experienced a steep decline in their math grades during their first months of junior high, those receiving the growth-mind-set intervention showed a significant rebound. Their math grades improved. Those in the control group, despite their excellent study skills intervention, continued their decline.

What's more, the teachers—who were unaware that the intervention workshops differed—singled out three times as many students in the growth-mindset intervention as showing marked changes in motivation. These students had a heightened desire to work hard and learn. One striking example was the boy who thought he was dumb. Before this experience, he had never put in any extra effort and often didn't turn his homework in on time. As a result of the training, he worked for hours one evening to finish an assignment early so that his

teacher could review it and give him a chance to revise it. He earned a $B+$ on the assignment (he had been getting Cs and lower previously).

Other researchers have obtained similar findings with a growth-mind-set intervention. Working with junior high school students, Good, Aronson, and Inzlicht (2003) found an increase in math and English achievement test scores; working with college students, Aronson, Fried, and Good (2002) found an increase in students' valuing of academics, their enjoyment of schoolwork, and their grade point averages.

To facilitate delivery of the growth-mind-set workshop to students, we developed an interactive computer-based version of the intervention called *Brainology*. Students work through six modules, learning about the brain, visiting virtual brain labs, doing virtual brain experiments, seeing how the brain changes with learning, and learning how they can make their brains work better and grow smarter.

When students believe that they can develop their intelligence, they focus on doing just that.

We tested our initial version in 20 New York City schools, with encouraging results. Almost all students (anonymously polled) reported changes in their study habits and motivation to learn resulting directly from their learning of the growth mind-set. One student noted that as a result of the animation she had seen about the brain, she could actually "picture the neurons growing bigger as they make more connections." One student referred to the value of effort: "If you do not give up and you keep studying, you can find your way through."

Adolescents often see school as a place where they perform for teachers who then judge them. The growth mind-set changes that perspective and makes school a place where students vigorously engage in learning for their own benefit.

Going Forward

Our research shows that educators cannot hand students confidence on a silver platter by praising their intelligence. Instead, we can help them gain the tools they need to maintain their confidence in learning by keeping them focused on the *process* of achievement.

Maybe we have produced a generation of students who are more dependent, fragile, and entitled than previous generations. If so, it's time for us to adopt a growth mind-set and learn from our mistakes. It's time to deliver interventions that will truly boost students' motivation, resilience, and learning.

References

Aronson, J., Fried, C., & Good, C. (2002). Reducing the effects of stereotype threat on African American college students by shaping theories of intelligence. *Journal of Experimental Social Psychology, 38,* 113–125.

Binet, A. (1909/1973). *Les idées modernes sur les enfants* [Modern ideas on children]. Paris: Flamarion. (Original work published 1909)

Blackwell, L., Trzesniewski, K., & Dweck, C. S. (2007). Implicit theories of intelligence predict achievement across an adolescent transition: A longitudinal study and an intervention. *Child Development, 78,* 246–263.

Cimpian, A., Arce, H., Markman, E. M., & Dweck, C. S. (2007). Subtle linguistic cues impact children's motivation. *Psychological Science, 18,* 314–316.

Doidge, N. (2007). *The brain that changes itself: Stories of personal triumph from the frontiers of brain science.* New York: Viking.

Dweck, C. S. (1999). *Self-theories: Their role in motivation, personality and development.* Philadelphia: Taylor and Francis/Psychology Press.

Dweck, C. S. (2006). *Mindset: The new psychology of success.* New York: Random House.

Ericsson, K. A., Charness, N., Feltovich, P. J., & Hoffman, R. R. (Eds.). (2006). *The Cambridge handbook of expertise and expert performance.* New York: Cambridge University Press.

Good, C., Aronson, J., & Inzlicht, M. (2003). Improving adolescents' standardized test performance: An intervention to reduce the effects of stereotype threat. *Journal of Applied Developmental Psychology, 24,* 645–662.

Grant, H., & Dweck, C. S. (2003). Clarifying achievement goals and their impact. *Journal of Personality and Social Psychology, 85,* 541–553.

Hong, Y. Y., Chiu, C., Dweck, C. S., Lin, D., & Wan, W. (1999). Implicit theories, attributions, and coping: A meaning system approach. *Journal of Personality and Social Psychology, 77,* 588–599.

Kamins, M., & Dweck, C. S. (1999). Person vs. process praise and criticism: Implications for contingent self-worth and coping. *Developmental Psychology, 35,* 835–847.

Mangels, J. A., Butterfield, B., Lamb, J., Good, C. D., & Dweck, C. S. (2006). Why do beliefs about intelligence influence learning success? A social-cognitive-neuroscience model. *Social, Cognitive, and Affective Neuroscience, 1,* 75–86.

Mueller, C. M., & Dweck, C. S. (1998). Intelligence praise can undermine motivation and performance. *Journal of Personality and Social Psychology, 75,* 33–52.

Nussbaum, A. D., & Dweck, C. S. (2007). Defensiveness vs. remediation: Self-theories and modes of self-esteem maintenance. *Personality and Social Psychology Bulletin.*

Sternberg, R. (2005). Intelligence, competence, and expertise. In A. Elliot & C. S. Dweck (Eds.), *The handbook of competence and motivation* (pp. 15–30). New York: Guilford Press.

CAROL S. DWECK is the Lewis and Virginia Eaton Professor of Psychology at Stanford University and the author of *Mindset: The New Psychology of Success* (Random House, 2006).

UNIT 5
Cognitive Processes

Unit Selections

Key Points to Consider

- With regard to thinking and cognition, do even experts make mistakes? Why and How?

- What is culture? In general, how does it affect us psychologically?

- How does culture affect the way we think, perceive, pay attention, and solve problems?

- Which came first—language or hand gestures?

- What is the current state of theory and research regarding the evolution of language?

Student Web Site

www.mhcls.com

Internet References

American Association for Artificial Intelligence (AAAI)
http://www.aaai.org/AITopics/index.html

Cognition and Thinking
http://library.thinkquest.org/26618/en-5.1.1=mental%20imagery.htm

© Stockbyte/Punchstock Images

As Rashad watches his four-month-old, he is convinced that the baby possesses some understanding of the world around her. In fact, Rashad is sure he has one of the smartest babies in the neighborhood. Although he is a proud father, he keeps his thoughts to himself so as not to alienate the parents of less intelligent babies.

Gustav lives in the same neighborhood as Rashad. Gustav doesn't have any children, but he does own two fox terriers. Despite Gustav's most concerted efforts, the dogs never come to him when he calls them. In fact, the dogs have been known to run in the opposite direction on occasion. Instead of being furious, Gustav accepts his dogs' disobedience because he is sure the dogs are just dumb beasts and don't know any better.

Both of these vignettes illustrate important and interesting ideas about cognition or thought processes. In the first vignette, Rashad ascribes cognitive abilities and high intelli-

gence to his child; in fact, Rashad perhaps ascribes too much cognitive ability to his 4-month old. On the other hand, Gustav assumes that his dogs are incapable of thought—more specifically, incapable of premeditated disobedience—and therefore forgives the dogs.

Few adults would deny the existence of their cognitive abilities. Some adults, in fact, think about thinking, something which psychologists call metacognition. Cognition is critical to our survival as adults. But are there differences in adult cognition? And what about other organisms? Can young children—infants, for example—think? If they can, do they think like adults? What about animals; can they think and solve problems? How has language evolved, and why is it only humans that have evolved such sophisticated means of communication? These and other questions are related to cognitive psychology and cognitive science, both of which are showcased in this unit.

What Was I Thinking?

Kahneman explains how intuition leads us astray.

ERIC JAFFE

This is a story without an ending. And that's not the only thing wrong with it.

In fact, there were a number of flaws in Nobel Laureate Daniel Kahneman's lecture "A Perspective of Flawed Thought," in March 2004 at the National Institutes of Health. Quite purposefully, the entire talk was full of them.

"I specialize in flaws," Kahneman said.

However appropriate that self-deprecating remark was to the topic, it hardly applied to the speaker's celebrated accomplishments. In addition to the 2002 Nobel Prize, which he received for his work applying psychologically realistic models to economic theory, APS Fellow Kahneman, Princeton University, has received most every award possible to a psychologist, including the 1990 APS William James Fellow Award.

Part of Kahneman's intent was to show that flawed thinking plays no favorites. Sure enough, despite his vast understanding of the subject, Kahneman himself claimed to be susceptible to misleading intuition, a realization he made while looking at the latest gallop poll, in which President George W. Bush's approval rating had shifted a statistically insignificant 2 percent from the previous week.

"I was influenced by this completely irrelevant data," he said. "I could not help myself from drawing inferences like, 'What happened this week?' or 'What's the explanation?' I was working on this intuitively and contrary to my better statistical judgment."

According to Kahneman, some human intuition is good, and some is erroneous. And like the incorrigible habit of the knuckle cracker, the bad ones are very difficult to correct.

One reason flawed intuition is allowed to permeate human thinking is its accessibility. For example, if the multiplication problem 17 times 24 is shown for only a moment before its answer, 408, is revealed, few solve it without a formal, lengthy act of computation. On the contrary, if the word "vomit" is displayed and immediately followed by the word "disgusting," it seems the accessible, almost instantaneous extension of the viewer's thinking.

"Intuitive impressions come to mind without explicit intention, and without any confrontation, and this is one of their distinctive aspects," he said.

To better understand the reasons for this accessibility, Kahneman has focused much of his research on expert intuitions. Expert intuitions are able to deal swiftly and decisively with a difficult matter—such as making a quick chess move or fighting a fire—that would seem to require extensive deliberation. Most of the time, a person with expert intuition is not really conscious of making a decision, but rather acts as though their instinctive choice is the only natural outcome of a circumstance.

"You can have a master chess player walking by a complicated chess position and, without slowing down, this player will say, 'White mates in three,'" Kahneman said. In the case of firefighters making perhaps life or death decisions, "something that is very close to the best solution came to mind, and nothing else."

APS Fellow Daniel Kahneman received the Nobel Prize in 2002 for his work applying psychologically realistic models to economic theory.

However, unless certain conditions of expertise—namely, prolonged practice and rapid, unequivocal feedback—are fulfilled, what develops is little more than the exigent knowledge of experience. This can lead to false impressions and overconfident experts, a subject explored by Kahneman and his longtime research partner, the late Amos Tversky.

"People jump to statistical conclusions on the basis of very weak evidence. We form powerful intuitions about trends and about the replicability of results on the basis of information that is truly inadequate," Kahneman said. For this reason, a person who is not an expert, even if thoroughly versed in a field of study, might make an intuitive mistake.

Kahneman leaned heavily on the closely related argument made by another, prominent psychologist, the late Paul Meehl. In the mid-1950s, Meehl gave clinicians personality information about individuals and asked that they predict behavioral outcomes. For example, the clinician might have been asked to decide whether a released prisoner would violate parole. The predictions were then compared to statistical models based on the subset of information available to the clinician.

In a study that still holds up over 50 years later, Meehl found that when the clinician competed with the statistical formula, the formula won almost every time. This finding has served as the basis for Kahneman's theory about overconfident experts.

"What you find is a great deal of confidence in the presence of very poor accuracy," Kahneman explained. "So the confidence people have is not a good indication of how accurate they are."

Overconfidence is accentuated by the failure of people to, in general, learn from their mistakes. "When something happens that a person has not anticipated, . . . they remain convinced that what they had predicted, although it didn't happen, almost happened," he said. The overconfidence is then propagated while the accuracy remains the same, and the cycle begins again.

In order to trace the roots of flawed intuition, Kahneman divided all thought into a two-system model, intuition and deliberate computation, whose particular attributes are almost completely opposite. Intuition is fast, uncontrolled, and, most importantly, effortless. Computation, on the other hand, is slow, governed by strict rules, and effortful.

"Most judgments in actions are governed by [intuitive thought]," he said. "Most of our mental life is relatively effortless." This is why effortful work, such as trying to remember a phone number of five years ago, is more susceptible to interference, and therefore less accessible.

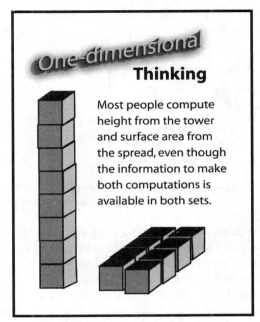

One-dimensional Thinking

Most people compute height from the tower and surface area from the spread, even though the information to make both computations is available in both sets.

"A **fully rational** agent would find it possible to answer both questions equally easily, regardless of the display," Kahneman said. "We do not use all the information that is actually available."

A bat and a ball together costs $1.10. The bat costs a dollar more than the ball. How much does the ball cost?

Interference is often enabled by poor monitoring, a shortcoming that results from our normally unconditional acceptance of intuition. Not surprisingly, according to Kahneman, **50 percent of Princeton students** incorrectly answered 10 cents when given this problem. "What happens to Princeton students is they don't check," said Kahneman. "It happens to MIT students too, though at a slightly lower rate," he joked (The answer for Princeton readers, is five cents.)

Interference is often enabled by poor monitoring, a shortcoming that results from our normally unconditional acceptance of intuition. In one study, Kahneman ran the following scenario past Princeton students: A bat and a ball together cost $1.10. The bat costs a dollar more than the ball. How much does the ball cost? Not surprisingly to Kahneman, 50 percent of Princeton students incorrectly answered 10 cents when given this problem in writing, because they unconditionally accepted their intuitions.

"What happens to Princeton students is they don't check," said Kahneman. "It happens to MIT students too, though at a slightly lower rate," he joked.

Take another common question eliciting intuitive flaw: When people were asked to guess how many murders there were in Michigan in a given year, and how many there were in Detroit, the median answers were 100 and 200, respectively.

"This by itself is not an error, but something is going on here that is not quite right," he said, referring to the presence of intuitive flaw. Occasionally someone asked about Michigan remembered Detroit is in Michigan, and their answer tended more toward 200, a meta-analytic process that reveals to Kahneman the ability of flawed thinking to mend itself if it recognizes all aspects of a situation.

"Accessibility, or the ease with which thoughts come to mind, has an influence not only on the operation of intuition—it almost defines intuition—but on the operations of computation," he said. "Our ability to avoid errors depends on what comes to mind, and whether the corrected thought comes to mind adequately."

But "what comes to mind" might actually be what does *not* come to mind. When looking at two sets of an equal number of cubes, one arranged vertically into a tower and the other spread flat, most people compute height from the tower and surface area from the spread, even though the information to make both computations is available in both sets.

"A fully rational agent would find it possible to answer both questions equally easily, regardless of the display," he said. "That's not what happens. We don't compute everything we could compute. We do not use all the information that is actually available."

For this reason, Kahneman argued that intuitive activities are very similar to perceptual activities, such as seeing and hearing. "These processes of perception are going to guide us in understanding intuition," he said. Take, for example, the following display sets, which are actually less defined than they appear:

Even though the B and the 13 are physically composed of the same elements, they are given context by association, and are rarely considered outside of this context. Though at the time this single-minded assessment doesn't seem wrong, it is in truth about as rational as peeking through the keyhole of a glass door, and grossly limits our understanding of the world. Flawed intuition occurs with similar blinders.

"When people make decisions, they tend to suppress alternative interpretations," Kahneman said. "We become aware only of a single solution—this is a fundamental rule in perceptual processing. All the other solutions that might have been considered by the system—and sometimes we know that alternative solutions have been considered and rejected—we do not become aware of. So consciousness is at the level of a choice that has already been made."

But despite all this understanding, Kahneman steered clear of offering a direct solution to flawed thinking—after all, he remained flummoxed by the gallop poll despite his 35 years studying flawed intuition. Besides, relying on computation instead of intuition would, according to Kahneman, create a slow, laborious, difficult, and costly world. What he did advocate is paying closer attention to the onset of faulty intuition.

"The alternative to thinking intuitively is mental paralysis," he said. "Most of the time, we just have to go with our intuition, [but] we can recognize situations in which our intuition is likely to lead us astray. It's an unfinished story." He paused. "So, it's an unfinished story, so . . ." Kahneman hesitated for words. Something made a succinct peroration inaccessible, but the audience intuited the talk was over, and was correct—most likely.

The Culture-Cognition Connection

Recent research suggests that Westerners and East Asians see the world differently—literally.

LEA WINERMAN

When you look at a picture [of a train] on the computer screen, where do your eyes linger longest? Surprisingly, the answer to that question might differ depending upon where you were raised. Americans stare more fixedly at the train in the center, while Chinese let their eyes roam more around the entire picture, according to research by psychologist Richard Nisbett, PhD.

That difference reflects a more general divide between the ways that Westerners and East Asians view the world around them, says Nisbett, who heads the Culture and Cognition Program at the University of Michigan. He and his colleagues explore how people's cultural backgrounds affect their most basic cognitive processes: categorization, learning, causal reasoning and even attention and perception.

The researchers have found increasing evidence that East Asians, whose more collectivist culture promotes group harmony and contextual understanding of situations, think in a more holistic way. They pay attention to all the elements of a scene, to context and to the relationships between items. Western culture, in contrast, emphasizes personal autonomy and formal logic, and so Westerners are more analytic and pay attention to particular objects and categories.

The idea that culture can shape the way people think at these deep levels is a departure for psychology, which as a field traditionally assumed that basic cognitive processes are universal, according to Nisbett. But it's an idea that has gained traction over the past decade or two.

Now, Nisbett and others are investigating the cognitive effects of the more subtle cultural variations between, for example, different areas of East Asia. They hope that these new studies will also help explain more precisely how and why culture and cognition interact.

Train Spotting

In a recent study, Nisbett and graduate student Hannah Faye Chua used a tracking device to monitor the eye movements of 25 American and 27 Chinese participants—all graduate students at Michigan—while the students stared for three seconds at pictures of objects against complex backgrounds. The 36 pictures included, among others, a train, a tiger in a forest and an airplane with mountains in the background.

The researchers found that the Americans focused on the foreground object 118 milliseconds sooner, on average, than the Chinese participants did, and then continued to look at the focal object longer. The Chinese tended to move their eyes back and forth more between the main object and the background, and looked at the background for longer than the Americans did.

The study, which was published in the *Proceedings of the National Academy of Sciences* in August (Vol. 102, No. 35, pages 12,629–12,633), complements earlier research that suggested—in a more general way—that Westerners and East Asians focus on different aspects of scenes.

In a 2001 study, for example, Nisbett and then-graduate student Takahiko Masuda, PhD, showed Japanese and American participants animated underwater vignettes that included focal objects—three big fish—and background objects like rocks, seaweed and water bubbles. When they asked participants to describe the scenes, Americans were more likely to begin by recalling the focal fish, while Japanese were more likely to describe the whole scene, saying something like "it was a lake or pond." Later, the Japanese participants also recalled more details about the background objects than the Americans did.

"Americans immediately zoomed in on the objects," Nisbett says. "The Japanese paid more attention to context."

Cognitive differences between Westerners and Asians show up in other areas as well. For example, in tests of categorization, Americans are more likely to group items based on how well the items fit into categories by type—so, say, a cow and a chicken might go together because they are both animals. Asians, in contrast, are more likely to group items based on relationships—so a cow and grass might go together because a cow eats grass.

Another difference between Westerners and Asians regards the fundamental attribution error—a mainstay psychological theory for the last 30 years that, it turns out, may not be so fundamental after all. The theory posits that people generally overemphasize personality-related explanations for others' behavior, while underemphasizing or ignoring contextual factors. So, for example, a man may believe he tripped and fell because of a crack in the sidewalk, but assume that someone else fell because of clumsiness.

But, it turns out, most East Asians do not fall prey to this error—they are much more likely to consider contextual factors when trying to explain other people's behavior. In a 1994 study, for example, psychologist Kaiping Peng, PhD, analyzed American and Chinese newspaper accounts of recent murders. He found that American reporters emphasized the personal attributes of the murderers, while Chinese reporters focused more on situational factors.

Frontier Spirit

Although such studies provide convincing evidence of cognitive differences between Asians and Westerners, says Nisbett, they don't explain why those differences occur.

"Our assertion is that these cognitive differences come from social differences," he says. "But that's a very tenuous connection. There's no direct evidence for it yet."

To find that evidence, psychologist Shinobu Kitayama, PhD—who co-chairs Michigan's culture and cognition program with Nisbett—is examining other cultures to determine how their different takes on collectivism, interdependence and other social attributes affect cognition. Kitayama is studying the cognitive style of residents of Hokkaido, Japan—what he calls Japan's "Wild West."

Settlers from the rest of Japan arrived there in the mid-19th century to seek their fortune in the wilderness. If this frontier spirit is associated with a kind of American-style individualism, Kitayama reasoned, then perhaps Hokkaido Japanese might look more like Americans than like other Japanese in their cognitive processes.

And indeed, in a study recently accepted for publication in the *Journal of Personality and Social Psychology,* he and his colleagues found that Hokkaido residents were nearly as likely as Americans to commit the fundamental attribution error.

"The frontier doesn't really exist anywhere anymore," Kitayama says, "but its myth and discourse are still powerful."

Another strand of evidence comes from Asian Americans, who often are raised with some blend of Asian and Western cultural traditions.

"In studies that look at Asians, European Americans and Asian Americans, Asian Americans usually fall somewhere in between the other two," Nisbett says.

Finally, Nisbett is beginning a series of studies that will examine cognitive differences between people in cultures that are quite similar in many ways, but differ in their degree of collectivism.

For example, Eastern and Western Europe, and Northern and Southern Italy—Eastern Europe and Southern Italy being generally more collectivist societies than Western Europe and Northern Italy.

"We've only done a couple of categorization tests," Nisbett says, "but so far we're finding the expected differences."

Why It Matters

In an increasingly multicultural world, these culture-induced cognitive differences can have practical implications, according to University of California, Santa Barbara, psychologist Heejung Kim, PhD. Kim, who is from South Korea, found her research inspiration in her experience as an international graduate student in the United States. In her graduate seminar classes, her inclination was to listen quietly and absorb what was going on around her—but she felt pressured to speak up.

"After struggling for a while, I began to think that someone should question whether the process of talking is valuable for everyone," she says, "because it certainly wasn't for me."

She decided to test European-American and first-generation Asian-American students by giving them a complex logic problem to solve. Control-group members solved the problem silently, while members of the experimental group had to talk out loud and explain their reasoning as they worked. Kim found that European Americans who talked out loud solved the problem just as well as those who stayed silent, but being forced to talk seriously undermined the Asian students' performance.

In general, Kim says, Asians may think and reason in a less readily "verbalizable" way than Westerners.

"It's more intuitive and less linear," she says. "So when you have to talk aloud, European Americans just vocalize their thoughts, but Asian Americans—on top of solving the problem—have to translate their thoughts into words."

In general, Nisbett says, he expects that over the next few decades work by researchers like Kim—and other Asian and Asian-American psychologists—will profoundly influence the way psychologists think about which aspects of thinking are universal and which are culture-specific.

"They're going to be bringing very different ways of thinking about cognitive psychology, social psychology, developmental psychology," he says. "They're going to change the field."

Talk to the Hand

New Insights into the Evolution of Language and Gesture

ERIC WARGO

In his book *Me Talk Pretty One Day*, humorist David Sedaris chronicled his pain at trying to learn French, in France, at age 41. His commiseration with a fellow language student sounds like it could be a dialogue between, say, two australopithecines, dimly anticipating the communicative achievements of their hominid descendents:

> "Sometimes me cry alone at night."
>
> "That be common for I, also, but be more strong, you. Much work and someday you talk pretty. People start love you soon. Maybe tomorrow, okay." (Sedaris, 2000)

Philosophers have always esteemed language among our most defining attributes, and the storytellers of every culture have tried to explain how humans acquired the gift. In Judeo-Christian myth, God granted Man the right to name things as he pleased, and later confused the world's tongues in retribution for human pride—leading to David Sedaris's predicament. Darwin supposed that language's origins were a more gradual and less deliberate outgrowth of animal communication: "Man not only uses inarticulate cries, gestures, and expressions, but has invented articulate language; if, indeed, the word *invented* can be applied to a process, completed by innumerable steps, half-consciously made" (Darwin, 1872/1998).

Accounting for these innumerable steps has been a challenge in the evolutionary psychology of language. What led our ancestors to become articulate? How did we finally learn to, you know, talk pretty?

It is intuitive to look to the vocal calls of primates for clues, and some primatologists still see this form of communication as the likeliest precursor for human language abilities. Yet evidence is accumulating that the "inarticulate cries" of monkeys appear to be controlled by different brain systems than those governing human language ability (Rizzolatti & Arbib, 1998), and psychologists interested in human and ape communication are turning with new interest to the properties of gesture. The story of language's "invention" may turn out to be more complicated than even Darwin could have imagined.

What is Language?

A language is a system that can express an infinite range of ideas using a finite set of sounds or word elements—a *discrete combinatorial system,* as APS Fellow and Charter Member Steven Pinker, Harvard University, calls it (Pinker, 1994). Simple sound elements like phonemes (for example, the sounds *ba, da,* and *pa;* some researchers even focus on smaller units called *articulatory primitives*—see Poeppel & Monahan, 2008), are combined into words standing for things or actions, which are combined into larger groupings like sentences that express ideas of varying levels of complexity—theoretically, infinite complexity (a language feature known as *recursion*).

The system that enables this infinite recombination from finite raw materials is *grammar,* and it is the element most conspicuously absent from all forms of animal communication. Vervet monkeys, for instance, have what could be called a vocabulary, a handful of distinct warning calls that are tied to specific threats in their environment like leopards, snakes, and eagles (see Cheney & Seyfarth, 2005); but there is no vervet grammar—the monkeys cannot mix and match their calls or use them to express new ideas (but see Zuberbühler, 2005). And as complex as some bird and whale songs are, grammatical rules enabling sentence-like recombination of ideas don't appear to exist in such animals either.

The linguist Noam Chomsky argued that humans uniquely are born with a *universal grammar,* an underlying set of rules that serves as the basis for language acquisition. His classic example was the made-up sentence "Colorless green ideas sleep furiously." It makes no sense—indeed, it consists of self-contradictory ideas—but the brain accepts it because it is grammatical; it obeys the rules of syntax. More recently, Pinker has upheld the Chomskyan view of the innateness of language ability in humans, calling language an "instinct" that humans are born with (Pinker, 1994).

According to Pinker, the instinct for language evolved as an adaptation for social coordination in our hunter-gatherer ancestors (Pinker, 1994), and its deep structure still bears evidence of the fundamental human priorities of manipulating the social and physical environment (Pinker, 2007). Somewhat controversially, Pinker also argues that language is a modular system that evolved independently from other human cognitive abilities—that it is its own unique tool in the toolbox that is the human brain. His view of the modularity of mental adaptations has been compared to that of University of California, Santa Barbara evolutionary psychologists (and APS Fellows) Leda Cosmides and John Tooby, who have likened the mind to a "Swiss Army knife" comprising numerous special-purpose adaptations for solving particular challenges.

Those who argue for a unique language-processing module in the brain make their case in opposition to connectionists, who emphasize that language arises from multiple distributed cognitive abilities and is inseparable from all the other intelligent feats humans can perform. Among those who are passionate about such subtleties, it is a hot debate. Neuroscientists are generally converging on a connectionist view of most cognitive abilities such as object recognition, categorization, and memory (see the April 2008 special issue of *Current Directions in Psychological Science:* "The Interface Between Neuroscience and Psychological Science"). It appears that different aspects of language also are handled by widely distributed, functionally interconnected brain areas. Speech perception and language comprehension, for example, are now known to involve a complex network of brain areas operating in parallel, including a "dorsal pathway" that maps auditory sound representations onto motor representations for producing speech sounds, and a "ventral pathway" that maps speech sound representations onto representations of word concepts (Poeppel & Monahan, 2008; see also Holt & Lotto, 2008).

Different systems also appear to handle semantics (meaning) and syntax (grammar). Recordings of event-related potentials—brain waves recorded with electrodes placed on the scalp—reveal that violations of semantics such as the sentence "He spread his warm bread with socks" causes something in the brain to balk, with a negative potential peaking at 400 milliseconds after the sense-violating word (in this case, the word "socks"; see Hagoort, 2008). However, an entirely different brain wave response betrays the brain's complaint at a violation of syntax. Like Chomsky's observation about colorless green ideas, something about the sentence "The boiled watering can smokes the telephone in the cat" is perfectly acceptable to brain's syntax enforcer even though it makes absolutely no sense. But a violation like "The boiled watering can *smoke* the telephone in the cat" causes a negative-amplitude spike at 600 milliseconds after the offending (grammatically incorrect) word "smoke"— evidence that syntax and sense-making are distinct cognitive functions (see Hagoort, 2008).

Particularity

Language has been called an instinct because it is so readily learned. Infants quickly begin to acquire language, without being actively taught: At 10 months of age, they know around 50 words (even though they do not say much), but by 30 months, they are already "social sophisticates," speaking in complete sentences with a production vocabulary of 550 words (Golinkoff & Hirsh-Pasek, 2006). Yet while it is instinctively

hungry to acquire language, the newborn brain is also completely unbiased to respond to the particular subset of possible sounds that constitute the spoken language of its parents—that is, when it comes to *phonetics,* it is a blank slate. That changes as the plastic brain quickly rewires (or prunes itself) to recognize only those sounds used in the language being spoken around it; older infants can only discriminate sounds from their own language (see Kraus & Banai, 2007), and adults learning a new language may have difficulty mastering its foreign sound distinctions (e.g., Japanese-speakers often have trouble distinguishing English "l" from "r").

This is one of the most interesting facts about language: you can't learn language without learning *a* language. Thus, while language requires an underlying mechanism (or mechanisms) common to everyone, and while language is used for the same purposes and in the same ways everywhere (i.e., it is a psychological universal), it is also a cultural system whose hallmark is particularity. There is no universal language any more than there is a "typical human." Languages, like people, are unique.

This is not merely an accident of history or evolution. One of the defining features of language, setting it apart from mere communication, is the feature known as *arbitrariness.* The Swiss linguist Ferdinand de Saussure noted that *signifiers* (e.g., words) by and large bear no necessary or logical connection to *signifieds,* or the things they stand for. There is no more reason to designate something you put on your head a "hat" than there is to call it a "chapeau." As such, the connection between the thing you put on your head and the word for it used in your community can only be a learned social convention. This is even true of onomatopoeia—words with a resemblance to natural sounds, the seeming exception to Saussure's rule. A Russian speaker will not recognize the onomatopoetic "bang" as the sound a gun makes, for example; where she grew up, she would have learned this sound as "batz."

The benefit of having to learn your lexicon instead of being born with it already hard-wired is that you are free to use words in novel and creative ways. It is possible to come up with other words for hats, or to lie about hats, or imagine a hat that doesn't exist yet, or wax nostalgic about hats in the past. It would be hard to imagine such human behaviors as tool-making, art, humor, long-term planning, or consciousness of self without the ability to represent abstractions, objects, and states of mind by words and other symbols that can be manipulated independently of what they stand for. The roots not only of abstract thought but also of culture lie in this radical disconnect between words and things.

Missing Links

On January 21st of this year, Alaskan octogenarian Marie Smith Jones died at her Anchorage home, at age 89. As a result, language conservationists moved her native tongue, Eyak, from the lists of "Endangered" to "Extinct." Smith had been the last living speaker of a language that, in prehistoric times, may have been spoken over much of Alaska's southeastern coast. The minor flurry of news reports of her passing briefly helped publicize the issue of language diversity and its rapid worldwide decline.

Despite the disappearance of languages like Eyak, there are still 6,000 languages spoken in the world today, give or take. They vary widely in the size of their lexicons, but in fundamental respects all these languages are pretty much alike. They are all fully modern and capable of expressing ideas of whatever complexity they are called upon to express. Linguists have observed the emergence of new languages, creoles, out of simplified pidgins that arise in trading communities and other situations when people who don't share a common language live with each other. But even creoles exhibit the complexity and syntactical capabilities of languages having long histories. No anthropologist has ever found, in some remote tribe, an evolutionary "missing link" between modern languages and the more rigid and stereotyped modes of communication used by animals.

Researchers attempting to explain how language could have evolved in humans inevitably return to the linguistic capabilities of other living primates for clues. The obvious social intelligence of apes, in particular, made them appealing candidates in some of the early experimental attempts to assess the language abilities of animals. Apes' vocal tracts cannot produce the sounds needed for spoken language, so in 1967, Beatrice and Allen Gardner (University of Nevada, Reno) tried raising a young chimp, Washoe, to communicate using American Sign Language (ASL), training her using operant conditioning techniques. Washoe's trainers reported that, by the time she died last year at age 42, she had learned around 250 signs and could even apply some of them in novel situations. Koko, a 37-year-old lowland gorilla, has been claimed by Stanford psychologist Francine Patterson to know over 1,000 ASL signs and to recognize over twice that many words of spoken English. Koko has gained a degree of fame for her sign-language abilities, being the subject of television documentaries and even taking part in an online "chat."

But many scientists have rejected the claims of the Gardners, Patterson, and other proponents of animal language, saying that researchers (and an eager public) have projected human-like mentality onto these animals in the absence of compelling evidence that they are doing much more than parroting their trainers or using linguistic signs in relatively rigid, nonlinguistic ways. The only ASL-fluent member of the Gardners' research team, for example, disputed Washoe's use of true ASL signs (see Pinker, 1994). These animals may display remarkable communication abilities, but communication—the ability to affect others' behavior—is not the same thing as language.

The most scientifically compelling case for rudimentary language abilities in apes comes from Kanzi, a bonobo who learned a system of communicating by pressing lexigrams (arbitrary symbols) on a keyboard. Unlike other ape language subjects, Kanzi was not raised by human parents, nor was his "language acquisition" a product of active training—he learned his first keyboard signs passively, as an infant, while his mother was being taught them by researcher Sue Savage-Rumbaugh at Georgia State University's Language Research Center, in the early 1980s. Kanzi, now 27, has shown remarkable abilities to understand spoken language, to link spoken words and things to corresponding lexigrams, and possibly to construct novel messages from combinations of signs. Savage-Rumbaugh claims that Kanzi is even able to understand the grammatical structure of some sentences (Savage-Rumbaugh, 1989). Whether the finite number of lexigrams available to Kanzi limits his ability to produce sentences as complex as the ones he understands (as Savage-Rumbaugh suggests), or whether there is some more basic linguistic threshold separating his abilities from full-blown language, remains an open question. But the case of Kanzi does appear to refute the notion that apes are only capable of parroting their human companions.

Much has been gained from observing the way primates communicate with each other in their natural environments. Many African monkeys, as well as chimpanzees, have been found to have repertoires of acoustically different alarm calls for different threats. APS Fellow Robert Seyfarth and his University of Pennsylvania colleague and wife Dorothy L. Cheney have found that such calls are highly dependent on social context; vervet monkeys, for example, seldom give an alarm if they are alone, and they are more likely to call in the presence of their own kin than in the presence of unrelated individuals (Cheney & Seyfarth, 2005).

Do monkeys understand the meaning of calls in the same way that humans understand the meaning of words? Is a vervet "leopard" alarm a word for a type of jungle cat, a recommendation ("run!"), or simply a symptomatic expression of a particular flavor of anxiety?

Primate calls are not simply reflexive; a monkey can decide whether or not to make a call based on who else is around. Such "audience effects," displayed by a number of species, are evidence for cognitive control and complexity in communication. But the evidence also suggests that despite the dependence on social context, monkeys lack theory-of-mind ability—the ability to conceptualize what other individuals may be thinking or how their knowledge may be changed by making (or not making) a vocalization. For Cheney and Seyfarth, this inability may be the key thing that distinguishes nonhuman primate communication from human language, and is probably at the root of their inability to generate new signals in creative ways or to utilize signals syntactically (Cheney & Seyfarth, 2005).

An interesting theme emerging in research on primate communication (as well as communication in other vocal animals such as parrots and dolphins) is the extreme asymmetry between vocal production and auditory comprehension. Animals are relatively inflexible and limited in the calls they can produce, yet they are often capable of much greater subtlety when it comes to grasping syntactical (i.e., causal) relationships, understanding the semantic meaning of calls, responding to the pragmatics (intentions and consequences) of calls, and even recognizing calls of other species. For example, Klaus Zuberbühler (University of St. Andrews) has found that Diana monkeys living among chimpanzees often made leopard alarm calls of their own when hearing chimpanzee leopard alarm screams, whereas Diana monkeys with less chimpanzee experience were more likely to hide silently (i.e., from the chimpanzees, who sometimes prey on the monkeys; Zuberbühler, 2005). Ape language experiments (and even everyday experience with pets) reflect the receptiveness and responsiveness to more sophisticated communication than animals are generally able to produce themselves. Zuberbühler suggests that the evolution of language in our species built on a basic competence in comprehension already existing in our primate ancestors.

How Necessary Was Speech?

The transition from hearing and understanding to actually talking required a revolution not only cognitively (e.g., theory-of-mind ability) but also in controlling the face and mouth. Humans uniquely are able to produce and combine a huge array of subtly distinct sounds (over 100 acoustically unique *phones* are listed in the International Phonetic Alphabet). The difference is partly due to the shape and position of the larynx (see below) and to finer motor control of the articulators—lips, tongue, jaw, and other structures that modify sounds. This fine motor control cannot be mastered by monkeys or apes (as the early ape language experiments showed), and it is now known to have a genetic component. In humans, the gene known as FOXP2 controls the facial and mouth motor abilities necessary for speech; damage to this gene causes inability to speak but few or no other cognitive handicaps. The normal human form of this gene dates to a mutation that was established about 200,000 years ago; this may have been a watershed event in the history of human speech (Zuberbühler, 2005).

But speech is not synonymous with language, and may not even be a prerequisite for it.

Most primates have a repertoire of vocal calls, but only we and our closest relatives, the apes, regularly communicate with our hands as well, suggesting that gesture may be a newer evolutionary development than the ability to vocalize. A counterintuitive theory that is gaining ground among researchers in a range of fields—from primatology, neuroscience, and even paleontology—is the notion that the driving force in language evolution may not have been the inarticulate cries of our primate ancestors, but their gestures (Corballis, 2003).

At Emory University, then-PhD-student Amy Pollick and her mentor Frans de Waal coded over 600 hours of videotaped interactions by chimpanzees and their relatively less-studied relatives, bonobos, in different captive groups. The aim was to compare the animals' gestural and vocal/facial communication. They found that the overwhelming majority of signals used to initiate social interactions in both species were either solely gestural or involved a combination of gestures and facial/vocal signals. According to Pollick, this finding was a surprise: Apes scream and hoot at each other a lot, and it would be easy for a casual observer to assume vocalization is these animals' dominant mode of initiating communication.

Ape vocalizations have been relatively less studied than those of monkeys (Zuberbühler, 2005), but recently Zuberbühler and his colleagues have found evidence for cognitive complexity and audience effects in chimpanzee screams. For example, during aggressive encounters, individuals varied their screams depending on the severity of an encounter, their own role in it, and who else was present to hear them; they even exaggerated calls for support (intensifying the severity of a call compared to the real severity of the encounter) if a higher-ranking male was

present (Slocombe & Zuberbühler, 2007). But most research so far shows that chimps' vocal signals are not much more complex than those of monkeys. Sounds are fairly highly stereotyped and are closely tied to particular emotions and situations (Pollick & de Waal, 2007). Social contexts eliciting particular facial/vocal displays in chimps reliably elicit the same displays in bonobos, and vice versa; and most vocalizations don't appear to have a targeted recipient.

By contrast, Pollick and de Waal found a highly nuanced hand-gesture vocabulary in chimps and bonobos, with great situational variation in use of gestures and combination with vocalizations, and a tendency to use gestures dyadically (i.e., more like conversational exchanges). The Emory researchers found that chimp and bonobo gestures were much less tied to particular emotions and situations than their vocalizations were. And hand gestures, even if they clearly evolved from basic object-related manual movements, were much more conventionalized (i.e., less stereotyped) and appeared to be deployed more deliberately—revealing greater cortical control over this mode of communication. Often the meaning of a particular chimp or bonobo gesture could only be extracted from its context.

The Emory researchers also found that, particularly in bonobos but to a lesser extent in chimps, gestures differed between different groups of the same species—evidence that, in these animals, gesture has truly begun to break from biology, becoming cultural. "Far more than facial expressions and vocalizations," they write, "gestures seem subject to modification, conventionalization, and social transmission" (Pollick & de Waal, 2007, p. 8188). Pollick and de Waal speculate that the flexible use of gestures and responsiveness to combined signals that they observed "may have characterized our early ancestors, which in turn may have served as a stepping stone for the evolution of symbolic communication" (p. 8188).

Talking with Our Hands

Pollick, who now works in Washington, DC as APS's Director of Government Relations, admits that her interest in ape gestures and the evolution of language isn't accidental. She is deaf and from a deaf family, so American Sign Language is, so to speak, her native tongue. "Having grown up with ASL, I was just naturally attuned to issues of communication," Pollick says. "I was also naturally attuned to gesture. All humans gesture, wherever they are, in all cultures. People gesture when they are not visible to the receiver, such as when they talk on the phone. Blind people gesture when talking to other blind people. This led me to think that gesture is deeply ingrained in human communication, and I began to wonder where this came from."

Pollick explains that in order to theorize about the relationship between ape gestures and human language, she drew a stricter distinction between hand gestures and other body movements than previous ape communication researchers had drawn. She also made finer-grained distinctions among different gestures—for example, determining that the meaning of an outstretched hand depended on the angle the hand was rotated at. Chimps, for instance, used an extended, upraised palm (i.e., "gimme") in a variety of situations: to request food, to request sex, to request to be groomed, or to implore the aid of another chimp. Sometimes the gesture was combined with a vocalization such as a scream. Bonobos mainly used the gesture to solicit play.

Humans use the "gimme" gesture too—as well as countless others. Linguists used to ignore the way humans use their hands when communicating, or relegate it to the subordinate category of "body language." But psychological research on human gesture is revealing that, as with chimps and bonobos, when humans talk with their hands it is far more than just an exception or a sideshow to the main attraction.

Important insights into the nature of language have come from studies of signing in the deaf. Linguists agree that human sign languages such as ASL are every bit as "linguistic" as spoken languages are—that is, they possess all the syntactical complexity and are just as flexible and open-ended as their spoken analogues. They are also just as readily learned. University of Toronto psychologist Laura-Ann A. Petitto found that deaf children exposed to ASL or the Quebec sign language, Langue des Signes Quebecoise, learned to sign at the same rate that hearing children acquire spoken language (Petitto, 2000). Other researchers have even suggested that deaf children acquire sign language on a faster developmental schedule than non-deaf learners of spoken language (Meier & Newport, 1990).

If a sign language doesn't happen to be available in a deaf child's environment, she will go ahead and invent one. APS Fellow and Charter Member Susan Goldin-Meadow (University of Chicago) studied profoundly deaf children in the United States and Taiwan who were raised by hearing parents and were unexposed to sign language. Such children spontaneously used gesture to communicate, and their gestures displayed the same structural properties (such as recursion and displaced communication—referring to things not present) that characterize natural spoken languages and sign languages (Goldin-Meadow, 2006).

The sign language instinct appears to exist also in hearing adults who have never learned a sign language. As Pollick notes, most people talk with their hands—that is, gesticulate to provide counterpoint, emphasis, or visual illustration of what they are saying with speech. Goldin-Meadow found that, when gesture accompanies speech, it lacks the fully linguistic properties observed in deaf people's spontaneous signing. In another study by Goldin-Meadow, non-deaf participants were asked to describe an event orally and also to attempt to describe it using only gestures. When they used speech, their hand gestures supported what they were saying imagistically, supporting the main spoken channel of communication by providing a kind of visual aid, but were not by themselves linguistic; however, when they had to describe an event solely through hand gestures, their gestures assumed the linguistic properties the researcher found in her studies with deaf children (Goldin-Meadow, 2006).

Goldin-Meadow's University of Chicago colleague, APS Fellow David McNeill, considers hand gestures to be intrinsic to language, driving thought and speech. Language, he argues, is a dialectic in which images (conveyed by the hands) work with and against speech, the tension between these two modes of thought propelling thought and communication forward. His studies of speakers' hand gestures revealed a temporal structure, distinct from ordinary syntax (sentence structure), in which gestural imagery and spoken content periodically resolved in what he dubs "growth points"—temporal boundaries of unfolding thought sequences that can be detected when a word or phrase synchronizes with gesture in a certain way (McNeill, 2006).

Speakers vary in how they use their hands when they are speaking. In another series of experiments, Goldin-Meadow compared learning and problem-solving ability in speaking children whose gestures matched (i.e., conveyed the same information as) their own or their teachers' verbal explanations of problems with the abilities of children whose gestures conveyed different information than what was being spoken. Children who used mismatching gestures or who were taught by teachers who used mismatching gestures learned faster and were more successful at solving problems than were those whose gestures merely supported the spoken communication. It suggests that this second, silent channel of nonverbal information may be an important helping hand (so to speak) to thought. According to Goldin-Meadow, "A conversation in gesture . . . appears to be taking place alongside the conversation in speech whenever speakers use their hands" (Goldin-Meadow, 2006, p. 37).

How Did We Get Here?

APS Fellow and Charter Member Michael Corballis (University of Auckland) is a proponent of the gesture-first scenario of language origins, arguing that it makes sense of a wide range of findings in various fields (Corballis, 2003). There is the paleontological evidence, for one thing: Sometime after the human lineage split from that of chimps and bonobos about six million years ago, our australopithecine ancestors became bipedal; whether or not gestural communication was a factor driving this shift, it did free the hands for greater manipulation of the physical environment, and likely facilitated communicative manipulation of the social environment. Australopithecine brains remained ape-like in most respects, as did their vocal tracts and breathing apparatus—meaning they couldn't talk—but expansion of the cortex, including specific brain areas governing language and gesture, is found in their tool-manufacturing descendent *Homo habilis*. Endocasts (casts of brain cases) of 2-million-year-old *H. habilis* skulls reveal an asymmetry that could correspond to expansion of areas on the left side of the brain, such as Broca's area, that have long been associated with language in humans (see Corballis, 2003).

In the 1990s, a group of neuroscientists at the University of Parma, Italy, made a discovery suggesting that the brain area in monkeys corresponding to Broca's area could have served as the platform for the emergence of language out of gesture in our deep primate past (Fogassi & Ferrari, 2007; Rizzolatti & Arbib, 1998). The homologue of Broca's area in the monkey brain, known as area F5, is involved in controlling manual gestures, not vocalizations; it also possesses a *mirror-neuron system*. Mirror neurons fire both when an animal (or person) initiates an action and when the animal perceives another individual make the same action (see "Mirror Neurons: How We Reflect on Behavior" in the May, 2007, issue of the *Observer*). Mirror neuron systems have been proposed as the basis for various forms of learning, social coordination, and even theory-of-mind abilities in animals and humans.

One category of mirror neurons in the monkey F5 fires both when the monkey makes a motor act with its forelimbs and when it hears the sound produced by the same action (e.g., by another monkey, or on a recording); another type of motor neuron in the same area specifically activates during observation of another monkey's mouth-communicative gestures like lip-smacking or tongue protrusion (Fogassi & Ferrari, 2007). Research in humans has revealed similar properties for Broca's area. It activates when people observe goal-related hand or mouth motor movements by other people, for example. And there is evidence for a matching mechanism whereby heard phonemes activate corresponding tongue motor representations in the cortex (Fogassi & Ferrari, 2007).

The neuroscience findings support a longstanding and influential theory of speech perception called the motor theory (Liberman & Mattingly, 1985). In this theory, linguistic primitives (basic elements) are not represented in the cortex as abstract sounds but as the motor signals that one would use to make those sounds. The picture is turning out to be more complicated—speech perception involves many more parts of the brain than just Broca's area. But the common neural basis of manual dexterity and important aspects of language means that the notion that language is a "tool" could be more than just a metaphor. Could tool use and language be flip sides of the same cognitive coin?[1]

Hand to Mouth

Corballis, like Zuberbühler, sees speech per se as a late development possibly occurring only with the rise of *Homo sapiens* around 170,000 years ago. Yet language, in some form, could well have been around for a long time before that. The beginnings of stone tool manufacture occurred around 2.5 million years ago, followed by a shift from forest dwelling to living and carrying materials on the open savannah around 2 million years ago. These developments hint at a level of abstract thinking and social coordination abilities that could have gone hand in hand (so to speak) with language skills.

One plausible scenario for the transition from gestural to vocal communication is that increased use of the hands for tool making and carrying drove greater use of the face for communication, and this ultimately led to speech. In modern sign languages, manual gestures convey semantic content and facial and body movements act as modifiers. Corballis suggests that facial movements could have become integrated into the manual sign system as carriers of syntax (Corballis, 2003) and this integration could have been an outgrowth of the mechanics of eating—an idea supported by mirror-neuron findings (Fogassi & Ferrari, 2007).

From this gesture–face integration, it would have been a small evolutionary step to add voicing to facial gesture to provide more range of meaning—perhaps made possible by the FOXP2 mutation mentioned earlier, as well as the descent of the larynx and changes to the muscles controlling breathing.[2] Corballis suggests that we should think of speaking not as the production of abstract phonemes but as a kind of noisy gesturing with our mouths (see Corballis, 2003).

Whatever its evolutionary origins, speech has acquired a great deal of autonomy from hand gestures. People can normally communicate on the phone, for example, with little loss of meaning, even if gesturing at the same time helps them think. The autonomy of speech has left many people with the natural impression that our linguistic abilities are more closely akin to animal vocalization than to other forms of communication. Since words and gestures don't fossilize, it may never be possible to answer the question "Where did language come from?" definitively. Pollick acknowledges that the theory that our language abilities evolved from gesture remains a "just-so story," even though the scientific evidence for pieces of the theory is compelling. Only further research, across a range of disciplines, can help settle the question of whether talking pretty piggybacked on gesture or the other way around—or whether language evolved in some completely different way.

Notes

1. The common neural origins of language and manual dexterity has been used to explain why nine out of ten humans are right-handed (Corballis, 2003). A bias toward right-handedness makes sense if manual dexterity developed in tandem with language ability, both sharing an underlying cortical substrate in the left hemisphere (which controls the right side of the body). However, recent discovery of handedness and hemispherical asymmetries in many other animal species, including many primates, may complicate this picture (see Hopkins & Cantalupo, in press).

2. The descent of the larynx, incidentally, made modern humans uniquely vulnerable to choking. Unlike other animals, we are prevented from breathing and swallowing at the same time, and, thus, are imperiled whenever we eat.

References

Cheney, D.L., & Seyfarth, R.M. (2005). Constraints and preadaptations in the earliest stages of language evolution. *The Linguistic Review, 22*, 135–159.

Corballis, M.C. (2003). From mouth to hand: Gesture, speech, and the evolution of right-handedness. *Behavioral and Brain Sciences, 26*, 199–260.

Darwin, C. (1998). *The expression of the emotions in man and animals.* New York: Oxford University Press. (Original work published 1872)

Fogassi, L., & Ferrari, P.F. (2007). Mirror neurons and the evolution of embodied language. *Current Directions in Psychological Science, 17*, 136–141.

Goldin-Meadow, S. (2006). Talking and thinking with our hands. *Current Directions in Psychological Science, 15*, 34–39.

Golinkoff, R.M., & Hirsh-Pasek, K. (2006). Baby wordsmith: From associationist to social sophisticate. *Current Directions in Psychological Science, 15*, 30–33.

Hagoort, P. (2008). Should psychology ignore the language of the brain? *Current Directions in Psychological Science, 17*, 96–101.

Holt, L.L., & Lotto, A.J. (2008). Speech perception within an auditory cognitive science framework. *Current Directions in Psychological Science, 17*, 42–46.

Hopkins, W.D., & Cantalupo, C. (in press). Theoretical speculations on the evolutionary origins of hemispheric specialization. Current Directions in Psychological Science.

Kraus, N., & Banai, K. (2007). Auditory-processing malleability: Focus on language and music. *Current Directions in Psychological Science, 16,* 105–110.

Liberman, A.M., & Mattingly, I.G. (1985). The motor theory of speech perception revisited. *Cognition, 21,* 1–36.

McNeill, D. (2006, September). *Gesture and thought.* Paper presented at the Summer Institute on Non-verbal Communication and the Biometrical Principle, Vietri sul Mare, Italy. Downloaded April 2, 2008, from http://mcneilllab.uchicago.edu/pdfs/dmcn_vietri_sul_mare.pdf

Meier, R.P., & Newport, E.L. (1990). Out of the hands of babes: On a possible sign language advantage in language acquisition. *Language, 66,* 1–23.

Petitto, L.A. (2000). On the biological foundations of human language. In H. Lane & K. Emmorey (Eds.), *The signs of language revisited* (pp. 447–471). Mahwah, NJ: Erlbaum.

Pinker, S. (1994). *The language instinct.* New York: HarperCollins.

Pinker, S. (1997). *The stuff of thought.* New York: Viking.

Poeppel, D., & Monahan, P.J. (2008). Speech perception: Cognitive foundations and cortical implementation. *Current Directions in Psychological Science, 17,* 80–85.

Pollick, A.S., & de Waal, F.B.M. (2007). Ape gestures and language evolution. *Proceedings of the National Academy of Sciences, USA, 104,* 8184–8189.

Rizzolatti, G., & Arbib, M.A. (1998). Language within our grasp. *Trends in Neurosciences, 21,* 188–194.

Savage-Rumbaugh, S., Shanker, S.G., & Taylor, T.J. (1998). *Apes, language, and the human mind.* New York: Oxford University Press.

Sedaris, D. (2000). Me talk pretty one day. In *Me talk pretty one day* (pp. 166–173). New York: Little, Brown.

Slocombe, K.E., & Zuberbühler, K. (2007). Chimpanzees modify recruitment screams as a function of audience composition. *Proceedings of the National Academy of Sciences, USA, 104,* 17228–17233.

Zuberbühler, K. (2005). The phylogenetic roots of language: Evidence from primate communication. *Current Directions in Psychological Science, 14,* 126–130.

UNIT 6
Emotion and Motivation

Unit Selections

Key Points to Consider

- What makes people successful? In what ways are our successes delusional?

- What is emotional intelligence and what role does it play in getting through everyday life?

- Why are some people more motivated (i.e. more likely to achieve their goals) than others?

- How is eating related to motivation? Why do some people overeat? Can psychologists help them change their habits?

- How can mothers model positive eating behaviors for their daughters?

- What causes people to "fly into a rage" and what are the negative impacts of doing so?

Student Web Site
www.mhcls.com

Internet References

Motivation
   http://chiron.valdosta.edu/whuitt/col/motivation/motivate.html
Emotion
   http://www.psychology.org/links/Environment_Behavior_Relationships/Emotion/
Mind Tools
   http://www.psychwww.com/mtsite/

Jasmine's sister was a working mother and always reminded Jasmine about how exciting life on the road as a sales representative was. Jasmine herself stayed home because she loved her children, 2-year old Min, 4-year-old Chi'Ming, and newborn Yuan. One day, Jasmine was having a difficult time with the children. The baby, Yuan, had been crying all day from colic. The other two children had been bickering over their toys. Jasmine, realizing that it was already 5:15 and her husband would be home any minute, frantically started preparing dinner. She wanted to fix a nice dinner so that she and her husband could eat after the children went to bed, then relax and enjoy each other.

This scenario was not to be. Jasmine sat waiting for her no-show husband. When he finally walked in the door at 10:15, Jasmine was furious. His excuse that his boss had invited the whole office for dinner didn't reduce Jasmine's ire. Jasmine reasoned that her husband could have called to say that he wouldn't be home for dinner; he could have taken 5 minutes to do that. He said he did but the phone was busy. Jasmine berated her husband. Her face was taut and red with rage. Her voice wavered as she escalated her decibel level. Suddenly, bursting into tears, she ran into the living room. Her husband retreated to the safety of their bedroom and the respite that a deep sleep would bring.

Exhausted and disappointed, Jasmine sat alone and pondered why she was so angry with her husband. Was she just tired? Was she frustrated by negotiating with young children all day and simply wanted another adult around once in a while? Was she secretly worried and jealous that her husband was seeing another woman and had lied about his whereabouts? Was she combative because her husband's and her sister's lives seemed so much fuller than her own life? Jasmine was unsure of how she felt and why she exploded in such rage at her husband, whom she loved dearly.

This story, while sad and gender stereotypical, is not necessarily unrealistic when it comes to emotions. There are times when we are moved by strong emotions. On other occasions, when we expect waterfalls of tears, we find that our eyes are dry or simply a little misty. What are these strange things we call

© Stockbyte/Punchstock Images

emotions? What motivates us to rage at someone we love? And why do Americans seem to autopsy every mood?

These questions and others have inspired psychologists to study emotion and motivation. Jasmine's story, besides introducing these topics to you, also illustrates why these two topics are usually interrelated in psychology. Some emotions are pleasant, so pleasant that we are motivated to keep experiencing them. Pleasant emotions are exemplified by love, pride, and joy. Other emotions are terribly draining and oppressive—so negative that we hope they will be over as soon as possible. Negative emotions are exemplified by anger, grief, and jealousy. Emotions and motivation, and their relationship to each other are the focus of this unit.

The Success Delusion

MARSHALL GOLDSMITH

Any human—in fact, any animal—will tend to repeat behavior that is followed by positive reinforcement. The more successful we become, the more positive reinforcement we get—and the more likely we are to experience the success delusion: *I behave this way. I am successful. Therefore, I must be successful because I behave this way.*

Wrong.

For leaders, the higher we move up the organizational ladder, the more our employees let us know how wonderful we are. Our behavior is often followed by positive reinforcement, even when this behavior makes absolutely no sense. One night over dinner, I listened as a very wise military leader shared his learnings from years of experience with an eager, newly minted general. "Recently, have you started to notice that when you tell jokes, everyone erupts into laughter—and that when you say something 'wise' everyone nods their heads in solemn agreement?" The new general said, "Why, yes, I have." The older general laughed. "Let me help you," he said. "You aren't that funny, and you aren't that smart. It's only that star on your shoulder. Don't ever let it go to your head."

We *all* want to hear what we want to hear. We want to believe the great things that the world is telling us about ourselves. And yes, our belief in ourselves helps us become successful and stay that way.

But it can also make it very hard for us to change, and most of us need to change: *We aren't really that funny, and we aren't really that smart.* We can all improve, but only it we are willing to take a hard look at ourselves. By understanding why changing behavior can be so difficult for successful leaders, we can increase the likelihood of making the changes that we need to make in our quest to become even more successful.

Why We Resist Change

UNUM, the insurance company, ran an ad some years ago showing a powerful grizzly in the middle of a roaring stream, with his neck extended to the limit, jaws wide open and teeth flaring. The bear was about to clamp on an unsuspecting salmon jumping upstream. The headline read: "You probably feel like the bear. We'd like to suggest that you are the salmon."

The ad was designed to sell disability insurance, but it struck me as a powerful statement about how we all delude ourselves about our achievements, our status, and our contributions. We often overestimate our contribution to a project, hold an elevated opinion of our professional skills and standing among our peers, and exaggerate our project's impact on profitability by discounting real and hidden costs.

Many of our delusions can come from our association with success, not failure. Since we get positive reinforcement from our past successes, we think that they are predictive of great things to come in our future.

Now, the fact that successful people tend to be delusional isn't all bad, Our belief in our wonderfulness gives us confidence. Even if we're not as good as we think we are, this confidence helps us be better than we would be if we didn't believe in ourselves. The most realistic people in the world aren't delusional—they're depressed! But while our self-confident delusions can help us achieve, they can make it difficult for us to change.

The fact that successful people tend to be delusional isn't all bad.

In fact, when others suggest that we need to change, we often view them with unadulterated bafflement. It's an interesting three-part response. First, we're convinced that the other party is confused: They are misinformed; they must have us mixed up with someone who truly does need to change. Second, as it dawns upon us that the other party may have accurate information about our perceived shortcomings—we go into denial mode. This criticism may be correct, but it can't be that important, or else we wouldn't be so successful. Finally, when all else fails, we attack the other party, trying to discredit the messenger. "Why is a winner like *me*" we conclude, "listening to a loser like *you?*"

Couple these denial mechanisms with the very positive interpretation that successful people assign to their past performance, their ability to influence their success (as opposed to just being lucky), their optimistic belief that their success will continue in the future, and their overstated sense of control over their own destiny (as opposed to being controlled by external forces), and you have a volatile cocktail of resistance to change.

Belief 1: I Have Succeeded, Therefore I Will Succeed

Successful people have one consistent idea coursing through their veins and brains: "I have succeeded. I have succeeded. I have succeeded." This strong belief in our *past* success gives us faith to take the risks needed for our *future* success.

You may think that this doesn't apply to you, that this is ego run amok. But look closely at yourself. How do you have the confidence to wake up in the morning and charge into work, filled with optimism and eagerness to compete? It's not because you are reminding yourself of the screw-ups you have created and the failures that you have endured. On the contrary: It's because you edit out failures and choose to run the highlight reel of your successes. If you're like the successful people I know, you're focused on the positives, calling up mental images of when you were the star, dazzled everyone, and came out on top. It might he those five minutes in the executive meeting when you had the floor and nailed the argument that you wanted to make. (Who wouldn't run that highlight in their head as if it were the SportsCenter Play of the Day?) It might be your skillfully crafted memo that the CEO praised and routed to everyone in the company. (Who wouldn't want to re-read that memo in a spare moment?) When our actions lead to a happy ending and make us look good, we love to replay it for ourselves.

When it comes to the thoughts successful people hold in our heads, we are not self-deprecating—we are self-aggrandizing. And that's a good thing! Without it, we wouldn't be so excited about getting up in the morning.

I once got into a conversation about this with a major-league baseball player. Every hitter has certain pitchers whom he historically hits better than others. He told me, "When I face a pitcher whom I've hit well in the past, I always go up to the plate thinking I 'own' this guy- That gives me confidence."

That's not surprising. To successful people, the past is made up of rose-colored prologue. But the ballplayer took that thinking one step further. "What about pitchers whom you *don't* hit well?" I asked. "How do you deal with a pitcher who owns *you?*" "Same thing," he said. "I go up to the plate thinking I can hit this guy. I have done it before with pitchers a lot better than he is."

In other words, not only did he lean on his past success to maintain his positive attitude, but he relied on it even when his past performance was *not* so rosy—i.e., when the evidence actually contradicted his self-confidence. Successful people don't drink from a glass that is half-empty!

When achievement is the result of a team effort—not just individual performance—we tend to overestimate our contribution to the final victory. I once asked three business partners to estimate their individual contribution to the partnership's profits. Not surprisingly, the sum of their answers amounted to over 150 percent of the actual profit.

This overestimation of our past success is true in almost any workplace. If you ask your colleagues (confidentially, of course) to estimate their percentage contribution to your enterprise, the total will always exceed 100 percent. There's nothing wrong with this. (If the total adds up to *less* than 100 percent, you probably need new colleagues!)

But "I have succeeded," positive as it is in most cases, can become a major obstacle when behavioral change is needed. Successful people consistently overrate themselves relative to their peers. Over the years, I have asked more than fifty thousand participants in my training programs to rate themselves in terms of their performance relative to their professional peers. Some 80 to 85 percent rank themselves in the top 20 percent of their peer group, and about 70 percent rank themselves in the top 10 percent. The numbers get even more ridiculous among professionals with higher perceived social status, such as physicians, pilots, and investment bankers. Physicians may be the most delusional. I once half-jokingly informed a group of doctors that my

extensive research had conclusively proven that half of all M.D.s had graduated in the bottom half of their medical-school class. Two of the doctors insisted that this was impossible!

We all tend to accept only the feedback from others that is consistent with the way we see ourselves. Successful people feel great about their previous performance. The good news is that these positive memories build our self-confidence and inspire us to try to succeed even more. The bad news is that our delusional self-image can make it hard to hear negative feedback and admit that we need to change.

Belief 2: I Have Earned My Success

Successful people believe themselves capable of having a positive influence on the world—and of making desirable things happen. It's not quite like a carnival magic act in which a mentalist purports to move objects on a table with her mind. But it's close. Successful people literally believe that through the sheer force of their personality, talent, and brainpower, they can steer a situation in their direction.

It's the reason why some people raise their hand and say, "Put me in, Coach" when the boss asks for volunteers—and others cower in the corner, praying that they won't be noticed.

This is the classic definition of self-efficacy, and it may be the most central belief driving individual success. People who believe they can succeed see opportunities, where others see threats. They are unafraid of uncertainty or ambiguity—indeed, they embrace it. They take more risks and achieve greater returns. Given the choice, they bet on themselves.

Successful people have a high "internal locus of control." In other words, they do not feel like victims of fate. They see their success as a function of their own motivation and ability—not luck, random chance, or fate. They carry this belief even when luck *does* play a crucial role in success.

Successful people don't drink from a glass that is half-empty!

Several years ago, six of my partners wanted to get involved in a very large deal. Since I was the senior partner, they needed my approval. I was dead set against the deal and told them that it was idiotic. I finally agreed, but kicking and screaming. Seven years later, my personal return from their "idiotic" investment exceeded seven digits to the left of the decimal. There was no way to credit my windfall other than pure, dumb luck. When I told this story to some of my successful friends, they refused to see it this way: They insisted that my good fortune was a deserved payoff for years of hard work and dedication. It was a classic successful person's response. Successful people tend to believe that good fortune is "earned" through an individual's motivation and ability, even when it clearly is not.

Of course, this belief makes about as much sense as inheriting money and believing that you are a self-made man. If you are born on third base, you shouldn't think you hit a triple. Successful people believe that there is a causal link between what they have done and the results that follow—even when no link exists. This belief is delusional, but it is also empowering.

This belief is certainly better than the alternative. Take the example of people who buy lottery tickets daily; they tend to be less successful. (This is why state-run lotteries are functionally a regressive tax on the poor.) If you believe success is a function of luck, you might as well buy lottery tickets; this is why you seldom see millionaires scratching tickets. To make matters worse, serious scratchers often blow the money if they actually win the lottery. Why? The same misguided beliefs that led to the purchase of the tickets are reinforced when they win.

Successful people trade this "lottery mentality" for an unshakable belief in themselves. This presents another obstacle in helping them change behavior. When we believe that our good fortune is directly and causally linked to our behavior, we can easily make a false assumption. *I behave this way. I am successful. Therefore, I must be successful because I behave this way.* It can be especially challenging to help successful leaders realize that their success is happening *in spite of* some of their behavior.

Belief 3: I will Succeed No Matter How Much I'm Asked to Do

Successful people are optimists. As anyone who has ever worked in sales knows: If you believe you will succeed you might not, but if you don't believe that you will succeed you definitely won't! Optimists tend to chronically over-commit. Why? We believe that we will get more done than we actually can.

It can be extremely difficult for an ambitious person with an "I will succeed" attitude to turn down desirable opportunities. The huge majority of leaders with whom I work today feel as busy—or busier—than they have ever felt in their lives. They are so busy not because they are losers but because they are winners. They are drowning in a sea of opportunity.

Optimists tend to chronically over-commit.

Perhaps this has happened to you. You do something wonderful at work. Suddenly, people want to associate themselves with your success. They think, quite logically, that since you pulled off a miracle once, you can do it again—this time for them. Soon opportunities are thrust upon you at a pace you have never seen before. Since you believe, "I will succeed," it is hard to say no. If not careful, you can get overwhelmed—and that which brought about your rise will bring about your fall.

In my volunteer work, one client was the executive director of an important human-services organization. His mission was to help the world's most vulnerable people. Unfortunately, his business was booming, and when people came to him for help, he didn't have the heart or inclination to say no. Everything was driven by his belief that "we will succeed." As a result, he promised more than even the most dedicated staff could deliver. His biggest challenge as a leader was not letting his personal optimism lead to staff burnout, turnover, and missed commitments.

This "I will succeed" belief can sabotage our chances for success when it is time for us to change behavior. I make no apology for the fact that I'm obsessed about following up with my clients to see if they actually use what I teach them and achieve positive change in behavior. Almost every participant who attends

my leadership-training program *intends* to apply what has been learned back at work. Most do—and they get better. Others do absolutely nothing and might as well have spent their time at home watching sitcoms. When I ask the do-nothings, "Why didn't you actually implement the behavioral changes that you said you would?", by tar the most common response is, "I meant to but just didn't have the time to get to it." In other words, they were over-committed. They sincerely believe that they would "get to it later," but "later" never came. Our excessive optimism and resulting over-commitment can be as serious an obstacle to change as our denial of negative feedback or our belief that our flaws are actually the cause of our success.

Belief 4: I Have Chosen Success, So I Can Choose to Change

Successful people believe that they are doing what they choose to do, because they choose to do it. They have a high need for self-determination. When we do what we *choose* to do, we are *committed.* When we do what we *have* to do, we are *compliant.*

A child can see the difference between commitment and compliance. Even a skeptical wise-guy teenager like me could see that some teachers had chosen the profession (and loved to teach) while others did it just to make a living—and the best teachers were clearly the former. They were committed to their students rather than being controlled by external forces (their paycheck). Successful people have a unique distaste for feeling controlled or manipulated. I see this daily in my work. Even when I've gotten great advance build-up as someone who can help people change for the better, I still meet resistance. I have made peace with the fact that I cannot *make* people change—I can only help them get better at what they choose to change.

Basketball coach Rick Pitino wrote a book called *Success Is a Choice.* I agree. "I choose to succeed" correlates closely with achievement in virtually any field. People don't stumble on success—they choose it. Unfortunately, getting successful people to say ". . . and I choose to *change*" is not an easy transition. It means turning that muscular commitment on its head. The more we believe that our behavior is a result of our own choices and commitments, the less likely we are to want to change that same behavior.

There's a reason for this, and it's one of the best-researched principles in psychology. It's called cognitive dissonance. It refers to the disconnect between what we want to believe and what we actually experience in the world. The underlying theory is simple: The more we are committed to believing that something is true, the less likely we are to believe that its opposite is true, even in the face of clear evidence that shows we are wrong.

Cognitive dissonance usually works in favor of successful people when they apply it to achieving their mission. The more we are committed to believing that we are on the right path, the less likely we are to believe that our strategy is flawed, even in the face of initial evidence that indicates we may be wrong. It's the reason successful people don't buckle and waver when times are hard. Of course, this same principle can work against successful people when they should change course. The old saying "winners never quit" often holds true, and not always for the best. Sometimes it's important for even the most successful people to quit doing something that isn't working.

These four success beliefs all filter through us and create in us something that we don't want to believe about ourselves. Our success delusion is actually a form of superstition.

"Who, me?" you say. "I'm an educated and logical person. I'm not superstitious!"

That may be true for childish superstitions such as bad luck ensuing from walking under a ladder, or breaking a mirror, or letting a black cat cross our path. Most of us scorn superstitions as silly beliefs of the primitive and uneducated. Deep down inside, we assure ourselves that we're above these silly notions.

Not so fast. To a degree, we're all superstitious. In many cases, the higher we climb the organizational totem pole, the more superstitious we become.

B.F. Skinner showed how hungry pigeons would repeat meaningless twitches when the twitches, by pure chance, were followed by random small pellets of food. In much the same way, successful leaders tend to repeat dysfunctional behavior when this behavior is followed by large pellets of money—even if the behavior has no connection with the results that led to the money.

Making the Necessary Changes

Now let's turn the spotlight on you, because few of us are immune to the success delusion. Pick one of your own quirky or unattractive behaviors, something that you know is annoying to friends, family, or co-workers. Now ask yourself: Do I continue to do this because I think it is somehow associated with the good things that have happened to me? Examine it more closely. Does this behavior help you achieve results—or is it one of those irrational, superstitious beliefs that have been controlling your life for years? The former is *because of* behavior, the latter *in spite of*.

Overcoming the success delusion requires vigilance and constantly asking, "Is this behavior a legitimate reason for my success, or am I just kidding myself?"

The first step in achieving positive change in behavior is to realize that it's hard for successful leaders to change, for all of the reasons I've mentioned. Realize that the same beliefs that have helped you get to where you are may be holding you back from where you want to go.

All of my personal coaching clients are either CEOs or people who have the potential to be CEOs in major corporations. I don't get paid if they don't achieve positive, measurable change—not as judged by themselves but, rather, as determined by their key stakeholders. These executives are brilliant people who have achieved amazing success and who want to get even better. Even with all of this motivation and ability, every one of my clients will verify that changing behavior may be simple, but it is far from easy.

How can you achieve positive change? Get in the habit of asking the key people in your life how you can improve. Recruit them in helping you get from where you are (which may be a pretty great place) to where you want to be (which can be even better). Realize that your first inclination when people point out your "areas for improvement" may well be to believe that they are simply mistaken. Accept the fact that your belief in your previous success—and your contribution to your team's success—is probably overstated.

Face the reality that you are likely to change only what you *choose* to change—and that the motivation and commitment to change must come from inside you. I have often heard Motorola CEO Ed Zander teach his high-potential leaders the value of encouraging participation, while also making clear that not every decision should be made by a vote or through achieving consensus. Leaders must make decisions. After listening to input from people you respect, work on only the changes that you believe are right for you and your organization.

Finally, watch out for over-commitment. Keep the change process positive, simple, focused, and fast. Realize that your natural inclination will be to think that you can do more than you actually will do. In the past, when I was young and idealistic, I suggested that leaders pick one to three areas for behavioral change. I now suggest that leaders focus on a single key behavior.

Ask the key people in your life how you can improve.

Keep on following up with the people whom you respect. One of my clients, Toyota Financial Services CEO George Borst, was very successful in changing the behavior that he picked for improvement: becoming a more effective coach. As we reviewed the positive results from his co-workers, he had a great realization: "If I am going to keep improving as a leader, I am going to have to be working on this stuff for the rest of my life—aren't I?"

As the wise older general noted, as you move up the ranks and get that star, don't let it go to your head. Realize that every promotion can make it harder to change. Always balance the confidence that got you where you are with the humility required to get you there—where you have the potential to go.

MARSHALL GOLDSMITH is co-founder of Marshall Goldsmith Partners, a network of top-level executive coaches; University Professor at Alliant International University's Marshall Goldsmith School of Management; and author or co-author of twenty-two books, most recently *What Got You Here Won't Get You There*, written with Mark Reiter.

Feeling Smart: The Science of Emotional Intelligence

A new idea in psychology has matured and shows promise of explaining how attending to emotions can help us in everyday life.

Daisy Grewal and Peter Salovey

Over the past decade almost everyone tuned in to American popular culture has heard the term *emotional intelligence*. As a new concept, emotional intelligence has been a hit: It has been the subject of several books, including a best seller, and myriad talk-show discussions and seminars for schools and organizations. Today you can hire a coach to help you raise your "EQ," your emotional quotient—or your child's.

Despite (or perhaps because of) its high public profile, emotional intelligence has attracted considerable scientific criticism. Some of the controversy arises from the fact that popular and scientific definitions of emotional intelligence differ sharply. In addition, measuring emotional intelligence has not been easy. Despite these difficulties, research on emotional intelligence has managed to sustain itself and in fact shows considerable promise as a serious line of scientific inquiry. It turns out that emotional intelligence can indeed be measured, as a set of mental abilities, and that doing so is an informative exercise that can help individuals understand the role of emotions in their everyday lives.

Ten years after the appearance of that bestselling book and a *TIME* magazine cover that asked "What's your EQ?" it seems sensible to ask what is known, scientifically, about emotional intelligence. In the history of modern psychology, the concept represents a stage in the evolution of our thinking about the relation between passion and reason and represents an important outgrowth of new theories of intelligence. Work in this subfield has produced a four-factor model of emotional intelligence that serves as a guide for empirical research. In this article we will explain ways of assessing emotional intelligence using ability-based tests and some of the findings that have resulted from this method.

Before "Emotional Intelligence"

Philosophers have debated the relation between thought and emotions for at least two millennia. The Stoics of ancient Greece and Rome believed emotion far too heated and unpredictable to be of much use to rational thought. Emotion was also strongly associated with women, in their view, and therefore representative of the weak, inferior aspects of humanity. The stereotype of women as the more "emotional" sex is one that persists today. Even though various romantic movements embraced emotion over the centuries, the Stoic view of emotions as more or less irrational persisted in one form or another well into the 20th century.

But many notions were upended during the rapid development of modern psychology in the 20th century. Setting the stage for a new way of thinking about emotions and thought, psychologists articulated broader definitions of intelligence and also new perspectives on the relation between feeling and thinking. As early as the 1930s, psychometrician Robert Thorndike mentioned the possibility that people might have a "social intelligence"—an ability to perceive their own and others' internal states, motivations and behaviors, and act accordingly. In 1934 David Wechsler, the psychologist whose name today attaches to two well-known intelligence tests, wrote about the "nonintellective" aspects of a person that contribute to overall intelligence. Thorndike's and Wechsler's statements were, however, speculations. Even though social intelligence seemed a definite possibility, Thorndike admitted that there existed little scientific evidence of its presence. A similar conclusion was reached by psychometric expert Lee Cronbach, who in 1960 declared that, after half a century of speculation, social intelligence remained "undefined and unmeasured."

But the 1980s brought a surge of new interest in expanding the definition of intelligence. In 1983 Howard Gardner of Harvard University became famous overnight when, in the book *Frames of Mind*, he outlined seven distinct forms of intelligence. Gardner proposed an "intrapersonal intelligence" very similar to the current conceptualization of emotional intelligence. "The core capacity at work here," he wrote, "is access to one's own feeling life—one's range of affects or emotions: the capacity instantly to effect discriminations among these feelings and, eventually, to label them, to enmesh them in symbolic codes, to draw upon them as a means of understanding and guiding one's behavior."

Is "emotional intelligence," then, simply a new name for social intelligence and other already-defined "intelligences"? We hope to clear up this thorny question by explaining just what we attempt to measure when assessing emotional intelligence. Certainly it can be seen as a type of social intelligence. But we prefer to explicitly focus on the processing of emotions and knowledge about emotion-related information and suggest that this constitutes its own form of intelligence. Social intelligence is very broadly defined, and partly for this reason the pertinent skills involved have remained elusive to scientists.

Emotional intelligence is a more focused concept. Dealing with emotions certainly has important implications for social relationships, but emotions also contribute to other aspects of life. Each of us has a need to set priorities, orient positively toward future endeavors and repair negative moods before they spiral into anxiety and depression. The concept of emotional intelligence isolates a specific set of skills embedded within the abilities that are broadly encompassed by the notion of social intelligence.

Emotion and Thinking

New understandings of the relation between thought and emotion have strengthened the scientific foundation of the study of emotional intelligence. Using a simple decision-making task, neurologist Antonio R. Damasio and his colleagues at the University of Iowa have provided convincing evidence that emotion and reason are essentially inseparable. When making decisions, people often focus on the logical pros and cons of the choices they face. However, Damasio has shown that without feelings, the decisions we make may not be in our best interest.

In the early 1990s Damasio had people participate in a gambling task in which the goal is to maximize profit on a loan of play money. Participants were instructed to select 100 cards, one at a time, from four different decks. The experimenter arranged the cards such that two of the decks provided larger payoffs ($100 compared to only $50) but also doled out larger penalties at unpredictable intervals. Players who chose from the higher-reward, higher risk decks lost a net of $250 every 10 cards; those choosing the $50 decks gained a net of $250 every 10 cards.

One group of participants in this study had been identified as having lesions to the ventromedial prefrontal cortex of the brain. Patients with this type of brain damage have normal intellectual function but are unable to use emotion in making decisions. The other group was normal, meaning that their brains were fully intact. Because there was no way for any of the players to calculate precisely which decks were riskier, they had to rely on their "gut" feelings to avoid losing money.

Damasio's group demonstrated that the brain-lesion patients failed to pay attention to these feelings (which he deems "somatic markers") and subsequently lost significantly more money than the normal participants. Therefore, defects in the brain that impair emotion and feeling detection can subsequently impair decision-making. Damasio concluded that "individuals make judgments not only by assessing the severity of outcomes, but also and primarily in terms of their emotional quality." This experiment demonstrates that emotions and thought processes are closely connected. Whatever notions we draw from our Stoic and Cartesian heritages, separating thinking and feeling is not necessarily more adaptive and may, in some cases, lead to disastrous consequences.

The Four-Branch Model

The term "emotional intelligence" was perhaps first used in an unpublished dissertation in 1986. One of us (Salovey), along with John D. Mayer of the University of New Hampshire, introduced it to scientific psychology in 1990, defining emotional intelligence as "the ability to monitor one's own and others' feelings, to discriminate among them, and to use this information to guide one's thinking and action."

Some critics have seen the concept of emotional intelligence as a mere outgrowth of the late-20th-century Zeitgeist—and indeed, as we reflect in the conclusion to this article, today the term has a vibrant pop-culture life of its own. But within psychology, the concept developed out of a growing emphasis on research on the interaction of emotion and thought. In the late 1970s psychologists conducted experiments that looked at a number of seemingly unrelated topics at the interface of feeling and thinking: the effect of depression on memory, the perception of emotion in facial expressions, the functional importance of regulating or expressing emotion.

Emotional intelligence is one of the concepts that emerged from this work. It integrates a number of the results into a related set of skills that can be measured and differentiated from personality and social skills; within psychology it can be defined as an intelligence because it is a quantifiable and indeed a measurable aspect of the individual's capacity to carry out abstract thought and to learn and adapt to the environment. Emotional intelligence can be shown to operate on emotional information in the same way that other types of intelligence might operate on a broken computer or what a photographer sees in her viewfinder.

Interested in helping the field of emotions develop a theory that would organize the numerous efforts to find individual difference in emotion-related processes, Salovey and Mayer proposed a four-branch model of emotional intelligence that emphasized four domains of related skills: (a) the ability to perceive emotions accurately; (b) the ability to use emotions to facilitate thinking and reasoning; (c) the ability to understand emotions, especially the language of emotions; and (d) the ability to manage emotions both in oneself and in others. This four-branch emotional intelligence model proposes that individuals differ in these skills and that these differences have consequences at home, school and work, and in social relations.

Perceiving and Using Emotions

The first domain of emotional intelligence, *perceiving emotions,* includes the abilities involved in identifying emotions in faces, voices, pictures, music and other stimuli. For example, the individual who excels at perceiving emotions can quickly tell when his friend is upset by accurately decoding his friend's facial expressions.

One might consider this the most basic skill involved in emotional intelligence because it makes all other processing of emotional information possible. In addition, our skill at reading faces is one of the attributes humans share across cultures. Paul Ekman of the University of California, San Francisco showed pictures of Americans expressing different emotions to a group of isolated New Guineans. He found that the New Guineans could recognize what emotions were being expressed in the photographs quite accurately, even though they had never encountered an American and had grown up in a completely different culture.

But emotion perception does vary across individuals. A study by Seth D. Pollak at the University of Wisconsin-Madison in 2000, for example, demonstrated that physical abuse might interfere with children's ability to adaptively perceive facial expressions.

Pollak asked abused and nonabused children, aged 8 to 10, to come into the laboratory to play "computer games." The children were shown digitally morphed faces that displayed emotional expressions that ranged from happy to fearful, happy to sad, angry to fearful, or angry to sad. In one of the games, the children were shown a single picture and asked to identify which emotion it expressed. Because all the faces expressed varying degrees of a certain emotion, the investigators were able to discover how the children perceived different facial expressions. They found that the abused children were more likely to categorize a face as angry, even when it showed only a slight amount of anger.

In addition, Pollak measured the brain activity of the children while completing this task using electrodes attached to their scalps. The abused children also exhibited more brain activity when viewing an angry face. This research shows that life experiences can strongly shape the recognition of facial expression. We can speculate that this difference in likelihood to perceive anger may have important consequences for the children's interactions with other people.

The second branch of emotional intelligence, *using emotions,* is the ability to harness emotional information to facilitate other cognitive activities. Certain moods may create mind-sets that are better suited for certain kinds of tasks.

In a clever experiment done during the 1980s, Alice Isen of Cornell University found that being in a happy mood helps people generate more creative solutions to problems. Isen brought undergraduates into the laboratory and induced either a positive mood (by showing them comedy clips) or a neutral mood (by showing them a short segment from a math film).

After watching one of the films, each student was seated at an individual table and given a book of matches, a box of tacks and a candle. Above the table was a corkboard. The students were given 10 minutes to provide a solution to the following challenge: how to affix the candle to the corkboard in such a way that it would burn without dripping wax onto the table. Those students who had watched the comedy films, and were therefore in a happier mood, were more likely to come up with

an adequate solution to the problem: They realized that the task can be easily accomplished by emptying the box, tacking it to the wall and using it as a platform for the candle. It appears that emotional intelligence can facilitate certain tasks; the emotionally intelligent person can utilize pleasant feelings most effectively.

Understanding and Managing Emotion

Mayer and Salovey classified the third and fourth branches of the emotional intelligence model as "strategic" (rather than "experiential") intelligence. The third branch, *understanding emotions,* is the ability to comprehend information about relations between emotions, transitions from one emotion to another, and to label emotions using emotion words. A person who is good at understanding emotions would have the ability to see differences between related emotions, such as between pride and joy. The same individual would also be able to recognize, for instance, that irritation can lead to rage if left unattended.

Boston College psychologist Lisa Feldman Barrett has demonstrated that the ability to differentiate one's emotional states has important implications for well-being. Feldman Barrett and her colleagues asked a group of 53 undergraduates to keep a daily diary of their emotions for two weeks. Specifically, they assessed the most intense emotional experience they had each day by rating the intensity of their experience of nine emotions, represented by words, on a scale from 0, *not at all,* to 4, *very much.* Four of the emotion words related to positive emotion (happiness, joy, enthusiasm, amusement); five related to negative emotion (nervous, angry, sad, ashamed, guilty).

Feldman Barrett and her colleagues then calculated the correlations between reported experiences of positive emotions and also looked at how correlated were reported experiences of negative emotions. A subject whose reports of positive emotions are highly correlated is perceiving less differentiation between positive states. Similarly, larger correlations between the reports of each negative emotion indicate less differentiation between negative states.

At the end of the study, all participants completed a questionnaire assessing the extent to which they engaged in various emotion-regulation strategies during the previous two weeks (for example, "talking to others"). Greater differentiation between positive emotional states had no effect on regulation strategies. But differentiation of negative states clearly did. That is, participants who were able to more specifically pinpoint *what* negative emotion they were feeling each day also engaged in more strategies for managing their emotions. This shows that the ability to distinguish and label emotions may represent an important skill in learning how to handle emotions successfully.

The fourth branch of emotional intelligence is the ability to manage one's emotions as well as the emotions of others. This skill of *managing emotions* is perhaps the most commonly identified aspect of emotional intelligence. Emotional intelligence is far more than simply being able to regulate bad moods effectively. It can also be important to maintain negative emotions when needed. For example, a speaker trying to persuade her audience of some injustice should have the ability to use her own outrage to stir others to action.

An example of how using different strategies for managing emotions can have different consequences is found in the work of James S. Gross of Stanford University, in experiments during the mid-1990s. Gross showed undergraduates video clips from medical procedures, such as amputation, that elicit disgust. The students were divided into three different groups. In the suppression condition, the students were instructed to hide their emotions during the film as much as possible by limiting their facial expressions. In the reappraisal condition, students were instructed to view the film as objectively as possible and to remain emotionally detached from what they were seeing. The third group was given no special instructions before viewing the film. All of the students' reactions to the films were recorded by video camera, and their physiological reactions, such as heart rate and skin conductance, were also measured. In addition, participants were asked to make self-reports of their feelings before, during and after watching the film.

The students in the suppression and reappraisal conditions had strikingly different experiences from watching the film. In the suppression condition, participants were able to successfully reduce the outward experience of their emotions by reducing their facial expressions and other behavioral reactions to the film. However, they showed heightened physiological arousal and reported feeling as much disgust as controls. The participants in the reappraisal condition reported lower levels of disgust upon watching the film while not displaying any heightened physical arousal (compared to controls). Gross's work demonstrates that there might be important, and sometimes hidden, physical costs for those individuals who chronically suppress expression of their negative emotions; nevertheless, monitoring and evaluating one's emotions may be strategically useful.

Measuring Emotional Intelligence

Any attribute being suggested as a form of intelligence must meet the standards of psychometrics, the field of psychological measurement. Scientists must be able to show that tests do not merely capture personality traits or information about other abilities. Three approaches to measuring emotional intelligence have been used: self-report tests, reports made by others and ability-based tests. Self-report tests were developed first and continue to be widely used, owing to the ease with which they can be administered and scored. Test-takers agree or disagree with items that attempt to capture various aspects of perceived emotional intelligence. For example, the popular Self-Report Emotional Intelligence Test (SREIT), authored by Nicola Schutte, asks respondents to rate how much they agree with such items as "I have control over my emotions," and "(other people find it easy to confide in me.)"

Reports made by others are commonly collected using "360" instruments. People who frequently interact with one another (such as friends and colleagues) are asked to rate one another's apparent degree of emotional intelligence. These instruments commonly contain items similar to those used in self-report tests, such as the statement "This person has control over his or her emotions."

Unfortunately, self-report tests assess self-estimates of attributes that often extend beyond definitions of emotional intelligence. They tend to incorporate facets of personality and character traditionally measured by existing personality tests.

Assessing emotional intelligence through self-report measures also presents the same dilemma one would face in trying to assess standard analytic intelligence by asking people, "Do you think you're smart?" Of course most people want to appear smart. Also, individuals may not have a good idea of their own strengths and weaknesses, especially in the domain of emotions. Similarly, although reports made by others seem more promising in providing accurate information, they are also highly vulnerable to biased viewpoints and subjective interpretations of behavior.

In an attempt to overcome these problems, the first ability-based measure of emotional intelligence was introduced in 1998 in the form of the Multi-factor Emotional Intelligence Scale (MEIS). An improved and professionally published version of the MEIS, from which problematic items were eliminated, was released in 2002 in the form of the Mayer-Salovey-Caruso Emotional Intelligence Test (MSCEIT, named for Mayer, Salovey and collaborator David R. Caruso of the EI Skills Group).

The MSCEIT consists of eight different tasks—two tasks devoted to each of the four branches of emotional intelligence. For example, the first branch, perceiving emotions, is tested by presenting participants with a photograph of a person and then asking them to rate the amount of sadness, happiness, fear etc. that they detect in the person's facial expression. Skill in using emotions is tested by having people indicate how helpful certain moods, such as boredom or happiness, would be for performing certain activities, such as planning a birthday party. The understanding-emotions portion of the test includes questions that ask participants to complete sentences testing their knowledge of emotion vocabulary and how emotions can progress from one to another. The test section addressing the fourth branch, managing emotions, presents participants with real-life scenarios. Participants are asked to choose, from several options, the best strategy for handling the emotions brought up in each scenario. After completing the MSCEIT, scores are generated for each of the four branches as well as an overall total score.

How Good Is the Test?

Marc A. Brackett of Yale University and Mayer calculated the extensive overlap between self-report tests of emotional intelligence and commonly used tests of personality. Many studies of personality are organized around The Big Five model of personality; they ask participants to self-rate how much they exhibit the following traits; neuroticism, extraversion, openness, agreeableness and conscientiousness.

Brackett and Mayer administered scales assessing The Big Five to a group of college students along with the MSCEIT and the SREIT. They found that scores on Big Five personality traits were more highly correlated with participants' scores on the SREIT than on the MSCEIT. The trait of "extraversion," for example, had a correlation of 0.37 with scores on the SREIT but only correlated 0.11 with scores on the MSCEIT. Therefore, it appears that self-report tests of emotional intelligence may offer limited information about a person above and beyond standard personality questionnaires.

The biggest problem one faces in trying to use an ability-based measure of emotional intelligence is how to determine correct answers. Unlike traditional intelligence tests, emotional intelligence tests can lack clear right or wrong solutions. There are dozens of ways one could handle many emotion-laden situations, so who should decide which is the emotionally intelligent way of doing things? Intrinsic to the four-branch model of emotional intelligence is the hypothesis that emotional skills cannot be separated from their social context. To use emotions in a useful way, one must be attuned to the social and cultural norms of the environment in which one interacts. Therefore, the model proposes that correct answers will depend highly upon agreement with others of one's own social group. Furthermore, experts on emotion research should also have the ability to identify correct answers, since scientific methods have provided us with good knowledge on correct alternatives to emotion-related problems.

Consequently, the MSCEIT is scored using two different methods: general consensus and expert scoring. In consensus scoring, an individual's answers are statistically compared with the answers that were provided by a diverse worldwide sample of 5,000 respondents aged 18 or older who completed the MSCEIT prior to May 2001. The sample is both educationally and ethnically diverse, with respondents from seven different countries including the United States.

In the consensus approach, greater statistical overlap with the sample's answers reflects higher emotional intelligence. In expert scoring, a person's answers are compared with those provided by a group of emotion experts, in this case 21 emotion investigators elected to the International Society for Research on Emotions (ISRE).

The amount of overlap between consensus and expert scoring has been carefully examined. Participants' responses have been scored first using the consensus method and then the expert method, and these results are then correlated with each other. The average correlation between the two sets of scores is greater than 0.90, indicating sizable overlap between the opinions of experts and the general consensus of test-takers. Laypeople and emotion experts, in other words, converge on the most "emotionally intelligent" answers. The scores of the experts tend to agree with one another more than do those of the consensus group, indicating that emotion experts are more likely to possess a shared social representation of what constitutes emotional intelligence.

The MSCEIT has demonstrated good reliability, meaning that scores tend to be consistent over time and that the test is internally consistent. In sum, given its modest overlap with commonly used tests of personality traits and analytic intelligence, the MSCEIT seems to test reliably for something that is distinct from both personality and IQ.

Putting Research to Work

Research on emotional intelligence has been put to practical use with unusual speed. The reason may be simple: Experiments suggest that scores on ability-based measures of emotional intelligence are associated with a number of important real-world outcomes.

Emotional intelligence may help one get along with peers and supervisors at work. Paulo N. Lopes of the University of Surrey in the United Kingdom spearheaded a study conducted at a Fortune 500 insurance company where employees worked in teams. Each team was asked to fill out surveys that asked individuals to rate other team members on personal descriptors related to emotions such as, "This person handles stress without getting too tense," or "This person is aware of the feelings of others."

Supervisors in the company were also asked to rate their subordinates on similar items. Everyone who participated in the study also took the MSCEIT. Although the sample of participants was small, employees who scored higher on the MSCEIT received more positive ratings from both their peers and their supervisors. Their peers reported having fewer conflicts with them, and they were perceived as creating a positive atmosphere at work. Supervisors rated their emotionally intelligent employees as more interpersonally sensitive, sociable, tolerant of stress and possessing more leadership potential. Higher scores were also positively associated with rank and salary in the company.

Emotional intelligence may also be important for creating and sustaining good relationships with peers. A different study conducted by Lopes and his collaborators asked German college students to keep diaries that described their everyday interactions with others over a two-week period. For every social interaction that lasted at least 10 minutes, students were asked to record the gender of the person they interacted with, how they felt about the interaction, how much they had wanted to make a certain impression, and to what extent they thought they succeeded in making that impression.

Scores on the using-emotions branch of the MSCEIT were positively related to how enjoyable and interesting students found their interactions to be, as well as how important and safe they felt during them. Scores on the managing-emotions branch seemed most important in interactions with the opposite sex. For these interactions, students scoring high on managing emotions reported more enjoyment, intimacy, interest, importance and respect. In addition, managing emotions was positively related to the students' beliefs that they had made the desired impression on their opposite-sex partners (coming across as friendly, say, or competent).

Brackett also investigated how scores on the MSCEIT relate to the quality of social relationships among college students. American college students completed the MSCEIT along with questionnaires assessing the quality of their friendships and their interpersonal skills, In addition, these students were asked to recruit two of their friends to evaluate the quality of their friendship. Individuals scoring high in managing emotions were rated as more caring and emotionally supportive by their friends. Scores on managing emotions were also negatively related to friends' reports of conflict with them. In another recent study by Nicole Lemer and Brackett, Yale students who scored higher in emotional intelligence were evaluated more positively by their roommates; that is, their roommates reported experiencing less conflict with them.

Emotional intelligence may also help people more successfully navigate their relationships with spouses and romantic partners. Another study headed by Brackett recruited 180 young couples (mean age 25 years) from the London area. The couples completed the MSCEIT and then filled out a variety of questionnaires asking about aspects of the couples' relationships, such as the quality of the interactions with their partners and how happy they were with the relationship. Happiness was correlated with high scores for both partners, and where one partner had a high score and the other a low score, satisfaction ratings tended to fall in the intermediate range.

The Future of Emotional Intelligence

Context plays an important role in shaping how these skills are put into action. We can all name people—certain notable politicians come to mind—who seem extremely talented in using their emotions in their professional lives while their personal lives seem in shambles. People may be more adept at using the skills of emotional intelligence in some situations than in others. A promising direction for future research is a focus on fluid skills rather than crystallized knowledge about emotions.

Although it has proved valuable so far as a test of general emotional intelligence, the MSCEIT requires refinement and improvement. We view the MEIS and the MSCEIT as the first in a potentially long line of improved ways of assessing emotional abilities.

We believe research on emotional intelligence will be especially valuable if focused on individual differences in emotional processes—a topic we hope will continue to generate more empirical interest. The science of emotion thus far has stressed principles of universality. Ekman's work on faces, mentioned above, and similar cross-cultural findings offer important insights into the nature of human emotional experience. However, in any given culture, people differ from one another in their abilities to interpret and use emotional information. Because individual deficits in emotional skills may lead to negative outcomes, anyone interested in improving emotional skills in various settings should focus on how and why some people, from childhood, are better at dealing with emotions than others. Such knowledge provides the hope of being able to successfully teach such skills to others.

The Popularization of "EQ"

Media interest in emotional intelligence was sparked by *New York Times* science writer Daniel Goleman's bestselling book *Emotional Intelligence* in 1995. In October of the same year came the *TIME* magazine cover and additional media coverage proclaiming emotional intelligence the new way to be smart and the best predictor of success in life.

The late 1990s provided the perfect cultural landscape for the appearance of emotional intelligence. The latest in a string of IQ controversies had broken out with the 1994 publication of *The Bell Curve,* which claimed that modern society has become increasingly stratified not by money, power or class, but by traditionally defined intelligence.

The Bell Curve was read as advocating a view that intelligence is the most important predictor of almost everything that seems to matter to most people: staying healthy, earning enough money, even having a successful marriage. Yet half the population, by definition, has below-average IQs; moreover, IQ is seen as difficult to change over one's lifespan. For many readers, *The Bell Curve* contained an extremely pessimistic message. As if to answer the growing fear that a relatively immutable IQ is the primary predictor of success in life, Goleman's book on emotional intelligence included the phrase, "Why it can matter more than IQ," right on the cover. The public responded favorably to this new promise, and the book soon became a staple on airport newsstands worldwide.

Skepticism over narrow definitions of the word "intelligence" resonated powerfully with a public that seemed to agree that something else—something more intangible—may more strongly determine the quality' of one's life. Evidence that the Scholastic Aptitude Test (SAT), which is highly correlated with IQ, fails to predict academic success especially well beyond the first year of college continued to fuel interest in how emotional skills, or something else beside traditional intelligence, may more significantly determine one's future accomplishments. Americans have always prided themselves on a strong work ethic; the motto that "slow and steady wins the race" represents an attitude that fits well with public conceptions of emotional intelligence as a mark of good character. Americans also have a strong collective self-image of equality, which popular views of emotional intelligence support by characterizing success as dependent on a set of skills that anyone can learn.

Goleman's book continues to be one of the most successful and influential of its genre, and other trade books concerned with emotional intelligence (or EQ, as it is referred to in the popular literature) have appeared in recent years. More than just a passing fad, or temporary backlash against standardized testing, emotional intelligence has captured the long-term interest of employers and educators. In just a few years, what started as a somewhat obscure area of science-driven research in psychology burgeoned into a multi-million-dollar industry marketing books, tapes, seminars and training programs aimed at increasing emotional intelligence.

Popularization has in some cases distorted the original scientific definition of emotional intelligence. Many people now equate emotional intelligence with almost everything desirable in a person's makeup that cannot be measured by an IQ test, such as character, motivation, confidence, mental stability, optimism and "people skills." Research has shown that emotional skills may contribute to some of these qualities, but most of them move far beyond skill-based emotional intelligence. We prefer to define emotional intelligence as a specific set of skills that can be used for either prosocial or antisocial purposes. The ability to accurately perceive how others are feeling may be used by a therapist to gauge how best to help her clients, whereas a con artist might use it to manipulate potential victims. Being emotionally intelligent does not necessarily make one an ethical person.

Although popular claims regarding emotional intelligence run far ahead of what research can reasonably support, the overall effects of the publicity have been more beneficial than harmful. The most positive aspect of this popularization is a new and much needed emphasis on emotion by employers, educators and others interested in promoting social welfare. The popularization of emotional intelligence has helped both the public and research psychology reevaluate the functionality of emotions and how they serve humans adaptively in every-day life. Although the continuing popular appeal of emotional intelligence is both warranted and desirable, we hope that such attention will stimulate a greater interest in the scientific and scholarly study of emotion. It is our hope that in coming decades, advances in cognitive and affective science will offer intertwining perspectives from which to study how people navigate their lives. Emotional intelligence, with its focus on both head and heart, may adequately serve to point us in the right direction.

Bibliography

Bechara, A., H. Damasio and A. R. Damasio. 2000. Emotion, decision making and the orbitofrontal cortex. *Cerebral Cortex* 10:295–307.

Brackett, M. A., and J. D. Mayer. 2003. Convergent, discriminant, and incremental validity of competing measures of emotional intelligence. *Personality and Social Psychology Bulletin* 29:1147–1158.

Daniasio, A. R. 1994. *Descartes' Error, Emotion, Reason, and the Human Brain.* New York: Putnam.

Ekman, P. 1980. *The Face of Man: Expressions of Universal Emotions in a New Guinea Village.* New York: Garland STPM Press.

Feldman Barrett, L., J. Gross, T. Christensen and M. Benvenuto. 2001. Knowing what you're feeling and knowing what to do about it: Mapping the relation between emotion differentiation and emotion regulation. *Cognition and Emotion* 15:713–724.

Gardner, H. 1983. *Frames of Mind.* New York: Basic Books.

Goleman, D. 1995. *Emotional Intelligence.* New York: Bantam Books.

Gross, J. J. 1998. Antecedent and response focused emotion regulation: Divergent consequences for experience, expression, and physiology, *Journal of Personality and Social Psychology* 74:224–237.

Isen, A. M., K. A. Daubman and C. P. Nowicki. 1987. Positive affect facilitates creative problem solving. *Journal of Personality and Social Psychology* 52:1122–1131.

Lopes, P. N., M. A. Brackett, J. Nezlck, A. Schutz, I. Sellin and P. Salovey. 2004. Emotional intelligence and social interaction. *Personality and Social Psychology Bulletin* 30:1018–1034.

Lopes, P. N., S. Côté, D. Grewal, J. Kadis, M. Gall and P. Salovey. Submitted. Evidence that emotional intelligence is related to job performance, interpersonal facilitation, affect and attitudes at work, and leadership potential.

Mayer, J. D., and P. Salovey. 1997. What is emotional intelligence? In *Emotional Development and Emotional Intelligence: Educational Implications,* ed. P. Salovey and D. Sluyter, pp. 3–31. New York: Basic Books.

Mayer, J. D., P. Salovey and D. Caruso. 2002. *The Mayer-Salovey-Caruso Emotional Intelligence Test (MSCEIT).* Toronto: Multi-Health Systems, Inc.

Mayer, J. D., P. Salovey, D. R. Caruso and G. Sitarenios. 2003. Measuring emotional intelligence with the MSCEIT V2.0. *Emotion* 3:97–105.

Pollak, S. D., and S. Tolley-Schell. 2003. Selective attention to facial emotion in physically abused children. *Journal of Abnormal Psychology* 22:323–338.

Salovey, P. and J. D. Mayer. 1990. Emotional intelligence. *Imagination, Cognition, and Personality* 9:185–211.

Salovey, P., J. D. Mayer and D. Caruso. 2002. The positive psychology of emotional intelligence. In *Handbook of Positive Psychology,* ed. C. R. Snyder and S. J. Lopez, pp. 159–171. New York: Oxford University Press.

DAISY GREWAL is a doctoral student in the social psychology program at Yale University. She received her B.A. in psychology from the University of California, Los Angeles in 2002 and her M.S. in psychology from Yale in 2004. Her research focuses on gender stereotypes and prejudice, particularly in organizational contexts. **PETER SALOVEY,** who earned his Ph.D. from Yale in 1986, is Dean of Yale College and Chris Argyris Professor of Psychology at Yale, where he directs the Health, Emotion, and Behavior Laboratory and holds additional professorships in management, epidemiology and public health, and social and political studies. His research emphases are the psychological significance and function of mood and emotion, and the application of principles from social and personality psychology to promoting healthy behavior. Address for Salovey: Yale University, Department of Psychology, 2 Hillhouse Avenue, New Haven, CT 06520-8205. Internet for both: daisy.grewal@yale.edu.peter.salovey@yale.edu

Ambition: Why Some People Are Most Likely to Succeed

A fire in the belly doesn't light itself. Does the spark of ambition lie in genes, family, culture—or even in your own hands? Science has answers.

JEFFREY KLUGER

You don't get as successful as Gregg Anddrew Shipp by accident. Shake hands with the 36-year-old fraternal twins who co-own the sprawling Hi Fi Personal Fitness club in Chicago, and it's clear you're in the presence of people who thrive on their drive. But that wasn't always the case. The twins' father founded the Jovan perfume company, a glamorous business that spun off the kinds of glamorous profits that made it possible for the Shipps to amble through high school, coast into college and never much worry about getting the rent paid or keeping the fridge filled. But before they graduated, their sense of drift began to trouble them. At about the same time, their father sold off the company, and with it went the cozy billets in adult life that had always served as an emotional backstop for the boys.

That did it. By the time they got out of school, both Shipps had entirely transformed themselves, changing from boys who might have grown up to live off the family's wealth to men consumed with going out and creating their own. "At this point," says Gregg, "I consider myself to be almost maniacally ambitious."

It shows. In 1998 the brothers went into the gym trade. They spotted a modest health club doing a modest business, bought out the owner and transformed the place into a luxury facility where private trainers could reserve space for top-dollar clients. In the years since, the company has outgrown one building, then another, and the brothers are about to move a third time. Gregg, a communications major at college, manages the club's clients, while Drew, a business major, oversees the more hardheaded chore of finance and expansion. "We're not sitting still," Drew says. "Even now that we're doing twice the business we did at our old place, there's a thirst that needs to be quenched."

Why is that? Why are some people born with a fire in the belly, while others—like the Shipps—need something to get their pilot light lit? And why do others never get the flame of ambition going? Is there a family anywhere that doesn't have its overachievers and underachievers—its Jimmy Carters and Billy Carters, its Jeb Bushes and Neil Bushes—and find itself wondering how they all could have come splashing out of exactly the same gene pool?

Of all the impulses in humanity's behavioral portfolio, ambition—that need to grab an ever bigger piece of the resource pie before someone else gets it—ought to be one of the most democratically distributed. Nature is a zero-sum game, after all. Every buffalo you kill for your family is one less for somebody else's; every acre of land you occupy elbows out somebody else. Given that, the need to get ahead ought to be hard-wired into all of us equally.

"For me, ambition has become a dirty word. I prefer hunger."

—Johnny Depp

And yet it's not. For every person consumed with the need to achieve, there's someone content to accept whatever life brings. For everyone who chooses the 80-hour workweek, there's someone punching out at 5. Men and women—so it's said—express ambition differently; so do Americans and Europeans, baby boomers and Gen Xers, the middle class and the well-to-do. Even among the manifestly motivated, there are degrees of ambition. Steve Wozniak co-founded Apple Computer and then left the company in 1985 as a 34-year-old multimillionaire. His partner, Steve Jobs, is still innovating at Apple and moonlighting at his second block-buster company, Pixar Animation Studios.

Not only do we struggle to understand why some people seem to have more ambition than others, but we can't even agree on just what ambition is. "Ambition is an evolutionary product," says anthropologist Edward Lowe at Soka University of America, in Aliso Viejo, Calif. "No matter how social status is defined, there are certain people in every community who aggressively pursue it and others who aren't so aggressive."

Dean Simonton, a psychologist at the University of California, Davis, who studies genius, creativity and eccentricity, believes it's more complicated than that. "Ambition is energy and determination," he says. "But it calls for goals too. People with goals but no energy are the ones who wind up sitting on the couch saying 'One day I'm going to build a better mousetrap.' People with energy but no clear goals just dissipate themselves in one desultory project after the next."

"Ambition is like love, impatient both of delays and rivals."

—Buddha

Assuming you've got drive, dreams and skill, is all ambition equal? Is the overworked lawyer on the partner track any more ambitious than the overworked parent on the mommy track? Is the successful musician to whom melody comes naturally more driven than the unsuccessful one who sweats out every note? We may listen to Mozart, but should we applaud Salieri?

Most troubling of all, what about when enough ambition becomes way too much? Grand dreams unmoored from morals are the stuff of tyrants—or at least of Enron. The 16-hour workday filled with high stress and at-the-desk meals is the stuff of burnout and heart attacks. Even among kids, too much ambition quickly starts to do real harm. In a just completed study, anthropologist Peter Demerath of Ohio State University surveyed 600 students at a high-achieving high school where most of the kids are triple-booked with advanced-placement courses, sports and after-school jobs. About 70% of them reported that they were starting to feel stress some or all of the time. "I asked one boy how his parents react to his workload, and he answered, 'I don't really get home that often,'" says Demerath. "Then he handed me his business card from the video store where he works."

Anthropologists, psychologists and others have begun looking more closely at these issues, seeking the roots of ambition in family, culture, gender, genes and more. They have by no means thrown the curtain all the way back, but they have begun to part it. "It's fundamentally human to be prestige conscious," says Soka's Lowe. "It's not enough just to be fed and housed. People want more."

If humans are an ambitious species, it's clear we're not the only one. Many animals are known to signal their ambitious tendencies almost from birth. Even before wolf pups are weaned, they begin sorting themselves out into alphas and all the others. The alphas are quicker, more curious, greedier for space, milk, Mom—and they stay that way for life. Alpha wolves wander widely, breed annually and may live to a geriatric 10 or 11 years old. Lower-ranking wolves enjoy none of these benefits—staying close to home, breeding rarely and usually dying before they're 4.

Humans often report the same kind of temperamental determinism. Families are full of stories of the inexhaustible infant who grew up to be an entrepreneur, the phlegmatic child who never really showed much go. But if it's genes that run the show, what accounts for the Shipps, who didn't bestir themselves until the cusp of adulthood? And what, more tellingly, explains identical twins—precise genetic templates of each other who ought to be temperamentally identical but often exhibit profound differences in the octane of their ambition?

Ongoing studies of identical twins have measured achievement motivation—lab language for ambition—in identical siblings separated at birth, and found that each twin's profile overlaps 30% to 50% of the other's. In genetic terms, that's an awful lot—"a benchmark for heritability," says geneticist Dean Hamer of the National Cancer Institute. But that still leaves a great deal that can be determined by experiences in infancy, subsequent upbringing and countless other imponderables.

Some of those variables may be found by studying the function of the brain. At Washington University, researchers have been conducting brain imaging to investigate a trait they call persistence—the ability to stay focused on a task until it's completed just so—which they consider one of the critical engines driving ambition.

The researchers recruited a sample group of students and gave each a questionnaire designed to measure persistence level. Then they presented the students with a task—identifying sets of pictures as either pleasant or unpleasant and taken either indoors or outdoors—while conducting magnetic resonance imaging of their brains. The nature of the task was unimportant, but how strongly the subjects felt about performing it well—and where in the brain that feeling was processed—could say a lot. In general, the researchers found that students who scored highest in persistence had the greatest activity in the limbic region, the area of the brain related to emotions and habits. "The correlation was .8 [or 80%]," says professor of psychiatry Robert Cloninger, one of the investigators. "That's as good as you can get."

It's impossible to say whether innate differences in the brain were driving the ambitious behavior or whether learned behavior was causing the limbic to light up. But a number of researchers believe it's possible for the nonambitious to jump-start their drive, provided the right jolt comes along. "Energy level may be genetic," says psychologist Simonton, "but a lot of times it's just." Simonton and others often cite the case of Franklin D. Roosevelt, who might not have been the same President he became—or even become President at all—had his disabling polio not taught him valuable lessons about patience and tenacity.

Is such an epiphany possible for all of us, or are some people immune to this kind of lightning? Are there individuals or whole groups for whom the amplitude of ambition is simply lower than it is for others? It's a question—sometimes a charge—that hangs at the edges of all discussions about gender and work, about whether women really have the meat-eating temperament to survive in the professional world. Both research findings and everyday experience suggest that women's ambitions express themselves differently from men's. The meaning of that difference is the hinge on which the arguments turn.

"Ambition makes you look pretty ugly."

—Radiohead

Economists Lise Vesterlund of the University of Pittsburgh and Muriel Niederle of Stanford University conducted a study in which they assembled 40 men and 40 women, gave them five minutes to add up as many two-digit numbers as they could, and paid them 50¢ for each correct answer. The subjects were not competing against one another but simply playing against the house. Later, the game was changed to a tournament in which the subjects were divided into teams of two men or two women each. Winning teams got $2 per computation; losers got nothing. Men and women performed equally in both tests, but on the third round, when asked to choose which of the two ways they wanted to play, only 35% of the women opted for the tournament format; 75% of the men did.

"Men and women just differ in their appetite for competition," says Vesterlund. "There seems to be a dislike for it among women and a preference among men."

"Ambition, old mankind, the immemorial weakness of the strong."

—Vita Sackville-West

To old-line employers of the old-boy school, this sounds like just one more reason to keep the glass ceiling polished. But other behavioral experts think Vesterlund's conclusions

go too far. They say it's not that women aren't ambitious enough to compete for what they want; it's that they're more selective about when they engage in competition; they're willing to get ahead at high cost but not at any cost. "Primate-wide, males are more directly competitive than females, and that makes sense," says Sarah Blaffer Hrdy, emeritus professor of anthropology at the University of California, Davis. "But that's not the same as saying women aren't innately competitive too."

As with so much viewed through the lens of anthropology, the roots of these differences lie in animal and human mating strategies. Males are built to go for quick, competitive reproductive hits and move on. Women are built for the it-takes-a-village life, in which they provide long-term care to a very few young and must sail them safely into an often hostile world. Among some of our evolutionary kin—baboons, macaques and other old-world monkeys—this can be especially tricky since young females inherit their mother's social rank. The mothers must thus operate the levers of society deftly so as to raise both their own position and, eventually, their daughters'. If you think that kind of ambition-by-proxy doesn't translate to humans, Hrdy argues, think again. "Just read an Edith Wharton novel about women in old New York competing for marriage potential for their daughters," she says.

Import such tendencies into the 21st century workplace, and you get women who are plenty able to compete ferociously but are inclined to do it in teams and to split the difference if they don't get everything they want. And mothers who appear to be unwilling to strive and quit the workplace altogether to go raise their kids? Hrdy believes they're competing for the most enduring stakes of all, putting aside their near-term goals to ensure the long-term success of their line. Robin Parker, 46, a campaign organizer who in 1980 was already on the presidential stump with Senator Edward Kennedy, was precisely the kind of lifetime pol who one day finds herself in the West Wing. But in 1992, at the very moment a President of her party was returning to the White House and she might have snagged a plum Washington job, she decamped from the capital, moved to Boston with her family and became a full-time mom to her two sons.

"Being out in the world became a lot less important to me," she says. "I used to worry about getting Presidents elected, and I'm still an incredibly ambitious person. But what I want to succeed at now is managing my family, raising my boys, helping my husband and the community. In 10 years, when the boys are launched, who knows what I'll be doing? But for now, I have my world."

But even if something as primal as the reproductive impulse wires you one way, it's possible for other things to rewire you completely. Two of the biggest influences on your level of ambition are the family that produced you and the culture that produced your family.

Donald Trump

Achievements

Before he ever uttered the words "You're fired," Trump developed more than 18 million sq. ft. of Manhattan real estate, naming most of it after himself.

Early Signs of Ambition

While in college, Donald read federal foreclosure listings for fun. It paid off: he bought his first housing project before he graduated.

Bill Clinton

Achievements

Former U.S. President, current global celebrity.

Early Signs of Ambition

At 16, he beat out some 1,000 other boys to win a mock state senate seat and a trip to Washington, where he knew "the action was." Once in the capital, he got himself into position to shake hands with his idol, President John F. Kennedy.

Oprah Winfrey

Achievements

Her $1 billion media empire includes movies, a magazine and her talk show, now in its 20th year.

Early Signs of Ambition

She could read at 2, and although she was just 5 when she started school, she insisted on being put in first grade. Her teacher relented. The next year young Oprah was skipped to third grade.

Tiger Woods

Achievements

At 21, he was the youngest golfer ever ranked No. 1 in the world. Now 29, he holds the record for most prize money won in a career—$56 million and counting.

Early Signs of Ambition

At 6, he listened to motivational tapes—"I will make my own destiny"—while practicing his swing in the mirror.

Martha Stewart

Achievements

The lifestyle guru rules an empire that includes one magazine, two TV shows, a satellite-radio deal, a shelf full of best sellers and a home-furnishings line at Kmart.

Early Signs of Ambition

As a grade-schooler, she organized and catered neighborhood birthday parties because, she says, the going rate of 50¢ an hr. for babysitting "wasn't quite enough money."

Vera Wang

Achievements

She turned one-of-a-kind wedding gowns into a $300 million fashion business.

Early Signs of Ambition

Although from a wealthy family, she spent her high school summers working as a sales clerk in a Manhattan boutique.

After college, she landed a job at *Vogue* magazine, where she put in seven-day workweeks, rose quickly and became a senior editor at 23.

Condoleezza Rice

Achievements

The current Secretary of State and former National Security Adviser was 38 when she became Stanford University's youngest, and first female, provost.

Early Signs of Ambition

A gifted child pianist who began studying at the Birmingham Conservatory at 10, the straight-A student became a competitive ice skater, rising at 4:30 A.M. to spend two hours at the rink before school and piano lessons.

Sean Combs

Achievements

Diddy, as he's now known, is a Grammy-winning performer and producer and a millionaire businessman with a restaurant, a clothing line and a marketing and ad agency.

Early Signs of Ambition

During his days at Howard University, he learned about business by doing: he sold term papers and tickets to dance parties he hosted.

Jennifer Lopez

Achievements

The former Fly Girl dancer has sold 40 million records, is the highest-paid Latina actress in Hollywood and has launched fashion and perfume lines.

Early Signs of Ambition

When she signed with Sony Music, she insisted on dealing with its chief, Tommy Mottola. She told him she wanted "the A treatment. I want everything top of the line."

Britney Spears

Achievements

Her first single and first four albums made their debut at No. 1. Since then she has sold 76 million records and amassed a $150 million fortune.

Early Signs of Ambition

Spears used to lock herself in the bathroom and sing to her dolls. After each number, she practiced smiling and blowing kisses to her toy audience.

Tom Cruise

Achievements

He's a movie superstar who gets $25 million a film, an accomplished actor with three Oscar nods and a gossip staple who has sold a zillion magazines.

Early Signs of Ambition

After his first role in a high school musical, he asked his family to give him 10 years to make it in show business. Within four, he was starring in the surprise hit film *Risky Business.*

There are no hard rules for the kinds of families that turn out the highest achievers. Most psychologists agree that parents who set tough but realistic challenges, applaud successes and go easy on failures produce kids with the greatest self-confidence.

What's harder for parents to control but has perhaps as great an effect is the level of privilege into which their kids are born. Just how wealth or poverty influences drive is difficult to predict. Grow up in a rich family, and you can inherit either the tools to achieve (think both Presidents Bush) or the indolence of the aristocrat. Grow up poor, and you can come away with either the motivation to strive (think Bill Clinton) or the inertia of the hopeless. On the whole, studies suggest it's the upper middle class that produces the greatest proportion of ambitious people—mostly because it also produces the greatest proportion of anxious people.

When measuring ambition, anthropologists divide families into four categories: poor, struggling but getting by, upper middle class, and rich. For members of the first two groups, who are fighting just to keep the electricity on and the phone bill paid, ambition is often a luxury. For the rich, it's often unnecessary. It's members of the upper middle class, reasonably safe economically but not so safe that a bad break couldn't spell catastrophe, who are most driven to improve their lot. "It's called status anxiety," says anthropologist Lowe, "and whether you're born to be concerned about it or not, you do develop it."

"Ambition is so powerful a passion in the human breast that however high we reach, we are never satisfied."

—Niccolo Machiavelli

But some societies make you more anxious than others. The U.S. has always been a me-first culture, as befits a nation that grew from a scattering of people on a fat saddle of continent where land was often given away. That have-it-all ethos persists today, even though the resource freebies are long since gone. Other countries—where the acreage is smaller and the pickings are slimmer—came of age differently, with the need to cooperate getting etched into the cultural DNA. The American model has produced wealth, but it has come at a price—with ambition sometimes turning back on the ambitious and consuming them whole.

The study of high-achieving high school students conducted by Ohio State's Demerath was noteworthy for more than the stress he found the students were suffering. It also revealed the lengths to which the kids and their parents were willing to go to gain an advantage over other suffering students. Cheating was common, and most students shrugged it off as only a minor problem. A number of parents—some of whose children carried a 4.0 average—sought to have their kids classified as special-education students, which would entitle them to extra time on standardized tests. "Kids develop their own moral code," says Demerath. "They have a keen sense of competing with others and are developing identities geared to that."

Demerath got very different results when he conducted research in a very different place—Papua, New Guinea. In the mid-1990s, he spent a year in a small village there, observing how the children learned. Usually, he found, they saw school as a noncompetitive place where it was important to succeed collectively and then move on. Succeeding at the expense of others was seen as a form of vanity that the New Guineans call "acting extra." Says Demerath: "This is an odd thing for them."

That makes tactical sense. In a country based on farming and fishing, you need to know that if you get sick and can't work your field or cast your net, someone else will do it for you. Putting on airs in the classroom is not the way to ensure that will happen.

Of course, once a collectivist not always a collectivist. Marcelo Suárez-Orozco, a professor of globalization and education at New York University, has been following 400 families that immigrated to the U.S. from Asia, Latin America and the Caribbean. Many hailed from villages where the American culture of competition is alien, but once they got here, they changed fast.

As a group, the immigrant children in his study are outperforming their U.S.-born peers. What's more, the adults are dramatically outperforming the immigrant families that came before them. "One hundred years ago, it took people two to three generations to achieve a middle-class standard of living," says Suárez-Orozco. "Today they're getting there within a generation."

So this is a good thing, right? Striving people come here to succeed—and do. While there are plenty of benefits that undeniably come with learning the ways of ambition, there are plenty of perils too—many a lot uglier than high school students cheating on the trig final.

Human history has always been writ in the blood of broken alliances, palace purges and strong people or nations beating up on weak ones—all in the service of someone's hunger for power There's a point at which you find an interesting kind of nerve circuitry between optimism and hubris," says Warren Bennis, a professor of business administration at the University of Southern California and the author of three books on leadership. "It becomes an arrogance or conceit, an inability to live without power."

While most ambitious people keep their secret Caesar tucked safely away, it can emerge surprisingly, even suddenly. Says Frans de Waal, a primatologist at the Yerkes Primate Center in Atlanta and the author of a new book, Our Inner Ape: "You can have a male chimp that is the most laid-back character, but one day he sees the chance to overthrow the leader and becomes a totally different male. I would say 90% of people would behave this way too. On an island with three people, they might become a little dictator."

But a yearning for supremacy can create its own set of problems. Heart attacks, ulcers and other stress-related ills are more common among high achievers—and that includes nonhuman achievers. The blood of alpha wolves routinely shows elevated levels of cortisol, the same stress hormone that is found in anxious humans. Alpha chimps even suffer ulcers and occasional heart attacks.

For these reasons, people and animals who have an appetite for becoming an alpha often settle contentedly into life as a beta. "The desire to be in a high position is universal," says de Waal. "But that trait has co-evolved with another skill—the skill to make the best of lower positions."

Humans not only make peace with their beta roles but they also make money from them. Among corporations, an increasingly well-rewarded portion of the workforce is made up of B players, managers and professionals somewhere below the top tier. They don't do the power lunching and ribbon cutting but instead perform the highly skilled, everyday work of making the company run. As skeptical shareholders look ever more askance at overpaid corporate A-listers, the B players are becoming more highly valued. It's an adaptation that serves the needs of both the corporation and the culture around it. "Everyone has ambition," says Lowe. "Societies have to provide alternative ways for people to achieve."

Ultimately, it's that very flexibility—that multiplicity of possible rewards—that makes dreaming big dreams and pursuing big goals worth all the bother. Ambition is an expensive impulse, one that requires an enormous investment of emotional capital. Like any investment, it can pay off in countless different kinds of coin. The trick, as any good speculator will tell you, is recognizing the riches when they come your way.

Eating into the Nation's Obesity Epidemic

Ann Conkle

"What product does the slogan 'Melts in your mouth, not in your hand' belong to?" Kelly Brownell challenged his listeners. They chuckled and shouted in unison "M&Ms." The audience hadn't expected a pop quiz when coming to hear Brownell's invited address, "Changing the American Diet: Real Change Requires Real Change," at the APS 18th Annual Convention. Next came "They're Grrreat!," "I'm lovin' it," "Break me off a piece of that . . . ," and finally "I go cuckoo for . . ." Of course, the audience knew every one. But they couldn't answer one question, what departments create the federal government's nutrition guidelines and, most importantly, what are they? "Well," answered Brownell, an APS Fellow from Yale University, "The real question is who has done your nutrition education? And most startlingly, who will do the nutrition education of your children? There's no question that the answer is the food industry."

With that, Brownell, who is among this year's *Time* 100, a list of people whose actions and ideas influence the world, began his introduction into the reality of nutrition in America. As the quiz shows, "little effort goes in on the government's part to show people how to eat in a healthy way." Meanwhile the food industry bombards us with messages about cheap, tasty processed foods, which are, of course, high in sugars and fats. People are broadly trained that fruits and vegetables are good for them, but many Americans also believe sugary cereals are part of a nutritious breakfast and any drink with fruit in its name is healthy.

Over the last few decades, America has experienced an "absolutely startling increase [in obesity]. Pandemic or epidemic is not overstating the situation." Some see this as a failure of personal responsibility, but evidence suggests that something larger in the environment is spurring this trend. There is no evidence to suggest that we are less responsible eaters than our grandparents. Studies of developing nations show that when packaged foods such as soft drinks and snack foods replace traditional diets, obesity increases. The obesity epidemic could feasibly have a genetic or biological basis, but then why has it happened so quickly and recently when the gene pool has not changed? Recent studies about the economy of food give some insight into the food landscape. Five factors influence food choice: accessibility, convenience, taste, promotion and cost. Unhealthy foods win out on all five. They are more accessible, more convenient, tastier, more heavily promoted and cheaper. No wonder we all eat so badly.

What Psychological Scientists Can Do

So, what roles can psychology play to alleviate this crisis? Many people jump to say that psychology could help with clinical interventions of the already obese, but sadly, the only treatment with impressive results for obesity is surgery, which is too costly and invasive to be a viable solution for treating the vast number of obese people in America today. Clinical treatments also ignore the larger public health issue. According to Brownell, treating obesity without looking at the broader health issues would be like treating lung cancer without addressing the fact that smoking causes lung cancer. "For every case we successfully treat," said Brownell, "thousands more are created because of the environment." According to him, a social movement against unhealthy eating, similar to the movement against tobacco, is the only way to improve the way America eats.

To be effective, psychologists must change their thinking and make novel connections with people outside their field. Researchers should also realize that they may have more influence than politicians because they are not caught in political messiness (some would say quagmire) between the government, the food industry, subsidies and giant agribusiness.

Brownell outlined several key research questions that psychologists will be instrumental in answering. In a broad sense, psychologists can investigate the behavioral economics of food—why do people make the eating decisions that they do?

Psychologists should investigate attitudes about food supply and processing. Over the last several decades, there was an increasing distance from food sources to our tables. Food moved from coming from the ground or an animal to coming from the super market or vending machine and is now often filled with ingredients whose names we can't pronounce and whose chemical effects are not completely understood. How does this affect consumption and health? In addition, Americans seem to have an ingrained "more for less is good" value when it comes to food, as has been dramatically exploited by the "supersize it" marketing campaigns at fast food restaurants and ballooning portion sizes (Super Big Gulp, anyone?). The quest for value clearly affects what and how much we eat.

A related issue is marketing. How does promotion affect food choice, particularly among children? As shown by the quiz at the beginning of the talk, food marketing is highly effective. We all know the jingles and take them with us all the way to the supermarket aisle. Brownell asks whether we can equate the food industry's kid friendly advertising (Ronald McDonald, Tony the Tiger, Toucan Sam, and others) to the cigarette industries' now infamous advertising campaigns aimed at children. This advertising could have life-long impacts on food choice.

Finally, can food be addictive? Clearly, most severely obese individuals have a toxic relationship with food. What causes the cravings and the inability to stop when one has gone from nourishing her or his body to killing it? How can this cycle be stopped? What about food enhanced with sweeteners? High fructose corn syrup may be metabolized differently than other foods, creating unforeseen effects on bodies as well as minds. Addiction research could change the whole political landscape by changing how we think about eating as a simple choice.

Brownell offered a challenge to the audience and the broader public with five action steps: foster a social movement for nutrition, emphasize strategic science, target frequent contributors to obesity (starting with soft drinks), transform the economics of food, and pressure politicians to change the way Americans are educated about nutrition. Maybe then we would know the answers to all the questions in Brownell's pop quiz.

A Nurturing Relationship

Mothers as Eating Role Models for Their Daughters

Recognizing that moms can have a huge impact on children's food habits goes a long way toward helping to break familial cycles of disordered eating behavior and dieting.

KINDY R. PEASLEE, RD

Confirming the reality of the previous dialogue, a recent *Teen People* magazine survey of 1,000 teens showed that 39% worry about weight. Many factors influence whether an adolescent will develop a positive or negative body image. When we look back in time at the evolution of the changing body shape and size of American women and girls, we see actresses' sizes decreasing and real women's sizes increasing. Regardless of the reason, the common trend points to a slenderizing standard of the female ideal. In a culture in which girls are bombarded with skinny, glossy, and superficial images, moms need to be a mirror their daughters can look into and see a reflection of understanding, reassurance, wisdom, and love.

The Biological Connection

Last September, I attended the Mother-Daughter Role Modeling Summit in New York City (www.mother-daughter.org/summit.html). This research presentation was organized to explore a mother's impact as a healthy behaviors role model for her daughter. Special guests included Joan Lunden, former cohost of ABC's *Good Morning America*, and her daughter. Both participate in a campaign to challenge mothers to pass on a new legacy of making better food and beverage choices, promoting positive self-esteem, and supporting physical activity to their daughters. The campaign aims to educate mothers about their influence in shaping their daughters' eating habits, dieting behaviors, and self-image.

As the first female role model, a mother's choice about what she eats and drinks impacts her daughter's choices and how she feels about her body. The mother-child bond is the first primary relationship we experience, and it powerfully impacts what we believe about ourselves. The evidence shows that, unintentionally, mothers often model both positive and negative behaviors.

Remember . . . Daughter See, Daughter Do . . .

"Mom, I am so fat! I look awful. I can't go to school today," my daughter, Kristin, pleaded.

"You are not fat. You look fine." I tried to answer calmly and confidently. We'd had this conversation before.

"I am fat. Look at my legs. I'd be fine if I could just cut my body off from the waist down. I feel awful," Kristin groaned. "Nothing I wear looks right. Isn't there a pill or something I can take to lose weight? I mean it. I can't go to school!"

Fear gripped my heart and stopped me dead in my tracks. I didn't know what to say. As a therapist, I was all too aware of the potential for eating disorders, as well as the epidemic of dieting among adolescent girls. "You are not fat, "I answered firmly.

"You just don't get it, Mom! You don't understand!" Kristin headed for her room, tears beginning to stream down her face.

"Maybe we can take an aerobics class together after school," I called after her, grasping at anything to turn the conversation in a more positive direction.

"I knew it!" Kristin cried harder. "You think I'm fat too!"

—Excerpt taken from the first chapter of *Mom, I Feel Fat! Becoming Your Daughter's Ally in Developing a Healthy Body Image*. Author Sharon Hersh shares a maddening moment that occurred with her daughter and planted a seed for her book.

"Mothers, especially, are very influential," says Debra Waterhouse, MPH, RD, presenter at the summit and author of *Outsmarting the Mother-Daughter Food Trap: How to Free*

Yourself From Dieting—and Pass on a Healthier Legacy to Your Daughter. Mothers "unknowingly pass the torch" to their daughters, says Waterhouse. She surveyed more than 100 mothers who had good and seemingly innocent food intentions toward feeding their preadolescent daughters, yet these good intentions still ultimately led to unhealthy eating behaviors for their daughters. Mothers were limiting junk food in their daughters' diets, putting them on low-fat diets, making sure no sweets were in the house, and not allowing for snacking between meals. Waterhouse discourages mothers from restricting their daughters' food intake, reminding them that daughters will react in one of two ways: rebelling and overeating when mom is not looking, or accepting and not eating at all when mom isn't looking.

"More mothers are dieting; more daughters are dieting. More mothers are disordered eaters; more daughters are disordered eaters. More mothers are overweight; more daughters are overweight. This sequence is not coincidental," says Waterhouse. She explains that if a mom is a disordered eater, she is more likely to try to control her daughter's eating, and her daughter is more likely to become a disordered eater and be overweight. However, if a mom is an intuitive eater, she is more likely to trust her daughter's eating decisions, and her daughter is more likely to become an instinctive eater and maintain a comfortable weight.

In her book, Waterhouse shares many mother and daughter examples. One is of a 26-year-old daughter who remembers, "My mother dieted every January and June, so I thought that it must be a normal part of womanhood to vow a 20 pound weight loss with each New Year's resolution and the same 20 pound loss with each presummer diet." Another daughter, aged 35, says, "My mother once told me that I had long, lovely legs and a short, fat waist. Twenty years later, I still like my legs but curse my waist each and every day." Once a mother's words are spoken, they are seldom forgotten. Perhaps your own mother's statements echo in your mind even now as an RD counseling others about nutrition and body image. Do any of these well-meaning comments sound familiar? "You're getting a little chunky, aren't you?" "Pull in your stomach and stand up straight. You'll look thinner." "Only wear dark colors. They will hide your fat." Or, "I want you to have a normal life, so please lose some weight."

The Legacy of Dieting

Every day, more than 56% of U.S. women are on diets. Parents, especially mothers, can do much to spare their children a lifelong struggle with eating and weight. In her counseling, author and therapist Sharon Hersh challenges moms to examine their own beliefs and prejudices about their weight and appearance. Her suggestion to mothers is to pull out photos of themselves at different ages. What photos are they drawn to? Why? Organize the photos chronologically. How has their body changed? When did they become aware of their body? When did they like their body or not like it? What was going on in their life then? Hersh believes that as a mother, it is important to communicate acceptance and respect to your own body regardless of weight,

which will reduce some pressure daughters may feel to change their bodies. Do not model or encourage dieting. Accept and talk about the fact that diets don't work and the dangers of altering one's body through dieting.

Moms preoccupied with dieting who try to influence their daughters' weight and eating habits may actually place them at risk for developing negative eating behaviors, such as the lack of response to internal cues to hunger and satiety.[1,2] Mothers who use pressure or coercive feeding strategies are more likely to have daughters who are picky eaters or at risk for obesity. Girls whose mothers criticize their eating habits or weight may develop lasting problems with body image and self-esteem. Restriction only cries out for self-indulgence.[3,4]

Yet, girls may still choose to diet even without a mother's dieting influence. Cheryl Rice, a nurse from upstate New York, was fortunate to grow up with a mother who didn't diet. However, she started dieting in high school and college and put pressure on herself to diet. Her mother never criticized her daughter's weight. Rice remembers that even her father never made negative comments on what she feels was her "chunky body type" growing up. It was only in later years, when her mom was in her 60s, that mother and daughter attended TOPS (Taking Pounds Off Sensibly) weight loss classes.

Role Modeling

"In order for role modeling to occur, the child must observe the model's behavior, have the ability to perform the behavior, and be motivated to perform the behavior," says Leann Birch, PhD, director of the Center for Childhood Obesity Research at Penn State University and one of the research presenters at the summit. "Same-sex models are more likely to be imitated. Mothers are more influential than fathers on their daughters." Mothers are strong influencers because they still have the primary responsibility for making food available in a family and providing food experiences for a baby during pregnancy and breast-feeding.

Mothers also play a role in modeling physical activity to their daughters. "Being a soccer mom isn't confined to a minivan: Moms can play or coach," says Christina Economos, PhD, assistant professor and New Balance Chair in Childhood Nutrition at the Friedman School of Nutrition Science and Policy at Tufts University. Economos, who presented research on physical activity topics at the summit, says that by modeling and engaging in the activity themselves, mothers with high levels of healthy activity were less overweight than mothers with lower levels of activity. The percentage of highly active girls was significantly higher when at least one parent provided physical activity support.[5] Recommendations from the American Academy of Pediatrics encourage parents to become good role models by increasing their own level of physical activity and incorporating an activity that family members of all ages and abilities can do together— not only daughters.[6]

As far as positive role modeling with eating behaviors, moms with a higher fruit and vegetable intake have daughters who consume more fruits and vegetables. Family meals provide opportunities for children to observe parental fruit and

For Your Clients: Top 10 Do's and Don'ts for Moms

Do's

1. **Appreciate your body.** If you appreciate your body, your daughter will learn to appreciate hers as well. Focus on your favorite features instead of complaining about what's less desirable.
2. **Consume a variety of fruits, vegetables, lean meats, low-fat milk, and whole grains daily.** Studies show that mothers who model healthy eating habits, such as drinking milk, are more likely to have daughters who do. If you want your daughter to fill her glass with milk instead of soda, you need to do the same.
3. **Serve milk at every meal.** Studies indicate that teens who drink milk instead of sugary sodas tend to weigh less and have less body fat. Drinking three glasses of low-fat milk per day is a healthy habit to promote strong bones and a lean, toned body.
4. **Be physically active and enjoy it.** Mothers who value the importance of exercise positively influence an active lifestyle in their daughters. Studies show that inactive mothers tend to have inactive daughters.
5. **Eat family meals at home.** Sharing meals together at home provides multiple opportunities for you to model healthy behaviors. Your own food and beverage choices may be more influential than any other attempt you make to control what your daughter eats and drinks.

Don'ts

1. **Do not criticize your daughter's body.** Compliment her positive attributes and teach by example. Research suggests that girls whose mothers criticize their eating habits or weight may develop lasting problems with body image and self-esteem.
2. **Do not be self-critical.** Studies have found a mother's concern about her own weight, dieting practices, and overeating are transmitted to her daughter. Mothers may unknowingly pass on poor body image and weight worries to their daughters.
3. **Do not let sugary beverages dominate.** Soft drinks and sugary fruit drinks are the No. 1 source of calories in a teen's diet. Plus, they're void of the vital nutrients your daughter needs. If you limit your intake, your daughter will likely do the same.
4. **Do not talk about your dieting.** Instead of talking about dieting around your daughter, educate her on foods that provide important nutrients she needs for building strong bones and a healthy body.
5. **Do not use pressure.** Pressuring your daughter to eat certain foods will likely backfire. Research suggests that modeling the desired behavior is a more effective approach for encouraging healthy choices.

—Source: www.mother-daughter.org/dos_donts.html

RDs as Role Models

- Educate mothers on the impact they have in shaping their daughters' eating habits, dieting behaviors, and self-image.
- Council parents about the importance of family meals at home and eating the foods and drinking the beverages they want their children to consume.
- Educate adolescent girls on the dangers of unhealthy dieting, the unrealistic thin ideal, and the realities of maturing female bodies.
- Discourage mothers from using pressure or restrictive feeding practices with their daughters. Encourage a role model approach, making healthful foods available.
- Ensure that parents are involved in childhood obesity prevention and treatment programs.
- Emphasize the importance of teachers, coaches, and principals to serve as positive role models for students and incorporate body image, self-esteem, and eating disorder prevention into health curricula.

vegetable consumption. When fruits and vegetables are available at home and adolescents are involved in meal preparation, they have lower intakes of fat and higher intakes of fruits, vegetables, folate, and vitamin A. Interestingly, mothers who pressure their daughters to eat are more likely to have picky eaters who consume significantly fewer fruits and vegetables than nonpicky eaters.[7,8]

Tamara Vitale, MS, RD, a department of nutrition and food sciences professor at Utah State University, raised two daughters (now aged 27 and 31) and taught them that healthy food doesn't taste bad. Both daughters say they still remember their mom teaching them how easy it is to make roasted vegetables and other fresh foods from scratch, which taste better than convenience foods. Even though most of their friends thought vegetables were gross, they remember always having vegetables on their plates—to them, eating vegetables wasn't a big deal. Vitale says both are now excellent cooks, at healthy weights, and one daughter is now passing the legacy of healthy eating onto her 11-month-old son, who eats a wide variety of healthy whole foods.

Vitale's older daughter, a vegetarian since the age of 12, says she remembers, "My mom told me that I could be a vegetarian as long as I figured out how to get protein, etc, from other foods; that empowered me to understand about food choices." Vitale says that now, whenever her daughters come home for a visit, they request a "10-a-day meal" (meaning lots of vegetables).

In our diet-crazed culture, this inspiring story about daughters experiencing healthy role modeling shows how children's balanced mealtime experience will affect their food choices for the rest of their lives. The rewards of knowing you are teaching your daughters how to eat for enjoyment is a true legacy to leave. We can be the next generation of women to be aware of our spoken and unspoken influence and, as mothers, be motivated to become healthier role models for our daughters.

As dietitians, let's continue to live and teach a nondiet lifestyle and stop the dieting mentality. Daughters also have a role to play and can help and encourage their mothers to live a diet-free life. Let's be the women who leave a new legacy for our daughters by ending the negative link between mothers, daughters, and dieting to bring about a healthier generation of daughters.

Resources
Web Sites
Finding Balance

Check out a newly launched video-on-demand resource Web site for eating and body image issues. www.findingbalance.com

F.I.T. Decisions

F.I.T. (Future Identity of Teens) hosts Girls Only!, a weekend conference for teenage girls to teach them how to live healthful, balanced lives. Nationally known speakers, drama skits, fashion shows, kick boxing, and snacks are part of the all-day workshop. www.fitdecisions.org

HUGS International, Inc.

HUGS for Better Health Web site features resources on how to build a nondiet lifestyle. www.hugs.com

Remuda Ranch

Remuda Ranch is an eating disorder treatment center devoted to the unique needs of women and girls and integrates specialized therapies such as art, equine, body image, and movement program components as part of the recovery treatment. www.remudaranch.com

Books

Brumberg JJ. *The Body Project: An Intimate History of American Girls.* New York: Random House; 1997.

Gaesser G. *Big Fat Lies: The Truth About Your Weight and Your Health.* Carlsbad, Calif.: Gürze; 2002.

Hersh S. *Mom, I Feel Fat! Becoming Your Daughter's Ally in Developing a Healthy Body Image.* Colorado Springs, Colo.: Waterbrook Press; 2001.

Hutchinson MG. *200 Ways to Love the Body You Have.* Freedom, Calif.: Crossing Press; 1999.

Jantz GL. *Hope, Help & Healing for Eating Disorders: A New Approach to Treating Anorexia, Bulimia, and Overeating.* Colorado Springs, Colo.: Waterbrook Press; 2002.

Rhodes C. *Life Inside the 'Thin' Cage: A Personal Look into the Hidden World of the Chronic Dieter.* Colorado Springs, Colo.: Waterbrook Press; 2003.

Tribole E, Resch E. *Intuitive Eating: A Recovery Book for the Chronic Dieter.* New York: St. Martin's Press; 1996.

KINDY R. PEASLEE, RD, is the founder of Kindy Creek Promotions, an upstate New York-based marketing firm specializing in the promotion of natural and organic food and beverage products. She can be reached at kindy@kindycreek.com. Visit her recipe Web site for parents: www.healthy-kid-recipes.com

For references, view article on our archive at www.TodaysDietitian.com.

Why So Mad?

Why Everyone Is So Angry and Why We Must Calm Down

ANDREW SANTELLA

You are better than this.
 You are not a hostile person, not a picker of fights. You're a Boy Scout troop leader, Friend of the Library, PTA volunteer. Last year, you even called in and donated money during a National Public Radio fund drive.

And yet you have these moments when the worst parts of your nature come to the fore. Moments when the world seems to be conspiring against you and the frustration builds inside you and the frustration turns to rage.

This morning, for example, you were running late for an 8:30 meeting and you just wanted to get your latte and bagel from Starbucks and run. Of course the guy in front of you in line had to spend 10 minutes talking to the woman behind the counter about that most fascinating of topics, the weather. You're ashamed to admit it now, but you were on the verge of balling up your $10 bill, throwing it across the counter, and screaming for service.

Actually, the whole day has been a little like this. At work, you had a tense exchange with your boss about what he called "peculiarities" in your expense account.

Then, on your way home, as you were inching toward a tollbooth on 294, it happened again. You had 20 minutes to get home, pick up your daughter, and drive her over to her dance lessons. No chance, right? The traffic was going nowhere when suddenly, thank God, another lane opened up. You went for it. So did the guy in your blind spot. A Hummer, cutting right across your bow like you weren't even there. And off you went, laying on the horn, screaming some embarrassingly unoriginal obscenities, spittle flying, face contorted. If you could have caught a peek of yourself in the rearview at that moment, you would have seen a person who appeared utterly insane.

Here's the thing—and maybe you'll find this comforting or maybe you'll find it frightening. There are a lot of you out there.

Rage seems to be all the rage lately. Look around; it's not difficult to conclude that the world is getting angrier and angrier. Our politics are angry, dominated by Bush-haters and Clinton-haters and even Nader-haters. Our popular music is angry, spiked with misogynistic rants and paranoid fantasies. Our highways run like rivers of anger. As Peter Wood points out in his book *A Bee in the Mouth: Anger in America Now* (Encounter, 2007), automakers are even making angrier-looking cars, with grills that seem to snarl at whatever gets in their way.

Are we really that angry? It's not an easy question to answer. There simply aren't a lot of practical ways to measure how pissed off people are. Judging by the space on the nation's bookshelves taken up by books about anger, we seem to be living in a golden age of Wrath Lit. You can find books about the perils of anger, books about how anger can work for you, and books that relate personal battles with rage.

Does this Wrath Lit explosion indicate a growing level of anger in the world or just a greater interest in the topic? Are we really angrier or just trying harder than ever to understand our anger? For that matter, is there more anger being released into our world or are our cameraphones just capturing more episodes of angry behavior and websites such as YouTube making them more accessible?

> **It's not just that people have such fury, it's that they are so proud of their rage, so eager to broadcast it, so determined to assert their rage as a badge of their identity. I'm pissed off, therefore I matter.**

"Have rates of public rage from seemingly normal people gone up, or has our awareness of it gone up?" Colorado State University psychologist Jerry Deffenbacher asks. "We don't know. But there are a lot of angry people out there."

Not even episodes of road rage are easy to quantify. In 1997 the American Automobile Association Foundation for Traffic Safety released a study that detailed an increase in road rage incidents of as much as 7 percent each year since 1990. Media outlets, already awash in trend stories about the road rage phenomenon, reported the study widely. *USA Today* described "an 'epidemic' of aggressive driving."

Then a piece by Michael Fumento in the *Atlantic Monthly* punched holes in the AAA study, arguing that any increase in reported incidents of road rage was the result of increased awareness. The newly coined road rage label had become a convenient way to describe episodes that might not have been reported at all in the past. The article quoted one researcher saying, "You get an epidemic by the mere coining of a term."

Barry Glassner, in his book *The Culture of Fear* (Basic, 2000), asked why journalists became so interested in the road rage "epidemic," when—even using AAA's numbers—angry drivers accounted for no more than one in a thousand roadway deaths between 1990 and 1997.

If measuring road rage is problematic, what about violent crime? Surely statistics on assaults, batteries, and murders would help measure a welling of anger in the world. Here, too, there is a problem. As Deffenbacher points out, violent crime figures seem to be going down.

Even though taking stock of our rage on the road and our angry assaults on others proves frustrating, it is possible to quantify one particular kind of anger epidemic, directed at one particular kind of victim. Call it Vending Machine Madness. A 1988 article in the *Journal of the American Medical Association* reported 15 serious injuries, three fatal, as a result of irate men rocking vending machines that had taken their money without giving them snacks.

How did it come to this? It's the kind of question that comes to you as you sit in your car in line at the tollbooth once you have emerged from your meltdown and regained some self-control. Is there something in the way we live our lives—maybe the frantic pace we set, maybe our relentless emphasis on personal fulfillment—that is bringing our rage to the surface? Or is it, as Wood suggests, that we have made a virtue of expressing our anger, so appearing pissed off, defiant, and aggressive is all just part of being authentic, keeping it real? Or, as Glassner argues, do Americans just have a knack for pessimistic panic-mongering so that we see crises wherever we look?

Certainly you've never thought you might need help. You are familiar with the anger management industry that has sprung up to provide that help, but the whole process makes too easy a target for it to be taken seriously. After all, you've seen the Adam Sandler–Jack Nicholson comedy *Anger Management.*

Then you remember to think about spouses trapped in angry, maybe violent, marriages, about kids being warped by a parent's misplaced rage. Ask one of them if the world is getting angrier or if they might not welcome some help for the scariest people in their worlds.

If that's a little too much for you, just ask one of those poor mopes lying flattened under a snack machine.

As one of the seven deadly sins, anger holds an exalted place but is a bit of a misfit in the group. It is the only one of the seven that doesn't pay off in our self-interest.

For people who have never been unusually prone to anger, that makes the emotion difficult to understand. There's no obvious payoff to a fit of anger. Only an outburst, hurt feelings, or, worse yet, violence. Hardly ever any real resolution to the problem that started the whole thing. Where's the temptation in that?

Lust we can understand. Gluttony we can understand. They may be wrong and hurtful, but we can acknowledge that it's sometimes hard to ignore that extra slice of pizza, hard to say no to the noontime quickie.

In *The Enigma of Anger* (Jossey-Bass, 2002), Garret Keizer writes that his anger "has more often distressed those I love and who love me than it has afflicted those at whom I was angry."

Knowing that anger doesn't always pay doesn't necessarily make it easier to control, which may help explain why anger is so prominent in our lives. The Christian religious tradition centers on a God who, when provoked, turned people to salt, drowned entire armies, and sent floods and pestilence as tokens of his wrath. The most famous episode of anger in the New Testament is Jesus lashing out at the money changers in the temple. It might be the most modern scene in the Gospels.

We're also deeply suspicious of our anger. The Romans preached self-control, and Renaissance essayist Michel de Montaigne advised marshaling anger and using it wisely. He urged people to "husband their anger and not expend it at random for that impedes its effect and weight. Heedless and continual scolding becomes a habit and makes everyone discount it."

That advice recognizes one of the paradoxes of anger: It's often destructive, it's often a waste, but every once in a while it works. It can fuel our drive to achieve, help us maintain our self-respect, stop the world from walking all over us.

The trick, apparently, is getting angry at the right times and not getting angry at the wrong ones. Sounds easy, right? Mark Twain suggested this: "When angry, count to four. When very angry, swear."

Wood, in *A Bee in the Mouth,* argues that one of the most telling signs of a national problem with anger is the hostile tone of our political discourse. He calls it a new style of anger. "For the first time in our political history," Wood writes, "declaring absolute hatred for one's opponent has become a sign not of sad excess, but of good character." As an example of political discourse that delights in its own vitriol, he cites Jonathan Chait's 2003 essay in the *New Republic,* which begins, "I hate President George W. Bush." Such language is typical of what Wood calls our "angriculture." It's not just that people have such fury, Wood argues, it's that they are so proud of their rage, so eager to broadcast it, so determined to assert their rage as a badge of their identity. I'm pissed off, therefore I matter.

Wood recognizes the vein of anger that has always run through American history, but he may not do full justice to the venom and the power of historical fury. Contemporary wrathmongers like Ann Coulter are loud and all too visible. But compare her to self-appointed avenger Preston Brooks, the South Carolinian who took a cane to Massachusetts senator Charles Sumner on the Senate floor in 1856. Clearly, extreme fury is nothing new in American politics.

The *Journal of the American Medical Association* reported 15 serious injuries, three fatal, as a result of irate men rocking vending machines that had taken their money without giving them snacks.

Often it changed our world for the better. American history owes a great deal to the motivational power of wrath. The abolition movement was largely fueled by rage, and so was the women's suffrage movement.

The abortion clinic bombers and schoolhouse shooters of recent decades may be the most violent examples of contemporary American rage. But don't forget strident bloggers, finger-pointing cable-news hosts, brawling professional athletes, bullying grade schoolers, and those Little League parents who go after umpires, veins bulging. It's likely that more often than not, anger plays itself out on the home front. The wife-beaters and screamers-at-kids are probably doing more damage with their anger than any of the more visibly angry people. Once you start looking for anger, you see it everywhere.

Then again, maybe we're not angry enough. Given war, environmental crisis, and economic injustice, maybe we should be out in the streets in force, demanding change. *New York Times* columnist Bob Herbert recently declared that the "anger quotient is much too low."

Too angry? Not angry enough? Not one of the sources I consulted suggested that we, as a society, have arrived at precisely the appropriate level of anger for our circumstances. Like perfect happiness, this "anger quotient" must be an elusive target.

So is there any hope for you and your anger? Is there any reason to believe that someday you will be able to survive the afternoon commute without screaming or tailgating or displaying choice fingers?

One option, of course, is to seek out some help with anger management. The very phrase has become such a familiar part of our lives—how often does a day pass without hearing of some offender being sentenced to attend anger management sessions?—that it's easy to forget that it is a relatively recent coinage. Raymond W. Novaco may have been the first to use the term, in his seminal 1975 work *Anger Control* (Lexington), but the term didn't begin appearing in the popular media until well into the 1980s.

Anger is often destructive, it's often a waste, but every once in a while it works.

One of the first and most influential popular books on anger was Carol Tavris' 1982 *Anger: The Misunderstood Emotion* (Simon & Schuster). Her book was a response to the then-popular "ventilationist" strategies that suggested that loudly articulating our anger would free us emotionally. Tavris insisted on a more subtle and complex approach to anger, one that even acknowledged its constructive aspects.

"I have watched people use anger, in the name of emotional liberation, to erode affection and trust, whittle away their spirits in bitterness and revenge, diminish their dignity in years of spiteful hatred," she wrote. "And I watch with admiration those who use anger to probe for truth, who challenge and change the complacent injustices of life."

Two decades later, researchers were still probing for the constructive aspects of anger. A January 2000 article in the journal *Health Psychology* suggested that calmly discussing angry feelings and working toward solutions with others can have health benefits. But the emphasis, the researchers pointed out, must be on solving problems, not merely venting feelings.

Anger management specialists usually work from a menu of strategies that include everything from deep-breathing exercises to muscle relaxation techniques to visualization exercises that help people regain their calm. Other interventions stress cognitive approaches that aim to change unhelpful patterns of thinking. And there are, as always, pharmaceutical options. Emil Coccaro, chair of psychiatry at the University of Chicago, has explored using Prozac to treat explosively angry people.

Psychologist Deffenbacher urges, among other things, using humor to defuse anger. The idea is that the next time you find yourself tempted to call someone a dumbass, you can merely picture that person as, say, a burro wearing a dunce cap. The image might be amusing enough to get you through your angry moment.

Whatever successes anger management professionals can claim, they are clearly dealing with new realities that make it all too easy to vent rage. John Duffy, a Chicago-area psychologist and life coach, says many of the teenagers he works with use text messaging and social networking sites such as MySpace to lash out at classmates or authority figures who have crossed them. This spring the *New York Times* reported on the popularity among high school students of "hit lists"—sometimes posted online, sometimes scrawled on a school wall—of people an angry student would like to harm. Part of the appeal is being able to spew bitter thoughts at targets without having to confront them and deal with them as human presences. Just as road ragers may find it easier to flip someone off when the gesture is mediated by a windshield, information technologies allow us to vent at a digital remove.

Anger has been called a sin. It has been called an emotion. Former secretary of state Alexander Haig once called it a "management vehicle."

One thing anger cannot be called, not yet anyway, is a mental disorder. *The Diagnostic and Statistical Manual of Mental Disorders*, psychiatry's official guidebook to mental illness, offers multiple varieties of depressions, anxieties, and phobias, but no specific category of disorders for which anger is the defining characteristic. The closest it comes is a mention of intermittent explosive disorder, which is marked by "aggressive impulses that result in serious assaultive acts" in which the aggressiveness "is grossly out of proportion" to the immediate provocation.

Anger experts want more. "We need probably a half-dozen anger disorders," says Deffenbacher. Such an array, he argues, would help legitimize the study of anger, and help researchers to understand it better and doctors to improve their interventions.

Not everyone agrees. Some people argue that making anger a disorder would give domestic abusers a get-out-of-jail-free card, allowing them to plead that they were at the mercy of an illness when they lashed out. Others simply object to the idea of labeling more and more behaviors as disorders, which they say only feeds the therapeutic and pharmaceutical industries.

Deffenbacher and other specialists in anger, however, say that recognizing dysfunctional anger as a disorder would help more troubled people recognize their problems and seek help. That argument should not be dismissed too easily. For most angry people, the real problem is not their anger. The problem is the endless series of people and things that keep provoking their anger. "Want me to stop being angry?" the angry guy asks. "Then tell the world to leave me alone."

Even the most patient of us can put together a long list of things that piss us off in the course of a day. What does it for you? People who fail to say "excuse me" when they run over your foot with their baby stroller? Drivers who drift across your lane when they make a left-hand turn in front of you? Bellicose vice presidents of the United States? Litterers who toss cigarette butts and Big Gulp cups out of car windows? Movie theater talkers? Cell phone loudmouths? E-mail nonresponders? Wiseass journalists?

What if they could all be convinced to disappear? What if all the things that pushed your buttons just went away? You're a decent person. At the core, your nature is good. Remember how you stayed late to clean up after the book group meeting last week, even though it wasn't your turn? If you could just avoid the jerks, the rude bastards, how much calmer would you be?

In *The Enigma of Anger*, Keizer writes about Abbot Ammonas, who lived in the fourth century as a hermit in a remote and desolate region of Egypt. Keizer points out that Ammonas, while doing his monkly spiritual exercises, never ceased praying to be delivered from his anger. Which raises the question: What exactly does a hermit have to get angry about?

Ammonas, whatever hardships he had to endure in the desert, was spared "Dixie" ringtones, telemarketers, and traffic jams. He was spared Bill O'Reilly. Yet he continued to struggle with his anger.

Maybe Ammonas' problem was that he was left, in the end, with the one thing that not even you—well-meaning and kindhearted as you are—can escape.

Your own angry self.

ANDREW SANTELLA (www.andrewsantella.com) has written for the *New York Times Book Review, Slate,* and *GQ*. Reprinted from *Notre Dame* (Summer 2007), a quarterly magazine produced by the University of Notre Dame.

UNIT 7

Development

Unit Selections

Key Points to Consider

- In what ways do infants learn about their world?

- How do children acquire a sense of humor?

- What is resilience in children? Why do some children develop resilience while others don't?

- Do adolescents spend too much time on computers and cell phones? What can their behavior while using these various media tell psychologists about them?

- What are the cornerstones of a successful marital or intimate relationship? What are some of the warning signs that a relationship is not faring well?

- Is the United States a death-denying society? What is the best way to interact with someone who has recently experienced death of a friend or significant other?

Student Web Site

www.mhcls.com

Internet References

American Association for Child and Adolescent Psychiatry
http://www.aacap.org
Developmental Psychology
http://psychology.about.com/od/developmentalpsychology/Developmental_Psychology.htm
The Opportunity of Adolescence
http://www.winternet.com/~webpage/adolescencepaper.html

The Garcias and the Szubas are brand new parents; in fact, they are still at the hospital with their newborns. When the babies are not in their mothers' rooms, both sets of parents wander down to the hospital's neonatal nursery where pediatric nurses care for both babies—José Garcia and Kimberly Szuba. Kimberly is alert, active, and often cries and squirms when her parents watch her. On the other hand, José is quiet, often asleep, and less attentive to external commotion when his parents view him in the nursery.

Why are these babies so different? Are the differences gender-related? Will these differences disappear as the children develop, or will they exaggerate? What does the future hold for each child? Will Kimberly excel at sports and José excel at art? Can Kimberly overcome her parents' poverty and succeed in a professional career? Will José become a doctor like his mother or a pharmacist like his father? Will both of these children escape childhood disease, maltreatment, and the other misfortunes sometimes visited upon American children?

Developmental psychologists are concerned with all of the Kimberlys and Josés of our world. Developmental psychologists study age-related changes in language, motor and social skills, cognition, and physical health. Developmental psychologists are interested in the common skills shared by all children, as well as the differences among children, and the events that create these differences.

In general, developmental psychologists are concerned with the forces that guide and direct development. Some developmental theorists argue that the forces that shape a child are found in the environment, in such factors as social class, quality of available stimulation, parenting style, and so on. Other theorists insist that genetics and related physiological factors such as hormones underlie human development. A third set of psychologists believe that a combination or interaction of all these factors are responsible for development.

© Singrid Olsson/Photo Alto

A Learning Machine
Plasticity and Change Throughout Life

LEAH NELSON

Drawing together five psychological scientists unlikely to cross paths outside of a conference, one of the APS 18th Annual Convention's themed programs, "Plasticity & Change: A Lifelong Perspective," showcased extraordinary research from various areas, all suggesting that the brain is almost infinitely adaptable from earliest infancy through latest adulthood. Although their research approached the topic from different angles, each presenter demonstrated the brain's extraordinary capacity to bend, stretch, expand, and specialize itself in response to challenges.

Gregg Recanzone, University of California, Davis, kicked off the discussion with a talk on animal models of adult neural plasticity. His findings indicate that the brain can be trained to increase its sensitivity to various stimuli. In one experiment, Recanzone exposed adult owl monkeys to two tones and decreasing the difference between them over time. After several weeks of training at this relatively simple task, their auditory sensitivity sharpened to a point at which they were able to easily discriminate between tones that were indistinguishable at the beginning of training. This increased sensitivity, Recanzone found, corresponded with a functional reorganization of the cerebral cortex—meaning that the activity of large populations of neurons in the monkeys' brains adapted. This evidence of plasticity in animal subjects' brains, Recanzone said, suggests that long-term levels of performance may be related to changes in neural activity.

Purposes of Plasticity

As a "learning machine," said the next presenter, Michael Merzenich of the University of California at San Francisco, the brain "has the incredible task . . . of recapitulating what we've learned in the history of our species." Merzenich has recently been researching plasticity among the elderly. Adult brains, he said, use plasticity for "purposeful" reasons, based on specific needs. For example, a professional musician might find it useful to train her brain to recognize absolute pitches, while a mechanic's brain would be better served by expanding its sensitivity to the precise differences among types of rumbles from a troubled car's insides. In contrast, during the "critical period" of childhood, the brain experiences "anything-goes plasticity," adapting itself to sort and interpret a huge variety of incoming data from the world. As individuals master major skill sets, massive cortical changes occur, said Merzenich. It is only after the development of *selective attention control*—the ability to sort and focus on preferred input—that plasticity shifts into a more purpose-driven, adult mode.

Like the adult monkeys' brain in Recanzone's experiment, the adult human brain can be trained to accommodate new skills. Merzenich said that his research is about "shaping the machinery of your brain . . . to develop the capacities of your life." As people grow older, he said, their brains become "noisier" because they are filled with more information, the management of which causes them to slow down. Increased noise degrades brains' learning-control machinery. But these changes are reversible, Merzenich said. In one experiment, he used adaptive computer games to rejuvenate the learning machinery of elderly subjects. His findings are striking: Through auditory training, people between the ages of 70 and 95 were able to recover the cortical plasticity of people 10 to 15 years younger than they. Visual training resulted in increased plasticity equivalent to that of brains 25 years younger. Countering conventional wisdom, which says that brains simply slow down with age, Merzenich said that it is "very easy to change cortical dynamics by training."

The Logic of Imagination

Merzenich focused on the elderly; Alison Gopnik of the University of California, Berkeley talked about plasticity in children's brains. In "The Logic of Imagination: How Children Change the World," she offered insight on the potential connection between children's imaginative capacity and the patterns of human evolution. "Everything in the environment we live in now was completely imaginary at one point in time," she said. "The deepest part of our human nature is that we are trying to escape human nature."

Evolution, Gopnik said, requires that we discover new things about how the world works and use this knowledge to imagine new things, to change the world based on our imaginings. Cognitive stretches are made possible by the brain's ability to create abstract representations of the world, imagine things that don't exist yet in those representations, and build them. Our ability to develop coherent theories about how things work—or might work—is what allows us to turn imagined worlds into real ones. Gopnik proposed that young children behave like scientists exploring the world for the first time: making predictions, testing them, comparing data, and forming new theories. She discussed an experiment in which young subjects were encouraged to hypothesize about the nature of an object that seemed to respond to both physical stimuli and vocal requests. Based on their knowledge of the world, the children all assumed initially that the object could not respond to their vocal commands. When it appeared to do just that, the children were able to override their assumptions and theorize that the object did in fact understand them. "Children do seem to begin with assumptions about how the world works, but can very rapidly use data to learn," Gopnik said. "Children are able to use this powerful computational machinery to imagine new things in the world, and they can use that new information to do new things in the world. . . . What children are doing is discovering new things about the world, and later on using that machinery to change the world." Like little scientists— and like every human who has ever imagined and invented anything new—children hypothesize, experiment, and make changes based on new data. Their ability to reshape their assumptions according to reality and then reshape reality based on their imaginings reflects the course of human evolution as a whole. It is the capacity for plasticity that makes it possible for children to learn and for the species to evolve, build, change, and grow.

Controlling Desires

In "Delay of Gratification Over Time: Mechanisms and Developmental Implications," Columbia University's Walter Mischel discussed another outcome of imaginative ability. With temptations of every kind constantly surrounding us, he asked, how do we learn to delay gratification? He proposed that the brain can conceive of two representations of every object—a "cool" representation of its abstract aspects and a "hot" representation of its rewarding traits. Anticipatory responses, such as salivation at the thought of delicious food, are "hot." Delayed gratification, said Mischel, an APS Fellow, is possible because we can also conceive of that same food in abstract terms—as fattening, for example, or likely to give us a stomachache.

From birth, children want instant gratification. But by stretching their brains to encompass abstract concepts and counterfactuals, they are able to train themselves to control their desires. "What's important is what kids are doing in their heads," Mischel explained. He described an experiment in which children were shown a real cake and a picture of a cake. When he told the children to imagine that the real cake was only a picture, they reported "cool" reactions and a decreased desire to eat the dessert. When the children were asked to imagine that the picture was a real cake, they had "hot" reactions even though they knew the cake wasn't really there. The degree of a child's power to delay gratification at an early age is a good predictor of later coping ability. Early delay skills protect against later vulnerability, Mischel said, so training children in "cooling strategies," like using their imaginations, can have a significant payoff later in life. "Delay makes it possible for people to cool it if and when they want to," Mischel said.

Effects of Deprivation

The symposium's final presenter, Sir Michael Rutter of King's College, underscored the limits of cortical plasticity with a somber report on "Long-Term Effects of Early Institutional Deprivation: Findings from an Adoption Study and Implications of Causal Mechanisms." Rutter and his associates followed the behavioral development of children who were adopted from Romanian orphanages by UK families after the fall of the Ceausescu regime. After evaluating them at the time of adoption, they studied a sample of such children at ages four, six, and eleven years, deploying a battery of cognitive and psychological tests to construct a theory about the results of profound deprivation followed by above-average living environments.

Some of their findings surprised them. "Like much of science, one has a mix of the expected and the totally unexpected," Rutter said. At arrival, most of the children tested as mentally retarded, but by age eleven, they were nearly normal. Variations tended to correlate to the amount of time spent in deprived conditions: Children who had been in orphanages for less than six months recovered most completely, while those who were there longer displayed more severe and longer-lasting deficits. What surprised researchers was that the nature of the deficits varied among the children: Instead of consistently suffering a similar set of problems, each child showed a different pattern of disturbance. This finding suggested to Rutter that plasticity must vary from child to child—that individual brains will respond to similar extreme circumstances in completely different ways. Unable to find a strong connection between adaptive ability and the characteristics of the households that adopted the children, Rutter concluded that, although psychosocial deprivation was the main risk factor for all the deficits the children displayed, its effects are neither universal nor fixed—a challenge to what some developmental theories would predict most researchers would expect. "Whatever theoretical explanation we end up with," Rutter concluded, "we'll have to account for these huge individual differences." Rutter also delivered the Keynote Address at the APS annual meeting.

The five presenters were delighted at the similarities they saw among their diverse fields. "We should change the way we do business," said Mischel. "Psychological science is at the point that it should become a big science. We should think about the way that chemistry and physics became great sciences. The time of each person in his own lab should maybe be over."

LEAH NELSON is a writer who lives in New York.

The Joke's in You

New research on how children develop a sense of humor is giving psychologists a window into social and mental development.

MICHAEL PRICE

One afternoon four years ago, Merideth Gattis, PhD, was putting groceries away in the kitchen while her 4-year-old daughter Ella looked on. After transferring eggs to the refrigerator, Gattis tripped slightly on her way to the trash can. The empty egg carton, with its top closed, threatened neither broken eggs nor a messy floor, but Gattis played it up for her daughter's amusement. She wobbled perilously, juggled the carton around, carefully steadied it, and made a comically grand show of relief—all to the giggling audience of Ella.

Gattis, a psychologist at Cardiff University in the United Kingdom, pondered the faux near-tragedy. What made that scenario funny?

Twenty years ago, scientists scoffed at the suggestion that studying humor was scientifically significant, but today psychologists are turning to humor as a tool for looking at development and cognition. In adults, a deficient sense of humor can signal a variety of disorders such as schizophrenia, autism and Asperger syndrome, and offers new insights into the nature of those conditions. In children, a developing sense of humor can serve as a weathervane for emerging cognitive features such as recognizing intentionality and understanding symbolism.

Humor's Building Blocks

Babies show their first signs of mirth within the first five weeks of life when they begin smiling in response to their parents' cooing and silly facial expressions. Most scientists think these smiles are an emotional response to social interaction, with different types of smiles for different situations. Peek-a-boo might elicit one type of smile, tickling another.

Three months later, laughter emerges, thrilling parents and grandparents and providing auditory evidence that the child is enjoying him- or herself. These behaviors aren't specific to humor, but they're the building blocks for expressing humor. As children get older, they begin to reliably laugh and smile at typically "funny" situations.

Psychologists' prevailing view of what makes a situation funny is known as the incongruity theory. Ithaca College psychologist Barney Beins, PhD, explains it like this: Something is funny when a real-world event doesn't match up with your mental model of what should happen. But the revelry's in the details, says Beins, who's been studying humor for 15 years.

"Humor is a very complicated psychological response; it's multifaceted," Beins says. And separating incongruous events into humorous and non-humorous situations depends on many factors, including mood and what children learn from others. "Children have to learn about humor. As kids start getting a bit older, their humor becomes more sophisticated."

So when Ella laughed at her mom's bumbling antics, she was recognizing the incongruity of someone trying desperately to save an empty egg carton from falling. But Gattis noticed a subtle kink in this theory: How did Ella know her mom was intentionally joking around with the egg carton rather than genuinely mistaken about its contents—or lack thereof?

As luck would have it, just a few days prior to the incident, Cardiff graduate student Elena Hoicka (who earned her PhD in June) approached Gattis about studying humor in children. Gattis credits the conversation with inspiring her to really take notice of her daughter's behavior. The two tried to break the problem down into smaller pieces for studying. Past research has shown that children as young as 14 months old can distinguish between intentional actions and unintentional ones. For instance, one study published in 1995 showed that 14- to 18-month-olds tend to copy intentional actions and correct unintentional mistakes. Gattis and Hoicka wanted to build upon this to see if toddlers could parse actions into either intentional joking or unintentional blunders.

Doing so requires that they first understand that a joke somehow deviates from the norm—for example, trying to write with a pencil's eraser or drinking from the bottom of a cup. Second, children must understand that someone intended for this deviation to happen, that it wasn't just an error. Finally, they must realize the performer knows that the children think it's a joke. If all of these cognitive pieces are in place, cue the laugh track; the child gets the joke.

Twenty years ago, scientists scoffed at the suggestion that studying humor was scientifically significant, but today psychologists are turning to humor as a tool for looking at development and cognition.

To look at the second step of this process, the researchers devised a way to measure whether children knew the performer intended to do the wrong thing. Gattis and Hoicka performed a variety of "incorrect" actions accompanied by either laughter and smiling or "Whoops!" and grimacing. Some were considered unambiguous jokes: Put a boot on your hand—laugh and smile. Others were unambiguous mistakes: Write with the wrong end of a marker—"Whoops!" And others were more ambiguous; sipping from the bottom of a cup could either be a mistake or a joke depending on the researcher's accompanying action. Because the toddlers were too young to simply tell researchers what they thought, Gattis and Hoicka watched to see whether the toddlers would copy or correct the actions.

According to results in press in *Cognitive Development* the 25- to 36-month-old toddlers aced the test. They copied all the actions marked by laughter and corrected those accompanied by "Whoops!" regardless of whether the actions were ambiguous. The 19- to 24-month-old group got tripped up on the ambiguous actions, but even at that age the children differentiated between intentional jokes and unintentional mistakes. As early as 19-months-old, the results suggest, children seem to distinguish between someone doing something wrong intentionally and doing something wrong accidentally—a big step in cognition. Grasping that others act intentionally is a fundamental part of theory of mind, or recognizing that others possess the same mental presence as oneself.

"Humor sets you up to understand that people can do things wrong and intend them to be wrong," Gattis says. That's an easy entry into duality—the idea that an action can mean more than one thing—a very difficult concept for young children, Gattis notes.

Humor Deficits

When the mind doesn't develop normally, people's sense of humor can become derailed. For instance, one study published in *Psychiatry Research* (Vol. 141, No. 2, pages 229–232) showed that people with schizophrenia don't perform as well as healthy participants on joke comprehension tests. Study author Joseph Polimeni, MD, and his research partner Jeffrey Reiss, MD, showed participants a variety of one-panel cartoons with captions beneath them. Some of the captions matched the cartoons, some didn't, and participants tried to identify those that matched.

"In general, people with a good sense of humor do pretty well [on the test]," Polimeni says. "Participants with schizophrenia did worse."

Also, he noted there is "a pretty high magnitude of difference" between the humor-recognizing abilities of people with schizophrenia and with bipolar disorder. As the two disorders are often mistaken for each other, it could provide a tool for more accurate diagnoses, Polimeni says, if further studies bear out the findings.

Polimeni, a psychiatrist at the University of Manitoba in Winnipeg, thinks the deficiency is related to schizophrenic people's frequent inability to connect the dots between associated ideas.

"A lot of humor has to do with associations," Polimeni says. "When you hear a punch line, everything in the joke has to come together. But if one of the associations isn't connecting, it's a lot harder to understand the joke."

A study published online in April of the *European Archives of Psychiatry and Clinical Neuroscience* offers an explanation: People with schizophrenia don't put in the extra cognitive effort required to understand jokes. Instead, they treat them purely as incongruent events, never making the leap to humor.

"It takes some effort to go beyond the surface of the joke to the hidden meaning, so schizophrenics who don't expend the extra effort would show less of a sense of humor," Barney Beins says.

Contrast this with cases of autism spectrum disorder and Asperger syndrome. Scientists agree that people with autism and Asperger have an impaired sense of humor similar to people with schizophrenia, but anecdotes abound of autistic and Asperger children and adults flirting with comedy. In a summary article published in 2004 in the *Journal of Autism and Developmental Disorders* (Vol. 34, No. 5), Viktoria Lyons and Michael Fitzgerald, PhD, examine the literature and arrive at an interesting suggestion: some people with autism and Asperger syndrome do understand humor—but at a mathematical level. Research has well established that many people with autism and Asperger have excellent mathematical reasoning skills, and these skills might cross over into the logical, formulaic patterns of certain types of humor, such as puns, the researchers say. But even at this level, the sense of humor appears to operate more at the intellectual level than at the emotionally expressive level, a bit like painting by numbers. They've figured out how humor "works," but a drama will still feel the same for them as a comedy.

Paul Rozin, PhD, a University of Pennsylvania psychologist who co-authored a 2006 article about patterns in humor and music in the journal *Emotion* (Vol. 6, No. 3, pages 349–355), thinks this equation-like understanding of humor might parallel the way people with autism process music. They can abstract relationships among ideas, he says, but have great difficulty fitting those ideas into a social framework.

"They're just as aware of [humor and music] as the normal person, but they're not as engaged in it," Rozin says. It's an area he'd like to see more work done in, he says, because humor is such a fundamental part of communication. "I think there's something really interesting here."

Figuring out what that something is will help scientists and parents alike understand what's behind laughter or the lack of it. Beins hopes that one day humor might be used as a diagnostic tool for discriminating conditions with otherwise similar symptoms. Further, understanding humor in normally developing children will help psychologists look at the cognitive processes that make humor possible in the first place. And parents can take pleasure in the fact that behind their children's giggling facade is a symphony of complex cognition.

A Question of Resilience

EMILY BAZELON

In the spring of 1993, when I was an intern at The New Haven Advocate, a local weekly, I met two girls named La'Tanya and Tichelle. La'Tanya was 13, Tichelle was 11 and, along with their two younger sisters, they had recently returned from a year in foster care to live with their mother, Jean. (I have used middle names to protect the family's privacy.) I was supposed to spend an hour or two with them and write an article for the paper about families that reunite. But I liked the girls, and I decided I needed to interview them again—the joy of being an intern, after all, is that no one really cares when you finish your article. The next time I showed up, about a week later, a worried-looking woman was talking to the girls. She was a prosecutor who was about to try Jean's boyfriend, Earl Osborn, for sexually abusing La'Tanya and Tichelle over several years and their 7-year-old sister, Charnelle, for a shorter period. The girls were her chief witnesses.

At the trial that May in a courtroom in New Haven, La'Tanya testified that Osborn started touching her when she was in kindergarten. She told her mother, and Jean put him out of the house. But somehow, though he wasn't violent, she couldn't make him stay out. She would later say that this was the greatest mistake of her life, but in court, she said as little as possible.

During the next five years, Jean warned Osborn to keep away from her daughters. He didn't. When La'Tanya and Tichelle were about 10 and 8, Jean testified, she put a lock on the door of their bedroom. Osborn broke the lock three times. Jean would find him lying on top of the girls, rubbing against them and putting his hands down their pajamas, or next to them masturbating. She gave her daughters a stick to sleep with. But she never banished him from their home.

In June 1991, after being tipped off that there might be a problem at home, a school social worker pulled La'Tanya out of her sixth-grade graduation party and asked if anyone was bothering her. La'Tanya shook her head no and then started to cry, and to talk. Jean lost cus-

tody of La'Tanya, Tichelle, Charnelle and their youngest sister, Chanté. That's when the girls lived in foster care, first with a family and then for several months with their grandmother. Osborn was arrested. In May 1993, on the strength of La'Tanya and Tichelle's testimony, a jury in New Haven convicted him of nine charges of sexual assault. Osborn was sentenced to 85 years in prison. The jury foreman was Jon Butler, a history professor, who is dean of the Yale Graduate School of Arts and Sciences. "The verdict hinged overwhelmingly on the credibility of the girls," he told me recently. "They were so good because they weren't so good. They weren't acting, this wasn't contrived, what happened had been deeply disturbing to them. They conveyed this with the kind of precision that made it completely believable."

During the summer after the trial, I spent time with the girls, taking them to the playground and the pool. I wrote about them for The Advocate. Then I left, as interns do. I did stay in touch with La'Tanya and Tichelle, because I was worried about them and because I admired them. They took care of each other, and they were resourceful. "They're very appealing kids, and I don't think anyone expected that, considering what they've been up against," Cecilia Wiederhold, the prosecutor, said in my Advocate article.

As the girls grew up, they kept exceeding my expectations. Study after study has shown that sexually-abused children—especially those who grow up in the sort of low-income, messy surroundings that the girls did—are more likely to develop a raft of emotional and health problems, including depression, post-traumatic stress disorder and suicidal thoughts. As adults, they are more likely to be unemployed, homeless, addicted to drugs or alcohol and alone. Now, at ages 26 and 24 respectively, La'Tanya and Tichelle are none of those things. La'Tanya works as a certified nursing assistant at St. Raphael's Hospital. She has her own apartment in a small town on the Connecticut shore. She is raising her two sons, who are 10 and 5. Tichelle is a computer operator for the city of Bridgeport.

She lives with her 1-year-old son in the same apartment complex as La'Tanya. Both sisters graduated from high school and have their own cars.

By middle-class standards, these accomplishments seem modest. But financial independence and stability are rare and hard-won for anyone in the poor black New Haven neighborhood where the sisters grew up. Jean raised her children on welfare and never learned to drive. La'Tanya and Tichelle's fathers have been almost entirely absent. On the blocks of row houses and vacant lots where they were raised, teenage mothers far outnumber married ones.

Over the years, I've wondered what accounts for their relative success. Were La'Tanya and Tichelle different, and if so, why? Weren't their lives supposed to have fallen into chaos? How is it that some children show a certain resilience after experiencing a trauma and others do not?

The everyday meaning of the word "resilience" extends to anything that bounces back. Estée Lauder makes Resilience Lift Eye Crème and Hanes makes Resilience Pantyhose. But in psychology, resilience has a specific meaning. It's the word for springing back from serious adversity, like abuse, war or natural disasters. You exhibit resilience (as opposed to plain competence) if you cope with terrible misfortune and live a relatively successful life as defined by mental health, success in school or at work or solid relationships. In studies of the long-term effects of physical and sexual child abuse, 20 to 40 percent of victims show few signs of behavioral or mental-health problems. And many of them don't appear damaged later in life. As Ann Masten, a resilience researcher, has written, resilient children have the benefit of "ordinary magic." When it comes to abuse victims, though, this finding is rarely trumpeted, for fear that saying abuse isn't always inevitably harmful is tantamount to saying it's not always bad.

Over the last several decades, a small group of researchers has tried to understand how a minority of maltreated children exceed expectations. The grandfather of resilience theory is Norman Garmezy, who by the 1960's had begun asking why some children of schizophrenics fared better than others. In the 1970's, Ann Masten joined Garmezy at the University of Minnesota, and the two, along with others, started a project spanning more than two decades. They looked at a child's personality, among other things, imagining resilience as a function of temperament, will or intelligence. While children of average intelligence or above were more likely to exhibit resilience, the researchers noted that good relationships with adults can exert an effect that is as powerful, if not more, in mitigating the effects of adversity.

In recent years, biological science has proposed a new paradigm. The latest research shows that resilience can best be understood as an interplay between particular genes and environment—GxE, in the lingo of the field. Researchers are discovering that a particular variation of a gene can help promote resilience in the people who have it, acting as a buffer against the ruinous effects of adversity. In the absence of an adverse environment, however, the gene doesn't express itself in this way. It drops out of the psychological picture. "We now have well-replicated findings showing that genes play a major role in influencing people's responses to adverse environments," says Sir Michael Rutter, a leading British psychiatrist and long-time resilience expert. "But the genes don't do anything much on their own."

Rutter opened a GxE research center because he was frustrated that most psychiatric studies tracked the effects either of genes or of environment rather than looking at them in tandem. Despite a few initial successes, like the discovery of the gene that causes Down syndrome, most searches for genes that fully explain psychiatric outcomes—"the alcoholism gene," "the schizophrenic gene"—have failed. Meanwhile, in the field of medicine, it's increasingly common to consider external factors when studying the effects of genes. "With heart disease and cancer, genetic researchers have always known to include factors like smoking and exercise," says Terrie Moffitt, who is on the faculty of Rutter's research center at the Institute of Psychiatry in London and of the University of Wisconsin. "We wanted to do the same thing for the study of behavior."

The breakthrough moment for GxE came in 2003, when Moffitt and her husband and co-investigator, Avshalom Caspi, published a paper in Science that discussed the relationship between the gene, 5-HTT, and childhood maltreatment in causing depression. Scientists have determined that 5-HTT is critical for the regulation of serotonin to the brain. Proper regulation of serotonin helps promote well-being and protects against depression in response to trauma or stress. In humans, each 5-HTT gene has two alleles, and each allele occurs in either a short or a long version. Scientists are still figuring out how the short allele affects serotonin delivery, but it seems that people with at least one short 5-HTT allele are more prone to depression. And since depression is associated with unemployment, struggling relationships, poor health and substance abuse, the short allele could contribute to a life going awry.

About one-third of the white population have two copies of the protective long allele. About one-half have one long allele and one short one. And about 17 percent have two short alleles. (African-Americans are less likely to have a short allele; Asians are more likely.) In their 2003 study, Caspi and Moffitt looked at 847 New Zealand adults and found a link between having at least one short 5-HTT allele and elevated rates of depression for people who had been mistreated as children or experienced several "life stresses"—defined as major setbacks with jobs, housing, relationships, health and money. Having two short alleles made it highly likely that people who had been mistreated or exposed to unhinging stress would suffer depression. One short allele posed a moderate risk of depression in these circumstances. Two long alleles, on the other hand, gave their carriers a good chance of bouncing back under negative circumstances. In other words, as a group, children with two risky alleles lost out badly when their environments failed them, children with one risky allele were at some risk and children with good resilience alleles often carried a shield. The risky variation of the gene doesn't confer vulnerability, though, if an individual who carries it never experiences abuse or serious stress—in other words, it's not a "depression gene" in any general sense. It seems that only under dire circumstances—abuse, the strife of war, chronic stress—is the gene triggered. Eventually scientists hope to understand more about other genes that most likely play a role like 5-HTT's.

Researchers who study humans cannot, of course, run controlled experiments by randomly assigning some children to abusive homes. But primatologists can. At a laboratory in rural Maryland, run by the National Institutes of Health, Stephen Suomi studies 500 rhesus monkeys. Each year, Suomi divides newborn monkeys into several groups. One group live with their mothers, much as they would in the wild (except for the indoor pens and the daily rations). Another group, created to mimic the experience of a neglected or abused child, never see their mothers, spending two weeks in an incubator and then moving into a small group of peers.

Rhesus monkeys share with humans about 96 percent of their genes—including the long and short variations of 5-HTT. Using DNA samples, Suomi is able to track which of his monkeys have which allele. In an ongoing study, Suomi has found that motherless, peer-raised monkeys who have a copy of the short 5-HTT allele are more likely to experience fear, panic and aggression (accompanied by low levels of serotonin acid in spinal fluid) when a strange monkey in a cage is placed next to them. Motherless, peer-raised monkeys with two long alleles, on the other hand, are more likely to take the presence of the stranger in stride, as mother-raised monkeys do. (Only a tiny number of monkeys have two copies of the short allele, so they're not studied.) "How you grow up affects your hormonal output and the structure and function of the brain," Suomi

says. "And these effects are tempered by the kind of gene the monkeys carry. So it's a true interaction."

In Suomi's lab, there's a room filled with large cages of 2- and 3-year-olds—adolescents approaching adulthood, in monkey years. "Go in quickly and quietly," Suomi tells me and then follows me through the door. Some of the monkeys stay in the middle of the cage, eyeing us without seeming preoccupied. Another group races to the back and huddles together in the farthest corner, their small fingers wrapping around one another's fur. They twitter and turn their faces away in distress.

The middle-of-the-cage monkeys were raised by their mothers. The freaked-out ones at the back raised one another. After a few minutes, some of the peer-raised monkeys begin to dart forward. After a few more minutes, they settle in with the mother-raised group. But others never move from the back of the cage. According to Suomi, you could approach the cage a hundred times and each time see the same result. And each time, the peer-raised monkeys would race to the back, and then a few would mirror human resilience by coming forward. And they would generally be the monkeys with two long 5-HTT alleles. The good version of the gene.

Suomi's peer-raised monkeys are deprived of their mothers and other adult monkeys. Abused children, by contrast, don't just live with other children. They may have in their lives grandparents, aunts, teachers, maybe an adult they know from church or a volunteer from a Big Brother or Big Sister program. And they are much more likely than other children to name one of these adults as the person on whom they most rely.

Caspi and Moffitt's research was important in showing a link between genes and an abusive environment, but they didn't explore the effect of mitigating factors in the abused children's lives. Joan Kaufman, a Yale psychiatry professor, has taken the next step by doing so. In a paper this month in the journal Biological Psychiatry, Kaufman reported on 196 children between the ages of 5 and 15, 109 of them removed from their homes in Connecticut because of reports of physical or sexual abuse or neglect. This group was compared with a second non-abused group with the same racial composition—about 28 percent white, 24 percent Hispanic, 28 percent African-American and 20 percent biracial—and the same income of $25,000 or less. (Physical and sexual abuse are more prevalent among poor families, though abuse happens at all economic levels. Studies like Caspi and Moffitt's, which include families of varied income, show that the resilience findings apply to middle- and upper-class kids as well as poor ones.)

Kaufman gave all 196 children a questionnaire about their moods, which measure mental health. She also used

DNA tests to check their 5-HTT alleles. Kaufman's abused children with two short 5-HTT alleles had a higher mean score for depression than the abused children with two long alleles and the nonabused children, no matter what their alleles. (In Kaufman's study, which was smaller than Caspi and Moffitt's, the moderate risk of depression posed by one short allele didn't show up, though that finding has been replicated by other researchers.)

In her recent paper and in earlier research, Kaufman also built on the work of psychologists who have measured the quality of abused children's relationships to adults, asking the children to name the person they most often "talk to about personal things, count on to buy the things they need, share good news with, get together with to have fun and go to if they need advice." The mean depression score for abused children with two short alleles who rarely saw the adults they named was off the charts. If the children with two short alleles saw the adults they counted on daily or almost daily, their depression scores were very close to the scores of the children with two long protective alleles—and within reach of the children who had not been abused. (The children with the protective version of the gene were far less affected by a lack of contact with their primary adult.) "Good support ameliorates the effect of abuse and of the high-risk genotype," Kaufman says. While he notes that Kaufman's research is preliminary, Dennis Charney, a psychiatry and neuroscience professor at Mount Sinai School of Medicine, says that the study used "solid methodology and yielded very interesting findings."

La'Tanya and Tichelle had relatively good support. When the state removed the girls and their sisters from their home, their grandmother took them in. "She did everything for us," La'Tanya remembers. Later, a half-sister who is 10 years older than La'Tanya began picking her up on weekends. "I spent a lot of time with her," La'Tanya says. "We'd rent movies, go places, do a lot of things together."

Having "good support" isn't just a question of good luck. Researchers have found that children who are resilient are skillful at creating beneficial relationships with adults, and those relationships in turn contribute to the children's resilience. La'Tanya and Tichelle were both good at forging these bonds. When I left New Haven in 1994, they wrote me. I moved back a few years later, and Tichelle called regularly, came to my office to meet me for lunch, asked me to stop by her house on the weekends. La'Tanya soon started calling, too. Sometimes the sisters were behind on their bills and, always with embarrassment, asked me for money. But more often they called, and still call, to check in, to ask after my kids or tell me about theirs. They let me know that I matter to them, and that has made them matter more to me.

In the last year or so, I've become more aware that La'Tanya and Tichelle are quite different and that the darkness of childhood seems to have left a more indelible mark on the older sister. La'Tanya and her sister were both molested. And they lived with their mother, who was remote—I don't think I ever saw Jean hug her daughters in the months surrounding the trial. But La'Tanya shouldered more of a burden than Tichelle did. As the oldest, La'Tanya often had to look after her sisters—make them dinner, put them to sleep. "La'Tanya raised us," Tichelle says. "She's more like a mom than a sister." La'Tanya wrote in her diary last year, "Ever since I can remember I've taken on more than any one person should have to."

In March 1994, when they were 14 and 12, the girls sent me letters. Tichelle wrote: "My grades are excellent. I got all A's and two B+'s. In school I am a cheerleader we cheer every Tuesday and Thursday. I am still in double dutch it's very fun." La'Tanya also reported her good grades. But mostly she described the heaviness of her world. "A lot of people have been getting killed," she wrote. "A house almost got burned down and nobody ever goes outside." A year later, La'Tanya ran away from home. She moved in with her 17-year-old boyfriend and decided to have a baby. The thread that runs through these decisions is her anger and disappointment with Jean. "I had a baby to be loved by someone," La'Tanya says. "When all the mess fell out, my mother didn't do anything about it. That's what made me think she didn't love us."

Tichelle, by contrast, forgave her mother and relies on her. "That's my mom, and I'm not going to let anyone take her away." On the day Tichelle went into labor last spring, the father of her baby was arrested for selling drugs. She called her mother, and after the birth Jean slept at the hospital with her daughter and grandson. Jean takes care of the baby every day while Tichelle is at work, as she has done for her other grandchildren.

Before her baby was born, Tichelle landed a permanent position in her office after impressing her boss as a temp. "I'm 23, and I know what I want for myself," she told me last year. La'Tanya, meanwhile, was struggling with crying spells and panic attacks. After a recurrent nightmare about Osborn, she would wake up and compulsively check and recheck the locks in her apartment. She couldn't stop thinking about Osborn's gun—"a black shotgun with a light brown barrel."

There are a lot of reasons that La'Tanya has had a harder time than her sister, not least of them that she was abused for a longer period of time. But reading all the GxE research made me wonder whether she was also more genetically vulnerable. I asked the girls if they'd be willing to be tested, and they agreed—they said they were curious. Last month, La'Tanya, Tichelle and Charnelle (who had been abused by Osborn for a shorter period when she was 3) sent cheek swabs with their DNA to a lab run by a Colorado-based company called NeuroMark, which tests for the 5-HTT alleles.

The study of resilience is nearly 50 years old. Yet its contribution to our understanding of the effects of child abuse has gained little traction beyond a small subset of academics. Historically, the study of resilience inadvertently collided with the movement to treat child abuse as a national cause for alarm. In the 1950's, experts like Alfred Kinsey minimized the damage of sexual abuse. The fright described by children who'd had sexual contact with adults was "nearer the level that children will show when they see insects [or] spiders," Kinsey wrote, as Joseph E. Davis, a sociologist, recounts in his recent book, "Accounts of Innocence." Until the mid 1970's, standard psychology textbooks also played down the effects of abuse and put the incidence of incest at one in a million.

By the beginning of the next decade, the textbooks were being rewritten. Led by Judith Lewis Herman, a professor of clinical psychiatry at Harvard, feminists shredded the myth that sexual abuse is rare and does little significant harm. They argued that even a brief, single incident of abuse could and often did scar victims for life. In 1980, Herman helped win an official psychiatric diagnosis for post-traumatic stress disorder, as a response to trauma that causes people to "dissociate," or fragment, by alternately feeling numb and reliving the event. According to its clinical definition, PTSD can strike a victim of rape or child abuse as easily as a combat veteran. The orthodoxy that abuse necessarily causes trauma grew and still remains entrenched. It has extensive institutional support—$29 million a year in government financing goes to a national "traumatic stress" center and 44 hospitals and community-based programs around the nation. "The problem in our country isn't that we overidentify trauma," said Ellen Gerrity, associate director for the national center. "It's that we underidentify it."

All along, a few experts have raised doubts about equating childhood sexual experience with trauma and about the assumption that abuse destroys victims' lives. But they got little attention—until an academic brush fire over terminology exploded into a public war. In 1998, Bruce Rind, Robert Bauserman and Philip Tromovitch published an article in Psychological Bulletin, a journal of the American Psychological Association, analyzing 59 studies of the long-term effects of sexual abuse and adult-child sexual contact on college students. "At the time, the starting hypothesis in the field was that child sexual abuse, broadly defined, was extremely harmful in all cases," Rind says. "Our idea was to take this very strong statement and to be statistically and methodologically rigorous about testing it."

The Rind paper found only a marginal difference between the psychological well-being of college students who'd been "sexually abused" and those who hadn't. But there was a catch: Some of the studies being analyzed defined sexual abuse broadly to include exhibitionism and consensual contact between teenagers and adults. When abuse was limited to lack of consent, force or incest, its deleterious effects were more pronounced. So Rind and his co-authors recommended narrowing the definition of abuse.

Conservatives condemned the Rind paper, and Congress denounced it. The uproar virtually derailed the hope of opening child sex studies to rigorous inquiry. "There had been an underestimation of the extent to which children can recover from sexual abuse," says David Finkelhor, a sociologist who directs the Crimes Against Children Research Center at the University of New Hampshire and who has found that pre-existing depression may make children vulnerable to sexual abuse and may help account for the problems some suffer afterward. "But that article started a trend in the opposite direction," he says—by discouraging investigations of the differences between harmful sexual abuse and other sexual contact.

Still, in trying to understand why some children are not scarred for life, resilience research brightens a picture that is often painted in black. And the promise of GxE brings with it new excitement—and grant money. Caspi and Moffitt, whose article about 5-HTT received widespread praise, didn't bother to try to get government money when they began collecting DNA data in 1998. Now they receive $500,000 a year in N.I.M.H. and U.K. government grants. Other researchers have similar support for GxE work.

If GxE pans out as the enthusiasts hope, it could change not just our understanding of the effects of abuse but also our treatment of it. Neurobiological research on mice and rats has begun to look at the effect that the 5-HTT gene has on the brain at the molecular level. Eventually, a designer drug might succeed in mimicking precisely what the long-allele variation of 5-HTT does to foster resilience. "A magic drug down the line—yes, that's the whole point of understanding the neurological mechanisms," Joan Kaufman says.

Other experts, however, are skeptical. Whatever an abused child's genes, they argue, she still needs the ingredients that promote resilience—adults she can trust, the reinforcements that make her believe in herself. "It's nice to know what's going on in the body," says Suniya Luthar, a psychology professor at Columbia University's Teachers College. "But what's the real promise here? We already know what people need to be resilient. From the standpoint of intervention, I'd rather see money go toward things that are more likely to make real change," like developing effective interventions. Luthar also worries about genetic profiling. "Are we going to think about genetic engineering" to weed out the high-risk variation of a gene? she asks.

Kaufman, too, warns that finding out which variation of 5-HTT you carry is not like getting a diagnosis. The short allele increases vulnerability across a large group rather than exposing any one person who has it. Other genes, as well as relationships, contribute. "Think about it as one factor on a scale," Kaufman says. "It can tip the scale toward depression or away from it. But other factors can tip the scale, more powerfully, in the opposite direction."

Still, the test results for La'Tanya, Tichelle and their younger sister Charnelle are intriguing. As it turns out, Tichelle carries only the protective version of the gene (two long alleles). So does Charnelle, who at 20 is thriving, with a steady job at a nursing home and an apartment she shares with a boyfriend whom her family likes.

La'Tanya, though, carries one copy of the short 5-HTT allele, putting her in the group of abused children who are at moderate risk of depression. Perhaps her genes help account for the times she has gone to the hospital because she's so anxious she can't breathe and the days she can't stop crying or get out of bed.

Yet, as Kaufman says, La'Tanya's genes don't doom her to unhappiness. She has good days too. Last year she signed up with a home-health-aide agency and was frustrated—and broke—because she was getting only scattered hours of work. She wanted a hospital job. But that required a state recertification. I gave her $700 for the four-week course she needed.

At the graduation ceremony last spring, two dozen students ate pizza next to the hospital beds and dummy patient they'd practiced on. "I got a 93 on the final," La'Tanya told me twice. She was wearing a pink turtleneck sweater, pressed jeans and high-heeled black boots. She'd taken out her lip piercing because the teacher said it might put off potential employers. "Now I just need to take the licensing test," she said to a friend. "When we leave from here I'm going over to sign up." She did. She passed. She got the hospital job she wanted. Keeping it hasn't been easy, especially because her younger son has been acting up in school. But she is doing it.

Next month, NeuroMark will begin selling the 5-HTT test to people whose doctors request it. The results won't solve the riddle of which survivors of abuse fare better than others. But they may provide a clue. "I think for me it helps explain things," La'Tanya said. "I feel a little better that there is a reason, another reason, for my life being hard. And I understand that what I'm able to do for myself and my kids, even with this, is good. It's good."

***

EMILY BAZELON is a senior editor at *Slate* and a recent Soros Media Justice Fellow.

Growing Up Online
Young People Jump Headfirst into the Internet's World

BRUCE BOWER

As a conversation unfolds among teenagers on an Internet message board, it rapidly becomes evident that this is not idle electronic chatter. One youngster poses a question that, to an outsider, seems shocking: "Does anyone know how to cut deep without having it sting and bleed too much?" An answer quickly appears: "I use box cutter blades. You have to pull the skin really tight and press the blade down really hard." Another response advises that a quick swipe of a blade against skin "doesn't hurt and there is blood galore." The questioner seems satisfied: "Okay, I'll get a Stanley blade 'cause I hear that it will cut right to the bone with no hassle. But . . . I won't cut that deep."

Welcome to the rapidly expanding online arena for teenagers who deliberately cut or otherwise injure themselves. It's a place where cutters, as they're known, can provide emotional support to one another, discuss events that trigger self-mutilation, encourage peers to seek medical or mental-health treatment, or offer tips on how best to hurt oneself without getting caught.

The conversation above, observed during a study of self-injury message boards, occupies a tiny corner of the virtual world that children and adolescents have aggressively colonized. Psychologist Janis L. Whitlock of Cornell University, the director of that study, and other researchers are beginning to explore how young people communicate on the Internet. The scientists are examining how various online contacts affect a youngster's schoolwork, social life, and budding sense of identity. Evidence also suggests that the Internet has expanded the reach of health-education efforts to teens in distant lands and provided unique leadership opportunities to a global crop of youngsters.

New findings, including six reports in the May *Developmental Psychology,* indicate that the Internet holds a special appeal for young people, says psychologist Patricia Greenfield of the University of California, Los Angeles (UCLA). That's because the Internet provides an unprecedented number and variety of meeting places, from message boards to instant messaging to so-called social networking sites such as *myspace.com.*

The one constant is that teens take to the Internet like ants to a summer picnic. Nearly 9 in 10 U.S. youngsters, ages 12 to 17, used the Internet in 2004, according to a national survey conducted by the Pew Internet & American Life Project in Washington, D.C. That amounted to 21 million teens, half of whom said that they go online every day. About three in four U.S. adults used the Internet at that time, Pew researchers found.

Teenagers, in particular, provide a moving target for Internet researchers, remarks psychologist Kaveri Subrahmanyam of California State University in Los Angeles. "By the time you publish research on one type of Internet use, such as blogging, teenagers have moved on to something new, such as *myspace,*" she says, with a resigned chuckle.

Express Yourself

Cyberspace offers a bevy of tempting opportunities to pretend to be who you're not. Yet teens don't typically go online to deceive others but to confront their own identities, according to recent studies. That's not surprising, Subrahmanyam notes, since adolescents typically seek answers to questions such as "Who am I?" and "Where do I belong?"

Consider the self-injury message boards studied by Whitlock's team. Five Internet search engines led the researchers to a whopping 406 such sites. Most of these attracted participants who identified themselves as girls between ages 12 and 20.

On message boards, as in chat rooms, participants register as members and adopt screen names, such as "Emily the Strange." In many cases, both members and nonmembers can view messages, although only members can post them.

> **"By the time you publish research on one type of Internet use . . . teenagers have moved on to something new."**
>
> —Kaveri Subrahmanyam,
> California State University

Whitlock and her coworkers studied the content of 3,219 messages at 10 popular self-injury message boards over a 2-month period in 2005. Many postings provided emotional support to other members. Participants also frequently discussed circumstances that triggered self-mutilation. These included depression and conflicts with key people in their lives. Some message senders detailed ways to seek aid for physical and emotional problems, but others described feeling addicted to self-injury.

More ominously, a substantial minority of messages either discouraged self-injurers from seeking formal medical or mental help or shared details about self-harm techniques and ways to keep the practice secret.

Online teen chat rooms generally don't have specific topics but, like message boards, attract a wide range of kids and present both helpful and hurtful communications. Subrahmanyam and her colleagues examined typical conversations at two online chat sites for teens. They monitored more than 5 hours of electronic exchanges selected at various times of the day during a 2-month stretch in 2003.

On one site, an adult monitored conversations for unacceptable language. The other site was unmonitored.

More than half of the 583 participants at both sites gave personal information, usually including sex and age. Sexual themes constituted 5 percent of all messages, corresponding to about one sexual comment per minute. Obscene language characterized 5 percent of messages on the unmonitored site and 2 percent on the monitored site.

One-quarter of participants made sexual references, which was not unexpected given the amount of daily sex talk that has been reported among some teens. In the chat rooms, however, all members were confronted with the minority's sexual banter.

The protected environment of the monitored chat room resulted in markedly fewer explicit sexual messages and obscene words than the unmonitored chat room did, Subrahmanyam says. Moreover, the monitored site attracted more participants who identified themselves as young girls than did the unmonitored venue, which featured a larger number of correspondents who identified themselves as males in their late teens or early 20s.

Much of the explicit sexuality on the unmonitored site amounted to degrading and insulting comments, adding to concerns previously raised by other researchers that youths who visit such sites are likely to encounter sexual harassment from either peers or adults.

Subrahmanyam's team also conducted in-person interviews with teens who hadn't participated in the chat room study. The results suggest that only a small minority ever pretend to be other people on the Internet.

Intriguingly, teens who write online journals, known as blogs, often forgo sex talk for more-mundane topics, such as daily experiences at home and school, Subrahmanyam adds. In 2004, she analyzed the content of 600 entries in 200 teen blogs.

Teen blogs offer an outlet for discussing romantic relationships and, especially for boys, disclosing hidden sides of themselves, says psychologist Sandra L. Calvert of Georgetown University in Washington, D.C. In a 2005 online report with David A. Huffaker of Northwestern University in Evanston, Ill., Calvert described entries in 70 teen blogs, evenly split between bloggers who identified themselves as girls and as boys. The ages given ranged from 13 to 17.

Bloggers routinely disclosed personal information, including e-mail addresses and other contact details, the researchers found. Half the blogs of both boys and girls discussed relationships with boyfriends or girlfriends. Ten boys, but only two girls, wrote that they were using the blogs to openly discuss their homosexuality for the first time.

"Teenagers stay closer to reality in their online expressions about themselves than has previously been suggested," Calvert asserts.

Net Gains

Give a middle school child from a low-income household a home computer with free Internet access and watch that child become a better reader. That's the conclusion of a new study that highlights potential academic consequences of the so-called digital divide separating poor kids from their better-off peers.

A team led by psychologist Linda A. Jackson of Michigan State University in East Lansing gave computers, Internet access, and in-home technical support to 140 children. The mostly 12-to-14-year-old, African-American boys and girls lived in single-parent families with incomes no higher than $15,000 a year. The researchers recorded each child's Internet use from December 2000 through June 2002.

Before entering the study, these children generally did poorly in school and on academic-achievement tests. However, overall grades and reading achievement scores—but not math-achievement scores—began to climb after 6 months of home Internet use. These measures had ascended farther by the end of the study, especially among the kids who spent the most time online.

Participants logged on to the Internet an average of 30 minutes a day, which isn't much in the grand scheme of teenage Internet use: Teens in middle- and upper-class families average 2 or more Internet hours each day. Only 25 percent of the children in the study used instant messaging, and only 16 percent sent e-mails or contributed to online chat. These low numbers probably reflect a lack of home Internet access among the kids' families and friends. Also, their parents forbade most of the participating kids from contacting strangers in chat rooms.

Still, text-heavy online sites seem to have provided reading experience that translated into higher reading scores and grades, the researchers suggest. Although participants remained below-average readers at the end of the study, their improvement showed promise, according to Jackson and her colleagues.

These findings raise the unsettling possibility that "children most likely to benefit from home Internet access are the very children least likely to have [it]," Jackson's team concludes.

In stark contrast to their poor peers, wealthier middle school and high school students spend much of their time on the Internet trading instant messages with friends, an activity with tremendous allure for young people trying to fit into peer groups, says psychologist Robert Kraut of Carnegie Mellon University in Pittsburgh.

For teens, instant messaging extends opportunities to communicate with friends and expands their social world, Kraut suggests. He and his colleagues probed instant messaging in interviews with 26 teens in 2002 and in surveys completed by 41 teens in 2004.

Instant messaging simulates joining a clique, without the rigid acceptance rules of in-person peer groups, in Kraut's view. Each user creates his or her own buddy list.

Within these virtual circles, teens become part of what they regard as a cool Internet practice and, at the same time, intensify feelings of being connected to friends, even when sitting by themselves doing homework, Kraut says.

Still, Internet-savvy youngsters typically have much to learn about the social reach and potential perils of online communication, says education professor Zheng Yan of the State University of New York at Albany.

Yan interviewed 322 elementary and middle school students in a New England suburb. Participants also drew pictures to show what the Internet looks like and, when told to think of the Internet as a city, what types of people one would see there.

By ages 10 to 11, children demonstrated considerable knowledge of the Internet's technical complexity, such as realizing that Internet sites act as data sources for many computers.

Not until ages 12 to 13, however, did youngsters begin to grasp the Internet's social complexity, such as the large numbers of strangers who can gain access to information that a person posts publicly. Even then, the kids' insight into the online social world's perils remained rudimentary compared with that previously observed in adults.

Children and teens plastering personal thoughts and images on Web sites such as *myspace.com* "often don't realize how many people have access to that information, including sexual predators," Yan asserts. He encourages parental monitoring of Internet activities and regular discussions of online dangers with children.

Worldwide Peers

Adolescents who form global Internet communities show signs of developing their own styles of leadership and social involvement, a trend that Northwestern University psychologist Justine Cassell and her coworkers view with optimism.

Cassell's team examined messages from an online community known as the Junior Summit, organized by the Massachusetts Institute of Technology. University officials sent out worldwide calls for youngsters to participate in a closed, online forum that would address how technology can aid young people. They chose 3,062 applicants, ages 9 to 16, from 139 countries.

Those selected ranged from suburbanites in wealthy families to child laborers working in factories. Computers and Internet access were provided to 200 schools and community centers in convenient locations for those participants who needed them.

During the last 3 months of 1998, children logged on to online homerooms, divided by geographic regions. Members of each homeroom generated and voted on 20 topics to be addressed by the overall forum. Topic groups then formed and participants elected a total of 100 delegates to an expenses-paid, 1-week summit in Boston in 1999.

Cassell's group found that delegates, whom the researchers refer to as online leaders, didn't display previously established characteristics of adult leaders, such as contributing many ideas to a task and asserting dominance over others. While the delegates eventually sent more messages than their peers did, those who were later chosen as online leaders—regardless of age or sex—had referred to group goals rather than to themselves and synthesized others' posts rather than offering only their own ideas.

> "Children most likely to benefit from home Internet access [may be] the very children least likely to have [it]."
>
> —Linda A. Jackson,
> Michigan State University

Without in-person leadership cues such as height or attractiveness, online congregants looked for signs of collaborative and persuasive proficiency, the researchers say.

Outside the controlled confines of the Junior Summit, teens even in places where few people own home computers find ways to obtain vital Internet information. Ghana, a western Africa nation in which adolescents represent almost half the population, provides one example.

Researchers led by Dina L.G. Borzekowski of Johns Hopkins Bloomberg School of Public Health in Baltimore surveyed online experiences among 778 teens, ages 15 to 18, in Ghana's capital, Accra.

Two-thirds of the 600 youngsters who attended high school said that they had previously gone online, as did about half of the 178 teens who didn't attend school. Among all Internet users, the largest proportion—53 percent—had sought online health information on topics including AIDS and other sexually transmitted diseases, nutrition, exercise, drug use, and pregnancy.

Out-of-school teens—who faced considerable poverty—ranked the Internet as a more important source of sexual-health information than the students did, the investigators say.

In both groups, the majority of teens went online at Internet cafés, where patrons rent time on computers hooked up to the Internet.

Internet cafés have rapidly sprung up in unexpected areas, UCLA's Greenfield says. She conducts research in the southeastern Mexico state of Chiapas, which is inhabited mainly by poor farming families.

Small storefronts, each containing around 10 Internet-equipped computers, now dot this hard-pressed region, Greenfield notes. Primarily young people frequent these businesses, paying the equivalent of about $1 for an hour of Internet surfing.

"Even in Chiapas, adolescents are in the vanguard of Internet use," Greenfield remarks.

Making Relationships Work

A Conversation with Psychologist

The best science we have on relationships comes from the most intense relationship of all—marriage. Here's what we know about it.

JOHN M. GOTTMAN

It has become common to extol the value of human relationships in the workplace. We all agree that managers need to connect deeply with followers to ensure outstanding performance, and we celebrate leaders who have the emotional intelligence to engage and inspire their people by creating bonds that are authentic and reliable. There's a large and fast-growing support industry to help us develop our "softer" relationship skills; many CEOs hire executive coaches, and libraries of self-help books detail how best to build and manage relationships on the way to the top.

Despite all the importance attached to interpersonal dynamics in the workplace, however, surprisingly little hard scientific evidence identifies what makes or breaks work relationships. We know, for instance, that the personal chemistry between a mentor and his or her protégé is critical to that relationship's success, but we don't try to work out what the magic is, at least not in any rigorous way. The absence of hard data and painstaking analysis exacts a heavy price: When relationships sour, as they easily can, there's little guidance on what you can do to patch things up. Even the best human resources officers may not know how or when to stage an intervention. If companies were more effective in helping executives handle their relationships through difficult times, they would see the company's productivity soar and find it much easier to retain leadership talent.

Good relationships aren't about clear communication—they're about small moments of attachment and intimacy.

But if there's little research on relationships at work, some is beginning to emerge on relationships at home. That's good news because the way that people manage their work relationships is closely linked to the way they manage their personal ones. People who are abusive at home, for example, are likely to be abusive at work. If you believe that—as most psychologists do—then the relevance of the work of those who study relationships at home immediately becomes obvious.

Few people can tell us more about how to maintain good personal relationships than John M. Gottman, the executive director of the Relationship Research Institute. At the institute's Family Research Laboratory—known as the Love Lab—Gottman has been studying marriage and divorce for the past 35 years. He has screened thousands of couples, interviewed them, and tracked their interactions over time. He and his colleagues use video cameras, heart monitors, and other biofeedback equipment to measure what goes on when couples experience moments of conflict and closeness. By mathematically analyzing the data, Gottman has generated hard scientific evidence on what makes good relationships.

HBR senior editor Diane Coutu went to the Seattle headquarters of the Relationship Research Institute to discuss that evidence with Gottman and to ask about the implications of his research for the work environment. As a scientist, he refuses to extrapolate beyond his research on couples to relationships in the workplace. The media have sensationalized his work, he says. However, he was willing to talk freely about what makes for good relationships in our personal lives.

Successful couples, he notes, look for ways to accentuate the positive. They try to say "yes" as often as possible. That doesn't mean good relationships have no room for conflict. On the contrary, individuals in thriving relationships embrace conflict over personality differences as a way to work them through. Gottman adds that good relationships aren't about clear communication—they're about small moments of attachment and intimacy. It takes time and work to make such moments part of the fabric of everyday life. Gottman discusses these and other nuances of his wisdom, acquired from experience and research, in this edited version of Coutu's conversation with him.

You're said to be able to predict, in a very short amount of time and with a high degree of accuracy, whether couples will stay together for the long term. How do you manage that?

Let me put it this way: If I had three hours with a couple, and if I could interview them and tape them interacting–in positive ways as well as in conflict–then I would say that I could predict a couple's success rate for staying together in the next three to five years with more than 90% accuracy. I've worked with 3,000 couples over 35 years, and the data support this claim, which have now been replicated by other scientists.

Could you train me to decide whether I should hire Dick or Jane?

I know this question has come up in the media, which have tried to sex up my work. But the reliability you see in my research has to do with studying relationships specifically. Just to predict whether an interviewee would be a good fit for a job—you couldn't do it. At least I know *I* couldn't do it. I rely on my research to be able to look at *couples*. And even with couples, I need to witness a sample interaction. The more emotional and the more realistic the situation is, the better I am at predicting with a high level of accuracy.

For instance, one test we've used for years is the "paper tower task." We give couples a bunch of materials, such as newspaper, scissors, Scotch tape, and string. We tell them to go build a paper tower that is freestanding, strong, and beautiful, and they have half an hour to do it. Then we watch the way the couples work. It's the very simple things that determine success. One time we had three Australian couples do the task. Beforehand, we had the couples talk on tape about each other and about a major conflict in their relationship that they were trying to resolve. So we had some data about how relatively happy or unhappy they were. When one couple who came across as happy started building their paper tower, the man said, "So, how are we going to do this?" The woman replied, "You know, we can fold the paper, we can turn the paper, we can make structures out of the paper." He said, "Really? Great." It took them something like ten seconds to build a tower. The wife in an unhappily married couple started by saying, "So how are we going to do this?" Her husband said, "Just a minute, can you be quiet while I figure out the design?" It didn't take much time to see that this couple would run into some difficulties down the line.

Your work depends heavily on your interviewing technique. How did you develop it?

My hero was Studs Terkel. I think he's by far the greatest interviewer ever. Bill Moyers is good. Barbara Walters is very good, too, but Terkel is amazing. In one interview, he went into a woman's attic and said to her, "Give me a tour, tell me what's up here." He had a big cigar in his mouth, but he was really interested. Acting as the tour guide, she said, "Well, I don't talk much about this doll." Terkel pointed out that it was not a new doll. "No," she said, "my first fiancé gave me this doll, before he was killed in a car accident. He was the only man I've ever loved." Surprised, Terkel remarked, "You're a grandmother; you must have married." She replied, "Yeah, and I love my husband, but just not like I loved Jack." The woman then launched into a great monologue, prompted by Terkel. We studied his tapes and based our interview technique on his approach.

What's your biggest discovery?

It sounds simple, but in fact you could capture all of my research findings with the metaphor of a saltshaker. Instead of filling it with salt, fill it with all the ways you can say yes, and that's what a good relationship is. "Yes," you say, "that is a good idea." "Yes, that's a great point, I never thought of that." "Yes, let's do that if you think it's important." You sprinkle yeses throughout your interactions—that's what a good relationship is. This is particularly important for men, whose ability to accept influence from women is really one of the most critical issues in a relationship. Marriages where the men say to their partners, "Gee, that's a good point" or "Yeah, I guess we could do that" are much more likely to succeed. In contrast, in a partnership that's troubled, the saltshaker is filled with all the ways you can say no. In violent relationships, for example, we see men responding to their wives' requests by saying, "No way," "It's just not going to happen," "You're not going to control me," or simply "Shut up." When a man is not willing to share power with his wife, our research shows, there is an 81% chance that the marriage will self-destruct.

When a man is not willing to share power with his wife, our research shows, there is an 81% chance that the marriage will self-destruct.

Does that mean that there's no room for conflict in a good relationship?

Absolutely not. Having a conflict-free relationship does not mean having a happy one, and when I tell you to say yes a lot, I'm not advising simple compliance. Agreement is not the same as compliance, so if people think they're giving in all the time, then their relationships are never going to work. There are conflicts that you absolutely must have because to give in is to give up some of your personality.

Let me explain by illustrating from personal experience. My wife is very bad at just sitting still and doing nothing. A couple of years ago I gave her a book called *The Art of Doing Nothing*. She never read it. She always has to be up and about doing things. I'm not like that. I don't multitask the way she does; if I take a day off, I want it to be a day off. I want to play music; I want to have a sense of leisure. We fight about this difference all the time. She wants me to do stuff around the house, and I want her to take it easy. And it's worth fighting about this because it's an important personality difference between us. I don't want to adopt her style, and she doesn't want to adopt mine.

Another common issue in many relationships is punctuality. People have huge differences in their attitudes toward it and fight about it constantly. And they should—because unless you do, you can't arrive at an understanding of your differences, which means you can't work out how to live with them.

What else do people in relationships fight about?

I actually analyzed about 900 arguments last summer. With the help of the lab staff, I interviewed people about their fights—we saw them fighting in the lab and then outside the lab, and we talked about the issue. What we learned from measuring all these interactions is that most people fight about nothing. Their fights are not about money, or sex, or in-laws—none of that stuff. The vast majority of conflicts are about the *way* people in the relationship fight. One fight we studied was about a remote control. The couple was watching television, and the man said, "OK, let me see what's on," and started channel surfing. At one point the woman said, "Wait, leave it on that program, it's kind of interesting." He replied, "OK, but first let me see what else is on." She kept objecting until he finally said, "Fine, here!" and handed her the remote. She bristled and said, "The way you said 'fine,' that kind of hurt my feelings." He shot back with, "You've always got to have it your way." It may seem really elementary, but that's what people fight about. Unfortunately, most of these issues never get resolved at all. Most couples don't go back and say, "You know, we should really discuss that remote control issue." They don't try to repair the relationship. But repair is the sine qua non of relationships, so everybody needs to know how to process those regrettable moments.

I want to stress that good relationships are not just about knowing when to fight and how to patch things up. We also need humor, affection, playing, silliness, exploration, adventure, lust, touching—all those positive emotional things that we share with all mammals. Something that's been so hard for me to convey to the media is that trivial moments provide opportunities for profound connection. For example, if you're giving your little kid a bath and he splashes and you're impatient, you miss an opportunity to play with him. But if you splash back and you clean up later, you have some fun together and you both get really wet, laugh, and have a beautiful moment. It's ephemeral, small, even trivial—yet it builds trust and connection. In couples who divorce or who live together unhappily, such small moments of connection are rare.

We can't splash around at work. Are there equivalent ways to achieve connections there?

There are many similar things you can do in a work environment. You can go into your friend David's office and say, "How's little Harry doing?" And he might say, "You know, he really likes his new school. He's excited by it, and in fact you know what he's doing now . . .?" The conversation might take five or ten minutes, but you've made a connection. This goes for the boss, too. A lot of times the person who's running an organization is pretty lonely, and if somebody walks into her office and doesn't talk about work but instead asks about her weekend, the message is, "Hey, I like you. I notice you independent of your position." Within organizations, people have to see each other as human beings or there will be no social glue.

What about intimate relationships at work–thumbs up or down?

That can be really problematic. Marriage researcher Shirley Glass did some terrific work on friendship in the work-place. She gave this wonderful example of a man who hadn't had sex for a long time. He and his wife had a new baby and were fighting a lot. Then after work one day, he and his coworkers went out to celebrate a really successful quarter at the company. Everybody had a good time. People eventually started to go home, but this man and a female coworker lingered. They were talking about the excellent fourth quarter earnings, and she said, "You know, George, this is the happiest I've seen you in months." Nothing untoward was happening, but he was enjoying the conversation in a way that he hadn't with his wife in a long time. So on the way home, he thought to himself, "You know, we laughed and shared a lot, and it was kind of intimate, and I should really go home and say, 'Nancy, I'm really kind of worried because I just had a conversation with a woman at work, and I felt closer to her than I've felt to you in months, and it scares the hell out of me, and we need to talk.' " But he knew exactly how his wife would react. She'd tell him to grow up and would say, "Hey, I have this baby sucking at my teats and now you're being a baby, too. I don't need this kind of crap from you, so just suck it up and get on with it. You're a new father, and quit having those conversations with that woman at work." So he decided not to share the experience with his wife because, he thought, "Nothing really happened anyway." But something did happen, and now he's got a secret. That's the beginning of betrayal.

Is there no difference between an emotional and a physical affair?

I honestly don't think so. I've seen this in my clinical work and in my research. Most affairs are not about sex at all; they're about friendship. They're about finding somebody who finds you interesting, attractive, fascinating. This can be on a physical or an emotional level–it all boils down to the same thing.

What contributes to a successful long-term relationship?

Look for the positive in each other. Robert Levenson, of the University of California at Berkeley, and I are in the 18th year of a 20-year longitudinal study in the San Francisco Bay area. We have two groups of couples who were first assessed when they were in their forties and sixties and are now, respectively, in their sixties and eighties. The surprising thing is that the longer people are together, the more the sense of kindness returns. Our research is starting to reveal that in later life your relationship becomes very much like it was during courtship. In courtship you find your new partner very charming and positive. It was all so new then. You de-emphasized the negative qualities and magnified the positive ones. In the long term, the same thing happens. You say, "She's a wonder woman. She can get us through anything." For instance, my wife and I have just moved out of the house we lived in for 14 years, and she orchestrated the entire thing. She was amazing. My genius was to sit back and say nothing. In good relationships, people savor the moments like this that they have together.

Is there such a thing as an ideal relationship?

I don't really know. Somebody I admired a long time ago was Harold Rausch, now retired, from the University of Massachusetts, who studied relationships and decided there was an optimal level of intimacy and friendship—and of conflict. He called couples who had achieved those levels "harmonious."

He said that couples who preferred some emotional distance in their relationships were psychologically brittle and not very oriented toward insight and deep understanding. Rausch identified another type of couple—those who fought a lot and were really passionate—and he said they're messed up, too.

We studied those three groups of couples as well, and our research showed that they could all be successful. The people who wanted more distant relationships and friendships valued loyalty, commitment, and dedication but weren't so interested in intimacy. Still, they could have very happy marriages. You might think, "OK, they don't fight a lot in order to avoid conflict, and maybe that's bad for the kids." It turns out that wasn't true at all. We followed the kids' emotional and intellectual development, and a distant relationship between the parents turned out to be fine for the children. Our research showed that bickering a lot can be fine, too, provided that both people in the relationship agree to it. People have different capacities for how much intimacy and passion they want and how much togetherness they want. The problem is when there's a mismatch.

Within organizations, people have to see each other as human beings or there will be no social glue.

Are the short-term factors for success in relationships different from the factors that make for long-term success?

We face this question about short- and long-term success when we study adolescents and their relationships. We don't necessarily want a 14-year-old's dating relationship to last, but we'd like it to be a positive experience, and we'd like to facilitate our kids' growth and not lead them down a negative path. Whether we look at teenagers or at older couples, it turns out again and again that respect and affection are the two most important things. Whatever your age, there are so many ways you can show respect for your partner. Express interest in the story she's telling at dinner, pay him compliments, listen to her ideas, ask him to watch a *Nova* special with you so that you can discuss it later. The possibilities abound.

What other advice emerges from your study of good relationships?

I think that men need to learn how to embrace their wives' anger. This message is particularly pertinent today because women are now being educated and empowered to achieve more economically, politically, and socially. But our culture still teaches women that when they assert themselves they are being pushy or obnoxious. Women who get angry when their goals are blocked are labeled as bitchy or rude. If men want to have a good relationship with women, they have to be sensitive to the changing dimensions of power and control in the Western world. And they have to accept the asymmetry in our relationships for the time being. The good news is that embracing your wife's anger just a little bit can go a long way toward unleashing feelings of appreciation and affection.

I had this funny experience when I sold my book *The Seven Principles for Making Marriage Work* to my publisher. I met with the head of the marketing department, a young guy who leaned back in his chair as if he were not at all impressed by any of my work. He pointed his finger at me and said, "All right, tell me one thing in the next 30 seconds that I can do to improve my marriage right now!" I told him that if I were to pick just one thing it would be to honor his wife's dreams. The guy jumped up, put on his coat, and left the room. I found out months later that he had immediately hopped on the subway to Brooklyn, where he surprised his wife, who was at home with a young baby. Her mouth dropped when he asked her what her dreams were. He told me later that she said she thought he would never ask.

What would you suggest we be on guard against in relationships?

What I call the Four Horsemen of the Apocalypse—criticism, defensiveness, stonewalling, and contempt—are the best predictors of breakup or continued misery. Readers familiar with my work will remember that I consider contempt to be the worst: It destroys relationships because it communicates disgust. You can't resolve a conflict with your partner when you're conveying the message that you're disgusted with her. Inevitably, contempt leads to greater conflict and negativity. Our research also shows that people in contemptuous relationships are more likely to suffer from infectious illnesses—flu, colds, and so on—than other people. Contempt attacks the immune system; fondness and admiration are the antidotes.

Are you in a successful relationship?

Yes, my wife and I have just celebrated our 20th wedding anniversary, but we both had disastrous first marriages. Mine failed because my first wife and I had opposite dreams. I really love children and wanted to be a father, but she wasn't so sure and that was a deal breaker. Could a therapist have saved that relationship? I don't think so. My need to be a father was too great. And I'm so glad I became a dad. It's the most important thing I've ever done.

Blessed Are Those Who Mourn— and Those Who Comfort Them

In our death-denying society, all too often the message is: Get over it and get back to normal. The fact is, the bereaved's "normal" never will be the same.

DOLORES PUTERBAUGH

Disbelief is the first thing you feel. The news does not make any sense. There is some mental scrambling around for an anchor. Is this real? How could this be? There is sadness and surprise and, perhaps hidden in the back of your mind, a sense of relief that it did not happen to you.

A friend, coworker, or extended family member has lost a loved one. Perhaps it was after a long illness, or maybe it was sudden and even violent: a crime, an accident, or suicide. The deceased may have been very old or an infant, perhaps not even yet born. Your friend's life has been irreparably changed, and you have an important role to play—even if you are "just" a coworker.

We live in a death-denying society. Most companies offer little time off for survivors, with many people using vacation days or even unpaid leave to accommodate vigils, funeral, and initial recovery. The physically and emotionally wounded survivors return to school or work within days, and often the expectation is that they will be "back to normal." The fact is, their "normal" has changed forever. Bereavement is a ripping away of part of one's heart. A hospice nurse told me the thing that strikes her most about bereavement counseling is that people always are taken by surprise at how powerful it is; the societal message of "getting over it" has infected most individuals.

Since we all will go through this—not once, but many times—it makes sense to figure out what to do to be helpful. Perhaps this will come back around to us, or perhaps we will just have the satisfaction of knowing that we tried to be supportive of a friend in need.

In *Healing Grief at Work: 100 Practical Ideas After Your Workplace Is Touched by a Loss,* clinician Alan Wolfelt reveals the experience of a client whose coworkers announced, one year after her child's death, that it was time to put away the picture on her desk and move on with her life. Knowing that this is shockingly inappropriate still does not provide guidance on how to behave. Of course, you would like to think you are more compassionate than that, but how can one act on that compassion?

Some simple aspects to being appropriately supportive are: be physically present; do not assume the "expert's" position; be a friend.

If a coworker has lost a loved one, you might not think it appropriate to go to the vigil or the funeral. Go! The vigil, visitation, and funerals, as well as the meal afterwards, not only are for the deceased—they are for the mourners, who need affirmation of their loss, recognition of their status as mourners, and support in their time of pain. Make sure you sign the guest book, greet the family, and participate in the rites whenever appropriate. Religious rites exist to help honor the deceased person and to provide comfort to the bereaved; every faith has developed rites to be celebrated in community, not alone. As part of the community of survivors, your role is to offer support.

In the weeks after the loss, continue to provide a physical presence. You may be rebuffed; deal with it and keep trying. This is not a time to keep score over whose turn it is to call whom, or who is next to invite whom to lunch. Prepare meals; invite the mourners over for food or call and invite yourself (with a prepared meal) over to their house. Show up with cleaning supplies or with a box of tissues. It can mean a lot to someone if you are able to help with the tasks that the deceased used to do. The survivor may be too upset or physically incapable of taking over the deceased's chores. Asking for help is difficult for most people, so volunteer your services.

Losing someone we love creates a tremendous void inside. The mourner may feel completely without anchor. This individual cannot be expected to hold up his or her end of the relationship with you at present. Saying, "Call me if you want to talk," is not good enough; be the one who calls and says, "How are you?" or "What about going out for breakfast on Saturday?" Evenings and weekends usually are hardest for those in mourning; make yourself available and be specific with your invitations.

Mourners often complain to me that friends, coworkers, and extended family analyze their (the mourners') grief process and mental health. This is not useful feedback. A common intervention by nonmourners is to provide unsolicited instruction on what stage of grief the mourner is experiencing. Some friends attempt to provide comfort by trying to put the loss into perspective. Another common error is to give mental health diagnoses and recommendations. Not only is this presumptuous, but it is self-aggrandizing on the friends', coworkers', or extended family's part. It is as if to say, "Let's look at you as a case study."

In a similar vein, more misused than any other expert is Elisabeth Kubler-Ross, whose 1969 work, *On Death and Dying,* was based on intensive interviews with the terminally ill and their families. She identified specific stages that occurred between the terminal diagnosis and death: denial and isolation; anger; bargaining; depression; acceptance; and hope. In the first stage, the reality is not accepted; the patient believes this is not happening. In the second stage, the reality begins to set in, but there is anger. From a psychological standpoint, anger is the emotion that accompanies the desire to change a situation; the dying person wants to fight the terminal condition. Next comes bargaining, generally with God: if you cure me, I'll never ———— or I'll always ————. This normal reaction can become paralyzing if the ill person is burdened with an ill-formed theology that believes in a higher power who doles out earthly experiences based on behavior. When bargaining fails, a depressed state of helplessness often ensues. It is beneficial if the dying are able to reach a stage of acceptance and hope. With all due respect to Kubler-Ross and her landmark work with the dying, many researchers and clinicians believe we cannot transfer her stages of dying on those in grief.

These normal reactions to terrible news often have been used to provide a template for grief. However, other researchers and specialists in the field offer different structures for making sense of the mourning process. J.W. Worden identified four primary tasks of grieving that assure a healthy outcome: accepting the fact of the death; working through the pain of the grief; adjusting to a world without the deceased; and renegotiating the internal relationship with the deceased so that the survivor can move forward with life.

Friends and coworkers should—at all costs—avoid announcing to the bereaved what stage, phase, or task they believe the mourner is experiencing at present, or should be. There are not very many "shoulds," if any, in grieving. Each person's experience of grief is unique and even experienced counselors are hesitant to assess any judgment on where someone "should" be at a given point in their grief. There are some specific things that must happen for a grief to become integrated into the person, but these happen gradually, with some overlapping, regressing, patience, and considerable pain.

Gaining Perspective

Another error often made by those trying to comfort grieving persons is attempting to put things into perspective. Survivors have been told to be grateful that someone who died unexpectedly "went quickly without suffering," while those whose loved ones died in hospice care are informed that they are fortunate that there was an opportunity to "say goodbye." Others who nursed dying loved ones for weeks, months, or even years have confided that friends are less sympathetic because they presume they "had a chance to prepare and could do their grieving in advance." Each person's experience of grief is unique, shaped by the relationship as well as their history, spirituality, and physical, emotional, and mental resources. Friends and family should refrain from rating someone else's grief.

This also is not a time to diagnose. As a mental health professional, I sometimes am asked about this: When is grieving "depression"? This question most often comes from friends of a survivor. My response is that it is normal to feel depressed after a tremendous loss. For some months, the bereaved can expect to have disruptions in sleep, appetite, and energy. Some people will sleep often; a bereavement counselor with more than 20 years in the field describes the experience of grief like recovering from major surgery: sleep and healthy foods are imperative parts of healing; take naps every day, she recommends. Others may suffer lack of sleep. They feel exhausted and crave the escape of sleep, but are restless. Some lose their appetite while others may gain weight by eating for comfort. Concentration may be very poor, and short-term memory temporarily may become impaired. Most mourners can benefit from carrying a small notebook and writing down all tasks, even the simplest, for a few months after the death.

Some mourners will suffer a terrifying inertia. Taking the initiative to call you will be overwhelming. Simple tasks often take twice as long as usual. Doing any chores around the house will feel exhausting, and it especially can be difficult to take over the things that the deceased used to do. Others may fly into a frenetic pace, using busyness as a kind of drug to keep the emotional darkness at bay.

It is important to take some kind of action if the person shows signs of suicidal planning, such as talking about "when I'm gone," giving away personal items, and suddenly seeming upbeat (a sign that he or she has come to a decision about how to handle things—by dying). In this case, immediately go to other family members, clergy, or consult a mental health professional on what to do.

This is not a time to preach. Even ordained clergy assert that it is not recommended at this juncture to teach the mourning about your particular theology of life and death. Accept them where they are and help them find comfort within their own tradition. Encourage and let yourself be part of the rituals of grieving: prayer services, memorial Masses, candles, planting trees, or otherwise offering memorial are important means to express formally the process of separation and loss.

Being a good friend, coworker, or family member to someone who is mourning is simple, but not always easy. In many ways, you should continue whatever your relationship was before the death. If you had lunch together, continue to have lunch together; if you rotated card games at one another's home, keep up the routine.

Do not be afraid to say the deceased person's name. If tears come, it is not because you reminded the mourner of the dead person. He or she was in no danger of forgetting! Most people want to hear people talk about the person they love. They want to hear the funny stories and warm memories you may have, or be given the opportunity to share some of their own. Let them tell you the same stories over and over. This narration of the life they shared is part of the healing process. Ask to see photo albums and to hear the tales of times past. Listen to the story of the death and surrounding experiences as often as you have to. They are integrating the story of the person they love and have lost into their life in the present.

Mourners may ask if they are "going crazy" based on poor concentration, edginess, thinking they see or hear the deceased, and either great tearfulness or an inability to cry. It would help if friends and coworkers were patient and accepting of these aspects to grief.

Keep in mind the anniversaries of the death and, if you were close to the people, any significant dates such as birthdays or wedding anniversaries. Monthly anniversaries of the death are very difficult and mourners are well aware of these dates. Send a card, bring in flowers, or invite your friend over for a meal.

Holidays will be terribly difficult: Do not wait until the last minute to invite someone in mourning over for Thanksgiving, a concert, and other holiday (or nonholiday) religious or social activities. If the person is "taken" for Thanksgiving, ask them for the next day. That typical four-day holiday weekend can be torture if it seems like everyone else is with people they love.

Let's Talk—Or Not

For many, talking about their feelings is difficult. Our voyeuristic television shows may indicate otherwise, but it often is hard to discuss one's innermost feelings. Activities done side-by-side, rather than face-to-face, may encourage gradual conversation and sharing of thoughts, feelings, and memories surrounding the deceased's life, death, and the survivor's life since the death. Fishing, walking, and long drives are great ways to let someone have an opportunity for private conversation.

When conversation can occur, hold back trite sayings such as "He's in a better place," or "She's your guardian angel," or (perhaps worst of all), "It was God's will." Without intimate familiarity with the mourner's theology, you risk hurting that individual terribly. People in mourning do not need fortune telling about their future prospects ("You'll have other children" or "You're young . . . you'll find someone else"). They do not need to be advised about having a "stiff upper lip" or "toughing it out."

Do not singlehandedly take on responsibility to spare this person from grief. If you are very close with the individual in mourning, be sure you have a support system of your own. Spending a lot of time with someone who is grieving can be upsetting. You may find yourself recalling your own grief experiences and feelings of loss. Share these, at first, with someone else in your circle rather than with the bereaved. They are not ready to commiserate until later in the process.

Most important, do not take a grieving person's anger, tears, rebuffs, or rejection personally. It will be healthier for you and more helpful for your friend if you bear in mind that terrible pain sometimes interferes with polite behavior. Respect people's desire for some time and privacy but do not give up, walk away, or leave them alone.

DOLORES PUTERBAUGH is a psychotherapist in private practice in Largo, Fla.

UNIT 8

Personality Processes

Unit Selections

Key Points to Consider

- How does being reared in one culture versus another influence the self-concept?

- How does a person with a high sensation-seeking trait behave? Is this trait good or bad?

- Can personality change? If so, what sorts of things can people do to improve their personality?

- Can optimism be learned? If so, how does one go about it?

Student Web Site

www.mhcls.com

Internet References

Great Ideas in Personality
   http://www.personalityresearch.org/
The Personality Project
   http://personality-project.org/personality.html

Sabrina and Sadie are identical twins. When the girls were young, their parents tried very hard to treat them equally. They dressed them the same, fed them same meals and allowed them to play with the same toys. Each had a kitten from the same litter. Whenever Sabrina received a present, Sadie received one, too, and vice-versa. Both girls attended dance school and completed early classes in ballet and tap dance. In elementary school, the twins were both placed in the same class with the same teacher. The teacher also tried to treat them the same.

In junior high school, Sadie became a tomboy. She loved to play rough-and-tumble sports with the neighborhood boys. On the other hand, Sabrina remained indoors and practiced the piano. Sabrina was keenly interested in the domestic arts such as painting, needlepoint, and crochet. Sadie was more interested in reading novels, especially science fiction, and watching adventure programs on television.

As the twins matured, they decided it would be best to attend different colleges. Sabrina went to a small, quiet college in a rural setting, and Sadie matriculated at a large public university. Sabrina majored in English, with a specialty in poetry; Sadie switched majors several times and finally decided on a psychology major.

Why, when these twins were exposed to the same early childhood environment, did their interests, personalities, and paths diverge later? What makes people—even identical twins—so unique, so different from one another? The study of individual differences is the domain of personality psychology. The psychological study of personality has included two major thrusts. The first has focused on the search for the commonalties of human behavior and personality. Its major question is: How are humans, especially their personalities, affected by specific events or activities? The second has focused on discovering the bases on which individuals differ in their responses to events. In its early history, this specialty was called genetic psychology because most people assumed that individual differences resulted from differences in inheritance. By the 1950s, the term genetic psychology had given way to the more current term: the psychology of individual differences.

Today, most psychologists accept the principle that both genes and the environment are important determinants of any

© Brand X/JupiterImages

type of behavior, whether it be watching adventure movies *or* sitting quietly and reading *or* caregiving to the elderly. Modern researchers devote much of their efforts to discovering how the two sources of influence interact to produce a unique individual. Thus, the focus of this unit is on personality characteristics and the differences and similarities among individuals.

Culture and the Development of Self-Knowledge

Although a great deal of work in the past decades has shown cultural variations in self-knowledge among adults, not until recently have researchers started to examine developmental processes and mechanisms that give rise to the variations. I discuss our research on the development of two kinds of self-knowledge: autobiographical memory and self-concept. Our findings indicate that children develop culture-specific self-knowledge early in life; the two kinds of self-knowledge reinforce each other at both individual and cultural levels; and early narrative practices constitute an important resource from which children draw cultural views about the self to incorporate into their self-understanding and remembering.

QI WANG

I am a wonderful and very smart person. A funny and hilarious person. A kind and caring person. A good-grade person who is going to go to Cornell. A helpful and cooperative girl.

I'm a human being. I'm a child. I like to play cards. I'm my mom and dad's child, my grandma and grandpa's grandson. I'm a hard-working good child.

The above self-descriptions were given by a Euro-American 6-year-old and a Chinese 6-year-old, respectively. While the first focuses on the child's own positive depositional traits and qualities, the second attends to the child's social roles and significant relations.

In the past two decades, a great deal of theoretical and empirical work has shown that self-knowledge in adults often integrates and reflects the prevailing cultural views of self (see Markus & Kitayama, 1991). In cultures that subscribe to an autonomous self and the inherent separateness of distinct persons, such as that of the United States, individuals often view themselves in terms of their unique personal attributes and qualities. In contrast, in cultures such as those of China and Japan, where prominence is given to interrelatedness and collectivity and the self is largely defined by one's place in a matrix of social networks, individuals tend to perceive themselves by focusing on their social roles and relationships. Yet not until recently have researchers started to examine the developmental origins of culture-specific self-knowledge.

Two Kinds of Self-Knowledge

My colleagues and I have studied the development of two kinds of self-knowledge: *autobiographical memory* and *self-concept* (Neisser, 1988). Autobiographical memory, or the "extended self," refers to long-lasting memory of significant personal experiences from an individual's life. Self-concept, or the "conceptual self," refers to an individual's conceptual representations of him- or herself. We view the development of self-knowledge as a process of cultural adaptation in which children, guided by socialization agents, internalize cultural views about the self into their own self-understanding and remembering (Wang, 2004; Wang & Ross, in press). This process is further facilitated by the interplay between the two kinds of self-knowledge: Self-concept enables privileged encoding of and access to autobiographical information that confirms the views about the self favored by the culture; autobiographical memory, in turn, sustains the development and maintenance of a self-concept that integrates cultural views about the self as its central component.

We use open-ended, free-narrative methods, which, compared with psychometric measures that have a preexisting norm often in favor of Western samples, allow children to describe themselves and their experiences in their own terms and from their own perspectives. Our findings address three interrelated questions, which I discuss in turn.

Does Culturally Construed Self-Knowledge Emerge Early?

Let's first consider self-concept. One important dimension of self-concept concerns whether individuals focus on their unique personal attributes or on their social roles and relationships in defining themselves. We have examined this self-dimension in children of different ages. Our youngest group was from an ongoing longitudinal study of Chinese families in China, first-generation Chinese immigrant families in the United States, and

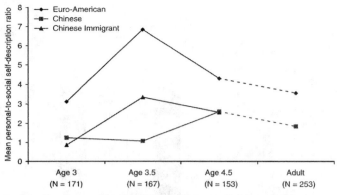

Figure 1 Mean personal-to-social self-description ratio as a function of culture and age. Children's responses were classified as "personal" when they referred to personal attributes, preferences, possessions, and behaviors unrelated to other people (e.g., "I'm happy," "I have a teddy bear") and as "social" when they referred to group memberships and interpersonal relations (e.g., "I am a girl," "I love my Mommy"). Some children did not provide any social self-descriptions, so the ratio was constructed for each child by dividing the number of personal self-descriptions by the number of social self-descriptions plus 1—that is, personal/(social + 1). The ratio represents a focus on personal relative to social aspects of self. The same ratio construct was used with the self-description data of Euro-American and Chinese adults. (The adult data come from Wang, 2001.)

Euro-American families. We interviewed children three times at home when they were 3, 3.5, and 4.5 years of age. We told children that we would like to write a story about them and asked them what things we should put in the story. Compared with their Chinese and Chinese immigrant peers, Euro-American youngsters were more likely to focus on their personal, as opposed to social, aspects of self across all age points (see Fig. 1). Interestingly, the pattern of cultural differences in preschool children's self-descriptions is not dissimilar to that of adults (Wang, 2001).

Cultural beliefs may also influence other dimensions of self-concept (Markus & Kitayama, 1991). The emphasis on autonomy in Euro-American culture endorses a context-independent self; such a self is defined by an individual's dispositional qualities and inner traits that are invariant over time and unconstrained by social situations. The high value placed on self-enhancement and self-esteem further encourages positive self-views that are considered crucial to one's psychological well-being. In contrast, the emphasis on social relatedness in Chinese culture advocates the situation boundedness of persons; in this view, the self is experienced and expressed in specific interpersonal contexts and characterized by an individual's overt behaviors. Self-criticism and humility are encouraged, to facilitate self-improvement and group solidarity.

In line with these analyses, I examined self-concepts in Euro-American and Chinese preschoolers, kindergartners, and second-graders (Wang, 2004). Children provided self-descriptions in a storytelling task. Across all age groups, Euro-American children described more abstract dispositions and inner traits (e.g., "I am smart") than did Chinese children, who referred to more situation-bound characteristics (e.g., "I play with my

friend Yin-Yin at school") and overt behaviors (e.g., "I practice the piano every day"). Euro-American children also gave more positive self-evaluations (e.g., "I'm beautiful") than did Chinese children, who more frequently described themselves in neutral terms. And again, Euro-American children focused more on their personal and less on their social aspects of self than did Chinese children.

Cultural views about the self can further shape how individuals sample, process, and retain autobiographical information; they thus affect memory *accessibility, style,* and *content.* An emphasis on autonomy may direct cognitive resources toward elaborate encoding of personal experiences, especially specific, one-moment-in-time events unique to the individual and focusing on the individual's own roles and perspectives (e.g., "the time I won the spelling-bee competition"). Such memories are likely to become richly represented and highly accessible during recall. They help individuals distinguish themselves from others and reaffirm their unique identity. An emphasis on relatedness may, instead, prioritize the retention of social knowledge critical for social harmony and group solidarity. Detailed remembering of one's own experiences may not be accentuated in this context. And when remembering the past, individuals may attend to generic routine events (e.g., "going to parties"), which, in contrast to memories of specific episodes, are often skeletal, have few sensory-emotional details, and generally serve to direct one's (appropriate) behavior in particular, oftentimes social, situations (Nelson & Fivush, 2004). Individuals may also focus on information about group activities and interactions, helping them relate to significant others and to the community.

Studies have supported this perspective. Compared with Asians, European and Euro-American adults are able to access more distant and more detailed very-long-term memories, such as early childhood experiences; retrieve more frequently unique, one-time episodes (as opposed to generic events); and focus more on their own roles and predilections (e.g., Mullen, 1994; Wang, 2001). We find the same pattern of cultural differences in children as young as age 3 or 4 (Han, Leichtman, & Wang, 1998; Wang, 2004). For instance, in Wang (2004), Euro-American and Chinese preschoolers, kindergartners, and second-graders were asked to recount four personal events such as a recent time when they did something special and fun. Across all age groups, Euro-American children provided lengthier, more detailed accounts and recalled more specific episodes than Chinese children did. They also more frequently commented on their preferences, opinions, and agency (e.g., "I liked the birthday present," and "My mom didn't let me go out but I did anyway") than did Chinese children, who more often spoke of other people relative to themselves (see Fig. 2).

Interestingly, Euro-Americans attend to specific episodes and focus on their own roles and perspectives not only when remembering events that happened to them personally but also when remembering things about other people. In a recent study (Wang, 2006), Euro-American and Taiwanese young adults were asked to recall their earliest childhood memories in response to cue words of self, mother, family, friend, and surroundings. Euro-Americans frequently reported specific events and focused on their own roles and predilections, even when recalling memories about their mother and their family. Taiwanese, in comparison, more often described generic events and emphasized the roles of others, across all memories.

How Are the Two Kinds of Self-Knowledge Related?

Given that self-concept and autobiographical memory are both culturally constructed from an early age, they may be linked not only at the cultural level but at the individual level as well. Thus, individuals with a greater autonomous sense of self should have more detailed, specific, and self-focused autobiographical memories. Consistent with this reasoning, our studies show that regardless of culture, children and adults who dwell more on personal attributes and qualities when describing themselves are more likely to provide detailed, specific, and self-focused memories, compared with those who dwell more on social roles and group memberships (Wang, 2001, 2004). In a more recent study, it was found that a focus on personal aspects of self in 3-year-olds uniquely predicted the amount of event details they recalled, independent of culture, gender, and language skills (Wang, in press).

Self-concept and autobiographical memory may further correspond across an individual's life periods. Theorists contend that individuals, no matter where they live, develop both personal (self-perceived distinctiveness) and social (self-perceived connectedness) identities in response to basic human needs and universal societal expectations (e.g., Kagitcibasi, 2005). The increasing autonomy and relatedness during ontogeny, then, should be reflected in individuals' lifespan retrieval. That is, when asked to recall personal experiences from their lives, individuals should exhibit an increase in both personal and social focuses in memories from earlier to later life periods. This prediction was confirmed in our study with Euro-American and Chinese middle-aged adults (Wang & Conway, 2004). Compared with participants' reported memories from childhood and youth, their memories from midlife periods were more likely to be specific episodes, focused more on the preferences and perspectives of the remember; midlife memories also attended more to social groups and significant others, independent of memory length. Thus, autobiographical remembering appears to be in concert with the lifespan development of personal and social identities.

If individuals possess both personal and social-relational aspects of self, it should be possible to prompt them to focus temporarily on either. We found that such shifts in attention can affect the content and accessibility of early memories (Wang & Ross, 2005). We asked European and Asian American adults to describe themselves by listing either ten unique personal attributes (personal prime) or ten memberships in social groups (relational prime). We then asked them to recall their earliest childhood memory. Regardless of culture, the personal prime elicited memories that focused more on the remember and less on social interactions than did the relational prime. The personal prime also helped Asians access more distant childhood memories, such that the first memories they reported were as early as those of Euro-Americans.

So, the focuses on autonomy and relatedness in self-views vary across individuals; they both increase within an individual with

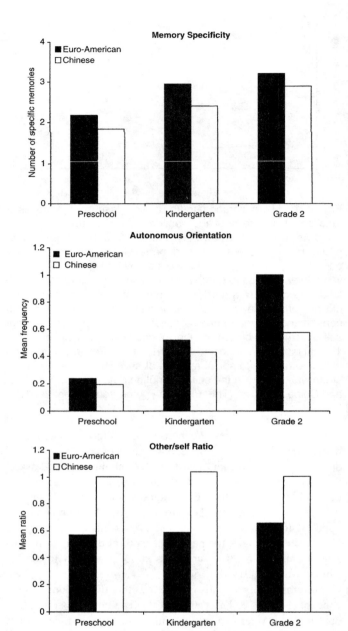

Figure 2 The specificity and content of children's autobiographical memories as a function of culture and age. Memory specificity (top panel) was scored based on the number of specific episodes (as opposed to generic events) children recalled, with a possible score range of 0 to 4. Autonomous orientation (middle panel) was scored by counting the number of instances children commented on their preferences, opinions, and agency per memory event. "Other/self ratio" (bottom panel), the number of times children mentioned other people over the number of times they mentioned themselves, captures the degree to which children attended to the roles of others versus themselves in their memories. The Euro-American group differed significantly from the Chinese group on all measures. From Wang (2004).

development; and they can change temporarily across circumstances, which further shape the content, style, and accessibility of autobiographical memories. These individual cognitive processes may elucidate how cultural differences in self-knowledge are formed and sustained: People incorporate into their self-concepts differing cultural views about the self that facilitate culture-specific forms of autobiographical remembering (i.e., which memories and which aspects of the memories are most likely to be accessible and enduring); their memories, in turn, support and regulate different modes of self-concept endorsed by their cultures.

Narrative Co-Construction of the Self

How do children come to incorporate cultural views of self into their own self-knowledge? Family memory sharing may serve as a critical forum for cultural transmission, in which parents model to children the appropriate ways of organizing, evaluating, and sharing their past experiences and further help children build the critical link between autobiographical memory and self-concept (Nelson & Fivush, 2004). This joint activity embodies rich cultural messages and parents' socialization goals pertaining to the self (Miller, Wiley, Fung, & Liang, 1997). A cultural emphasis on individuality and the use of memory to promote an autonomous sense of self may encourage memory sharing as a means of helping children construct elaborate personal stories to build a unique individual identity; a cultural emphasis on relatedness and collectivity may prioritize the use of memory sharing to instill social knowledge and a sense of belonging.

In a series of studies, we observed Euro-American and Chinese mothers sharing memories at home with their 3-year-olds in semi-structured interviews (see Wang & Ross, in press). Mothers selected past events in which both mother and child had participated, and then discussed the events with their children. Euro-American mothers frequently supplemented embellished information and commented and expanded on children's

memory responses (e.g., "Yes, you got a balloon! A yellow balloon doggy. That was exciting."). In doing so, they scaffolded children's participation and meanwhile provided a narrative structure for the construction of elaborate personal stories. Furthermore, the conversations often centered on the child, and mothers frequently referred to the child's roles and predilections. Chinese mothers, in comparison, tended to take a directive role in posing pointed questions to children and provided less embellishment or feedback. They frequently referred to social norms and behavioral expectations and placed past events in a more social-relational context. These cultural differences are illustrated in the conversational excerpts about an emotionally salient event between two mother–son pairs (Table 1).

Here, both conversations were about an incident involving conflicts between the child and adults and, given the emotional nature of the events, both mothers referred to their children's feeling states. However, the style and content focus of the two conversations differed. The Euro-American mother frequently confirmed and elaborated on her child's speech. She focused the discussion on the child's actions and predilections, and further acknowledged the child's emotional tantrum as an expression of individuality. Such conversations facilitate children's detailed remembering of personal experiences that highlight their uniqueness and socialize children into an autonomous sense of self. In contrast, the Chinese mother initiated a directive and didactic talk with her child. The focus of the conversation was not to construct an elaborate personal story but to instill proper behavioral conduct in the child. The child's emotions were treated as part of his wrongdoing, which resulted in punishment so that a lesson could be learned. Such conversations situate children in a relational hierarchy, encourage them to abide by rules and develop a sense of belonging, and yet downplay the use of memory to construct a unique individual identity.

Table 1   Mother (M) and Child (C) Conversation Excerpts

Euro-American mother and son

M: Tell me about the craft fair. Mommy and Daddy went to the craft fair. What did we go there for, do you remember?

C: Yeah. Christmas time.

M: It was Christmas time, we were getting some Christmas presents. Did you want to be there?

C: No.

M: And what did you start to do?

C: Hit.

M: You started to hit and what else?

C: Scratch.

M: Do you remember why you were so mad?

C: Yell.

M: You were yelling very loud, I sure agree with that.

C: And crying.

M: And crying too. Why were you so mad?

C: Because I just want to do whatever I want to do.

M: You want to do whatever you want to do. I see.

Chinese mother and son

M: What story did Teacher Lin tell you at school?

C: "Qiu Shao-yun." He didn't move even when his body was on fire.

M: The teacher taught you to follow the rules, right?

C: Um.

M: Then why did you cry last night?

C: You and Grandma didn't let me watch TV.

M: Do you know why we didn't let you watch TV?

C: You were worried that my eyes would get hurt. I wanted to watch "Chao-Tian-Men." I was mad. I insisted on watching it.

M: So you got spanked, right?

C: Um.

These different narrative practices are mirrored in children's developing self-knowledge. Euro-American youngsters focus more on their unique attributes in defining themselves and provide more detailed and self-focused autobiographical accounts than their Chinese peers do (e.g., Han et al., 1998; Wang, 2004). Our longitudinal data (Wang, 2005) further showed that, regardless of culture, children whose mothers more frequently engaged them in the construction of elaborate personal stories came to recall more detailed and self-focused autobiographical memories. Maternal style further served as a potent mediator in explaining cultural differences in children's memories (Wang, in press). These findings suggest that family memory sharing directly contributes to the development of culturally construed self-knowledge.

Future Directions

The development of self-knowledge diverges early across cultures. It is a process taking place through individual cognitive processes and in adult-guided participation in the sharing of memory narratives. Our findings highlight the importance of studying developmental origins in order to understand cultural diversity in human cognition and behavior. Future research will continue to identify mechanisms for the development of culture-specific self-knowledge. For example, at which stage(s) of personal remembering (e.g., encoding, retention, retrieval) does culture exert an influence? How do children develop culture-specific self-knowledge in different life domains (e.g., family, school life)? How do language and culture interact in the process of narrative self-making? More specifically, which aspects of cultural self-knowledge most reflect the linguistic constraints of a language, and which aspects are relatively independent of language influences? It is also timely to study the impact of immigration and intercultural exchange on self-development to uncover the dynamic and adaptive nature of the cultural construction of the self.

References

Kagitcibasi, C. (2005). Autonomy and relatedness in cultural context: Implications for self and family. *Journal of Cross-Cultural Psychology, 36,* 403–422.

Han, J.J., Leichtman, M.D., & Wang, Q. (1998). Autobiographical memory in Korean, Chinese, and American children. *Developmental Psychology, 34,* 701–713.

Markus, H.R., & Kitayama, S. (1991). Culture and the self: Implications for cognition, emotion, and motivation. *Psychological Review, 98,* 224–253.

Miller, P.J., Wiley, A.R., Fung, H., & Liang, C.H. (1997). Personal storytelling as a medium of socialization in Chinese and American families. *Child Development, 68,* 557–568.

Mullen, M.K. (1994). Earliest recollections of childhood: A demographic analysis. *Cognition, 52,* 55–79.

Neisser, U. (1988). Five kinds of self-knowledge. *Philosophical Psychology, 1,* 35–59.

Nelson, K., & Fivush, R. (2004). The emergence of autobiographical memory: A social cultural developmental theory. *Psychological Review, 111,* 486–511.

Wang, Q. (2001). Cultural effects on adults' earliest childhood recollection and self-description: Implications for the relation between memory and the self. *Journal of Personality and Social Psychology, 81,* 220–233.

Wang, Q. (2004). The emergence of cultural self-construct: Autobiographical memory and self-description in American and Chinese children. *Developmental Psychology, 40,* 3–15.

Wang, Q. (2005, April). The socialization of self in Chinese and immigrant Chinese families. In R. Chao & H. Fung (Co-chairs), *Cultural perspectives of Chinese socialization,* Invited symposium conducted at the biennial meeting of the Society for Research in Child Development, Atlanta, Georgia.

Wang, Q. (2006). Earliest recollections of self and others in European American and Taiwanese young adults. *Psychological Science, 17,* 708–714.

Wang, Q. (in press). The relations of maternal style and child self-concept to autobiographical memories in Chinese, Chinese immigrant, and European American 3-year-olds. *Child Development.*

Wang, Q., & Conway, M.A. (2004). The stories we keep: Autobiographical memory in American and Chinese middle-aged adults. *Journal of Personality, 72,* 911–938.

Wang, Q., & Ross, M. (2005). What we remember and what we tell: The effects of culture and self-priming on memory representations and narratives. *Memory, 13,* 594–606.

Wang, Q., & Ross, M. (in press). Culture and memory. In H. Kitayama & D. Cohen (Eds.), *Handbook of Cultural Psychology.* New York, NY: Guilford Publications.

Address correspondence to Qi Wang, Department of Human Development, Cornell University, Ithaca, NY 14853 4401; e-mail: qw23@cornell.edu.

Acknowledgments—Part of the research was supported by NIMH Grant R01-MH64661 to the author. I thank Charles Brainerd, Lee Lee, and the Editor for helpful comments.

From *Current Directions in Psychological Science,* Vol. 15, No. 4, pp. 182–187. Copyright © by the Association for Psychological Science. Reprinted by permission of Blackwell Publishing, Ltd.

Frisky, but More Risky

High sensation-seekers' quest for new experiences leads some to the high-stress jobs society needs done but makes others vulnerable to reckless behavior.

CHRISTOPHER MUNSEY

In the early 1960s, University of Delaware psychology professor Marvin Zuckerman, PhD, and his fellow researchers noticed something unique about the young men volunteering for their sensory-deprivation experiments: Many were free-spirited types, wearing motorcycle jackets and favoring long hair over the close-cropped style still prevalent in those years. Yet it seemed to Zuckerman, initially at least, that the experiment couldn't have been more dull: Participants lay motionless for hours on an air mattress in a darkened, double-walled sound-proof room, the monotony broken only by restroom breaks and cold sandwiches.

Puzzled at the incongruity, Zuckerman then found out what was behind it: Some participants had supposedly experienced hallucinations during prior sensory-deprivation experiments conducted by other scientists, according to newspaper reports. Some of the volunteers now showing up for Zuckerman's experiments came seeking the same hallucinogenic sensations, he says.

He found that these volunteers scored high on a measure he developed to gauge sensation-seeking, and that high sensation-seekers also were more likely to volunteer for experiments on hypnosis and the testing of hallucinogenic drugs.

The discovery helped Zuckerman develop a new sensation-seeking construct for personality, one recognizing the role that an individual's desire for varied, complex, novel and intense stimulation plays in determining personality and behavior. In 1971 in the *Journal of Consulting and Clinical Psychology* (Vol. 36, No. 2, pages 45–52), he published the Sensation Seeking Scale Form IV, a personality test designed to measure a person's predilection for thrill- and adventure-seeking, experience-seeking, disinhibition and boredom susceptibility.

Subsequent research suggests that high sensation-seeking reaches into every aspect of people's lives, affecting engagement in risky sports, relationship satisfaction before and during marriage, tastes in music, art and entertainment, driving habits, food preferences, job choices and satisfaction, humor, creativity and social attitudes.

Compared with low sensation-seekers, high sensation-seekers are more likely to smoke, abuse alcohol and use drugs, and are more attracted to high-stress careers. Probing further, Zuckerman has found evidence for both a physiological and biochemical basis for the sensation-seeking trait: High sensation-seekers appear to process stimuli differently, both in the brain and in physiological reactions.

High sensation-seekers, who crave novel experiences, are at one end of the scale, while low sensation-seekers, who actively avoid excitement, are at the other end. Most people fall in the middle, with a moderate inclination to seek out new experiences, but a disinclination to push too far, he says.

What's Different

When presented with new stimuli, high sensation-seekers have a different orienting reflex (OR) than that of low sensation-seekers. As defined by Zuckerman, the OR is a measure of arousal and interest triggered by any novel object appearing in a perceptual field.

One study found that when subjects with high disinhibition scores were presented with a moderate-intensity tone, their heart-rates slowed down on the first exposure, while the heart rates of low sensation-seekers quickened.

Another of his studies, published in the *Journal of Personality* (Vol. 58, No. 1, pages 313–345) in 1990, indicates that the differences between high and low sensation-seekers extend to the cortex of the brain, with high sensation-seekers showing an "augmenting" electrochemical reaction, or increasing amplitude of cortical-evoked potentials (EPs) in response to increasing intensities of stimulation. Low sensation-seekers, however, demonstrate a reducing reaction, showing little EP increase in relation to increasing stimulus intensity, and sometimes showing a reduction in EP amplitudes at the highest intensities of stimulation.

The personality trait may have a biochemical basis as well. High sensation-seekers have lower levels of monoamine

Psychologists Are Thrill-Seekers Too

Come Memorial Day weekend, you can usually find Frank Farley, PhD, and a band of about a half-dozen devoted fellow psychologists in the stands at the Indianapolis 500 waiting for the green flag to signal the race's start.

"When those incredibly powerful engines start up, the roar is deafening, and the whole racetrack shakes and reverberates," says Farley, a Temple University professor.

Yet Farley sees something deeper at work than just spectacle at the Indy 500—namely, the human desire to pursue thrills for their own sake.

"It's kind of a focused example of thrill-seeking, of the vicarious enjoyment of thrills," he says.

He started coming to the race in part because of his friendship with Richard Hurlbut, PhD, a former president of the Wisconsin Psychological Association and clinical psychologist in Stevens Point, Wis. Hurlbut arranges the tickets and hotel rooms for psychologists making the annual pilgrimage.

Hurlbut's father owned an auto parts store and got free tickets to the race when he was a boy. Hurlbut stopped going for a while during his college years and first career as a high school English teacher, but started attending again with his psychologist colleagues in the early 1980s.

Together, they observe the full range of human behavior—"from the most classy things to the most debasing things," Hurlbut says—at what's been described as the largest regularly scheduled gathering of humanity in North America. It's all there, from drivers performing at their mental and physical peak, roaring more than 220 miles per hour six inches from the lip of a concrete wall, to the beer-belly bacchanalia among the tens of thousands of fans packed in the infield. There's slightly less inebriation than in years past, though, when at least one old, beat-up car would be doused with gasoline and ceremonially torched once the race started, he says.

Besides watching their fellow fans, the psychologists follow the careers of the drivers such as Rick Mears, a four-time Indy winner who has gone on to become a successful coach. Despite suffering a crushing foot injury during his driving career, Mears worked his way back into racing and recovered his ability to maintain a constant speed, completing lap after lap on the 2.5 mile track with times varying by as little as two-hundredths of a second.

"The people that get to that level are remarkably good, and remarkably devoted to what they're doing, and they risk their lives," Hurlbut says.

Back home at his practice, Hurlbut sometimes draws on Indy 500 lore to help treat people with chronic pain. His favorite is the tale of a 1920s race winner whose leg welded to the manifold after some protective metal ripped loose. It wasn't until after the driver completed the 200-lap, 500-mile race that he noticed that the heat had severely burned his leg.

Just like the driver, people can sometimes overcome their pain if they're intensely focused on something else, Hurlbut says.

—C. Munsey

oxidase (MAO) type B, an enzyme involved in the regulation of neurotransmitters, particularly dopamine, according to Zuckerman's book "Behavioral Expressions and Biosocial Bases of Sensation Seeking" (Cambridge University Press, 1994) and a research review chapter he wrote in the book "Biology of Personality and Individual Differences" (Guilford Press, 2006).

Moreover, research Zuckerman published with M. Neeb in *Personality and Individual Differences* (Vol. 1, No. 3, pages 197–206) in 1980 determined that sensation-seeking, which is higher in men than in women, peaks in the late teens and early 20s and gradually declines with age, along with levels of testosterone. MAO, which is low in high sensation-seekers, increases with age in the blood and brain.

Since the development of the sensation-seeking scale, Zuckerman has developed the Zuckerman-Kuhlman Personality Inventory measuring impulsive sensation-seeking as a major trait of personality, along with four other major traits: sociability, neuroticism-anxiety, aggression-hostility and activity.

Zuckerman emphasizes that high sensation-seeking is a normal personality trait, despite its association with risky behavior. For example, the trait plays a role in bringing people into prosocial occupations such as law enforcement, firefighting and emergency room medicine—high-stress jobs that would shut down low sensation-seekers.

"In a diverse society, you need both types," he says. "You need people to keep the books and make laws and have families, and you need your adventurers like Columbus to explore and find excitement."

Now a professor emeritus at Delaware, Zuckerman is preparing to publish his third book on sensation-seeking, "Sensation Seeking and Risky Behavior," through APA later this fall.

Looking to the future, Zuckerman says researchers need to learn more about how people's genetic makeup, family environment and social life interact to determine the sensation-seeking aspect of their personalities.

The Big T Personality

How a person's thrill-seeking traits fit into the larger society—and how society can channel positive aspects of thrill-seeking and dampen negative aspects—is a question that fascinates Temple University psychologist Frank Farley, PhD. A former APA president, Farley has developed a personality model that describes the Big T (thrill-seeking) personality.

"To me, one of the deepest motivations in the human spirit is to lead an exciting, interesting and thrilling life. It's not for everybody, but it's a powerful force," he says.

Farley's study of thrill-seeking has taken him to Nepal, where he interviewed Mount Everest climbers, to China and later to the Baltic states where he participated as a crew member in cross-country hot air balloon racing. He travels the world seeking extreme risk-takers, who provide him, he argues, a more valid profile than college students do.

"If I want to study major risk-taking, I've got to go to where the major risk-takers are," he says.

"To me, one of the deepest motivations in the human spirit is to lead an interesting, exciting, and thrilling life. It's not for everybody, but it's a powerful force."

—Frank Farley
Temple University

In Farley's model, the Big T "positive" personality can account for involvement in entrepreneurship, extreme sports such as parachuting and hang-gliding, or creative science and art. By contrast, the Big T "negative" personality may turn to crime, violence or terrorism "for the thrill of it"—embracing the destructive, dark side of the trait.

A Big T positive personality can find thrills in physical or mental activities. Albert Einstein, for example, was a Big T "mental" personality who found intellectual discovery thrilling.

Farley sees thrill-seeking everywhere, from special effects-laden Hollywood blockbusters to the hundreds of thousands of fans who gather annually at the Indianapolis 500 motor race, enjoying the vicarious thrill of watching hurtling race cars (see sidebar). It extends to the highest reaches of creativity and innovation in science, business and education, as he outlined in a chapter in "Fostering Creativity in Children, K–8: Theory and Practice" (Allyn and Bacon, 2001).

Farley theorizes that in a country such as the United States—a Big T nation built on the risky adventure of immigration—thrill-seekers are given more freedom to pursue their quest for bigger thrills and risks than in countries with more structured cultures, such as China.

Often democratic societies benefit economically, as risk-takers become ever more creative in their endeavors, says Farley. He cites as an example of a creative risk-taker Microsoft founder Bill Gates—a college dropout whose ideas helped revolutionize how society uses computers.

Despite America's tradition of thrill-seekers, Farley sees a constant tension between thrill-seekers and people who want stricter safety regulations, citing the ongoing debate over the toll of climbers killed on Mount Everest every year. Mountain climbers think the chance to reach the top is worth it, despite the risk of dying.

"Their view is, 'We're all going to die. I'd rather die undertaking a grand adventure than in bed with tubes running through my body,'" he says.

A Sense of Calm

While psychologists like Farley research thrill-seekers, others like Chris Carr PhD, focus their practice on them. Carr works with athletes who might be considered sensation-seekers and thrill-seekers by anyone not involved in their sports.

An Indianapolis-based sport psychologist, Carr served as team psychologist for the U.S. men's alpine skiing team from 1992 to 2002 and is currently working with the U.S. national diving team. He also consults with Rising Star Driver Development, a Chicago-based firm that helps younger race car drivers transition into professional racing. The skiers he's worked with rocket down icy slopes at speeds topping 70 miles per hour, while the divers leap off platforms more than 32 feet above a pool, twisting and turning to the water below.

Interestingly to him, the elite athletes he works with don't talk so much about the thrill of pulling off such physically challenging feats, but rather about the sense of calm they feel when performing at their peak, Carr says.

"I think they love the sensation of moving; they love the sensation of being in control when maybe everyone else would feel out of control," he says.

Second Nature

Your personality isn't necessarily set in stone with a little experimentation, the ornery and bleak can reshape their temperaments and inject pluck and passion into their lives.

KATHLEEN MCGOWAN

Call it the cult of the ugly duckling. We devour stories of personal transformation: the uptight guy who learns to cut loose, the wallflower who becomes the life of the party. It's the staple of self-help books and romantic comedies—as well as the primary reason that people drag themselves to high-school reunions. ("Can you believe that guy who never talked is now a real estate mogul?") But psychologists have long believed that major personality makeovers are impossible. In fact, the big themes of personality—whether you are shy or outgoing, relaxed or a worrywart—seem to be scripted at a very young age.

Recently, however, personality researchers have begun looking more closely at the smaller ways we can and do change. Positive psychologists, who investigate human talents, have identified 24 character strengths—familiar qualities we admire, such as integrity, loyalty, kindness, vitality—and are limning them to find out why these faculties come so naturally to some people. What they're discovering is that many of these qualities amount to habitual ways of responding to the world—habits that can be learned.

"The evidence is good that most of these things can be changed," says Christopher Peterson, professor of psychology at the University of Michigan. "That doesn't mean it's easy. It doesn't come in a flash." Psychologists talk about personality change the way doctors talk about the biological set point for weight: Nature designed some of us to be heavy, and others to be slim. It's not impossible to alter your weight, but it requires going against your own grain.

But eventually, the new way of being can come to feel like second nature. Peterson cites himself as an example. Inherently introverted, he realized early on in his career as an academic that his reticence would prove disastrous in the lecture hall. So he learned to be more outgoing, to crack jokes, and to entertain big classes full of psychology students. "Do I still have an introverted temperament? Yes, in that if I'm in a big crowd, I get anxious," he says. "But my behavior is consistently extroverted, because I've worked to make it that way. Now, it's very spontaneous."

Whether Peterson's personality has truly changed is almost beside the point. He may not be an extrovert, technically speaking, but he behaves like one, and is treated like one. Tweaking the way you interpret and react to the world can be a transformative experience, freeing you up to act in new ways. At first, it feels awkward, even bizarre. But with new behaviors come new experiences, creating a feedback loop that, over time, reinforces the transition.

Some sought-after qualities are easier to develop than others. Courage, joy, passion, and optimism are among the more amenable to cultivation, but each requires mastering a different—and sometimes surprising—set of skills. To bring more joy and passion into your life, you must paradoxically be more open to experiencing sadness, anxiety, and fear. Learning to think like an optimist, it turns out, is less important than acting like one. And being courageous has nothing to do with how afraid you are: It's a matter of how strongly you feel about your goals. Cultivating these characteristics puts you on the road to that blend of happiness, satisfaction, and purpose that is the height of human functioning, what positive psychologists call "the good life."

Optimism: Make the Road by Walking

When David Fajgenbaum was 18 years old, he had a horrible shock. Just as he was gearing up for his new life at Georgetown University, his mother was diagnosed with brain cancer. Instead of jumping into the freshman whirlwind of libraries, parties, and football games, he spent every weekend at home with his family. "I had three feelings: I felt alone, I felt helpless, and I felt guilty for being at school," he says now.

Before his mother's death, an idea struck him: To honor her, he'd reach out to others who were going through the same thing. Back on campus, he quickly found that beyond ordinary counseling, the university had no services for grieving students. So Fajgenbaum launched a support group, Students of Ailing Mothers and Fathers.

The project snowballed. Both affected students and their friends wanted to do something useful to combat their terrible feelings of helplessness, and so the group organized fundraisers for research money, and began helping younger kids in high schools. The organization now has more than 20 chapters, and even earned a "Brick" award, a national prize for youth service.

Even after his mother died, Fajgenbaum did not withdraw. Instead, he spent three to four hours every day building his group. "I invested everything I had in it" Fajgenbaum says now. "And it's the most rewarding thing, to honor somebody and at the same time be able to have an impact." He took action despite his own pain—a mainstay of the optimistic mind-set.

Optimists seem to be sprinkled with fairy dust. They suffer less and recover quicker. They're healthier and better-liked and have stronger marriages and more fun. It's enough to make the rest of us gloomy—except that psychologists believe that a lot of these qualities stem from cognitive habits that can be learned. More than any other major personality trait, optimism is a matter of practice.

More than any other major personality trait, optimism is a matter of practice.

The key to increasing optimism lies in understanding its true nature. It's not relentless cheer or "positive thinking." It has more to do with how you behave, says Suzanne Segerstrom, an associate professor of psychology at the University of Kentucky in Lexington. "I think an optimistic outlook can be cultivated, but it's even better to cultivate optimistic behavior—engagement and persistence toward one's goals," she says.

Anticipating a better future, an optimist takes the steps necessary to create it. If Fajgenbaum, now 23, were more pessimistic, he'd probably have given up when he found out that Georgetown didn't have the support networks he sought, figuring that it was impossible for him, a bereaved freshman, to do anything about it. Instead, he resolved to build them himself.

Pessimists are skeptical that their own actions can lead to good results and tend to overlook positive outcomes when they do occur. To overcome this stumbling block, Segerstrom recommends in her recent book, *Breaking Murphy's Law: How Optimists Get What They Want from Life—and Pessimists Can Too,* that you train yourself to pay attention to good fortune. Keep a log in which you write down three positive things that come about each day. This will help you convince yourself that favorable outcomes actually happen all the time, making it easier to begin taking action.

Keep a journal, too, but don't write down your darkest thoughts and fears. Instead, envision a future that you desire and describe how it could evolve out of your present circumstances. By clarifying exactly what you'll need to do to get what you want, you can create your own map to a more hopeful state of mind.

Then, with the pump primed, it'll be easier to make small moves that lead to gratifying results, building further enthusiasm

that will protect you from setbacks. Fajgenbaum was a finalist for the Rhodes scholarship, but didn't get the award. Never mind. He's now finishing his master's degree in public health at Oxford—thanks to a different award—and after that, will go on to medical school at the University of Pennsylvania to study oncology. He thinks he has a shot at curing cancer. The rest of us might call that Pollyannaish, but he's just calling it his life's work.

Passion: Taking the Plunge

You know it when you see it. Someone who is fully engaged, deeply involved, totally dedicated—a person brimming with passion. But you've probably never seen it take the form of a 525-foot dive straight down into the depths of the ocean. Tanya Streeter, 35, is the Tiger Woods of freediving, the sport of plunging deep into the water without tanks or other breathing equipment. Beginning in 1998, she set nine world records, often besting both men and women. An average person can hold her breath for one minute. Streeter can do it for six.

The physical stamina required for this sport is intense. But the psychological demands were even more overwhelming—and for Streeter, that was the allure. Sure, she was terrified some of the time. Who wouldn't be? But she learned to untangle her fears from her judgment of what her body and mind could do. "In my career as a competitive freediver, there was a limit to what I could do—but it wasn't anywhere near where I thought it was" she says. "When I did my first deep dive, it was 100 feet. I thought I'd never go any farther."

Passions don't arrive like bolts out of the blue. They build slowly, through the process of gradual mastery.

By 2003, Streeter had smashed every record she worked against, and saw no point in rehashing old glories. So she switched to another extreme sport: television hosting. She'd always been passionate about the ocean. Now, she had the opportunity to promote conservation and environmentalism using her celebrity and her amazing swimming skills to introduce viewers to the wonders of the sea.

We spend so much time experimenting with foods, with ways to organize our houses, and so little time experimenting with all the ways we can act as a person.

Streeter was not a natural in front of the camera. The first day of filming her first ocean documentary, she was painfully self-conscious. "I was horrible," she says. "I sucked." When it was over, she strapped on her fins and took off for a reef for a good cry. But as she's become better at hosting, she's enjoyed it more and more. "It's just so difficult to be relaxed and calm and who you are on camera," she says. "That's the endless—and the most satisfying—challenge."

It's tempting to brand Streeter as a fundamental go-getter, born with fire in her belly. But finding a pursuit that pushes your buttons can infuse anyone with sudden zeal for life. The secret about consuming passions, though, is that while they appear effortless, they require discipline and ability. If they were easy, they wouldn't be so rewarding. Such passions—anything from becoming an opera aficionado to a black belt in karate—tend to be "very open-ended in the amount of skill or knowledge required," says psychologist Paul Silvia of the University of North Carolina at Greensboro. The Holy Grail comes in moments of "flow," when you are so absorbed in what you're doing that you lose yourself. This, in turn, generates feelings of mastery, well-being, and enduring satisfaction.

Many people have at least one such passion. Streeter already has two. But for those who are seeking this sense of fulfillment, there are a few tricks, suggests Todd Kashdan, a psychologist at George Mason University. The first step is to commit to learning a bit about a subject. Passions don't arrive like bolts out of the blue. They build slowly, through the process of gradual mastery. "Passion and interest, the research is clear, come out of practice and expertise," says Peterson.

As a greenhorn, you also have to put up with feeling like an idiot—to tolerate and laugh at your own ignorance. "You must be willing to accept the discomfort and negative feelings that come your way," says Kashdan.

In fact, those butterflies in your stomach will probably be the first sign that you've hit upon a potential pursuit, says Streeter. "The thing that scares you the most tends to be the most fulfilling," she says. "It doesn't have to be something great. It has to be something that you aren't sure you can do."

Joy: The Art of Loving Life

Mauro Zappaterra was in the fast lane of the fast track, among the elite of young physician-scientists. After grueling training at Harvard Medical School, in January of 2004 he plunged into the research he'd been longing to do, the project that would earn him his Ph.D.

The problem: He was miserable. "I've always been really excited about life," he says. "And then I got to the lab, and it wasn't working" His research didn't mesh with his curiosity about healing, which was what had brought him into medicine. And he was preoccupied with the future. His girlfriend urged him to take some time off, but "vacation" and "break" are foreign concepts to M.D./Ph.D. students. Finally, he did—and it was a transforming experience. During eight months in Santa Fe, Zappaterra soaked up everything he could about healing techniques not taught at Harvard: polarity therapy, meridians, trauma resolution. "I was interested in how compassion, healing, and medicine could be intertwined," he says.

When he got back from Santa Fe, Zappaterra switched labs to study how cerebrospinal fluid nourishes and protects the developing nervous system. This cutting-edge research project also connects to his ongoing training in craniosacral therapy, an alternative medical practice in which the cranial bones, spine, and connective tissue are subtly contacted to bring harmony to the nervous system and thereby treat pain, stress, and injuries.

He also vowed to live more fully in the present moment, and to look for the joy in everything, including failure, disappointment, and sickness. He used meditation, focusing methods, and techniques learned from craniosacral therapy to reach his goals. That's when Zappaterra stumbled upon one of the counterintuitive realities of personality change: The kind of joy he found was often quiet and reflective rather than loud and exuberant. The way Zappaterra, now 32, describes it today, it's as if he feels all of his feelings more deeply, and takes pleasure even from sadness. "I can be joyous, even when I'm not in a joyful mood," he says. In the lab, failure is a constant. For every experiment that goes well, 99 don't work at all. But Zappaterra now believes that these frustrations and setbacks help him learn—about both his research and himself.

Bad things will come find you. . . . For the positive stuff, you have to open the door, go hunt for it, and find it.

Essentially, what he trained himself to do is what Loyola University psychologist Fred Bryant calls "savoring": the art of managing positive feelings. Whereas coping well means dealing successfully with problems and setbacks, savoring—glorying in what goes right—is an equally crucial emotional competence. "If all you're doing is trying to get by, trying to avoid the bad, you're missing half of life," says Bryant, author of *Savoring: A New Model of Positive Experience.* Although people tend to think that taking pleasure in good things comes naturally, it's really a skill. "Bad things will come and find you, knock down your door, and make you deal with them," he adds. "The positive stuff ain't like that. You have to open the door, go hunt for it, and find it."

To heighten joy in life, Bryant suggests that when something good happens, you make time to pay attention to it. Share the experience: The happiest people celebrate triumphs with others. Take a "mental photograph" in which you describe the positive event and its circumstances to yourself in great detail.

Joy can also be held back by rigidity. Kashdan recommends scrutinizing the prohibitions and barriers that structure your life. "The way to living a more zestful life is to be guided and flexible rather than governed," says Kashdan. Zappaterra's turn-around came when he realized that he needed to take time off, even though it violated the creed of M.D./Ph.D. students.

Try paying more attention to your mind-set, Kashdan adds. Are you concentrating on avoiding failure or looking forward to an opportunity to do something well? "The protection mode—focusing on being safe—might get in the way of your reaching your goals." For example, are you hoping to get through a business lunch without embarrassing yourself, or are you thinking about how riveting the conversation might be? That slight difference in mentality "changes how you think, how you feel, what parts of the brain light up," says Kashdan. It subtly inflects your interactions with the world, and is one simple way to have more fun with what you already do.

As with other changes, learning to be more joyous does not come quickly. When Zappaterra got back from Santa Fe, he planted a dozen seeds from a split-leaf philodendron, a slow-growing houseplant that eventually produces huge, glossy leaves. Zappaterra tended the seedlings as a daily reminder of how long it takes to make a real change in a human life. Nearly three years later, he's learned to get better at seeing the good in things. And he's enjoying his big, beautiful plants.

Courage: Doing the Right Thing

Usually, we think of courage as physical bravery—the backbone it takes to face enemy fire or stand up to a dictator. But ordinary life demands its own style of bravery, more humble and harder to spot. Day-to-day courage might involve confronting a bullying boss. It could mean stepping up to take responsibility for a mistake. For industrial engineer Kenneth Pedeleose, it meant speaking out against something he thought was wrong.

Pedeleose, an analyst at the Defense Contract Management Agency, which monitors federal military contracts, was stationed at a plant in Marietta, Georgia, where military cargo planes were being built. His job was to oversee the contracts, and he didn't like what he saw: high prices for spare parts ($714 for rivets and $5,217 for brackets) on one project and serious safety violations on another. In 2002, he and other engineers went "public" sending a report to the Congress members making decisions about military operations.

The Department of Defense launched a major investigation of the project, and an inspector general's report later substantiated many of Pedeleose's allegations. The agency found it would be too dangerous to use these planes for their main purpose: dropping equipment and troops into hostile areas. In 2006 the contract was restructured to include more oversight and accountability—and lower prices.

Was Pedeleose honored for his vigilance? Not exactly. He was labelled a whistleblower, suspended twice in the past four years, and had to fight to get his back pay reinstated (he won). The experience was stressful and draining, he says. Pedeleose estimates he has spent 2000 hours over the years uncovering fraud and abuse, and defending himself against retaliation. Nonetheless, he is now working on his fifth report, which he also plans to send to Congress.

"What I saw sickened me," he says now. "If I could have stopped an airplane from crashing, and I just sat back and didn't do anything about it, I couldn't have looked at myself in the mirror." Pedeleose was in the position to make a difference, and had the knowledge and the authority to call attention to the wrongs he had witnessed. Another key: He prepared his case meticulously, marshalling all the facts and documenting every allegation. "Bravery would play into it, but I calculated it so I had a high chance of success. It means more when you can prove what you're saying."

Pedeleose's story illuminates a widely misunderstood truth about courage: It is motivated not by fearlessness, but by a strong sense of duty. People who behave bravely often say they were afraid at the time, finds Cynthia Pury, a psychologist at Clemson University. But their principles forced them to take action. Her survey research revealed that whether a student acted courageously had more to do with how strongly he or she felt about the situation than with how frightening it was.

Pury believes that people can learn to become more courageous. Many of her students described doing the same things before they took action. Faced with a risky situation, they first tried to calm themselves down. They prepared for the situation, looking for a way to mitigate the danger, just as Pedeleose did by documenting his allegations. And they focused on what they were trying to accomplish, and how important it was. "I don't think any intervention about courage is going to go that far unless you help people decide what's important," she says.

"Being courageous is really a large number of moments in which, in the face of feeling uncomfortable, you still went forward," says Kashdan. Set up small behavioral experiments for yourself, he suggests. Try a few episodes of sticking your neck out. "We spend so much time experimenting with foods, with different ways to organize our houses, and so little time experimenting with all the ways we can act as a person." Flexibility is the hallmark of psychological health, and it can be energizing and even thrilling to step out of your habits.

Over the long term, picking up a new character trait may help you inch toward being the person you want to be. And in the short term, the effort itself could be surprisingly rewarding, a kind of internal adventure—a way to see the world from a different angle—without ever leaving home.

KATHLEEN MCGOWAN is a former senior editor at *PT* and a freelance science writer living in New York City.

UNIT 9
Social Processes

Unit Selections

Key Points to Consider

- Why are social behaviors the domain of psychologists and not just sociologists?

- Can the same person be both good and bad? What causes a person to flip-flop between the two?

- What is prejudice? Discrimination? An implicit bias? If people deny or are unaware of their own biases, how can psychologists possibly study them?

- Are humans destined to seek out the company of others? If yes, why?

- Is modern technology driving us away from or toward others? How has technology changed the way we interact with one another?

Student Web Site
www.mhcls.com

Internet References

Nonverbal Behavior and Nonverbal Communication
   http://www3.usal.es/~nonverbal/
The Social Psychology Network
   http://www.socialpsychology.org/

Everywhere we look there are groups of people. Your introductory psychology class is a group. It is what social psychologists would call a secondary group—a group that comes together for a particular, somewhat contractual reason, and then disbands after its goals have been met. Other secondary groups include athletic teams, church associations, juries, and committees. Can you think of other examples of secondary groups?

There are other types of groups, too. One is the primary group. A primary group has much face-to-face contact, and there is often a sense of "we-ness" in the group (or cohesiveness, as social psychologists would call it). Examples of primary groups include families, suite mates, sororities, and teenage cliques. What other primary groups have punctated your life?

Collectives, or very large groups, are loosely-knit, massive groups of people. A stadium full of football fans would be a collective. A long line of people waiting to get into a rock concert would also be a collective. A mob in a riot would be construed as a collective, too. As you might guess, collectives behave differently from primary and secondary groups. What examples of collectives can you think of?

Mainstream American society and any other large group that shares common rules and norms are also groups, albeit extremely large groups. Although we might not always think about our society and how it shapes our behavior and our attitudes, society and culture nonetheless have a measureless influence on us. Psychologists, anthropologists, and sociologists alike are all interested in studying the effects of a particular culture on its group members. In this unit we will look at both positive and negative forms of social interaction.

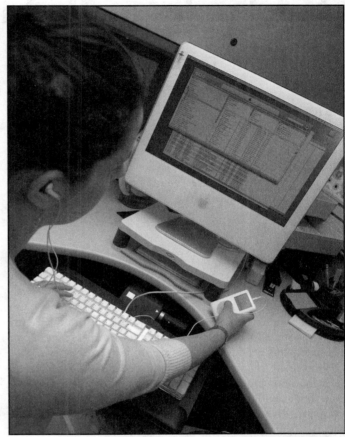

© The McGraw-Hill Companies, Inc./John Flournoy, photographer

Bad Apples or Bad Barrels?

Zimbardo on 'The Lucifer Effect'.

Eric Wargo

It is rare when a social scientist actually embraces theologically loaded words like "good" or "evil." Most prefer to speak in more muted terms of violence and aggression, or use the sanitized, judgment-free language of psychopathology—the language of disorders.

Not so, Philip Zimbardo.

"Psychologists rarely ask the big questions," the eminent Stanford psychologist said, addressing a standing-room-only crowd gathered to hear his talk, "The Lucifer Effect: Understanding How Good People Turn Evil," at the APS 18th Annual Convention. "We have all kinds of great techniques for answering small questions. We've never bothered to ask the big questions. It's time we asked the big questions like the nature of evil."

In a young century already dominated by iconic images of evil, the photographs with which he opened his presentation were both familiar and hard to watch. "This," he said, "is the ultimate evil of our time: The little shop of horrors, the dungeon, Tier 1A, the night shift, at Abu Ghraib." The pictures, a few of which had become well known from media reports of the prison, showed Army reservist guards torturing and humiliating Iraqi prisoners—naked prisoners stacked in pyramids or crawling on the floor with leashes; a prisoner standing in a black hood with electrodes on his fingertips; naked terrified prisoners being threatened with attack dogs or having guns pointed at their genitals by hideously masked guards; and worse.

"Pretty horrible," Zimbardo said, breaking the stunned silence in the room.

All of the photographs, he explained, were what he called "trophy photos" that had come from the guards' digital cameras. Zimbardo had access to them because he had served as an expert witness for the defense of one of the guards who had been tried for the atrocities. Despite the natural repulsion it was easy to feel toward those guards, Zimbardo's aim was to show how readily, given the right circumstances, almost any normal person can become an agent of evil.

Their accusers called them "bad apples"—a dispositional account that simply blames the individual for wrongdoing. But as psychologists, Zimbardo said, it is necessary to assume that the perpetrators of the abuses at Abu Ghraib and other prisons in Iraq "didn't go in there with sadistic tendencies, this is not part of their whole lifestyle, they are not serial murderers and torturers." Rather, they were transformed into perpetrators of evil by their situation, the "bad barrel" of war.

Known to everyone in the audience as the researcher who conducted the famous 1971 Stanford Prison Experiment, Zimbardo is probably the best-positioned psychologist in the world to deliver such a situational analysis of atrocity. "We imagine a line between good and evil," he said, "and we like to believe that it's impermeable. We are good on this side. The bad guys, the bad women, they are on that side, and the bad people never will become good, and the good never will become bad. I'll say today that's nonsense. Because that line is . . . permeable. Because sometimes, just like human cells, material flows in and out. And if it does, then it could allow some ordinary people like you to become perpetrators of evil."

From Jekyll to Hyde

Beginning with the classic studies of diffusion of responsibility, Zimbardo walked his engrossed audience through a great tradition of 20th-century social-psychological research seemingly tailor-made to understanding the situation at Abu Ghraib.

Ask a classroom of students who would be willing to pull the trigger to execute a condemned traitor; no one will raise their hands. Alter the conditions such that one would be part of a large firing squad in which there is only one real bullet, no one knowing who had fired the fatal shot, resistance to committing the deed lessens. "If you can diffuse responsibility, so people don't feel individually accountable, now they will do things that they ordinarily say 'I would never do that.'" This basic psychological principle is just one ingredient in the potion that can turn good Dr. Jekylls into sadistic Mr. Hydes.

Many of the other ingredients were revealed in Stanley Milgram's classic 1961 study of obedience to authority—in which over two thirds of subjects in a study ostensibly about memory went all the way in delivering what they thought was a lethal shock to another person (actually an actor feigning agony) when ordered to do so by an authority figure in a lab coat. Subsequent studies by other researchers in which male and female psychology students delivered actual nonfatal but painful shocks to a puppy (causing it to yelp and cry)—they were led to believe they would get a failing grade if they failed to condition the puppy—further revealed how easily people's scruples can evaporate when something even as minor as a grade is at stake.

From such studies, Zimbardo said, we can learn important principles about how to create obedience. He listed several, including the importance of a legitimate-sounding cover story (e.g., a memory study, or "national security"), a legitimate-seeming authority figure, and rules that are vague enough that they are hard to understand or remember. You also, he said, need a model of compliance that, ironically enough, allows room for dissent (" 'Yes, I can understand. Yeah, cry, go ahead and cry. Just keep pressing the button' "). Showing slides of the mass suicide/execution of 912 People's Temple cult members in Guyana in 1978, Zimbardo added that it is also important to "make exiting difficult. This is one of the big things all cults do: They literally create a barrier to leaving [by saying] 'If you exit, you're going to end up mentally impaired.' Literally a lot of people in practicing cults are there because they don't know how to exit."

Situations in which people are depersonalized are good breeding grounds for evil, Zimbardo said. Among the most disturbing of the Abu Ghraib photographs showed an Army reservist guard with his face painted like a hideous skeleton (modeled after the violent rock group "Insane Clown Posse"). "Can you imagine what it must have been like to be a prisoner, watching one of your guards look like this?" Zimbardo discussed a number of deindividuation studies in which disguises such as hoods facilitated overcoming moral barriers to hurting another person. He also cited anthropological research showing that warriors in cultures that donned masks or costumes before engaging in battle were significantly more likely to torture, mutilate, and kill their enemies than warriors in cultures that didn't engage in self-disguise. "Masks have terrible power, they're a medium of terror. And of course the first terrorists in the United States were the Ku Klux Klan." Military uniforms, like disguises, are tools of deindividuating a person. And depersonalizing the enemy—if only through linguistic labels—is the flip side of the coin: He cited a study by Albert Bandura in which students delivered much higher electric shocks to another group of participants merely if they had overheard that those students from the other college seemed like "animals."

Zimbardo's famous Prison Study exemplifies all of the above principles and how they can be used to create evil. After randomly assigning 24 normal, psychologically healthy college students to roles of prisoner and guard, giving each group suitably depersonalizing attire (the guards wore reflective sunglasses, for example—an idea Zimbardo said he got from the movie *Cool Hand Luke*)—the students began very quickly to lose their everyday personalities and fulfill their assigned roles. Guards quickly began giving prisoners humiliating menial tasks, then forced them to strip naked and subjected them to sexual degradation. "Within 36 hours, the first normal, healthy student prisoner had a breakdown. . . . We released a prisoner

each day for the next five days, until we ended the experiment at six days, because it was out of control. There was no way to control the guards."

Ordinary People, Extraordinary Conditions

The parallels between the Stanford Prison Experiment and Abu Ghraib are striking. "What we've done is substituted social psychology for Dr. Jekyll's chemical—transforming good ordinary people into perpetrators of evil. So essentially we took the chemical out of Dr. Jekyll's hand. It's not necessary. You can do it using social psychology."

Thus Zimbardo's role as a witness for the defense of the reservist sergeant in charge of Tier 1A (where the infamous abuses were committed) made perfect sense. "This is Chip Frederick," he said. "He is the one who got the idea for the iconic image of torture, the hooded man"—referring to the now-famous photograph of a hooded Iraqi prisoner—"He put electrodes on his fingers, he put him on a box, and said, 'You get tired, you fall off, you get electrocuted.' Imagine the terror. But what was Frederick like before going out into the desert to do that terrible stuff?"

Like any of the students in Zimbardo's study, or any of the hundreds of participants in Milgram's or other similar studies, Frederick is—and was, before his fateful tour of duty—a normal healthy person. He had a distinguished work and military record and a healthy family life. "I had the army's permission to have a whole battery of psychological tests conducted by an assessment expert," Zimbardo said. "I interviewed him at my home. Normal. No evidence of any psychopathology. No sadistic tendencies. His only negatives were obsessive about orderliness, neatness, discipline, personal appearance—all of which was absent at Abu Ghraib." A series of slides of Frederick and his family taken both before and after his hellish experience in Iraq—including a charming photo of Zimbardo and Frederick embracing like old friends—drove his normality home.

According to Zimbardo, the inhuman conditions at the prison—which had been Saddam Hussein's torture chamber before the war—created the situation necessary to effect a Jekyll/Hyde transformation in Frederick's (and his fellow guards') character. Forced to work 12-hour shifts, seven nights a week, for 40 days without a break, in hellishly filthy conditions (without toilets or running water) and under constant enemy bombardment, it sounds like a picture of hell. "Frederick was in charge of 1,000 prisoner, 12 reservist guards, 60 Iraqi police guards who were smuggling weapons and drugs to the Iraqi prisoners. They had no training. There was never supervision on anyone's part. [Frederick] rarely left the prison. . . . Tier 1A became his total reference group, and we know what that means."

The situationist explanation does not absolve Frederick and the other guards from responsibility, Zimbardo emphasized. "What happened at Abu Ghraib was terrible. By understanding the processes we don't excuse it. These people are guilty." But for Zimbardo, the military leadership that had implicitly condoned torture and averted its eyes from what was happening at Abu Ghraib prison deserved the bulk of the blame. He made evident that in his analysis it was the military command and the Bush Administration that created the evil system that created the bad barrel that corrupted once-good American soldiers.

The more than a thousand attendees gladly stayed well over the allotted hour to hear Zimbardo finish his presentation. "I want to end on a positive note," he said, to relieved laughter. "Not all good people turn bad. People resist." Turning around Hannah Arendt's famous phrase "the banality of evil," Zimbardo coined the term "the banality of heroism" to describe the soldier—another otherwise undistinguished, normal guy— who blew the whistle on what was happening at Abu Ghraib by turning over a CD of the soldiers' trophy photographs to the authorities. "Heroic action by ordinary people . . . is more common than the few lifelong heroes," he said.

Zimbardo's address exemplified how social psychology— even the most depressing studies of human weakness—can actually be inspiring. "There will come a time in your life," he said, "when . . . you have the power within you, as an ordinary person, as a person who is willing to take a decision, to blow the whistle, to take action, to go the other direction and do the heroic thing." That decision is set against the decisions to perpetrate evil or to do nothing, which is the evil of inaction. Zimbardo concluded with a thought from Alexandr Solzhenitsyn, the Russian poet imprisoned under Stalin: "The line between good and evil lies at the center of every human heart." He added, "it is not an abstraction out there. It's a decision you have to make every day in here." With the last of Zimbardo's 150 slides and three video clips, came an extended standing ovation—rare among psychology audiences.

From *APS Observer,* August 2006, pp. 33–34, 45. Copyright © 2006 by American Psychological Society. Reprinted by permission via the Copyright Clearance Center.

Young and Restless

Saudi Arabia's baby boomers, born after the 1973 oil embargo, are redefining the kingdom's relationship with the modern world.

AFSHIN MOLAVI

Scented smoke from dozens of water pipes mingled with Lebanese pop music at Al-Nakheel, a seaside restaurant in the Red Sea port of Jeddah. Saudi men in white robes and women in black *abayas,* their head scarves falling to their shoulders, leaned back on red cushions as they sipped tea and shared lamb kebab and hummus. Four young Saudi women, head scarves removed, trailed perfume as they walked past. Nearby, a teenage boy snapped photos of his friends with a cellphone. At an adjoining table, two young men with slicked-back hair swayed their heads to a hip-hop song echoing from the parking lot.

"Look around," said Khaled al-Maeena, editor in chief of the English-language daily *Arab News.* "You wouldn't have seen this even a few years ago."

Saudi Arabia, long bound by tradition and religious conservatism, is beginning to embrace change. You can see it in public places like Al-Nakheel. You hear it in conversations with ordinary Saudis. You read about it in an energetic local press and witness it in Saudi cyberspace. Slowly, tentatively, almost imperceptibly to outsiders, the kingdom is redefining its relationship with the modern world.

The accession of King Abdullah in August has something to do with it. Over the past several months he has freed several liberal reformers from jail, promised women greater rights and tolerated levels of press freedom unseen in Saudi history; he has reached out to marginalized minorities such as the Shiites, reined in the notorious religious "morals" police and taken steps to improve education and judicial systems long dominated by extremist teachers and judges. But a look around Al-Nakheel suggests another reason for change: demography.

Saudi Arabia is one of the youngest countries in the world, with some 75 percent of the population under 30 and 60 percent under 21; more than one in three Saudis is under 14. Saudi Arabia's changes are coming not only from the authorities above, but also from below, driven by this young and increasingly urban generation. Even as some of them jealously guard parts of the status quo and display a zeal for their Islamic faith unseen in their parents' generation, others are recalibrating the balance between modernity and tradition, directing bursts of new energy at civil society and demanding new political and social rights. "We must face the facts," said al-Maeena, who is 54. "This huge youth population will determine our future. That's why we need to watch them carefully and train them well. They hold the keys to the kingdom."

Saudi Arabia, home to a quarter of the world's known oil reserves, is one of the United States' key allies in the Middle East. Yet its baby boom was launched by an act of defiance—the 1973 oil embargo, in which King Faisal suspended supplies to the United States to protest Washington's support for Israel in its war with Egypt and Syria. As oil prices rose, cash-rich Saudis began having families in record numbers. The kingdom's population grew about 5 percent annually from 6 million in 1970 to 16 million in 1989. (The current growth rate has slowed to about 2.5 percent, and the population is 24 million.)

Those baby boomers are now coming of age. And as Saudi analyst Mai Yamani writes in her book *Changed Identities: The Challenge of the New Generation in Saudi Arabia,* "Their numbers alone make them the crucial political constituency."

Their grandparents largely lived on subsistence farms in unconnected villages where tribe, clan and ethnicity trumped national identity. Their parents (at least the men) worked in the burgeoning state bureaucracy and trained with the foreign engineers and bankers who flocked to the kingdom; they lived in an era when television, foreign travel, multilane highways, national newspapers and mass education were novelties. But the boomers live in a mass culture fed by satellite TV and the Internet, consumerism, an intellectual glasnost and stirrings of Saudi nationalism. "I'm not sure young Saudis grasp the enormity of the changes in just three generations," al-Maeena told me. "It is like night and day."

The boomers, however, did not grow into fantastic wealth. In 1981, the kingdom's per capita income was $28,000, making it one of the richest countries on earth. But by 1993, when I first met al-Maeena in Jeddah during a year I spent there on a journalism exchange program, the kingdom was recovering from both a long recession (oil prices had dwindled) and a war on its border (the Persian Gulf war of 1991). Per capita income was declining rapidly; and boomers were straining the finances of a largely welfare-driven state. Government jobs and scholarships for foreign study grew scarce. (In 2001, per capita income was a quarter of what it had been in 1981.)

Arabic satellite television was in its infancy and state censorship was pervasive—in August 1990 the Saudi government prohibited the media from publishing news of Iraq's invasion of Kuwait for three days. But as the '90s progressed, technology forced change. Long-distance telephone service became affordable. The Internet began to shrink the world, Aljazeera became a boisterous news channel breaking social, political and religious taboos: Many young Saudis began to feel they were living in a country with outdated institutions: an education system that favored rote learning over critical thinking, a religious establishment that promoted an intolerant brand of Islam and a government that was falling behind its neighbors in economic development.

"I'm not sure young Saudis grasp the enormity of the changes in just three generations. It is like night and day."

"The 1990s were not a good decade for young people," said one young Saudi civil servant, who asked not to be named because he works for the government. "We didn't have the secure jobs of our parents' generation, and our government was basically incompetent and getting too corrupt." In the private sector, employers preferred skilled foreigners to newly minted Saudi college graduates. "We were just sitting still while everyone else seemed to be moving forward," the civil servant added.

Then came September 11, 2001, and with it the revelation that 15 of the 19 men who launched the attacks on the United States were Saudis—acting under the auspices of another Saudi, Osama bin Laden. "That event and the [West's] anti-Saudi reaction made me feel more nationalist," said Khaled Salti, a 21-year-old student in Riyadh. "I wanted to go to America and defend Saudi Arabia in public forums, to tell them that we are not all terrorists. I wanted to do something for my country."

Ebtihal Mubarak, a 27-year-old reporter for the *Arab News,* said the attacks "forced us to face some ugly truths: that such terrible people exist in our society and that our education system failed us." She called May 12, 2003, another infamous date for many Saudis: Al Qaeda bombed an expatriate compound in Riyadh that day, killing 35, including 9 Americans and 7 Saudis. A series of attacks on Westerners, Saudi government sites and Arabs ensued, leaving hundreds dead. (In late February, Al Qaeda also took responsibility for a failed attempt to blow up a Saudi oil-processing complex.)

Most violent opposition to the ruling al-Saud family comes from boomers—jihadists in their 20s and 30s—but those extremists are hardly representative of their generation. "When we think of youth in this country, two incorrect stereotypes emerge," Hani Khoja, a 37-year-old business consultant and television producer, told me. "We think of the religious radical who wants to join jihadist movements, like the 9/11 guys, or we think of extremist fun-seekers who think only of listening to pop music and having a good time. But the reality is that most young Saudis are somewhere in the middle, looking for answers, curious about the world and uncertain of the path they should take."

In dozens of conversations with young Saudis in five cities and a village, it became obvious that there is no monolithic Saudi youth worldview. Opinions vary widely on everything from internal reform to foreign policy to the kingdom's relations with the United States and the rest of the West. Regional, ethnic and religious differences also remain. Young Saudi Shiites often feel alienated in a country whose religious establishment often refers to them as "unbelievers." Residents of Hijaz, a cosmopolitan region that encompasses Mecca, Jeddah and Medina, regularly complain about the religious conservatism and political domination of the Najd, the province from which most religious and political elites hail. Some Najdis scorn Hijazis as "impure Arabs," children fertilized over the centuries by the dozens of nationalities who overstayed a pilgrimage to Mecca. And loyalty to tribe or region may still trump loyalty to the state.

But despite these differences, the kingdom's baby boomers seem to agree that change is necessary. And collectively they are shaping a new national identity and a common Saudi narrative.

Ebtihal Mubarak is one of several talented female reporters and editors on the *Arab News* staff. That in itself is a change from my days at the paper more than a decade ago. In recent years the *News* has doubled its full-time Saudi female staff and put more female reporters out in the field. Mubarak reports on the small but growing movement for greater political and social rights for Saudis. Persecution by extremists is a common theme in her work. As she surfed Saudi Internet forums one day last fall, she came across a posting describing an attack on a liberal journalist in the northern city of Hail. "A journalist's car had been attacked while he was sleeping," she said. "A note on his car read: 'This time it's your car, next time it will be you.'"

"The *hijab* is such an overexamined issue in the West. I like wearing it. We as women face more serious issues."

A few years ago, such an episode would probably have ended with the Hail journalist intimidated into silence. But now, Mubarak worked the phones, speaking with the journalist, the police and outside experts, and put together a story for the next day's paper, quoting the journalist: "What happened to me is not just a threat to one individual but to the whole of society." Thanks to the Internet, the episode became a national story, and the subject of vigorous debate.

And yet: after Mubarak exercised the power of the press, she faced the limited power of Saudi women. Once she filed her story, she hung around the newsroom, glancing at her watch—waiting for a driver, because under a patriarchal legal system Saudi women may not drive. "I feel like I'm always waiting for someone to pick me up," she said. "Imagine a reporter who cannot drive. How will we beat the competition when we are always waiting to be picked up by someone?"

Mubarak reflects how much Saudi society has changed, and how much it hasn't. Like her generational peers, she comes from the urban middle class. Yet as a working woman, she represents a minority: only 5 percent of Saudi women work outside the home. Most are stifled by a patriarchal society and a legal system that treats them like children.

Beyond matters of mobility and employment opportunity is the issue of spousal abuse, which, according to Saudi newspapers, remains prevalent. In one high-profile case, the husband of Rania al-Baz, the country's first female broadcaster, beat her nearly to death in 2004. Saudi media covered the case with the zeal of British tabloids, creating widespread sympathy for the victim and sparking a national debate on abuse. The case even made it to "Oprah," where al-Baz was hailed as a woman of courage. Once the spotlight dimmed, however, the broadcaster succumbed to pressure from an Islamic judge and from her own family to forgive her husband.

Tensions between the old and the new aren't always so consequential, but they persist. Hani Khoja, the TV producer, told me that he "wanted to show that it is possible to be religious and modern at the same time" on the popular youth-oriented show "Yallah Shabab" ("Let's Go Youth"). Another program that promotes a more modern view of Islam is "Kalam Nouam" ("Speaking Softly"). One of its hostesses, Muna Abu Sulayman, embodies that blend. Born in 1973, Abu Sulayman followed her father, a liberal Islamic scholar, around the globe, including nine years in the United States, where she studied English literature. (Saudi universities opened their doors to women in 1964.) Today, in addition to her television work, she advises billionaire businessman Prince Al-Waleed bin Talal on philanthropic activities that seek to build links between the Islamic world and the West.

The prince's company, Kingdom Holdings, has the only known Saudi workplace that allows Muslim women to choose whether to wear the *hijab* (the Islamic veil and other modest apparel) or Western dress. (The prince also employs the only female Saudi pilot.) Kingdom Holdings' quarters look more Beirut than Riyadh, with fashionable women in corporate attire shuffling between offices. Abu Sulayman, however, chooses to wear the hijab—on the day I met her, a striking green head scarf and shirt ensemble. "The hijab is such an over-examined issue in the West," she told me. "I like wearing it. We as women face more serious issues."

And even as she acknowledges that "the opportunities available to me today were unavailable a generation ago," she says, "We are hopeful to achieve more. I expect my daughter to be living in an entirely different world."

"I want to get things done. . . . I will try to do it quietly and not just to score political points against the extremists."

"I am from Burayda, that famous city you Western journalists are curious about," Adel Toraifi said when we met at a Holiday Inn in Riyadh. He was smiling—Burayda is the heartland of Wahhabi Islam. Toraifi, now 27, came of age in one of the most conservative regions of the kingdom.

More than two centuries ago, Sheikh ibn Abd al Wahhab emerged from the desert there with a puritanical vision of Islam focused on the concept of *tawhid,* or the oneness of God. At the time, he made a key alliance with the local al-Saud ruler, who pledged to support the passionate preacher in return for support from the religious establishment. Eventually, Wahhabism spread across central Arabia, even when the al-Sauds lost power twice in the 19th century (to regain it again in the early 20th). When King Abdulaziz ibn Saud, the founder of modern Saudi Arabia, began his march across the Arabian Peninsula in the early 20th century to reclaim his tribal lands, he revived the bargain with the descendants of Sheikh ibn Abd al Wahhab, known today as the al-Alsheikh family.

The essential outlines of that relationship remain intact. Wahhabi preachers hold the highest positions of religious authority while the al-Sauds hold political authority. Today's Saudi Wahhabist is quick to condemn those who belong to other schools of religious thought as impure or, worse, kufr, unbelievers. That explains part of the political radicalism of young Saudi jihadists—but only part.

Another explanation might lie in the evolution of Saudi Arabia's education system. In the 1960s and '70s, the kingdom fought a rear-guard battle with Egypt for regional hearts and minds. To counter Gamal Abdel Nasser's secular pan-Arab nationalism, the Saudis promoted a conservative pan-Islamism. While Egypt, Syria and Jordan were expelling Islamist radicals, many of whom were college graduates, Saudi Arabia welcomed them as teachers.

When Toraifi was 13, he decided to become a religious scholar in the Wahhabi tradition. For five years, he led an ascetic life, studying the Koran and the sayings of the Prophet Muhammad several hours a day. "I was not a radical," he said, "but my mind was not open, either. I dreamed of becoming a respected scholar, but I had never read a Western book or anything by an Islamic modernist or Arab liberal."

As he walked home from evening prayer one day, he was hit by a car. After three months in a coma, he spent more than a year recuperating in a hospital, thinking and reading. "I thought to myself: I did everything right. I prayed. I fasted. I learned the Koran by heart, and yet I got hit by a car. It was troubling to me."

Once recovered, Toraifi took to reading Western philosophy and Arab liberals with a seminarian's zeal. He studied engineering, but political philosophy was his passion. After taking a job as a development executive with a German technology company, he began writing articles critical of Wahhabism—including one published shortly after the May 12, 2003, attacks warning that a "Saudi Manhattan" was coming unless religious extremism was checked. He was excoriated in some religious Internet forums, but the government largely let it pass.

Then Toraifi repeated his views on Aljazeera, whose coverage had often been critical of the royal family. That, apparently, crossed a line: afterward, Toraifi said, Saudi intelligence detained him for several days before letting him go with a warning. Then an establishment newspaper offered him a column—writing about foreign, but not domestic, affairs. The gesture was seen as an attempt to bring a critic into the mainstream. But he dismisses concerns that he might have been co-opted. "I will continue speaking about the importance of democracy," he told me. (In December, he accepted a fellowship at a British think tank, where he is writing a paper on Saudi Arabia's reform movement.)

The Al-Sauds number some 7,000 princes and princesses. The most senior princes are sons of the late Ibn Saud, who died in 1953, and most are in their 60s, 70s and 80s. Their sons include Prince Bandar bin Sultan, the former Saudi ambassador to the United States, and Prince Turki al-Faisal, the former director of Saudi intelligence and the current ambassador to the United States. Third- and fourth-generation princes have just begun to make their marks, and while the occasional rumor about corruption or a wild night in a European disco makes the rounds, several third-generation princes are becoming important drivers of modernization.

"I was not radical but my mind wasn't open, either. . . . I had never read a Western book or anything by an Islamic modernist."

Mohammed Khaled al-Faisal, 38, is one of them. The Harvard MBA runs a conglomerate of diverse businesses, including a world-class industrialized dairy farm. When I visited his Riyadh office, he proudly described an initiative that his company had taken to hire village widows and unmarried women to work at the dairy.

"In order to circumvent protest from local religious authorities, we reached out to them and asked them to consult with us on the proper uniforms the women should wear on the job," he said. "We didn't ask them if we could employ women; we simply brought them into the discussion, so they could play a role in how we do it. I am a businessman. I want to get things done. If my aim is to employ more women, I will try to do it quietly and not just to score political points against the extremists."

Economic reform, he went on, is "the chariot that will drive all other reforms." What Saudi Arabia needs, in his judgment, is more small and medium-sized businesses and the jobs they would provide.

"I see my older brother unemployed," said Hassan, a dimpled 14-year-old. "I'm afraid that will happen to me too." The four other students in the room, who ranged in age from 13 to 16, nodded their heads in agreement.

They and their teacher met me in an office in Qatif, in the oil-rich Eastern Province—home to most of Saudi Arabia's Shiite Muslims. Some of the most vitriolic abuse from Saudi religious authorities and ordinary citizens is directed at Shiites, who make up only 15 percent of the population. Though they share job anxiety with their Sunni peers, they feel that upward mobility belongs primarily to Sunnis.

Two of the youths attend a village school several miles away; while the other three go to the local public high school. The lack of a college in Qatif, many Shiites say, is an example of the discrimination they feel.

I asked if teaching had improved since 9/11. "The new teachers are good," said Ali, a smiling 15-year-old, "but the old ones are still around and still bad." The students said their teachers praised bin Laden, ridiculed the United States or described Shiites as unbelievers.

Recently, Ali said, he had brought sweets to school to celebrate the birthday of a prominent Shiite religious figure, and his teacher reprimanded him with anti-Shiite slurs.

I asked if they ever thought of leaving Saudi Arabia.

"No, Qatif is my home," said Hassan. "I am proud to be from Qatif."

Are they proud to be from Saudi Arabia?

Mohammad, who had spoken very little, answered: "If the government doesn't make us feel included, why should we be proud to be from Saudi Arabia? If they did include us more, then I think we would all be proud."

"I see my older brother unemployed," says one of the students in the room. "I'm afraid that will happen to me too."

Public pop concerts are banned in the kingdom, so musically inclined young Saudis gather at underground events or in small groups. Hasan Hatrash, an *Arab News* reporter and musician, took me to a heavy-metal jam session in Jeddah.

Hatrash, who abstains from drink and covers the hajj, the annual Islamic pilgrimage, for local papers, had spent the past two years in Malaysia, waiting tables and playing guitar in bars. When I asked about his eclectic tastes, he said, "I am a Hijazi. We have DNA from everywhere in the world!"

At a walled villa in Jeddah, young men were tuning guitars and tapping drums. Ahmad, who is half-Lebanese and half-Saudi, is the lead singer of a band known as Grieving Age. He introduced me around. A few of the musicians, including Ahmad, had long hair and beards, but most did not. One wore a Starbucks shirt—for his job, afterward. Another worked as an attendant on Saudia, the national airline, and a third worked in insurance. All seemed exceedingly polite.

They played songs from the genre heavy-metal fans call "melodic death." It had a haunting appeal, though the lyrics were, predictably unintelligible amid the heavy bass. On the walls, a poster of the British band Iron Maiden competed for space with one of Mariam Fares, a sultry Lebanese pop star.

When Hatrash took the stage, he played a series of guitar favorites, such as Jimi Hendrix's Purple Haze and softer rock, to the seeming delight of the heavy-metal aficionados. Throughout the evening, more young men arrived—but no women. Some took turns playing; others just watched. By midnight, the jam session had wound down. "This is a tame event, as you can see," Hatrash said. "There is no drinking or drugs. We are just enjoying the music."

I asked if he could envision a day when he could play in public, instead of behind closed doors.

He just smiled and launched into another song. Someone jumped up to accompany him on the bass, and Ahmad mouthed the lyrics. The guy in the Starbucks shirt rushed out the door, late for his shift.

AFSHIN MOLAVI, a fellow at the New America Foundation, has covered the Middle East for many publications.

We're Wired to Connect

Our brains are designed to be social, says bestselling science writer Daniel Goleman—and they catch emotions the same way we catch colds.

MARK MATOUSEK

Have you ever wondered why a stranger's smile can transform your entire day? Why your eyes mist up when you see someone crying, and the sight of a yawn can leave you exhausted? Daniel Goleman, Ph.D., has wondered, too, and just as he helped revolutionize our definition of what it means to be smart with his 1995 blockbuster, *Emotional Intelligence,* the two-time Pulitzer nominee and former science reporter for *The New York Times* has dropped a bombshell on our understanding of human connection in his startling new book, *Social Intelligence* (Bantam).

For the first time in history, thanks to recent breakthroughs in neuroscience, experts are able to observe brain activity while we're in the act of feeling—and their findings have been astonishing. Once believed to be lumps of lonely gray matter cogitating between our ears, our brains turn out to be more like interlooped, Wi-Fi octopi with invisible tentacles slithering in all directions, at every moment, constantly picking up messages we're not aware of and prompting reactions—including illnesses—in ways never before understood.

"The brain itself is social—that's the most exciting finding," Goleman explains during lunch at a restaurant near his home in Massachusetts. "One person's inner state affects and drives the other person. We're forming brain-to-brain bridges—a two-way traffic system—all the time. We actually catch each other's emotions like a cold."

The more important the relationship, the more potent such "contagion" will be. A stranger's putdown may roll off your back, while the same zinger from your boss is devastating. "If we're in toxic relationships with people who are constantly putting us down, this has actual physical consequences," Goleman says. Stress produces a harmful chemical called cortisol, which interferes with certain immune cell functions. Positive interactions prompt the body to secrete oxytocin (the same chemical released during lovemaking), boosting the immune system and decreasing stress hormones. As a doting grandparent himself (with author-therapist wife Tara Bennett-Goleman), the author often feels this felicitous rush. "I was just with my two-year-old granddaughter," he says. "This girl is like a vitamin for me.

Being with her actually feels like a kind of elixir. The most important people in our lives can be our biological allies."

The notion of relationships as pharmaceutical is a new concept. "My mother is 96," Goleman goes on. "She was a professor of sociology whose husband—my father—died many years ago, leaving her with a big house. After retiring at 65, she decided to let graduate students live there for free. She's since had a long succession of housemates. When she was 90, a couple from Taiwan had a baby while they were living there. The child regarded her as Grandma and lived there till the age of two. During that time, I swore I could see my mother getting younger. It was stunning." But not, he adds, completely surprising. "This was the living arrangement we were designed for, remember? For most of human history there were extended families where the elderly lived in the same household as the babies. Many older people have the time and nurturing energy that kids crave—and vice versa. If I were designing assisted-living facilities, I'd put daycare centers in them and allow residents to volunteer. Institutions are cheating children," he says. "And we older people need it, too."

Positive interactions can boost the immune system: "The most important people in our lives can be our biological allies."

Young or old, people can affect our personalities. Though each of us has a distinctive temperament and a "set point of happiness" modulating our general mood, science has now confirmed that these tendencies are not locked in. Anger-prone people, for example, can "infect" themselves with calmness by spending time with mellower individuals, absorbing less-aggressive behavior and thereby sharpening social intelligence.

A key to understanding this process is something called mirror neurons: "neurons whose only job is to recognize a smile and make you smile in return," says Goleman (the same goes for frowning and other reactions). This is why, when you're smiling, the whole world does indeed seem to smile with you. It also explains the Michelangelo phenomenon, in which long-term partners come to resemble each other through facial-muscle mimicry and "empathic resonance." If you've ever seen a group with a case of the giggles, you've witnessed mirror neurons at play. Such mirroring takes place in the realm of ideas, too, which is why sweeping cultural ideals and prejudices can spread through populations with viral speed.

This phenomenon gets to the heart of why social intelligence matters most: its impact on suffering and creating a less crazy world. It is critical, Goleman believes, that we stop treating people as objects or as functionaries who are there to give us something. This can range from barking at telephone operators to the sort of old-shoe treatment that long-term partners often use in relating to each other (talking at, rather than to, each other). We need, he says, a richer human connection.

Unfortunately, what he calls the "inexorable technocreep" of contemporary culture threatens such meaningful connection. Presciently remarking on the TV set in 1963, poet T.S. Eliot noted that this techno-shredder of the social fabric "permits millions of people to listen to the same joke at the same time, and yet remain lonesome." We can only imagine what the dour writer would have made of Internet dating. And as Goleman points out, this "constant digital connectivity" can deaden us to the people around us. Social intelligence, he says, means putting down your BlackBerry, actually paying full attention—showing people that they're being experienced—which is basically what each of us wants more than anything. Scientists agree that such connection—or lack of it—will determine our survival as a species: "Empathy," writes Goleman, "is the prime inhibitor of human cruelty."

And our social brains are wired for kindness, despite the gore you may see on the nightly news. "It's an aberration to be cruel," says Goleman. Primitive tribes learned that strength lay in numbers, and that their chances of surviving a brutal environment increased exponentially through helping their neighbors (as opposed to, say, chopping their heads off). Even young children are wired for compassion. One study in Goleman's book found that infants cry when they see or hear another baby crying, but rarely when they hear recordings of their own distress. In another study, monkeys starved themselves after realizing that when they took food, a shock was delivered to their cage mate.

Perhaps the most inspiring piece of the social-intelligence puzzle is neuroplasticity: the discovery that our brains never stop evolving. "Stem cells manufacture 10,000 brain cells every day till you die," says Goleman. "Social interaction helps neurogenesis. The brain rises to the occasion the more you challenge it."

MARK MATOUSEK'S *The Art of Survival* (Bloomsbury) will be published next year.

UNIT 10

Psychological Disorders

Unit Selections

Key Points to Consider

- What is Attention Deficit Disorder? How does it develop?

- What effects does combat have on soldiers' psyche?

- What is post-traumatic stress disorder? Who is likely to suffer from it? How can such individuals be treated?

- What sorts of experiences contribute to the development of anxiety and phobias?

Student Web Site

www.mhcls.com

Internet References

American Association of Suicidology
http://www.suicidology.org
Ask NOAH About: Mental Health
http://www.noah-health.org/en/mental/
Mental Health Net Disorders and Treatments
http://www.mentalhelp.net/
National Clearinghouse for Alcohol and Drug Information
http://ncadi.samhsa.gov
National Women's Health Resource Center (NWHRC)
http://www.healthywomen.org

© BananaStock/PunchStock

Jay and Harry were two brothers who owned a service station. They were the middle children of four. The other two children were sisters, the oldest of whom had married and moved out of the family home. Their father retired and turned the station over to his sons.

Harry and Jay had a good working relationship. Harry was the "up-front" man. Taking customer orders, accepting payments, and working with parts distributors, Harry was the individual who dealt most directly with the public, delivery personnel, and other people accessing the station. Jay worked behind the scenes. While Harry made the mechanical diagnoses, Jay was the mastermind who did the corrective work. Some of his friends thought Jay was a veritable mechanical genius; he could fix anything. Preferring to spend time by himself, Jay had always been a little odd and a bit of a loner. Jay's friends thought his emotions had always been inappropriate and more intense than other people's emotional states, but they passed it off as part of his eccentric talent. On the other hand, Harry was the stalwart of the family. He was the acknowledged leader and decision-maker when it came to family finances.

One day Jay did not show up for work on time. When he did, he was dressed in the most garish outfit and was laughing hysterically and talking to himself. Harry at first suspected that his brother had taken some illegal drugs. However, Jay's condition persisted and, in fact, worsened. Out of concern, his family took him to their physician, who immediately sent Jay and his family to a psychiatrist. After several visits, the doctor informed that Jay suffered from schizophrenia. Jay's maternal uncle had also been schizophrenic. The family somberly left the psychiatrist's office and went to the local pharmacy to fill a prescription for anti-psychotic medications.

What caused Jay's drastic change in mental health? Was Jay destined to be schizophrenic because of his family tree? Did competitiveness with his brother and the feeling that he was less revered than Harry cause his descent into mental disorder? How can psychiatrists and clinical psychologists make accurate diagnoses? Once a diagnosis of mental disorder is made, can the individual ever completely recover? These and other questions are the emphasis in this unit.

A New Approach to Attention Deficit Disorder

It's not a simple behavior disorder but rather a complex syndrome of impairments in the management system of the brain.

Thomas E. Brown

As burgeoning numbers of children and adolescents are being diagnosed with attention deficit disorders, parents are increasingly asking teachers, "Do you think my child has ADD or ADHD?" Some insist that their child receive multiple accommodations for presumed ADD/ADHD. Many teachers and school administrators are uncertain about how to respond. They are also unsure about which interventions are appropriate when a student appears to be impaired by attention disorders but the parents are skeptical or refuse to consider that possibility.

A recent study conducted by the U.S. Centers for Disease Control found that approximately 7.8 percent of U.S. children ages 4–17 are currently diagnosed with Attention Deficit Disorder (ADD) or Attention Deficit/Hyperactivity Disorder (ADHD) (*Journal of the American Medical Association,* 2005). This means that most teachers are likely to have at least a couple of students with ADD/ADHD[1] in every class they teach. However, few educators are familiar with major findings from recent scientific studies of attention deficit disorders or with the implications of these findings for schools.

For decades, most educators, physicians, psychologists, and parents have thought of ADD as a cluster of behavior problems, a label for children who can't sit still, won't stop talking, and often are disruptive in class. Discussion has centered mainly on controversy over whether children with this diagnosis should be treated with stimulant medication, which, paradoxically, calms down overactive bodies and brains. However, recent research offers a new way of understanding this disorder and a different view of how medication treatment actually works in the brain.

The Symphony of the Brain

Few researchers still think of ADD as a simple behavior disorder. Increasingly, specialists are recognizing that it is a complex syndrome of impairments in development of the brain's cognitive management system, or executive functions. The disorder affects one's ability to

- Organize and get started on tasks.
- Attend to details and avoid excessive distractibility.
- Regulate alertness and processing speed.
- Sustain and, when necessary, shift focus.
- Use short-term working memory and access recall.
- Sustain motivation to work.
- Manage emotions appropriately. One way to imagine the cluster of cognitive functions involved in the new model of ADD is to visualize a symphony orchestra composed of talented musicians. Regardless of their expertise, the musicians need a competent conductor who will select the piece to play, make sure they start at the same time and stay on tempo, fade in the strings and then bring in the brass, and manage them as they interpret the music. Without an effective conductor, the symphony will not produce good music.

In individuals with ADD, the parts of the brain that correspond to the individual musicians often work quite well. The problem is with the conductor, with those executive functions that, in a healthy individual, work together to accomplish a task. ADD impairs neural circuits that function as the conductor of the symphony.

Take James, for example. He's a bright 6th grader who enthusiastically participates in class discussions that relate to science or social studies. He often contributes examples from shows he has watched on the Discovery Channel or History Channel or from the many books he has read. However, he rarely completes homework assignments, can't keep track of his papers or books, and often claims that he can't recall what he has just finished hearing or reading in class.

Julie has her own set of challenges with accomplishing school tasks. A quiet, intelligent 9th grader, she was on the honor roll every year—until she got to high school. Halfway through freshman year, she is in danger of failing most of her major classes because of missing homework and low test grades. Her parents say that although she spends many hours each night doing homework, she loses track of what she needs to hand in for each class. As she works to catch up on overdue work in one course, she falls behind in others. She also studies hard for tests and knows all the answers when others quiz her on the material, but on the following day when she takes the test, she's unable to recall most of the information. Both James and Julie display executive function impairment.

The Six Executive Functions

One model describing the executive functions emerged from my research with children, adolescents, and adults. Although each of the six components of the model has a single-word label, they are not unitary variables like height, weight, or blood pressure. Instead, each is like a basket containing a cluster of related cognitive functions. The six executive functions that work together in various combinations are

- *Activation:* organizing, prioritizing, and activating for work.
- *Focus:* focusing, sustaining, and shifting attention to tasks.
- *Effort:* regulating alertness and sustaining effort and processing speed.
- *Emotion:* managing frustration and modulating emotions.
- *Memory:* using working memory and accessing recall.
- *Action:* monitoring and self-regulating action.

In daily life, these clusters of cognitive functions operate, often without our conscious involvement, in integrated and dynamic ways to accomplish a wide variety of tasks. They do not continually work at peak efficiency for any of us; everyone has difficulty with some of them from time to time. However, those diagnosed with ADD—James and Julie, for example—are substantially more impaired in their ability to use these executive functions than are most other people of the same age and developmental level.

Approximately 7.8 percent of U.S. children ages 4–17 are currently diagnosed with ADD or ADHD.

We no longer see ADD as an all-or-nothing concept. It's not like pregnancy, where one either is or isn't pregnant, with nothing in between. Diagnosing ADD is more like distinguishing clinical depression from normal fluctuations in mood. Although everyone feels sad from time to time, treating a person for depression only makes sense when he or she is significantly impaired by depressive symptoms over a substantial period of time. Similarly, the diagnosis of ADD/ADHD is not warranted for people who have occasional difficulty with the relevant symptoms but rather for those who are significantly impaired by the cluster of ADD symptoms over a longer period of time.

Differences in Development

As teachers know, a student's capacity to exercise these various self-management functions develops slowly from early childhood through late adolescence or early adulthood. We hold different expectations for 8-year-olds than for 5-year-olds in their capacity to sustain attention, follow directions, remember information, and so on. We also know that within any given age group, some children develop these abilities more quickly and in more refined ways than others do. A diagnosis of ADD/ADHD is appropriate only when the individual's impairment is significantly greater than that of most other children of the same age and developmental level.

Scientific evidence has now demonstrated that although some basic elements of executive functions emerge during early childhood, these complex self-management networks are not fully developed until the late teens or early twenties (Brown, 2005). Accordingly, most governments will not allow their citizens to drive a motor vehicle until they are at least 16 years old. This is not because the drivers' legs are too short for their feet to reach the pedals; rather, it is because the crucial executive functions of the brain that enable an individual to manage the complexities and high-stakes responsibilities of driving a car do not develop sufficiently until middle or late adolescence.

Because normal development of executive functions is not complete until late adolescence or early adulthood, it is not always possible to identify, during childhood, students with impairments in these functions. For some students, ADD impairments become obvious during preschool. These students may be wildly hyperactive or unable to sit still or follow even the most basic directions. Other students may learn and behave quite well during elementary school, showing signs of ADD impairments only when middle school challenges their self-management abilities as they leave behind a classroom in which a single teacher has helped guide their executive functions.

Some students do not manifest their ADD impairments in noticeable ways until they encounter the more demanding world of high school, where they may be unable to cope with the ongoing conflicts and demands of study, classroom performance, homework in several subjects, and family and social interactions. Other students with ADD do not have noticeable symptoms until even later. Their parents may have built such successful compensatory scaffolding around them that their ADD impairments do not become apparent until the scaffolding is suddenly removed—as when the student moves away from home to attend a college or university.

Why Here and Not There?

The most perplexing aspect of an ADD diagnosis is the situational specificity of the symptoms. Every child, adolescent, and adult with ADD whom I have ever seen has a few types of activity in which they effectively exercise cognitive functions that are quite impaired in almost every other circumstance.

Take Larry, for example, a high school junior who was the goaltender for his ice hockey team. His parents brought him in for evaluation the day after the team won the state championship. As they described his performance, it was clear that he was an extraordinary goalie who kept careful track of the puck throughout each game. He was bright; his IQ was in the very superior range. However, he was always in trouble with his teachers. They reported that although he occasionally made impressively perceptive comments in class, most of the time he was distracted and "out to lunch," unable to follow the class discussion. "If you can pay attention so well when you're playing hockey," they would ask him, "then why can't you pay attention in class?"

Not all individuals with ADD focus best in sports; some get intensely involved in such activities as playing video games, drawing, building with Legos, or completing mechanical tasks. All seem to have a few specific activities in which they can focus well and for long periods of time. Yet they have difficulty focusing on many other tasks that they recognize are important and that they want to do well, such as completing an essay or preparing for a major exam. People often see ADD as a problem of willpower: "You can do it here," they say. "Why can't you do it there?" ADD is *not* a problem of willpower, however. It is a chronic impairment in the chemistry of the management system of the brain.

A Word about Medications

Evidence now shows that ADD is a highly heritable disorder, with impairments related to problems in the release and reloading of two crucial neurotransmitter chemicals made in the brain: dopamine and norepinephrine. These chemicals play a crucial role in facilitating communication within neural networks that orchestrate cognition. A massive body of evidence indicates that 8 of 10 individuals with the disorder experience significant improvement in their functioning when treated with appropriately fine-tuned medications. These treatments can compensate for inefficient release and reloading of essential neurotransmitters at countless synaptic connections in the brain.

However, ADD is not like a strep infection, where you can take a course of antibiotics and knock out the infection. It's more like a vision problem: Appropriately prescribed eyeglasses can improve impaired vision, but not cure it. Similarly, medications for ADD may help alleviate symptoms, but only for those hours of the day when the medication is active in the brain. During these times, some students under treatment can perform most self-management tasks quite well. For others, medication alone is not sufficient.

Approximately 50 percent of students with ADD have one or more specific learning disorders. If students with concurrent ADD and learning disabilities do not receive adequate treatment for their ADD impairments, it is unlikely that they will benefit from special education instruction because they will not be in a state that makes them available to learn. But medication alone will not alleviate their learning disability problems. Students with both ADD and learning disabilities often require accommodations or special education services.

The Difficulties of Diagnosis

When we considered ADD/ADHD a simple behavior disorder, it was easy to diagnose. Teachers could readily spot students who were chronically inattentive, restless, and impulsive in the classroom and on the playground. However, the new model of ADD—as a developmental impairment of executive functions—requires a different kind of evaluation, an approach that can pick up more subtle cognitive impairments. These may or may not be accompanied by hyperactivity or other readily observable symptoms. For example, a student may appear to be paying attention in class when he is actually drifting off and thinking of unrelated things. Another student may diligently read her assignment but then be unable to recall what she's just read.

To begin with, the most important assessment element is an individual clinical interview to query the student about a variety of daily cognitive functions. This requires a clinician who is well trained to recognize ADD and differentiate it from other learning, emotional, and behavioral problems. The evaluating clinician also needs to gather information from parents and teachers that describes the student's strengths and impairments as he or she encounters such tasks as keeping track of assignments, doing homework, reading for understanding, organizing thoughts for writing projects, and socially interacting both in and out of school. Rating scales—such as the Conners Rating Scale, Behavior Assessment System for Children (BASC), or Brown ADD Scales—can be helpful in gathering data for evaluation, but none is sufficient in itself for making or ruling out a diagnosis of ADD.

Nor can standard IQ scores or achievement test scores help an evaluator diagnose ADD. However, IQ index scores on the Wechsler Intelligence Scale for Children (WISC-IV) or Wechsler Adult Intelligence Scale (WAIS-III) can suggest ADD impairments if the student's score for the Working Memory and/or Processing Speed Index is one standard deviation or more below that student's index score for Verbal Comprehension or Perceptual Organization. Any student who underachieves in school and displays such discrepancies between basic cognitive abilities and indices of executive functions should be carefully evaluated for possible ADD.

ADD impairs the neural circuits that function as the conductor of the symphony of the brain.

Three specific groups of students with ADD tend to be overlooked: bright students, female students, and students under stress. Adults often think that very bright students who underachieve are lazy, the assumption being that one cannot be bright and, at the same time, have significant ADD impairments. In fact, individuals with ADD are found at all IQ levels. Female students with ADD may be difficult to spot because they generally don't call attention to themselves with dramatic, disruptive behavior. Finally, adults often explain away the achievement problems of students coming from families with multiple social stressors, such as divorce, unemployment, poverty, and multiple relocations. Teachers may assume that poor achievement is just the student's reaction to these difficulties. They may not realize that ADD is more common in families under psychosocial stress.

Importance of Early Identification

When a student with or without hyper-activity or behavior problems chronically underachieves, educators should consider evaluating the student for ADD/ADHD. To start the process, school staff should systematically gather relevant information from teachers and the school psychologist about specific impairments observed in the student's academic work, classroom performance, or social interactions. They should present this information to parents with suggestions about how the parents can arrange for an appropriate evaluation to identify causes of the student's chronic difficulties and possible options for intervention.

Before school staff can adequately assist parents in identifying students for a possible ADD/ADHD evaluation, however, teachers, school psychologists, and administrators need to develop a solid understanding of the new model for attention deficit disorders. Resources are available online at http://help4ADHD.org, a Web site funded by the U.S. Centers for Disease Control, or in the *CHADD Educator's Manual* available at http://chadd.org.

Early identification of students with ADD is important because appropriate interventions can prevent a student from becoming demoralized by repeated experiences of frustration and failure. With appropriate intervention, most students with ADD/ADHD can achieve at the level of their abilities.

Note

1. I use the terms ADD and ADHD interchangeably in this article.

References

Brown, T. E. (2005). *Attention deficit disorder: The unfocused mind in children and adults*. New Haven, CT: Yale University Press.

Journal of the American Medical Association. (2005, November 9). 18, 2293–2295.

THOMAS E. BROWN is Associate Director of the Yale Clinic for Attention and Related Disorders, Department of Psychiatry, Yale University School of Medicine. He is the author of *Attention Deficit Disorder: The Unfocused Mind in Children and Adults* (Yale University Press, 2005) and the developer of the Brown ADD Scales for Children, Adolescents, and Adults (Psychological Association, 1996, 2001); www.drthomasebrown.com.

Treating War's Toll on the Mind

Thousands of Soldiers Have Post-Traumatic Stress Disorder. Will They Get the Help They Need?

BETSY STREISAND

As they take their seats in the movie theater, Eric and Raquel Schrumpf could be any young couple out on a summer night in Southern California. No one notices as Schrumpf, 31, a former Marine sergeant who served in Iraq, scans the rows for moviegoers who may be wired with explosives under their jackets. No one pays attention as a man who appears to be Middle Eastern, wearing a long coat with bulging pockets, takes a seat in the same row as the Schrumpfs and Eric starts watching him intently. No one listens as Schrumpf instructs his wife to "get as low to the ground as you can if something happens." Then something does. Schrumpf hears metal jangling as the man reaches into his pocket. Convinced he is a suicide bomber about to strike, Schrumpf lunges at him. The man jerks away and his deadly weapon falls to the floor: a can of Coke.

Schrumpf has everyone's attention now, as he and his wife quickly leave the theater. The Schrumpfs can't even remember what movie they went to see. Not that it would have mattered. Eric Schrumpf had room for only one movie in his head, the one where he is in Iraq. Now, more than two years later, Schrumpf has a good job, a strong marriage, a couple of pets, and a life that looks startlingly like everyone else's in Orange County, Calif. But he is still never more than a sound, smell, or thought away from the war. He gets anxious in a crowd, has been known to dive for cover, even indoors, at the sound of a helicopter, reaches for nonexistent weapons to be used in nonexistent circumstances, and wakes up screaming from nightmares about burning bodies and rocket-propelled grenades. "I'll never be the same again," says Schrumpf, who as a weapons and tactics instructor with the 5th Marine Regiment was part of the initial push into southern Iraq in 2003. "The war will be part of my life and my family's life forever."

Reliving the war. Like thousands of soldiers who have returned from Iraq and Afghanistan, Schrumpf is suffering from post-traumatic stress disorder, a chronic condition whose symptoms include rage, depression, flashbacks, emotional numbness, and hypervigilance. It can be brought on by a single event, such as when a grenade landed next to Schrumpf, ticking off his death and then failing to explode. Or it can be the result of repeated exposure to trauma such as house-to-house firefights or the accidental killing of civilians. "Soldiers who are routinely exposed to the trauma of killing, maiming, and dying are much more likely to bring those problems home," says Army Col. Kathy Platoni, a clinical psychologist and leader of a combat stress-control unit that works with soldiers on the battlefield. At its most basic, PTSD is the inability to flip the switch from combat soldier to everyday citizen and to stop reliving the war at so high a frequency that it interferes with the ability to function.

The problem is as old as war itself. But this time, American soldiers have been assured by the government and the military that the solution will be different: Iraq will be nothing like Vietnam, with its legacy of psychologically scarred veterans whose problems went unrecognized, undiagnosed, and untreated. "The hallmark of this war is going to be psychological injury," says Stephen Robinson, a Gulf War vet and director of government relations for Veterans for America in Washington, D.C. "We have learned the lessons of Vietnam, but now they have to be implemented."

Since the war began, the departments of Defense and Veterans Affairs have stepped up efforts to address the mental health needs of soldiers before, during, and after they are deployed. And more effective treatments for PTSD have been developed. But as the war drags on, the psychological costs are mounting and so is the tab for mental health care. Troop shortages are driving already traumatized soldiers back into combat for three and sometimes four tours of duty. Those who make it home often feel too stigmatized to ask for treatment lest they jeopardize their military careers. And if they do ask, they often can't get the care they need when they need it.

In addition, there are concerns among veterans groups that the Bush administration is trying to reduce the runaway cost of the war by holding down the number of PTSD cases diagnosed (and benefits paid), and that the promise to protect the mental health of nearly 1.5 million troops is not being kept.

"Throughout this war, everything has been underestimated–the insurgency, the body armor, the cost, and the number of troops," says Paul Rieckhoff, an Iraq war vet and founder of Iraq and Afghanistan Veterans of America in New York. "Now, the psychological problems and the needs of these soldiers are being underestimated, too."

Just how many troops will bring the war home with them is impossible to know at this point. But the numbers could be substantial. In a study published in 2004 in the *New England Journal of Medicine,* researchers at the Walter Reed Army Institute of Research found that nearly 17 percent of soldiers who have returned from Iraq, or nearly 1 in 6, showed signs of major depression, generalized anxiety, or PTSD. A report in the *Journal of the American Medical Association* earlier this year found that 1 in 5 soldiers met the risk for concern. And those numbers are virtually certain to grow as the war enters its fourth year. "I do think we're going to see a whole lot more PTSD as time goes on," says Platoni.

The VA, short of doctors, therapists, and staff in some areas, is straining to meet the mental health needs of the troops who have already returned from Iraq and Afghanistan. Soldiers often wait weeks or even months to see a psychiatrist or psychologist. A 2004 study by the Government Accountability Office found that six of the seven VA medical facilities it visited "may not be able to meet" increased demand for PTSD. "I don't think anybody can say with certainty whether we are prepared to meet the problem because we don't know what the scope is yet," says Matthew Friedman, a psychiatrist and executive director of the VA's National Center for PTSD in White River Junction, Vt. "What we do know is that the greater the exposure to trauma, the greater the chance that someone will have PTSD."

PTSD is the inability to flip the switch from combat soldier to everyday citizen.

Danger zone. There may be no war better designed to produce combat stress and trauma. Operation Iraqi Freedom is a round-the-clock, unrelenting danger zone. There are no front lines, it's impossible to identify the enemy, and everything from a paper bag to a baby carriage is a potential bomb. Soldiers are targets 24–7, whether they are running combat missions or asleep in their bunks. "There is no moment of safety in Iraq," says Andrew Pomerantz, a psychiatrist and chief of the Mental Health and Behavioral Science Service at the VA Medical Center in White River Junction. "That's one of the things we're seeing in people when they come back–a feeling of an absolute lack of safety wherever they are."

Stories of vets who sleep with guns and knives and patrol the perimeters of their homes obsessively are as common as tales of valor. Marine Lt. Col. Michael Zacchea, 38, who trained Iraqi troops and was in about 100 firefights, knows that paranoia all too well. "Every time I get on the road," says Zacchea, who commutes from Long Island to Wall Street, "it's like I'm back in the streets of Baghdad in combat, driving and running gun battles, with people throwing grenades at me." Zacchea, a reservist, is now being treated for PTSD at a VA hospital, but had it not been for chronic dysentery, migraines, and shrapnel wounds in his shoulder, he says he probably would have been redeployed in September, emotional scars and all.

And he still may be. The military's need to maintain troop strength in the face of historic recruiting lows means many service members, including some suffering from psychological problems like Zacchea, have no choice but to return. President Bush recently authorized the Marine Corps to call up inactive reservists, men and women who have already fulfilled their active-duty commitment. "They're having to go deep into the bench," says Robinson, "and deploy some people who shouldn't be deployed."

Multiple tours. Robinson is referring to the increasing number of reports of service members who stock antidepressants and sleeping pills alongside their shampoo, soap, and razor blades. The Defense Department does not track the number of soldiers on mental health medications or diagnosed with mental illnesses. But the military acknowledges that service members on medication who may be suffering from combat-induced psychological problems are being kept in combat. "We're not keeping people over there on heavy-duty drugs," says Army Surgeon General Kevin Kiley, who estimates that 4 to 5 percent of soldiers are taking medications, mostly sleeping pills. "Four to five percent of 150,000, that's still a lot of troops. But if it's got them handling things, I'm OK with that."

Handling things is a relative term. Army Pvt. Jason Sedotal, 21, a military policeman from Pierre Part, La., had been in Iraq six weeks in 2004 when he drove a humvee over a landmine. His sergeant, seated beside him, lost two legs and an arm in the explosion. Consumed by guilt and fear, Sedotal, who suffered only minor injuries, was diagnosed with PTSD when he returned from his first tour in early 2005 and given antidepressants and sleeping pills. Several months later, while stationed at Fort Polk, La., he sought more mental health care and was prescribed a different antidepressant.

Last November, Sedotal was redeployed. "They told me I had to go back because my problem wasn't serious enough," Sedotal said in an interview from Baghdad in mid-September. Sedotal says he started "seeing things and having flashbacks." Twice a combat stress unit referred him to a hospital for mental health care. Twice he was returned to his unit, each time with more medication and the second time without his weapon. "I stopped running missions, and I was shunned by my immediate chain of command and my unit," says Sedotal, who returned to Fort Polk last week.

Cases like Sedotal's prompted Congress earlier this year to instruct the Department of Defense to create a Task Force on Mental Health to examine the state of mental health care for the military. It is expected to deliver a report to Secretary of Defense Donald Rumsfeld in May 2007 and make recommendations for everything from reducing the stigma surrounding disorders to helping families and children deal with the traumatized soldier.

Sending military members who suffer from PTSD back into combat goes straight to one of the toughest issues of the war: how to protect soldiers' mental health and still keep them fighting. It is well-established that repeated and prolonged exposure to combat stress is the single greatest risk factor in developing PTSD.

At the same time, there is tremendous resistance to sending home soldiers who are suffering from psychological wounds, in all but the most severe cases. "If a soldier has some PTSD symptoms," says Kiley, "we'll watch him and see how he does." The expectation "is that we're all in this boat together and we need to drive on to complete the mission," he says, adding that if the situation gets worse, the soldier would most likely be given a couple days of rest to see if he recovers. Once soldiers are evacuated, "they are much less likely to come back."

There are no front lines, it's impossible to identify the enemy, and everything from a paper bag to a baby carriage is a potential bomb.

With that in mind, the DOD has designed a program to manage combat stress and identify mental health problems when they occur. It will include so-called battle-mind training for recruits, which focuses on the emotional fallout of seeing and contributing to the carnage of war and how to deal with it. Once they are in Iraq, there are psychologists and combat stress-control teams, such as Platoni's, who work side by side with troops to help them deal with their emotions and decompress immediately after battle. "Soldiers suffering from combat stress do better if they are treated early, efficiently, and as close to the battlefield as possible," says Col. Charles Hoge, chief of the Department of Psychiatry and Behavioral Sciences at Walter Reed Army Institute of Research.

Currently, there are more than 200 psychiatrists, therapists, social workers, and other mental health experts working with soldiers "in theater." They lend an ear, encourage soldiers to talk about their experiences with each other, and administer whatever short-term remedies they can, including stress-reduction techniques, anger-management strategies, or medications. However, their mission, first and foremost, is to be "force multipliers" who maintain troop strength. Their success is judged by their ability to keep soldiers from going home for psychological reasons. Soldiers are often their allies in this effort, as they feel such guilt and shame over abandoning their units they'll most likely say anything to keep from leaving. "It's a very sticky wicket," says Platoni. "We don't know if our interventions are enough to help them stay mentally healthy, or if they'll suffer more in the long term."

Last year, for instance, Platoni spent four months in Ar Ramadi, near Baghdad, where her battalion was under constant attack by insurgents. "They were watching their fellow soldiers burning to death and thinking they might be next," says Platoni. When a break came, one platoon was removed from combat for 48 hours so they could rest, shower, have a hot meal, and talk to psychologists about what they'd been through. "When they returned to the fighting," says Platoni, "they were able to deal with their fears better and focus on what needed to be done."

When soldiers do return home, the true emotional trauma of war is often just beginning. They go through a cursory post-deployment medical screening and a quick interview with a healthcare worker, who may or may not specialize in mental health. And returning soldiers are far more likely to downplay emotional problems for fear of being shifted from the "go home" line into the "further evaluation" line and being prevented from seeing families and friends.

Macho warrior. Three to six months after they return—the time when PTSD symptoms are the most likely to start becoming obvious—troops are given another mental health screening and may be referred for further evaluation, although the chances are slim. A GAO report issued in May, for instance, found that of the 5 percent of returning veterans between 2001 and 2004 who tested as being at risk for PTSD, fewer than one quarter were referred for further mental health evaluations. William Winkenwerder, assistant secretary of defense for health affairs, took issue with the study: "We're doing more than any military in history to identify, prevent, and treat mental health concerns among our troops. It is a top priority for us." Even with a referral, many veterans and active-duty soldiers will not seek help for fear of being stigmatized. To help break down the barriers, the DOD has begun encouraging high-ranking soldiers to openly discuss the effects that combat and killing can have on a person's psyche. Even so, the military remains dominated by the image of the macho warrior who sucks it up and drives on. According to the VA, the number of PTSD cases has doubled since 2000, to an all-time high of 260,000, but fewer than 40 percent of veterans from Iraq and Afghanistan have sought medical treatment. "This is the military culture," says Schrumpf, who now gets regular therapy and takes medication to help with his PTSD. "If it gets out that you even went to see the medical officer, and it always does, then you're done as a career marine."

In a surprising admission, former Georgia Sen. Max Cleland, who lost three limbs in Vietnam, announced in August that he is being treated for PTSD in the hopes of encouraging other vets to do the same. One of the biggest problems for Vietnam veterans, for instance, was that their psychological wounds went unrecognized and unattended for so long that, by the time they got treatment, many were past the point of being helped. Cleland is one of a growing crowd of Vietnam vets who are finally seeking help—and competing for VA services—as a result of long-buried feelings stirred up by the Iraq war.

In the past few years, in part because of events such as September 11, there have been advances in therapies for PTSD. "Just because you have PTSD, it doesn't mean you can't be successful in daily life," says Harold Wain, chief of the psychiatry consultation and liaison service at Walter Reed Army Medical Center in Washington, D.C., the main Army hospital for amputees. Many of the patients Wain sees have suffered catastrophic injuries and must heal their bodies as well as their minds.

As the war drags on, psychological costs are mounting and so is the tab for mental health care.

Reimagining the trauma again and again, or what's known as exposure therapy, has long been believed to be the most effective way of conquering PTSD. It is still popular and has been made even more effective by such tools as virtual reality. However, therapists are increasingly relying on cognitive behavior therapy or cognitive reframing, putting a new frame around a thought to shift the way a soldier interprets an event. A soldier who is racked with guilt because he couldn't save an injured buddy, for instance, may be redirected to concentrate on what he did do to help. Other approaches such as eye movement desensitization and reprocessing use hypnosis to help soldiers.

For some soldiers, simply talking about what happened to them can be therapy enough. When Zachary Scott-Singley returned from Iraq in 2005, he was haunted by the image of a 3-year-old boy who had been shot and killed accidentally by a fellow soldier. With a son of his own, Scott-Singley couldn't get the picture of the child and his wailing mother out of his head and became increasingly paranoid about his own child's safety. "I was constantly thinking about how people were going to attack me and take him," he says. Scott-Singley twice sought mental health care from the Army. The first time he says he was told that since he wasn't hurting anybody, he didn't have PTSD. The next counselor suggested he buy some stress-management tapes on the Internet and practice counting to 10 whenever he felt overwhelmed. (The VA is legally precluded from discussing a soldier's medical records.) Ironically, Scott-Singley found his therapy on the Web anyway, with his blog A Soldier's Thoughts (*misoldierthoughts.blogspot.com*). "It feels so much better to know I am not alone."

Outcry. Many veterans say they would also find it therapeutic to hear Bush acknowledge PTSD and the psychological costs of the war instead of downplaying them. Earlier this year, for instance, the Institute of Medicine was asked by Congress to re-evaluate the diagnostic criteria for PTSD, which was established by the American Psychiatric Association in 1980. Critics claim the review was ordered by the Bush administration in an effort to make it harder to diagnose PTSD, which would in turn reduce the amount of disability payments. The number of veterans from all wars receiving disability payments for PTSD, about 216,000 last year, has grown seven times as fast as the number receiving benefits for disabilities in general, at a cost of $4.6 billion a year. And that figure does not include most of the more than 100,000 Iraq and Afghanistan veterans who have sought mental health services. The IOM report, released in June, supported the current criteria for diagnosing PTSD.

Now the institute is looking at the accuracy of screening techniques and how to compensate and treat vets with PTSD, widely regarded as an easy condition to fake. And in another move that infuriated veterans groups, the VA late last year proposed a review of 72,000 cases of vets who were receiving full disability benefits for PTSD to look for fraud. The move prompted such an outcry that it was called off.

Studies and reviews aside, there isn't enough help available to veterans with PTSD. According to a report from the VA, individual veterans' visits to PTSD specialists dropped by 20 percent from 1995 to 2005–"a decrease in capacity at a time when the VA needs to reach out," the report stated. Secretary of Veterans Affairs James Nicholson says the VA sees 85 percent of new mental health patients within 30 days. "But that still leaves 15 percent and that's a big number. Could we do better? Yes."

Bush has called for a record $80.6 billion in the 2007 VA budget. That includes $3.2 billion for mental health services, a $339 million increase over this year's budget. However, those increases are being met by increasing demands for care, as well as rising cost-of-living allowances and prescription drug prices. "The bigger budget doesn't really add up to much," says Rieckhoff.

However frustrating and exhausting the process, most vets can avoid getting help only so long before friends and family push them into counseling or they get in trouble with the law. "It's almost like your family has its own form of PTSD just from being around you every day," says a former Army sergeant who worked as an interrogator in Iraq and asked that his name be withheld. "When I came back I was emotionally shut down and severely paranoid. My wife thought I was crazy and my son didn't realize who I was. Because of them, I got help."

Like many soldiers, he found it at one of more than 200 local Veterans Centers, which offer counseling for PTSD and sexual assault, a growing concern for women in the military. Vet Centers are part of the VA but operate like the anti-VA, free of the delays and bureaucracy. There is almost no paperwork, and the wait to see a counselor is rarely more than a week. It's no coincidence that when *Doonesbury* character B.D. finally went for help with his PTSD, he went to a Vet Center (story, Page 182). The centers are small and staffed mostly by vets, which creates the feel of a nurturing social environment rather than an institutional one. The free coffee is strictly decaf, and the approach is laid back. "Someone may come in asking about an insurance problem, and as we answer their questions, we ask them how are they feeling," says Karen Schoenfeld-Smith, a psychologist and team leader at the San Diego Vet Center, which sees a lot of Iraq vets from nearby Camp Pendleton. "That's how we get them into it." Many come just to talk to other vets.

It is that same need to talk that keeps Schrumpf e-mailing and phoning fellow marines and returning to Camp Pendleton every couple of weeks to hang out. "It is the only place I can talk about the killing," he says. Next month, Schrumpf will leave California for his home state of Tennessee, where he says it will be easier to raise a family. He's not worried about taking the war with him. In fact, in many ways he is more worried about leaving it behind. "The anger, the rage, and all that is just there," says Schrumpf. "And honestly, I don't want it to leave. It's like a security blanket." Or a movie, that just keeps on playing.

Soldier Support

Psychologists help troops handle the stresses of combat in Iraq and the anxieties of coming home.

CHRISTOPHER MUNSEY

Last fall near the city of Ar Ramadi in Iraq, the strain of combat was beginning to overwhelm a platoon from an Army unit supporting infantry pursuing insurgents, says Lt. Col. Kathy Platoni, PsyD, an Army psychologist. The soldiers were worn down by a constant toll of attacks from insurgents, pushed close to the edge of panic by fear.

"They were afraid to die, because so many of them had," Platoni says.

The insurgents' most frequent method of attack came via improvised explosive devices (IEDs), bombs planted by insurgents on roads and highways used by U.S. forces, but other soldiers had been killed or wounded by small arms fire, rocket-propelled grenades and sniper bullets. "They watched their beloved fellow soldiers being blown up all the time, burning to death right in front of them," she says.

Concerned about the soldiers' ability to continue functioning given their level of fear and sheer physical exhaustion, Platoni worked with the unit's leadership to give many of them a 48-hour reprieve from operations.

During the break, the soldiers got a chance to sleep, take a shower, eat a hot meal and talk to mental health professionals about their experiences, if they wanted to talk. Following the brief respite, the soldiers returned to their duties, still facing constant danger, but better able to manage their fears and concentrate on the job at hand.

Platoni, a mobilized Army reservist and private practitioner in Beavercreek, Ohio, organized the reprieve project with fellow soldier and mental health specialist Sgt. George McQuade during a 10-month stint working at forward operating bases in Iraq last year. Nicknamed FOBs in military lingo and scattered across Iraq, the bases are where U.S. servicemen and-women live and operate from while serving in the country.

The need for psychological services, she says, is evident in the sobering statistics: As of mid-March, 2,302 service members had been killed in action in Iraq and more than 17,124 had been wounded. Every day in Iraq, psychologists like Platoni are helping soldiers, Marines, sailors and airmen cope with the traumatic effects of combat and the stresses of living and working far from home and family in austere, dangerous conditions. They're also helping service members adjust to life after Iraq when they return home.

How Therapy Is Delivered

In fact, the Army has redoubled its mental health efforts, making psychologists and combat stress-control teams more accessible to deployed soldiers, instituting more stress-control training for deploying soldiers and surveying individual units for problems.

For example, working with the Marines, Navy medicine has adopted a new approach called OSCAR, for Operational Stress Control and Readiness. Instead of assigning a Navy psychologist from outside the unit's existing medical support staff, the program matches psychologists with Marine regiments in the months before a deployment, continuing during a rotation in Iraq, then back home, so that closer relationships can be built between psychologists and a unit's leadership.

Psychologists across military branches say their goal is keeping service members mentally focused during deployment and fostering resilience that encourages service members to rely on both their individual and unit strengths. Keeping soldiers or Marines focused can help them stay sharp in a hazardous environment requiring constant vigilance, psychologists say.

Often, doing that requires psychologists to get out from behind a desk in the larger, relatively more secure FOBs and experience firsthand what some service members see patrolling the roads and neighborhoods of Iraqi cities and towns every day.

"Just living in this environment can be overwhelming."

Bret Moore
U.S. Army

Different Types of Stress

Psychologists say service members encounter two broad kinds of stress in Iraq. The first is combat stress, created by directly experiencing roadside bomb explosions, suicide vehicle bomber attacks and combat operations. Besides the threat of IEDs, service members also have to deal with the unnerving threat of lethal mortar and rocket attacks targeting service members where they work and sleep.

The second is operational or deployment stress, created by being deployed overseas and working in harsh conditions. Service members live with very little privacy and typically sleep jammed together in tents, trailers and bunkers, all while enduring an outside environment with temperatures topping 130 degrees in the summer and cold rain and mud in the winter.

And while the immediacy of e-mail makes it much easier for family members to stay in touch, it sometimes exacerbates stress when spouses relay bad news and expect help with financial problems and kids in trouble back home.

Psychologists say they help service members cope with the different types of stress in a number of ways. Working from a FOB in northern Iraq, Army Capt. Bret Moore, PsyD, is the officer-in-charge of a three-person preventive team from the 85th Medical Detachment, making care available to about 5,000 soldiers. "Just living in this environment can be overwhelming," Moore says.

The Army deals with soldiers experiencing combat stress using a set of precepts, BICEPS. The acronym stands for:

- *Brevity.* Treatment will be short, addressing the problem at hand.
- *Immediacy.* An intervention will take place quickly, before symptoms worsen.
- *Centrality.* Treatment will be set apart from medical facilities, as a way to reduce the stigma soldiers might feel about seeking mental health services.
- *Expectancy.* A soldier experiencing problems with combat stress is expected to return to duty.
- *Proximity.* Soldiers are treated as close to their units as possible and are not evacuated from the area of operations.
- *Simplicity.* Besides therapy, the basics of a good meal, hot shower and a comfortable place to sleep ensure a soldier's basic physical needs are met.

All told, Moore says about 98 percent of soldiers sent to restoration areas come back to their units.

If a soldier isn't sent to a restoration area for 48- to 72-hour respite, Moore says he's only got enough time for between five and six therapy sessions with each soldier. The therapy's goal is keeping the soldier with his or her unit and functioning, he says. Moore uses a variety of techniques, ranging from cognitive-behavioral therapy to handing out CDs explaining deep breathing and other relaxation practices. To strengthen resiliency, he advises soldiers to exercise every day—preferably through a team sport—to eat balanced meals and to sleep when they can, he says.

It's not just Army psychologists helping care for soldiers. Another psychologist, Air Force Capt. Michael Detweiler, PhD, runs a life skills support center at an overseas base in Southwest Asia.

Detweiler describes himself as the only mental health provider for about 10,000 service members, mostly Army and Air Force personnel. Besides assisting soldiers in dealing with trauma, he often helps service members get along better.

"We live with the same people we work with . . . so the same people who drive you crazy at work are the same people you live with," Detweiler says.

Other important roles for psychologists in Iraq are helping leaders understand morale problems or handle interpersonal difficulties within units. Navy psychologist Lt. Cmdr. Gary Hoyt, PsyD, served with two Marine regimental combat teams in 2004 in Iraq, during which he regularly went out on patrols. Being present and exposed to the same dangers helped him earn the trust of junior enlisted Marines.

If the tempo of operations was too high, if they weren't getting enough sleep or if they were struggling with the big-picture "whys" of their mission in Iraq, Hoyt says he heard about it. With his access to leaders, Hoyt served as a conduit for those concerns, letting battalion-level officers know what was bothering junior Marines.

"There's no way they're going to hear this input directly from the junior ranks," he says. Besides talking to senior leadership, Hoyt says he stressed education and training of small-unit leaders about combat stress so Marines could spot problems themselves and help each other tackle them before the problems worsened.

Follow-up Care Strengthened

Besides offering mental health treatment for deployed soldiers, the Army also seeks to detect symptoms of post-traumatic stress disorder or other combat-related psychological problems when they return home, says Col. Bruce Crow, PsyD, the Army's chief psychologist. Currently, the best estimates are that about 15 percent of soldiers returning from Iraq will show symptoms of post-traumatic stress, Crow says.

As part of a military-wide initiative, all service members receive a health screening about 90 days after they return home. In addition, all soldiers and their families can tap into counseling through the Deployment Cycle Support Program.

Aiding in this effort is Lt. Col. Platoni, who works with returning combat soldiers on adjusting to life in the civilian world.

We Love to Be Scared on Halloween

But fears and phobias are no laughing matter.

RICHARD HÉBERT

It seems we humans spend a good deal of time and energy in pursuit of thrills, chills, and spills, especially at this time of year. From haunted houses to ghoulish get-ups, we love to be scared.

Even when it's not Halloween, scary pursuits are commonplace. For fun we jump off bridges tethered to bungee cords or drive fast cars or swim with sharks. Or watch others do it. On the face of it, these fear-seeking behaviors seem contrary to our basic instincts of self-preservation. But it could be that they are vestiges of our genetic and environmental past.

"Many individuals are motivated to seek increased arousal," explains Fordham University's Dean McKay, whose research focuses on obsessive compulsive disorder and anxiety disorders. "Intense experiences such as bungee jumping or extreme rock climbing satisfy this need. Most individuals seek this out in some way, whether by direct experience or (vicariously) by observation."

High jinks and thrills aside, fear is an excellent survival tool handed down by our cave-dwelling ancestors who probably learned fear in order to avoid saber-toothed tigers and woolly mammoths. Today's world can be quite scary, too; we teach life-preserving fears to our children—warning them about cliff edges and hot stovetops and talking to strangers.

So, fear is a good thing. But like so many good things, too much of it can be a problem. Too much fear can be debilitating, and the result can be an anxiety disorder or phobia.

At some point in our lives, about three in 10 of us experience an anxiety disorder severe enough to meet diagnostic criteria for impairment, according to APS Fellow and Charter Member David Barlow, Director of Boston University's Center for Anxiety and Related Disorders. And 11 percent of us meet criteria for a specific phobia.

Control is the key, McKay says. Halloween revelers and thrill-seekers have it; phobics and victims of anxiety disorder don't. When systems that serve a critical need malfunction, the result is disease. Think of phobias and anxiety disorders as "diseases" of the brain's "fear system."

Our understanding of phobias has been undergoing a revolution. "For a long time," says Barlow, "we thought that people with phobias must have had some traumatic experience that created the fear. Now we know that's not true. Only a minority of people with specific phobias have actually had a bad incident."

Fear of water can show up in children too young to have any meaningful experience with water, he says. And when you compare people who have a fear of dogs with others who don't, about the same number in each group have had a bad experience with a dog. The dog attack might precipitate phobia in those already vulnerable, but it doesn't cause it.

It's more often quite the opposite, according to research by Ross Menzies, University of Sydney, Australia. Most stuntmen, he found, have histories of serious childhood accidents. Far from making them phobic, they embraced the wellspring of their fear and built a livelihood around mastering it.

Phobias are not learned: We're born with them and "events previously thought to bring about phobias actually lead to greater approach for the object."

McKay says this demonstrates that phobias are not learned: We're born with them and "events previously thought to bring about phobias actually lead to greater approach for the object."

But don't go looking for a "phobic gene." According to Barlow, the inherited DNA codings are a bit more complex than that. "We're now learning that they're not single genes, they're variations in genetic structure, certain genes with certain patterns of alleles that, when they're turned on by events in the environment, would make us more susceptible."

So yes, genetic inheritance does play a role, accounting for perhaps a third to half of the variance between those who develop phobias and those who don't, "but it's misleading to talk like that. The genetic piece means nothing unless it's part of the feedback system."

He likens that system to an "intricate dance" of "triple vulnerabilities," genetics being only one dancer. The other two are psychological vulnerabilities—one generalized, based on early experiences developing a sense of control over events or lack of it, and the other more specific, in which one learns to focus anxiety on specific objects or situations. "When these three vulnerabilities line up, then you're at substantial risk for developing a phobia," Barlow says. "If they don't line up, if you just have one and not the others, you're at much less risk.

"There was always this myth that somehow anxiety disorders were due to chemical imbalance and could be treated with pills, whereas the psychological myth was that it was some distorted cognition or learning. We now know all these things are in it and interrelated. It's all a system. You have to change the whole system, not just neurotransmitter endings."

One of the most successful ways to counter the genetic vulnerability, he says, is by changing the internal and external environment. This "could be behavior, regulating your emotions, or learning new ways to respond to stress, which in turn will influence brain functioning."

Not All Phobias Are Alike

Of course, not all phobias are alike. They are typically grouped under three headings: specific phobias (like fear of heights, dogs, or water); social phobias, now more often called social anxiety disorders; and panic disorders—inexplicable panic attacks.

More than simple fear is involved, McKay says. It's also disgust, "a pretty powerful emotion for engendering avoidance. In the past two or three years, we've seen a big upswing in this kind of work, where an effort is being made to isolate the way disgust contributes to phobias." He is currently co-editing a book on the subject with Bumni Olatunji of Vanderbilt University, to be published in 2007.

How phobias are treated is another of the major turnarounds prompted by psychological research over the past few years. "Up until recently," Barlow says, "the usual approach was to see patients once a week and have them do a lot of prescribed exercises between sessions." Treatment lasted 10 to 12 weeks. The innovation, pioneered by Lars-Göran Öst, Stockholm University, "was simply to do it all at once in an intensive fashion," says Barlow, who now treats phobic patients using Öst's method—in a single four- to six-hour session, "more equivalent to doing surgery."

In that session, a patient gets intensive exposure to the thing or situation that triggers the terror. A patient might be shown insects, or small animals brought in from a pet store. The acrophobe may be taken to high places and a claustrophobe to enclosed spaces. Guided by the psychologist, the patient learns to "extinguish" the fear by learning to control it.

"The success rates, particularly for adults, seem to be up in the 80 to 90 percent range," Barlow says, "so it's clearly the treatment of choice" for specific phobias. Only about 10 to 15 percent of the patients relapse, and even then "it's fairly easy to go back and have a booster session."

More generalized social anxiety and panic disorders still require long-term therapy or medication, which are about equally effective, says Barlow. The drugs are either antidepressants, such as selective serotonin reuptake inhibitors (SSRIs), or high-potency tranquilizers, although the latter are used much

less and typically as adjuncts to therapy because patients can develop dependence on them.

While some patients prefer the "quick fix" of a pill, especially when they see it promoted on television, surveys have shown that around 75 percent prefer therapy that teaches them to master their fears. This is due primarily to the side effects of the medications, but also because relapse is more common with drugs.

"Psychological treatments are more durable," Barlow says. "The patients actually seem to learn something that has lasting benefit." As for combining drugs and therapy for anxiety disorders, he says, "Surprisingly, there does not seem to be any advantage to combining the two. It's more expensive and there's no evidence that the treatments are additive."

> **"Psychological treatments are more durable," Barlow says "The patients actually seem to learn something that has lasting benefit."**

Exposure therapy teaches patients to regulate and master their emotional response "and to accept that there has to be some confrontation with both the internal and external situation that provoked the phobic response," Barlow says.

The main disadvantage of the new one-day treatments is that they aren't readily available. "These intensive treatments came into their own in the past five years, but are still not widespread," he says. "Our biggest obstacle is actually getting them out there to the consumers. They require a lot of training, and that expertise is just not widely available yet."

Barlow's center at Boston University is now experimenting with intensive exposure therapy for panic disorders and social phobias as well. It recently received a five-year National Institute of Mental Health grant of $2 million to test one-day exposure therapy on 50 adolescents with panic disorders, comparing their results to patients who received more traditional care. The investigators are beginning with adolescents because the need is greater: It's harder for schoolchildren to get to a clinic every week than for adults.

A similar study using adult patients has also been started, and the center has a pilot project to treat severe social anxiety by putting small groups of patients together for several hours a day for a week. After their group interactions, they are sent out on assignments to interact socially in public, such as at a coffee shop.

Relapse is Tied to Context

The therapy springs from intriguing results in animal research. Mark Bouton, University of Vermont, has been working with laboratory rats since 1979, building on Pavlov's work on conditioned responses in dogs almost a century ago. Bouton demonstrated that a rat learns to fear a certain sound because it is always accompanied by an electric shock, then "extinguishes" that fear response by repeatedly hearing the tone without the shock. But he never "unlearns" the original fear; it lives on alongside the new learning, ready to spring alive again—in the right context.

He discovered this by teaching rats fear in one chamber, teaching them to extinguish it in a different chamber, then putting them back in the original chamber. When the tone sounded in the original chamber, the rats once again froze in fear, even after the fear was extinguished in the second chamber. It also happened if they were placed in a neutral third chamber and received the shock with the bell tone. The fear came rushing back to the fore.

"The fact that the original performance can recover after extinction may be an important insight into understanding relapse after therapy," Bouton and his colleagues write in their chapter in a newly published book on fear and learning (Bouton 2006). "(M)any manipulations of the context can cause an extinguished fear . . . to recover or return."

Their recent research has focused on how to take advantage of this context-dependency to prevent relapse into the original fear reaction, without much success. "(A)s far as we have been able to determine," they write, "extinction can often still remain surprisingly sensitive to the context (and the original responding thus susceptible to relapse) even after extinction procedures that have been designed to optimize the new learning."

The one approach they say "appears especially promising" at preventing relapse is building treatment "bridges," such as conducting therapy in the very situations that usually trigger the fright.

They offer multiple ways of doing this: "Conducting exposure therapy in the context where relapse is going to be a problem provides the most direct bridge," they write. "Retrieval cues for extinction provide another kind of bridge in the sense that they bring a piece of therapy to the relapse context. Occasional reinforced trials in extinction are another kind of bridge because they allow extinction in the presence of a cue (a new reinforced trial) that may be a strong stimulus for relapse."

Bouton is now studying time as context. "Extinction is specific to the temporal context in which it is learned," he explains, "just as it appears to be specific to the room in which it is learned. We are therefore looking at a lot of implications of this idea that are leading us in some interesting new directions. One practical implication is that extinction trials—therapy sessions—that are widely spaced in time should protect the system from relapse that might otherwise occur at intervals shorter than the interval between extinction trials."

Given that relapse rates for specific phobias are so low, the research appears to have greater significance for social anxiety and panic disorders, where relapse is more common. "I think of our research as a kind of caution sign," Bouton says.

A Clearer Picture in the Brain

Thanks both to animals like Bouton's rats and brain-imaging research, we now also have a better idea of what's happening in the brain when phobias strike. "It's very clear that the amygdala is a central player from the animal research," says Scott Rauch, MD, Associate Chief of Psychiatry for Neuroscience Research

at Massachusetts General Hospital, "but it's just one part of a larger network. At least two other key areas play a role. The ventromedial prefrontal cortex (vmPFC) probably plays a critical role in the capacity to recall extinction memory, whereas the hippocampus plays an important role in the context" in which that memory was acquired.

Raffael Kalisch and colleagues at the University of Hamburg, Germany, are looking in the other direction—removing context from the equation. They have conducted the first study of fear extinction's context-dependence in humans. "A key feature of this study," they write in the *Journal of Neuroscience* (in press), "is that our design allows delineation of the neural circuitry involved in that function, using a psychological manipulation that engenders recall of extinction memory in the appropriate context.

"Clinically, contextual restrictions on extinction can considerably complicate anxiety therapy. . . . For therapeutic purposes, therefore, it often may be desirable to create non-contextualized extinction memories." They say their data suggest this might be achieved by making the vmPFC-dependent recall of the extinction memory—the therapy—independent of the hippocampus.

A clearer picture of how the three realms of the brain interact is slowly emerging, says Rauch. In patients with post-traumatic stress disorder (PTSD), "quite an array of data from a variety of imaging tools" shows that "the amygdala is hyper-responsive, and that the vmPFC and hippocampus are both structurally small and of reduced function. It is hypothesized (but not yet shown) that the reduced function results in insufficient inhibition of the amygdala."

The amygdala also plays a role in learning about safety, he says, but "it seems to take the prefrontal cortex to recall that extinction learning and to suppress the amygdala's response."

Rauch and colleague Mohammed Milad also have shown that the thickness of an individual's vmPFC correlates with the ability to recall the fear-extinction, and that may link it to personality as well. "The thicker the area, the more extroverted a person might be. The idea being, if you're able to extinguish these adverse associations effectively, it enables you, when you have a bad experience, to limit that to the situation in which it occurred and not to over-generalize it. It allows you to be somebody who is more courageous or outgoing in the way you attack life."

There are differences, of course. It's generally believed that anxiety disorders and PTSD have similar brain mechanisms, he says, "but we also know these disorders are distinct one from another, and there ought to be some differences. That's precisely where the science is right now, trying to understand what the similarities and differences are."

For example, data from imaging studies "suggest that PTSD and panic subjects show exaggerated amygdala responses to general threat-related stimuli as well as stimuli related to their particular fears, whereas for (specific) phobias, exaggerated amygdala responses may be limited to the stimuli related to their particular fears."

Panic attacks are also being re-examined in light of human imaging studies, Rauch says. Historically, panic disorder attacks were thought to arise spontaneously, but research shows the amygdala can be activated subconsciously. This opens the door to reinterpreting "spontaneous" panic attacks. "It opens the possibility that, even though the individual is not aware of what stimulus in the environment tweaked their amygdala, it doesn't mean there wasn't any stimulus, just that they didn't know what it was."

For the most disabling cases that require more aggressive treatments—panic disorders, PTSD, obsessive-compulsive disorder—Rauch says, "as we come to understand underlying mechanisms and brain circuitry, it may be possible to develop newer and better medications, or use treatments to influence the limbic system circuitry, known to play a critical role in anxiety disorders."

Experimental procedures being investigated include lesions that cut the circuitry at targeted locations; "deep brain stimulation," in which implanted electrodes modulate the circuitry; electro-convulsive therapy; and trans-cranial magnetic stimulation—putting a magnet against the head to create a magnetic field that influences brain activity.

Whatever technology comes along for extreme cases, however, it is clear that for the foreseeable future behavioral therapy, and especially the innovative intense exposure therapies being developed by psychological science, will be called upon to carry the load in treating most patients with phobias and anxiety disorders.

Reference

Bouton, M.E., Woods, A.M., Moody E.W., Sunsay, C. & García-Gutiérrez, A. (2006). "Counteracting the Context-Dependence of Extinction: Relapse and Some Tests of Possible Methods of Relapse Prevention," In *Fear and Learning: Basic Science to Clinical Application* (175–196). In M.G. Craske, D. Hermans, & D. Vansteenwegen (Eds.), Washington, DC: American Psychological Association.

RICHARD HÉBERT is an *Observer* contributor.

UNIT 11

Psychological Treatments

Unit Selections

Key Points to Consider

- What is couple therapy? Does it work?

- What factors contribute to the high suicide rate among American Indians? What is being done to treat it?

- What are the different means by which psychologists approach the treatment of post-traumatic stress disorder?

- Which methods of treating post-traumatic stress disorder appear to be the most effective?

- Psychologists often treat psychological disorders through therapy and some advise their clients to seek drug treatments. Are these approaches to treating psychological disorders effective? Given the evidence to date, which approach appears to be more effective?

Student Web Site

www.mhcls.com

Internet References

Abraham A. Brill Library
http://plaza.interport.net/nypsan/service.html
The C.G. Jung Page
http://www.cgjungpage.org
Knowledge Exchange Network (KEN)
http://www.mentalhealth.org
NetPsychology
http://netpsych.com/index.htm
This is a basic cybertherapy resource site.
Sigmund Freud and the Freud Archives
http://plaza.interport.net/nypsan/freudarc.html

Have you ever had the nightmare of being trapped in a dark, dismal place? No one lets you out. Your pleas for freedom go unanswered and, in fact, are suppressed or ignored by domineering authority figures around you. You keep begging for mercy but to no avail. You are fortunate to awake to your normal bedroom and to the realities of your daily life. For the mentally ill, the nightmare of institutionalization, where individuals can be held against their will in what are sometimes terribly dreary, restrictive surroundings, is a reality. Have you ever wondered what would happen if we took perfectly normal individuals and institutionalized them in such a place? In one well known and remarkable study, that is exactly what happened.

In 1973, eight people, including a pediatrician, a psychiatrist and some psychologists, presented themselves to psychiatric hospitals. Each claimed that he or she was hearing voices. The voices, they reported, seemed unclear but appeared to be saying "empty" or "thud." Each of these individuals was admitted to a mental hospital, and most were diagnosed as being schizophrenic. After admission to the hospital, the "pseudopatients" or fake patients gave truthful information and thereafter acted like their usual, normal selves.

Their hospital stays lasted anywhere from 7 to 52 days. The nurses, doctors, psychologists, and other staff members treated them as if they were schizophrenic and never saw through their trickery. Some of the real patients in the hospital, however, recognized that the pseudopatients were perfectly normal. After their discharge almost all of the pseudopatients received the diagnosis of "schizophrenic in remission," meaning that they were still clearly defined as schizophrenic; they just weren't exhibiting any of the symptoms at the time of release.

What does this study demonstrate about mental illness? Is true mental illness always readily detectable? If we can't always pinpoint mental disorders (the more professionally accepted term for mental illness), how can we treat them appropriately? What treatments are available, and which treatments work better for various diagnoses? The treatment of mental disorders is a challenge. The array of available treatments is ever increasing and can be downright bewildering—and not just to the patient or

© David Buffington/Getty Images

client! In order to demystify and simplify your understanding of treatments and interventions for mental disorders, we will look at them in this unit.

Couple Therapy

Psychotherapy for Two and Two for Psychotherapy

The problems that confront the clients and patients of mental health professionals arise mostly in marriages and other intimate relationships. Marriage and family difficulties account for about half of all visits to psychotherapists, family therapy is increasingly popular as a mental health specialty, and most family therapists work chiefly with couples. The term "couple therapy" (or "couples therapy") is gradually replacing the older "marital therapy" in order to include unmarried and gay couples.

Licensed couple therapists include psychiatrists, psychologists, clinical social workers, psychiatric nurses, pastoral counselors, and marriage and family therapists who have taken specialized courses and undergone supervised training in the field. The therapist assumes that the unhappiness of a couple amounts to more than the sum of their individual problems and symptoms. They may be concerned about emotional distancing, power struggles, poor communication, jealousy, infidelity, sexual dissatisfaction, and violence. The therapist helps them examine their lives together and decide what changes are needed. They work on eliminating mutual misunderstandings, unreasonable expectations, and unstated assumptions that perpetuate conflict.

Couple therapists make little use of psychiatric diagnosis, but they do use many of the same methods employed by individual therapists: interpreting emotional conflicts and the influence of the past; assigning exercises for behavior change; challenging beliefs; offering advice, reassurance, and support; teaching social skills and problem solving. If the relationship is moribund, some couple therapists believe that they can help the couple make a break with a minimum of recrimination, bitterness, and suffering.

Family Systems and Patterns

Family systems theory was once dominant and is still influential as a blueprint for couple therapists. It emphasizes the patterns of communication, action, and reaction that create and reinforce a family environment. In an unhappy couple, the system resists change because it has reached a maladaptive equilibrium, just as individual symptoms may resist change because they preserve individual emotional balance. The couple may have unknowingly set rules for themselves that are working poorly. The therapist helps them become aware of these rules and patterns as a prerequisite to changing them.

Sometimes each partner demands too much of the same thing from the other—service, protection, care. Sometimes they adopt complementary roles. One member of the couple takes charge and the other becomes incompetent. An overbearing and emotionally distant husband responds to his dependent or melodramatic wife by becoming still more overbearing. A strong wife is constantly angry at her passive husband, whose passivity only increases. The husband or wife of a depressed and hypochondriacal person may act as a healer and savior.

Couple therapists try to help both individuals understand the function of their contributions to the system. The passive partner might learn about his need to suppress rather than productively express anger. "Saviors" may see how that role helps them deny their own sense of helplessness. An emotionally distant husband could learn about the fear of strong emotion. A dependent wife might confront her wish to avoid managing her own anxieties. By acknowledging their own contributions to the conflict, members of a couple can begin to weigh the benefits and costs of the bargain they've made with a partner.

When the two are not communicating well, verbally or nonverbally, each one may behave as though certain principles are accepted when they are not. For example, one partner believes the other has agreed that he or she can stay at work as long as he or she thinks is necessary, but the other thinks he or she has implicitly agreed to be home for dinner. Other misunderstood implicit promises include: I need a certain amount of sex, a certain degree of financial security, or a certain number of friends.

Family systems therapists often employ the concept of the double bind, a situation that results when members of a couple send mutually contradictory messages—often one in words and the other through the silent communication of emotion. The partner must not acknowledge the contradiction or respond to the underlying intentions if he or she wants to maintain the relationship. For example, one partner asks the other to come to him or her and stiffens at the other's approach. The second partner withdraws, and the first one says, "Why are you so cold?" The second person has no response: To point out what is going on would only alienate the first partner further. Eventually people who are communicating—or failing to communicate—in this way find it difficult to say what they mean, understand what the other person means, or even distinguish real from simulated feelings. Family systems therapy is designed to uncover and solve problems of this kind.

Behavioral Couple Therapy

Behavioral treatment of couples provides three kinds of help: behavioral exchange, communication training, and problem-solving training.

In behavioral exchange, each partner is helped to identify a desired change in the other partner's behavior, and they agree to reciprocate. The therapist encourages them to follow through and show gratitude. Communication training shows the couple how to listen sensitively and express their needs without accusations. From exercises in problem solving, they learn how to define the issues that generate conflict, find specific solutions, negotiate, and compromise.

Either during therapeutic sessions or as homework, behavior therapists may prescribe tasks that reveal maladaptive patterns. A woman might be told to exaggerate her criticism of her partner until he challenges her. If a couple is drifting apart, the therapist might arrange for the man (or woman) to be sure to come home for dinner four or five nights a week.

Today many behavior therapists also try to change the way each member of the couple responds to undesired behavior. They may also employ cognitive restructuring—changing the way the partners interpret one another's behavior. They learn to avoid using words like "always" and "never," to examine evidence before blaming the other, and to consider the consequences of living by doubtful implicit assumptions (such as the belief that you should never be angry at your partner).

Emotionally Focused Couple Therapy

Another kind of treatment, drawing on ideas from the client-centered therapy of Carl Rogers (see *Mental Health Letter*, January 2006) as well as family systems theory, concentrates on emotion rather than behavior. The therapist helps the couple recognize the emotions that drive their conflict as a precursor to stopping the resulting troublesome behavior patterns. They expose their vulnerability and express unacknowledged feelings, then reconsider their situation in the light of these feelings to work out new solutions.

Often the problem is stated as a matter of interrupting or escaping from rigid response patterns or cycles. In one pattern that arises repeatedly, an angry, critical, complaining partner confronts one who is defensive and withdrawn. The therapist helps the angry partner to feel his or her desperation about not getting through and the consequent fear of abandonment, while urging the withdrawn partner to temporarily disregard the feeling of being attacked and—instead of acting defensively—to listen to the concerns and respond with support.

Emotionally focused couple therapy may encourage the couple to reframe their problems in terms of attachment needs. The premise of attachment theory is that a safe emotional bond with another person is a basic survival need, providing a home base in the world. From infancy on, we all need contact with others who care for us and respond sensitively to our needs. Attachment patterns usually appear first in the relationship between parent and child and are often repeated throughout life.

A secure attachment provides both comfort and room for independent exploration. When attachment is insecure, people may become angry, and—if there is no response—depressed and despairing. They may also develop a distorted attachment that takes the form of anxious clinging, or a combination of the two, exemplified by the double bind: "Come here to me, I need you" and "You are dangerous, go away."

Couples often seek help when they have sustained an "attachment injury"—a crisis involving infidelity, financial deception, violence, deeply insulting words, or another apparent betrayal. One of the partners may feel emotionally abandoned at a critical moment such as job loss or serious illness. Divorce or separation may be threatening.

In therapy, at first the injured partner may angrily or sadly recount the incident while the offending partner minimizes the damage or becomes defensive. The injured partner is encouraged to show grief and fear instead of anger, and the offending partner is encouraged to acknowledge responsibility and show remorse. Then the injured partner may ask for comfort and care that was unavailable at the time of the incident, and the offending partner may come through, helping heal the attachment injury.

An example: Mary has discovered that her husband John had an affair three years ago. They've never discussed it, but John complains that she repeatedly reminds him of it. It is a typical pattern of anger and defensiveness. She worries about what he does when he goes out alone, and when he is at home he feels under siege and retreats to a room alone. Over a period of several months, the therapist helps him talk about his feelings of shame, and he tearfully expresses his sorrow and his love for her. As the complete range of their feelings becomes more apparent to both of them, she begins to move past her injury and expresses genuine forgiveness.

Psychodynamic Couple Therapy

Psychodynamic therapists believe that the way adult couples treat each other is strongly influenced by patterns established in childhood—lessons learned, mostly unconsciously, in their birth families. The therapist emphasizes unconscious wishes and the defenses, also mostly unconscious, that divert or prevent the full expression of those wishes.

Psychodynamic couple therapists sometimes pay special attention to projective identification, a defense that involves disavowing your own impulses or wishes, attributing them to another person, and behaving in a way that elicits responses that convince you that your attributions are right. A husband can't bear his own dependency or weakness and overcompensates by being controlling and rigid as an expression of strength. This evokes dependent behavior in his wife—which he can both identify with *and* resent. Projective identification can perpetuate a painful attachment when, as often happens, the partner uses the defense in a complementary way. In this example, the wife may need to disavow her own aggression, so her dependency also evokes even more rigidity and hostility in her husband. Such complementary patterns, psychodynamic therapists believe, often originate in childhood relationships with parents.

Psychodynamic therapists explore the influence of the past partly by pointing out how feelings originally directed at members of the birth family have been transferred to the partner, and sometimes to the therapist, too. They also show how emotionally charged fantasies blend with present reality. If all goes well, the members of the couple succeed in separating their feelings about one another from their feelings about their own parents and past experiences.

The Individual and the Couple

Individual psychiatric symptoms and the problems of couples are related in complicated ways. Often there is a vicious cycle in which a relationship is endangered by the withdrawal and irritability of a depressed person, the aggressive and impulsive behavior associated with mania, the need for constant reassurance resulting from anxiety, or the multifarious ravages of alcoholism and drug addiction. Conflict between the members of the couple exacerbates these symptoms until it is difficult to tell where the cycle began. According to some versions of family systems theory, individual symptoms serve to maintain arrangements that prevent change both partners need but fear.

Couple therapists may concentrate on specific actions that exacerbate individual symptoms, or they can enlist one partner as a surrogate therapist or coach. Partners can help with treatments such as relaxation training, exposure and response prevention, or cognitive restructuring, while monitoring changes as the therapy progresses and providing the therapist with information.

Alcoholism has been treated successfully with forms of behavioral couple therapy called community reinforcement and Project CALM (Counseling for Alcoholic Marriages). Emotionally focused couple therapy may be helpful for depressed people when the depression is associated with an insecure attachment. It has also been used for survivors of child abuse and Vietnam veterans suffering from traumatic stress reactions. Dialectical behavior therapy (see *Mental Health Letter,* August 2002) for couples can relieve depression and reduce emotional volatility in people with borderline personality disorder.

Individual and couple therapy are often combined. For example, a woman marries a divorced man with two young sons from a previous marriage, gives birth to a girl, and develops a postpartum depression. Her stepsons, already feeling displaced by the new baby, become angry and defiant. She is reminded of her own unhappy relationship with her stepmother and feels as though she is turning into an evil stepmother herself. The marriage is affected, and the couple seeks therapy. Her depression is part of the problem and might best be treated additionally with medications and her own psychotherapy.

In cases of serious domestic violence, the trend today is to separate the partners instead of treating them jointly. Some professionals reject the idea of couple therapy for batterers because it may suggest that someone or something other than the instigator of violence is to blame. But others believe that a combination of individual and couple therapy may be workable as long as the violence has stopped, the victim does not fear retaliation, and the perpetrator admits responsibility. The therapist must always make it clear that no alleged provocation justifies violence.

How Effective Is Couple Therapy?

Most studies find that couple therapy can be helpful, at least for a while, but not all studies meet the highest standards. It's also unclear whether the treatment can transform unhappy relationships into satisfactory ones, and whether the effects last. Behavioral couple therapy and emotionally focused couple therapy have been found more effective than a waiting list in controlled studies. The American Psychological Association approves behavioral couple therapy as "well established" and emotionally focused couple therapy as "probably efficacious." Other reviews support the value of cognitive behavioral couple therapy and family systems therapy.

Some of the research has raised doubt about whether all the components of behavioral or emotionally focused couple therapy are necessary, and whether these techniques work in the way that the underlying theory proposes.

Improvement is usually maintained for six months, but often there is a relapse after a year or two. In a four-year follow-up, the longest so far, researchers found that 38% of couples treated with behavioral couple therapy were divorced. But in some cases, a divorce—especially if it is amicable—may represent a good outcome. A recent two-year follow-up indicated that a year of therapy for a couple in which one partner was depressed gave better results—and produced fewer dropouts—than antidepressant drug treatment.

There is only a little evidence on who couple therapy works best for. Younger couples seem to improve more in some studies. One study found that couples did better when they had been together longer; another, that couples with the most serious problems were least likely to benefit; and still another, that in heterosexual couples, therapy worked out better when the woman was the main problem solver in the family.

Like individual therapists, couple therapists are becoming more eclectic in their approach. A method called integrative couple therapy combines emotional acceptance with behavioral strategies. Therapists are also trying different approaches with different couples, or emphasizing features that all treatments have in common, such as the therapeutic alliance.

According to the United States Department of Health and Human Services, the number of specialists in marriage and family therapy has increased from about 2,000 in 1966 to almost 50,000 today. The American Association for Marriage and Family Therapy estimates that more than 3% of the nation's 57 million married couples see a psychotherapist for marital difficulties each year. The line between enhancement and therapy is becoming blurred with the development of programs aimed at preventing marital conflict and improving relationships. Because it is increasingly understood that emotional disturbances and behavior problems originate *between* people as well as within them, psychotherapy for two will continue to thrive.

References

Cournos F. "Psychodynamic Couples Therapy," in Hersen M, et al., eds, *Encyclopedia of Psychotherapy.* Academic Press, 2002.

Gurman AS, et al. "The History of Couple Therapy: A Millennial Review," *Family Process* (June 2002): Vol. 41, No. 2, pp. 199–260.

Makinen JA, et al. "Resolving Attachment Injuries in Couples Using Emotionally Focused Therapy: Steps toward Forgiveness and Reconciliation," *Journal of Consulting and Clinical Psychology* (December 2006): Vol. 74, No. 6, pp. 1055–64.

O'Farrell TJ, et al., eds. *Behavioral Couples Therapy for Alcoholism and Drug Abuse,* Haworth Press, 2006.

Snyder DK, et al. "Current Status and Future Directions in Couple Therapy," *Annual Review of Psychology* (2006): Vol.57, pp. 317–44.

'A Struggle for Hope'

Armed with funding and cultural insights, psychologist-designed programs seek to reduce the alarmingly high suicide rate among American Indians.

LAURIE MEYERS

D
ifferent tribes, different languages, but a common thread: despair.

After generations of displacement, forced assimilation, poverty and neglect, many American Indians are trapped in a cycle of hopelessness that often leads to substance abuse, violence and in many cases suicide, say experts. In fact, according to the Indian Health Service, the suicide rate for American Indians is two and a half times higher than the national average. The rate for Indian youth and young adults 15 to 24 years old is over three times higher than the national average for this age group.

But there appears to be a glimmer of optimism for this long-ignored population. Community leaders, Indian psychologists and government agencies such as the Indian Health Service and the Substance Abuse and Mental Health Services Administration are working to identify the factors that contribute to suicide and to design interventions to help prevent it in those most at risk.

"The suicide rate did increase markedly in the 1970s and 1980s and then leveled off at very high rates," says psychologist Jon Perez, PhD, former director of the Behavioral Health Unit of the Indian Health Service (IHS). "However, now it's looking like there might be some hope that we can attenuate the rate."

New federally funded programs and tribal initiatives are working to do just that. In 2003, the IHS established its Suicide Prevention Committee, which established a national network with 50 to 60 people who train communities in how to prevent and react to clusters of suicides, which have become a frequent problem on reservations.

Also, last year the Substance Abuse and Mental Health Services Administration (SAMHSA) announced that it was providing $9.6 million in grant money over three years for eight youth suicide prevention programs, many of which target American Indian and Alaska Native communities. SAMHSA also recently awarded $49.3 million in grant funding for 14 new and one supplemental grant to tribal organizations for mental illness and substance abuse prevention, treatment and recovery support programs. The tribes will use the grants to fund culturally appropriate programs addressing issues such as suicide in schools, programs for children with severe emotional disturbances and alcohol- and methamphetamine-abuse prevention programs.

These programs will embrace methods specific to each culture, drawing on native traditions to promote understanding and healing.

A History of Trauma

Many Indian psychologists believe that the root of the population's suicide problem is the combination of generational trauma and loss of ethnic identity.

As psychologist Tawa M. Witko, PhD, notes in her book, "Mental Health Care for Urban Indians: Clinical Insights From Native Practitioners" (APA, 2006), Europeans' effort to "civilize" Indians changed their culture in ways that are still being felt. In fact, until a generation ago, Indian children were still taken from their families and tribes and sent to boarding schools to assimilate into white culture. In the process, many customs that should have been handed down from generation to generation have been lost, notes Witko.

The intergenerational trauma, compounded by extreme poverty, lack of economic opportunity and widespread substance abuse, has shattered these communities, Perez says. "Suicide is a single response to a multiplicity of problems," he emphasizes. "If you have these things going on, and you don't see any hope for the future, suicide seems like an option."

Hope can often be hard to come by when there are not enough jobs on the reservation and you don't have a car or enough money for gas or even food, says Diane Willis, PhD, a Kiowa tribe member and professor emeritus at the University of Oklahoma Health Sciences Center. Willis, who has worked with tribes across the country teaching locals about infant mental health, says the economic situation is so dire that some Indians are starving. At one reservation—where the average resident income is $2,900 a year—she saw an 18-month-old little girl who was so hungry, that she grabbed for a freshly poured bowl of soup and burned herself. At another reservation, 40 people had attempted suicide within the last six months and approximately half succeeded.

Substance abuse—particularly alcohol—has fueled and compounded the misery, says psychologist Marlene EchoHawk, PhD, a member of the Otoe Missouria tribe and director of the Indian Health Service's Suicide Prevention Committee. In her community, alcohol became more prevalent when young Indian men returned from World War II with a newfound taste for alcohol and suffering from what is now recognized as post-traumatic stress disorder. They used the alcohol to stop the pain, but it only increased the depression, notes EchoHawk, who has seen this pattern repeat itself with tribe members returning from Vietnam and now from Iraq.

Young people in Indian communities are turning to alcohol at a very young age, setting them up for a lifetime of alcohol abuse and an increased risk of suicide, says Willis. Indeed, in one community, almost 20 percent of middle school students admitted to having attempted suicide in the last six months, psychologist Teresa LaFromboise, PhD, an associate counseling psychology professor and chair of Native American Studies at Stanford University, found in a recent survey.

"Our children and grandchildren are carrying all the pain of the generations that came before," says Ethleen Iron-Cloud Two Dogs, a member of the Ogalala Lakota tribe and director of Wakanyeja Pawicayapi (The Children First), Inc., a non-profit community mental health organization on the Pine Ridge Indian reservation in South Dakota.

Hope in a Return to Tradition

Historically, suicide was rare in American Indian culture, and the stigma attached to it is still very strong, notes LaFromboise. Many communities are just now coming out of denial and starting to address the problem, she adds.

Because the community emphasis on suicide is relatively new, there isn't a lot of research on what works. Many of the SAMHSA-funded programs will use evidence-based practices and tailor them to community culture and needs.

"Our children and grand-children are carrying all the pain of the generations that came before."

—Ethleen Iron-Cloud Two Dogs
Wakanyeja Pawicayapi
(The Children First), Inc.

Indian psychologists believe that letting the community determine what it needs and allowing residents to incorporate traditions will produce the best results.

Indeed, community-oriented suicide prevention can significantly decrease suicidal gestures and acts, sociologist Philip A. May, PhD, found in a 15-year study published in the *American Journal of Public Health* (Vol. 95, No. 7, pages 1238–1244).

"We do have strength and we do have resources," maintains Shannon Crossbear, a member of the Ojibwe tribe and of the board—which Iron-Cloud Two Dogs is also vice president of—at First Nation Behavioral Health, a mental health advocacy group for American Indians and Alaska Natives. Her community has revived coming-of-age ceremonies for young girls, and in the short time they have been doing it, they have seen changes like fewer girls getting pregnant at a young age and greater engagement in community rituals.

EchoHawk's tribe has started performing a ceremony that emphasizes spirituality and reintegrating into the community for those returning from Iraq. In the IHS youth centers, they are also using traditional practices where possible, and the young people are using them, she adds.

LaFromboise developed the American Indian Life Skills Development Curriculum, designed to reduce suicidal and other destructive behavior by giving students coping and problem-solving skills. The curriculum addresses specific problems in Indian students' lives such as substance abuse, dysfunctional family environments and violence, and builds self-esteem by encouraging students to learn about and take pride in their cultural heritage. In the process, students also learn how to help a suicidal friend get help within the community. The program, initially developed for the Zuni tribe in collaboration with the Cherokee Nation, has been adapted in several other communities.

In communities where there have been clusters of suicides, the solution appears to lie not within clinical methods, but in the response of the community itself, says Perez. How quickly and effectively they respond has been a much better predictor of reducing suicide rates than any clinical methods outside agencies have provided. Economic empowerment is also critical, adds Willis.

Traditionally American Indians are taught to view neighbors as family, notes Crossbear, and this can be an essential strength.

"In American Indian communities we have to be family," she says.

Further Readings

LaFromboise, T.D. (1996). *American Indian life skills development curriculum.* Madison, Wisc.: University of Wisconsin Press.

Witko, T.M., Ed. (2006). *Mental health care for urban Indians: Clinical insights from native practitioners.* Washington, DC: American Psychological Association.

PTSD Treatments Grow in Evidence, Effectiveness

Several psychological interventions help to significantly reduce post-traumatic stress disorder symptoms, say new guidelines.

Tori DeAngelis

It's a bittersweet fact: Traumatic events such as the Sept. 11 attacks, Hurricane Katrina, and the wars in Iraq and Afghanistan have enabled researchers to learn a lot more about how best to treat post-traumatic stress disorder (PTSD).

"The advances made have been nothing short of outstanding," says Boston University psychologist Terence M. Keane, PhD, director of the behavioral science division of the National Center for Post-Traumatic Stress Disorder and a contributor to the original PTSD diagnosis. "These are very important times in the treatment of PTSD."

In perhaps the most important news, in November, the International Society for Traumatic Stress Studies (ISTSS), a professional society that promotes knowledge on severe stress and trauma, issued new PTSD practice guidelines. Using a grading system from "A" to "E," the guidelines label several PTSD treatments as "A" treatments based on their high degree of empirical support, says Keane, one of the volume's editors. The guidelines—the first since 2000—update and generally confirm recommendations of other major practice-related bodies, including the U.S. Department of Veterans Affairs (VA), the Department of Defense, the American Psychiatric Association, and Great Britain's and Australia's national health-care guidelines, he says.

In other PTSD-treatment advances, researchers are adding medications and virtual-reality simulations to proven treatments to beef up their effectiveness. Clinical investigators are also exploring ways to treat PTSD when other psychological and medical conditions are present, and they are studying specific populations such as those affected by the Sept. 11 attacks.

Though exciting, these breakthroughs are somewhat colored by an October Institute of Medicine (IoM) report that concludes there is still not enough evidence to say which PTSD treatments are effective, except for exposure therapies. Many experts, however, disagree with that conclusion, noting that a number of factors specific to the condition, such as high dropout rates, can lead to what may seem like imperfect study designs (see sidebar).

Treatments That Make a Difference

The fact that several treatments made the "A" list is great news for psychologists, says Keane. "Having this many evidence-based treatments allows therapists to use what they're comfortable with from their own background and training, and at the same time to select treatments for use with patients with different characteristics," he says.

Moreover, many of these treatments were developed by psychologists, he notes.

They include:

- **Prolonged-exposure therapy,** developed for use in PTSD by Keane, University of Pennsylvania psychologist Edna Foa, PhD, and Emory University psychologist Barbara O. Rothbaum, PhD. In this type of treatment, a therapist guides the client to recall traumatic memories in a controlled fashion so that clients eventually regain mastery of their thoughts and feelings around the incident. While exposing people to the very events that caused their trauma may seem counterintuitive, Rothbaum emphasizes that it's done in a gradual, controlled and repeated manner, until the person can evaluate their circumstances realistically and understand they can safely return to the activities in their current lives that they had been avoiding. Drawing from PTSD best practices, the APA-initiated Center for Deployment Psychology includes exposure therapy in the training of psychologists and other health professionals who are or will be treating returning Iraq and Afghanistan service personnel (see sidebar on page 45).

- **Cognitive-processing therapy,** a form of cognitive behavioral therapy, or CBT, developed by Boston University psychologist Patricia A. Resick, PhD, director of the women's health sciences division of the National Center for PTSD, to treat rape victims and later applied to PTSD. This treatment includes an exposure component but places greater emphasis on cognitive strategies to help people alter erroneous thinking that has emerged because of the event. Practitioners may work with clients on false beliefs that the world is no longer safe, for example, or that they are incompetent because they have "let" a terrible event happen to them.

- **Stress-inoculation training,** another form of CBT, where practitioners teach clients techniques to manage and reduce anxiety, such as breathing, muscle relaxation and positive self-talk.

- **Other forms of cognitive therapy,** including cognitive restructuring and cognitive therapy.

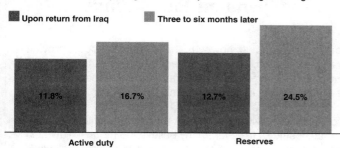

Percentage of soldiers reporting mental health problems during screenings

■ Upon return from Iraq   ■ Three to six months later

11.8%   16.7%   12.7%   24.5%

Active duty   Reserves

Delayed reaction   When troops returning from Iraq are screened a second time, the proportion who report mental health problem rises.

Source: Journal of the American Medical Association

- **Eye-movement desensitization and reprocessing,** or EMDR, where the therapist guides clients to make eye movements or follow hand taps, for instance, at the same time they are recounting traumatic events. It's not clear how EMDR works, and, for that reason, it's somewhat controversial, though the therapy is supported by research, notes Dartmouth University psychologist Paula P. Schnurr, PhD, deputy executive director of the National Center for PTSD.
- **Medications,** specifically selective serotonin reuptake inhibitors. Two in particular—paroxetine (Paxil) and sertaline (Zoloft)—have been approved by the Food and Drug Administration for use in PTSD. Other medications may be useful in treating PTSD as well, particularly when the person has additional disorders such as depression, anxiety or psychosis, the guidelines note.

Spreading the Word

So promising does the VA consider two of the "A" treatments—prolonged exposure therapy and cognitive-processing therapy—that it is doing national rollouts of them within the VA, notes psychologist Antonette Zeiss, PhD, deputy chief consultant for mental health at the agency.

"Enhancing our ability to provide veterans with the psychotherapies for PTSD that have the strongest evidence base is one of our highest priorities," Zeiss says. In fact, the VA began training psychologists to provide the two approaches more than a year before the Institute of Medicine released its report of successful treatments, she says. "We're pleased that the report confirms our emphasis on this training."

The VA system's structure and philosophy make it possible to test the results of treatments in large, realistic samples—a clinical researcher's dream, notes Schnurr, who has conducted a number of such studies, most recently in a study of female veterans that led to the rollout out of prolonged exposure therapy. That study was reported in the Feb. 28, 2007, issue of *The Journal of the American Medical Association* (Vol. 297, No. 8, pages 820–830).

"The VA was able to support the science, so the research didn't just sit around in a journal and get discussed," Zeiss says. "They put money toward it, and they asked us to help them do a major rollout of the treatment."

Boosting Effectiveness

Meanwhile, other researchers are experimenting with add-ons to these proven treatments to increase their effectiveness. Some are looking at how virtual reality might enhance the effects of prolonged-exposure

therapy. By adding virtual reality, whereby clients experience 3-D imagery, sounds and sometimes smells that correspond with a traumatic event, "we think it might be a good alternative for people who are too avoidant to do standard exposure therapy, because it puts them right there," says Emory University's Rothbaum.

Other researchers are adding a small dose of an old tuberculosis drug, D-cycloserine, or DCS, to treatment to see if it can mitigate people's fear reactions. Rothbaum's team, which includes psychologist Mike Davis, PhD, and psychiatrist Kerry Ressler, MD, PhD, have recently shown that the drug helps to extinguish fear in animals, so they're hoping for a similar effect in people.

In one study with veterans of the current Iraq war, Rothbaum's team is giving all participants a type of virtual reality that simulates combat conditions in Iraq, then randomizing them into a drug condition where they get DCS, a placebo, or the anti-anxiety drug alprazolam (Xanax).

In a similar vein, researchers at the Program for Anxiety and Traumatic Stress Studies at Weill Cornell Medical College are using virtual reality and DCS to treat those directly affected by the 2001 World Trade Center attacks, including civilians who were in the towers or nearby buildings, witnesses, and firefighters and police officers who were first responders.

Participants receive standard cognitive behavioral treatment enhanced with virtual reality, where they see graded versions of a Twin Towers scenario, starting with simple images of the buildings on a sunny day, and progressing gradually to include the horrific sights and sounds of that day. They also randomly receive either a small dose of DCS or a placebo pill before each session.

While neither study is complete, the researchers say the treatments appear to significantly reduce participants' PTSD symptoms. Rothbaum has recently submitted a grant proposal for a study where she plans to compare traditional and virtual-reality exposure therapies—which hasn't yet been done—in combination with DCS or a placebo.

Addressing Comorbidity

Other psychologists are starting to think about ways to treat PTSD when it is accompanied by other psychiatric and health conditions. Psychologist John Otis, PhD, of Boston University and VA Boston, for instance, is testing an integrated treatment that aims to alleviate symptoms of both PTSD and chronic pain in Vietnam veterans and veterans of Operation Iraqi Freedom and Operation Enduring Freedom. The treatment combines aspects of cognitive processing therapy for trauma and cognitive behavioral therapy for chronic pain.

"We think these two conditions may interact in some [psychological] way that makes them more severe and challenging to treat," Otis says. In particular, he and others posit that "anxiety sensitivity"—fear of experiencing one's anxiety-related symptoms—may increase the odds that certain PTSD sufferers have more problems than others.

Again, while the study is not yet finished, results are encouraging, reports Otis. "Many of the veterans who are getting the integrated treatment are experiencing partial or complete remission of both kinds of symptoms," he says.

On a broader scale, the National Center for PTSD's Keane believes that much more research is needed on treating PTSD and psychiatric comorbidities such as depression, anxiety, substance abuse, personality disorders and psychosis—a common situation that escalates the more severe a person's PTSD symptoms are, he says.

He, for one, would like to examine possible applications to PTSD of the concept of a "unified protocol," a theory and methodology being developed by Boston University psychotherapy researcher David Barlow, PhD, to treat concurrent problems such as panic attacks, anxiety and phobias.

PTSD Treatments Demand More Study, Independent Panel Finds

Inserting a cautionary note in the enthusiasm about effective treatments for post-traumatic stress disorders (PTSD), an Institute of Medicine (IoM) panel concluded in October that only exposure therapies such as prolonged exposure and cognitive-processing therapy have enough evidence to recommend them for treatment. The independent review was requested by the Department of Veterans Affairs (VA).

"At this time, we can make no judgment about the effectiveness of most psychotherapies or about any medications in helping patients with PTSD," states Alfred O. Berg, MD, the University of Washington professor of family medicine who chaired the IoM committee. "These therapies may or may not be effective—we just don't know in the absence of good data."

In a review of 53 drug studies and 37 psychotherapy studies, the seven-member panel concluded that many PTSD studies are flawed in terms of design and high dropout rates, which limit their generalizablity. Moreover, most drug studies were funded by pharmaceutical companies, and many psychotherapy studies were conducted by people who developed the techniques or by their close collaborators, the report finds.

Besides listing a number of drugs that need more independent investigation, the panel asserted that the following psychotherapies need better evaluation:

- Eye-movement desensitization and reprocessing.
- Cognitive restructuring.
- Coping-skills training.
- Group psychotherapy.

This said, the findings shouldn't be interpreted to mean that exposure therapies are the only treatments that should be used to treat the condition, the report adds. The reports' authors do suggest, however, that Congress should provide resources to the VA and other federal agencies to fund high-quality PTSD research that includes veterans and other affected groups in research planning.

Psychologists expert in PTSD commended the committee for its critical review and the VA for commissioning the independent study. However, many believe the report is flawed in several ways, including that it fails to address the difficulties in conducting PTSD research and to take into account existing reviews and guidelines conducted by other independent bodies.

"I think [the IoM panel] raised the bar too high and they're not realistic about what PTSD is and how hard it is to study and to keep people in treatment," says PTSD expert Barbara O. Rothbaum, PhD, director of the Trauma and Anxiety Recovery Program at Emory University. "High dropout is endemic in PTSD."

Dartmouth Medical School psychologist Paula P. Schnurr, PhD, well-known for her rigorous, large-scale studies of PTSD populations, says that in her view, the literature "differs from the conclusions of the report, in that there's good evidence that a wider range of cognitive behavioral therapies are effective."

In addition, the panel's findings are at odds with many reviews already done in the field, Rothbaum says. As one example, the committee did not support the evidence base on any drug at all, even though the Food and Drug Administration has approved the selective serotonin reuptake inhibitors paroxetine (Paxil) and sertaline (Zoloft) to treat PTSD. "There have been a number of reviews out there, and none has concluded that only one intervention works," she says.

—T. DeAngelis

That said, the recent advances promise to help many more people suffering from a condition they did not bring on themselves, says Zeiss.

"While there is still more to learn, we have taken significant steps in developing treatments that have been shown to be effective and that will be increasingly provided both in VA and other mental health care settings," says Zeiss. "Those affected by combat stress and other traumas will be able to reach out for care without feeling ashamed or hopeless."

TORI DEANGELIS is a writer in Syracuse, N.Y.

When Do Meds Make the Difference?

For most nonpsychotic conditions, empirically supported therapies and medications yield similarly good results, but therapy is better over the long haul, research finds.

Tori DeAngelis

As new psychotropic drugs enter the marketplace, and more psychologists gain the ability to prescribe, an inevitable question arises: Are drugs, therapy or a combination the best form of treatment?

Research shows fairly consistent results: For most nonpsychotic disorders, behavioral interventions are just as effective as medications, and they hold up better over time.

"When researchers have directly compared empirically supported therapies with drugs in nonpsychotic populations, they hold their own very nicely," says Vanderbilt University depression expert Steven D. Hollon, PhD. Such therapies are also stronger in terms of enduring effects, he says. "People come away from treatment not only having their symptoms relieved, but learning something they can use the next time," he notes.

The British government, for one, is taking strong action with such findings: The United Kingdom's National Health Service is investing millions of dollars over the next few years to train more psychologists in evidence-based practices, making these interventions the treatment of choice over medications.

Meanwhile, research is continuing on combining drugs and therapy in treatment, and there, results are more mixed, says David H. Barlow, PhD, director of Boston University's Center for Anxiety and Related Disorders. In some cases, one treatment may boost the other. In other cases, there is no effect. Other times, combining the two may undermine an effective treatment. In addition, combination studies have been hobbled by theory and design problems, but research is improving and eventually should lead to clearer outcomes, Barlow says (see sidebar on page 50).

As the research continues to unfold, practicing psychologists—whether they prescribe themselves or collaborate with physicians—should educate themselves on psychopharmacological findings, says Jeff Matranga, PhD, one of two psychologists at the group practice Health Psych Maine who has completed postdoctoral psychopharmacology training.

"It is critically important that we gain information about the relative merits of medications, psychotherapy, a combination or a sequence for a given clinical problem," says Matranga, who lectures frequently on the topic. "Thankfully, this type of research has been increasing, and it is quite valuable for the treating clinician to help guide treatment choices."

The Word on Depression

Research on depression shows that medications and empirically supported therapies such as cognitive behavioral therapy (CBT) and interpersonal therapy are equally effective, with each modality helping about 60 percent of clients, notes Hollon. Combined treatments produce even better results: In a literature review in the April 2005 *Journal of Clinical Psychiatry* (Vol. 66, No. 4, pages 455–468), Hollon and colleagues found that, in general, combining medication and therapy raised treatment effectiveness to as much as 75 percent.

"While that's not a huge increment in terms of the likelihood that someone will get better, you get a faster, more complete and more enduring response when you put drugs and therapy together," Hollon says.

One subgroup of depressed clients seems particularly amenable to combined treatment: severely and chronically depressed adults. One large multisite study was reported in the May 2000 *New England Journal of Medicine* (Vol. 342, No. 20, pages 1462–1470), and conducted by Brown University psychiatrist Martin B. Keller, MD, Virginia Commonwealth University psychologist James P. McCullough Jr., PhD, Stony Brook University psychologist Daniel Klein, PhD, and colleagues. In the study, researchers randomized patients with major depression either to a depression-focused CBT developed by McCullough, or to the antidepressant Serzone (nefazodone).

"The combination of the two was whoppingly more effective than either one alone," says Klein. About three-quarters responded to the combination, compared with about 48 percent for each individual condition. "People suffering from chronic depression often have longstanding interpersonal difficulties, and the virtue of combined treatment in this case may be that it simultaneously targets both depressive symptoms and social functioning," he says.

Weighing in on Anxiety Disorders

Likewise, large-scale studies on anxiety disorders find that people do equally well with medication or CBT, but that fewer people relapse with CBT than with medication, says Barlow, a lead researcher in the area. Unlike with depression, however, combined treatments don't seem to confer extra benefits, he notes.

"The ultimate positive circumstance is to have as many tools as you can."

—Richard G. Heimberg
Temple University

The same pattern holds true for social phobia, says Temple University's Richard G. Heimberg, PhD, who has conducted a number of studies in the area. "You might get a bigger short-term burst from medication, but CBT is about as effective, and it's also associated with better protection against relapse," he says.

A long-standing line of research on obsessive-compulsive disorder (OCD) that has tested therapy and medication interventions has yielded what is considered a "best practice" for the disorder: a cognitive behavioral treatment for OCD combining exposure and ritual prevention, known as EX/RP. In this line of research, University of Pennsylvania researcher Edna Foa, PhD, and colleagues have conducted systematic studies to identify the active ingredients of EX/RP. In one set of studies, the team compared separate components of EX/RP and found that exposure only and ritual prevention only were not as effective as the combination of the two. In another line of research, they compared the efficacy of the trycyclic antidepressant clomipramine with EX/RP. They found that EX/RP reduced symptoms more than clomipramine and that EX/RP improved the effects of clomipramine, but the reverse was not the case.

The results of these studies "show that EX/RP is the treatment of choice for OCD, both as a treatment by itself and as an augmentation to medication," says Foa. She has found similar results with children and adolescents, though a related study on young people at Duke University did find an optimal effect by combining the selective serotonin reuptake inhibitor (SSRI) Zoloft (sertraline) and EX/RP, she notes.

Foa and her colleagues are now looking at how to improve OCD treatment further. In a current study, for instance, they're exploring how adding different conditions and more time might influence outcome. In the first part of the study, they're examining what happens when they give OCD sufferers not responding well to an SSRI an additional treatment

Combined-Treatment Research Gains Sophistication

Results of combined-treatment studies can be varied and confusing, as a result of methodology, researcher bias and patient characteristics, experts say. In fact, even the order in which you give treatments may make a difference, as may patients' treatment preference, notes Stony Brook University psychologist and depression researcher Daniel Klein, PhD.

Fortunately, research on combined treatments is becoming more sophisticated in design, theory and potential application, says David H. Barlow, PhD, director of Boston University's Center for Anxiety and Related Disorders. This evolution bodes well both for research and treatment, he believes.

The original studies on combined treatments tested drugs and therapy at the same time. The problem with this approach was a lack of theoretical rationale and hence a conflicting record of results. "No one provided a really good reason as to why these treatments might do better than one treatment alone," Barlow says.

A more sensible strategy that's being increasingly used examines "sequential" treatments, where researchers start with one treatment and either add or substitute a second one if the first isn't producing adequate results. This methodology promises to help tailor treatments and save money, Barlow says.

Now, researchers are launching what Barlow thinks may be the most effective research design yet: combining therapy with drugs developed specifically to work with a given psychological treatment—so-called "synergistic" treatments. For example, scientists are adding D-cycloserine—an old tuberculosis antibiotic recently shown to help extinguish fear in animals—as a complement to psychological treatments for conditions such as obsessive-compulsive disorder and post-traumatic stress disorder (PTSD). (See the January *Monitor* for its application to PTSD.)

Likewise, they're looking into possible applications of the hormone oxytocin to treat people with social anxiety, Barlow says. Traditionally used to stimulate labor and breastfeeding in women, oxytocin also helps to promote trust and bonding, which could help people with social anxiety overcome their fears, he notes.

—T. DeAngelis

of either EX/RP or the antipsychotic medication risperidone. In the second part, they're extending the length of each additional treatment for those still not experiencing much symptom relief.

Real-World Considerations

Transporting such findings into the real world can, of course, be challenging. Unlike the relative purity of the lab, the treatment world is a teeming bazaar of providers—many of whom do not have the credentials or training of psychologists—turf issues, cost concerns and varying patient inclinations and needs, experts say.

In the provider domain, practitioners both in psychology and medicine often are not as up to date on empirically tested treatments as researchers, Hollon says. "There's a large discussion in the literature about how few people in the real world tend to practice therapies with empirical support, and the same thing is true with pharmacotherapy," he notes.

And, of course, not everyone has access to mental health care. Even if they do, says Foa, "It's not easy for people to find this treatment, because there aren't a lot of experts in the area."

Meanwhile, cost issues can prevent the most effective treatments from being used, those involved say. For instance, therapy may be more expensive up front, though studies show it is often more cost-effective over the long run, Matranga notes.

Insurers are sometimes more willing to pay for medications than for therapy, and some primary-care physicians are more likely to prescribe medications before therapy for a range of psychological conditions, he says, particularly if they don't have easy access to someone trained in these therapies.

Patient variables present a mystery in need of greater understanding as well, says Heimberg: Some people don't believe that "talking" can help, others are too anxious to try medications on one side or therapy on the other, and still others can't tolerate medication side effects, for example.

> **"There's a large discussion in the literature about how few people in the real world tend to practice therapies with empirical support, and the same thing is true with pharmacotherapy."**
>
> —Steven D. Hollon
> Vanderbilt University

Likewise, research is beginning to show that clients' preferences make a huge difference in outcome, says Klein. "They're more willing to stick with and invest in something they believe will work," he notes.

Finally, drugs and therapy each carry pros and cons that need to be assessed when finding the right treatment for someone, Hollon says. With therapy, there's a learning curve; with drugs, there are side effects, he says.

Given that we're moving into an era where pharmacological and behavioral strategies will be increasingly used and blended, it's wise to be as informed as possible, Heimberg emphasizes.

"The ultimate positive circumstance," he says, "is to have as many tools as you can."

TORI DEANGELIS is a writer in Syracuse, N.Y.

Test-Your-Knowledge Form

We encourage you to photocopy and use this page as a tool to assess how the articles in *Annual Editions* expand on the information in your textbook. By reflecting on the articles you will gain enhanced text information. You can also access this useful form on a product's book support Web site at *http://www.mhcls.com*.

NAME: DATE:

_____

TITLE AND NUMBER OF ARTICLE:

_____

BRIEFLY STATE THE MAIN IDEA OF THIS ARTICLE:

_____

LIST THREE IMPORTANT FACTS THAT THE AUTHOR USES TO SUPPORT THE MAIN IDEA:

_____

WHAT INFORMATION OR IDEAS DISCUSSED IN THIS ARTICLE ARE ALSO DISCUSSED IN YOUR TEXTBOOK OR OTHER READINGS THAT YOU HAVE DONE? LIST THE TEXTBOOK CHAPTERS AND PAGE NUMBERS:

_____

LIST ANY EXAMPLES OF BIAS OR FAULTY REASONING THAT YOU FOUND IN THE ARTICLE:

_____

LIST ANY NEW TERMS/CONCEPTS THAT WERE DISCUSSED IN THE ARTICLE, AND WRITE A SHORT DEFINITION:

We Want Your Advice

ANNUAL EDITIONS revisions depend on two major opinion sources: one is our Advisory Board, listed in the front of this volume, which works with us in scanning the thousands of articles published in the public press each year; the other is you—the person actually using the book. Please help us and the users of the next edition by completing the prepaid article rating form on this page and returning it to us. Thank you for your help!

ANNUAL EDITIONS: Psychology 09/10

ARTICLE RATING FORM

Here is an opportunity for you to have direct input into the next revision of this volume.
We would like you to rate each of the articles listed below, using the following scale:

1. **Excellent: should definitely be retained**
2. **Above average: should probably be retained**
3. **Below average: should probably be deleted**
4. **Poor: should definitely be deleted**

Your ratings will play a vital part in the next revision.
Please mail this prepaid form to us as soon as possible.
Thanks for your help!

RATING	ARTICLE	RATING	ARTICLE
	1. Why Study Psychology?		22. Eating into the Nation's Obesity Epidemic
	2. Does Psychology Make a Significant Difference in Our Lives?		23. A Nurturing Relationship
			24. Why So Mad?
	3. The 10 Commandments of Helping Students Distinguish Science from Pseudoscience in Psychology		25. A Learning Machine
			26. The Joke's in You
			27. A Question of Resilience
	4. Science vs. Ideology		28. Growing Up Online
	5. The Amazing Brain		29. Making Relationships Work
	6. The Threatened Brain		30. Blessed Are Those Who Mourn—and Those Who Comfort Them
	7. Phantom Pain and the Brain		
	8. The Home Team Advantage . . . and Other Sex Hormone Secrets		31. Culture and the Development of Self-Knowledge
			32. Frisky, but More Risky
	9. Extreme States		33. Second Nature
	10. A Matter of Taste		34. Bad Apples or Bad Barrels?
	11. What Dreams Are Made Of		35. Young and Restless
	12. About Face		36. We're Wired to Connect
	13. Conversing with Copycats		37. A New Approach to Attention Deficit Disorder
	14. Move Over, Mice		38. Treating War's Toll on the Mind
	15. The Perils and Promises of Praise		39. Soldier Support
	16. What Was I Thinking?		40. We Love to Be Scared on Halloween
	17. The Culture-Cognition Connection		41. Couple Therapy
	18. Talk to the Hand		42. 'A Struggle for Hope'
	19. The Success Delusion		43. PTSD Treatments Grow in Evidence, Effectiveness
	20. Feeling Smart: The Science of Emotional Intelligence		
			44. When Do Meds Make the Difference?
	21. Ambition: Why Some People Are Most Likely to Succeed		

BUSINESS REPLY MAIL
FIRST CLASS MAIL PERMIT NO. 551 DUBUQUE IA

POSTAGE WILL BE PAID BY ADDRESSEE

McGraw-Hill Contemporary Learning Series
501 BELL STREET
DUBUQUE, IA 52001

ABOUT YOU

Name   Date

Are you a teacher? ❑ A student? ❑
Your school's name

Department

Address   City   State   Zip

School telephone #

YOUR COMMENTS ARE IMPORTANT TO US!

Please fill in the following information:
For which course did you use this book?

Did you use a text with this ANNUAL EDITION? ❑ yes ❑ no
What was the title of the text?

What are your general reactions to the Annual Editions concept?

Have you read any pertinent articles recently that you think should be included in the next edition? Explain.

Are there any articles that you feel should be replaced in the next edition? Why?

Are there any World Wide Web sites that you feel should be included in the next edition? Please annotate.

May we contact you for editorial input? ❑ yes ❑ no
May we quote your comments? ❑ yes ❑ no